AF705337

ASCENT

CENTER FOR TECHNICAL KNOWLEDGE

3DEXPERIENCE CATIA 2026x Transition to the 3DEXPERIENCE Platform for CATIA V5 Users

Learning Guide

Edition 1.0

ASCENT - Center for Technical Knowledge®
3DEXPERIENCE CATIA 2026x
Transition to the 3DEXPERIENCE Platform for CATIA V5 Users

Edition 1.0

Prepared and produced by:

ASCENT Center for Technical Knowledge
11201 Dolfield Blvd, Suite 112
Owings Mills, MD 21117

866-527-2368
www.ASCENTed.com

Lead Contributor: Mark Potrzebowski

ASCENT - Center for Technical Knowledge (a division of Rand Worldwide Inc.) is a leading developer of professional learning materials and knowledge products for engineering software applications. ASCENT specializes in designing targeted content that facilitates application-based learning with hands-on software experience. For over 25 years, ASCENT has helped users become more productive through tailored custom learning solutions.

We welcome any comments you may have regarding this guide, or any of our products. To contact us please email: feedback@ASCENTed.com.

AS-3DE26-TCV51-SG // RS-3DE26-TCV51-SG

Contents

Preface

The *3DEXPERIENCE CATIA 2026x: Transition to the 3DEXPERIENCE Platform for CATIA V5 Users* guide is for experienced users of CATIA V5 who are migrating to the 3DEXPERIENCE platform. This guide explores the 3DEXPERIENCE platform and how to work with various apps, including CATIA Part Design and CATIA Assembly Design.

Topics Covered

- 3DEXPERIENCE Platform Overview
- 3DEXPERIENCE Platform PLM Objects
- Launching the 3DEXPERIENCE Platform
- 3DEXPERIENCE Platform User Interface
- Customizing the 3DEXPERIENCE Platform
- Creating a New 3D Part
- Managing Object Lifecycles
- Engineering Connections and Constraints
- Completing Weight Calculations
- Designing in Context
- Using Catalogs
- Analyzing Assemblies
- Working with Drawings in the 3DEXPERIENCE Platform

Prerequisites

- Access to the 3DEXPERIENCE CATIA 2026x platform, including access to the CATIA Part Design, CATIA Assembly Design, CATIA Drafting, ENOVIA Collaborative Lifecycle, ENOVIA Product Finder, and ENOVIA Design IP Classification apps, to ensure compatibility with this learning content. Future software updates that are released by Dassault Systèmes may include changes that are not reflected in this content. The practices and files included might not be compatible with prior versions of the software (e.g., 3DEXPERIENCE CATIA 2025x).
- Permission to import 3DXML files.

Note on Software Setup

This guide assumes a standard installation of the software using the default preferences during installation. Lectures and practices use the standard software templates and default options for the Content Libraries.

Note on Learning Guide Content

ASCENT's learning guides are intended to teach the technical aspects of using the software and do not focus on professional design principles and standards. The practices aim to demonstrate the capabilities and flexibility of the software rather than following specific design codes or standards.

Lead Contributor: Mark Potrzebowski

Mark is a seasoned trainer and curriculum designer with more than 15 years of experience in the PLM industry. With a primary focus on CATIA, Creo, and PLM systems, Mark uses his Instructional Design skills and comprehensive CAD experience to develop training products at ASCENT, including learning content for print and web, as well as instructional videos and presentations.

Mark holds a bachelor's degree in Computer Graphics Technology from Purdue University, West Lafayette, Indiana.

Mark Potrzebowski has been the Lead Contributor for *3DEXPERIENCE CATIA 2026x: Transition to the 3DEXPERIENCE Platform for CATIA V5 Users* since 2021.

In This Guide

The following highlights the key features of this guide.

Feature	Description
Practice Files	The Practice Files page includes a link to the practice files and instructions on how to download and install them. The practice files are required to complete the practices in this guide.
Chapters	A chapter consists of the following: Learning Objectives, Instructional Content, and Practices. • **Learning Objectives** define the skills you can acquire by learning the content provided in the chapter. • **Instructional Content**, which begins right after Learning Objectives, refers to the descriptive and procedural information related to various topics. Each main topic introduces a product feature, discusses various aspects of that feature, and provides step-by-step procedures on how to use that feature. Where relevant, examples, figures, helpful hints, and notes are provided. • **Practice** for a topic follows the instructional content. Practices enable you to use the software to perform a hands-on review of a topic. It is required that you download the practice files (using the link found on the Practice Files page) prior to starting the first practice.

Practice Files

To download the practice files for this guide, use the following steps:

1. Type the URL *exactly as shown below* into the address bar of your Internet browser to access the Course File Download page.

   Note: If you are using the ebook, you do not have to type the URL. Instead, you can access the page by clicking the URL below.

   https://www.ascented.com/getfile/id/cinereumPF

2. On the Course File Download page, click the **DOWNLOAD NOW** button, as shown below, to download the .ZIP file that contains the practice files.

3. Once the download is complete, unzip the file and extract its contents.

   The recommended practice files folder location is:
   C:\3DEXPERIENCE Transition Practice Files

   Note: It is recommended that you do not change the location of the practice files folder. Doing so may cause errors when completing the practices.

Stay Informed!

To receive information about upcoming events, promotional offers, and complimentary webcasts, visit:

www.ASCENTed.com/updates

Chapter 1

Overview

This chapter provides an overview of the 3DEXPERIENCE platform. You will understand the various components comprising the platform, and how working with 3DEXPERIENCE differs from CATIA V5.

Learning Objectives

- Understand the 3DEXPERIENCE platform.
- Understand the various components of the platform, including the 3DDashboard, various apps, and the database.
- Understand the compatibility between CATIA V5 and 3DEXPERIENCE objects.
- Understand the licensing and platform deployment schemes.
- Become familiar with 3DEXPERIENCE platform PLM objects and the 3DEXPERIENCE product structure.
- Learn the general process for accessing the system and search for objects.
- Learn how to import, export, and open objects.

1.1 3DEXPERIENCE Platform Overview

The 3DEXPERIENCE platform is a unified database and interface from Dassault Systèmes that provides a platform in which business software and applications can run, particularly programs related to the design, development, and manufacturing industries, as shown in Figure 1–1.

Figure 1–1

3DDashboard

The 3DDashboard, shown in Figure 1–2, is a front home page for your projects. In here, you can gather information from a variety of sources – reports, 3D models, files, group communications – to gain a holistic view of the project.

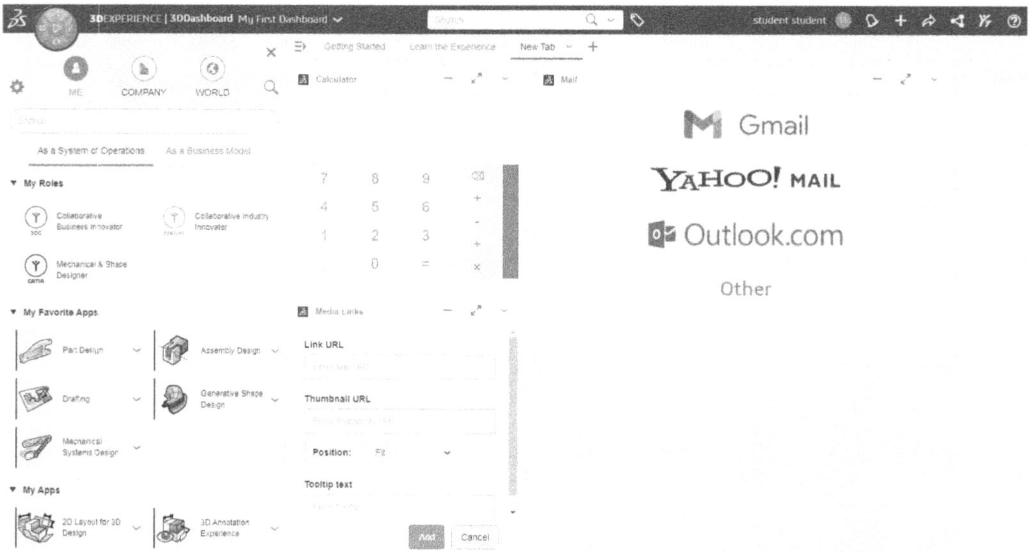

Figure 1–2

Apps

Applications (apps) are the various programs that run in the 3DEXPERIENCE platform. These are equivalent to workbenches in V5. Several apps are shown in Figure 1–3. Each application is made of several commands related to a common task. For example, the CATIA Part Design application contains commands used to build 3D solid models.

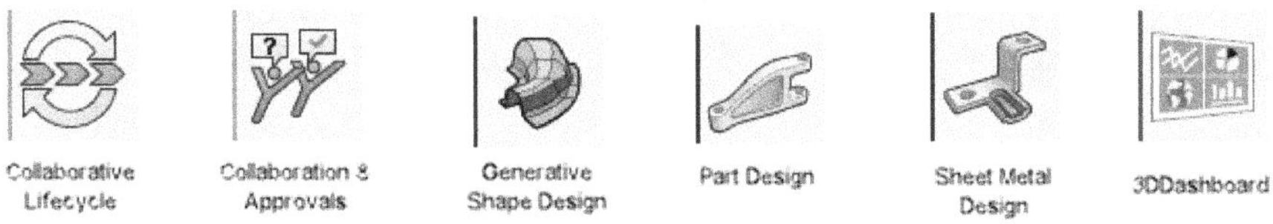

Figure 1–3

Compass

Apps are accessible through the Compass. The Compass is a reimagined version of the Start menu from V5. The Compass is broken into two selectable regions – the **Play** button (inner circle) and the **Roles, Apps & Solutions portfolio** button (outer ring). Selecting the **Play** button in certain applicable apps will start interactions like simulations and animations. The **Roles, Apps & Solutions portfolio** button lists all the available roles and apps that are accessible on the 3DEXPERIENCE platform, as shown in Figure 1–4.

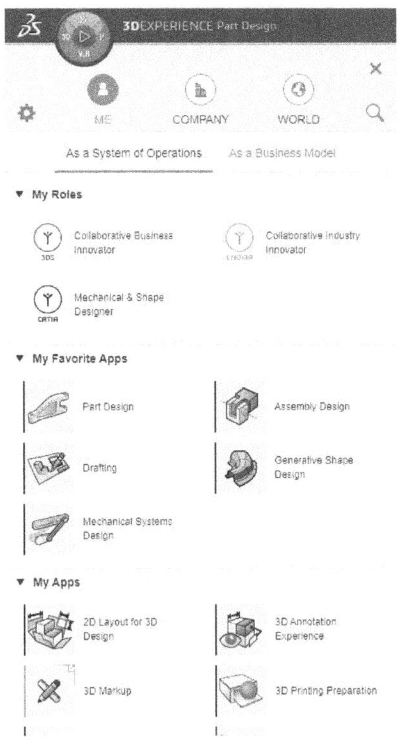

Figure 1–4

While the **Roles, Apps & Solutions portfolio** area works as a single button to access apps, there are general categories that a number of these apps fall under. Below is a list of some of the modules capable of being implemented within 3DEXPERIENCE.

Social and Collaborative Apps

- **ENOVIA** – Collaborative innovation, document revisions, and database management
- **3DEXCITE** – Marketing in the age of relationships

3D Modeling Apps

- **CATIA** – Product development and shape creation
- **Solidworks** – Inspiring innovation
- **Geovia** – Virtual planet
- **Biovia** – Virtual biosphere and materials

Content and Simulation Apps

- **Simulia** – Simulation for product, nature, and life
- **DELMIA** – Digital manufacturing and global industrial operations
- **3DVIA** – The consumer experience brand

Information Intelligence Apps

- **NETVIBES** – Dashboard intelligence
- **EXALEAD** – Data in business

Database

The goal of the 3DEXPERIENCE platform is to integrate the various disconnected 3D processes. By tying different aspects of product creation, development, and manufacturing, the platform becomes a single source of truth to define the product. As such, all file information is stored in a shared database.

As opposed to simply storing files in folders, a database creates relations between files so that they may be searched, filtered, and connected in meaningful ways that create value and usefulness, making it easier to work with large sets of data and provide individual users with the knowledge that they need.

This database can be accessed through a variety of methods:

- Webclient
- Windows integration
- Tablet
- Mobile

Since the 3DEXPERIENCE platform is based on a relational database, instead of saving individual files into folders on a network or local drive, all files are stored in the database. This alleviates issues with version control and data backup.

In the database, files can be locked or unlocked to prevent accidental overwriting (check in and check out). Version control can be applied to models. Different revisions and variations can easily be made. Non-CAD data and information can be stored, broadening the files' scope and depth of use.

Compatibility

CATIA V5 and 3DEXPERIENCE use the same geometry modeling engines. Models from the same release can be transferred back and forth while maintaining feature history, as shown in Figure 1–5.

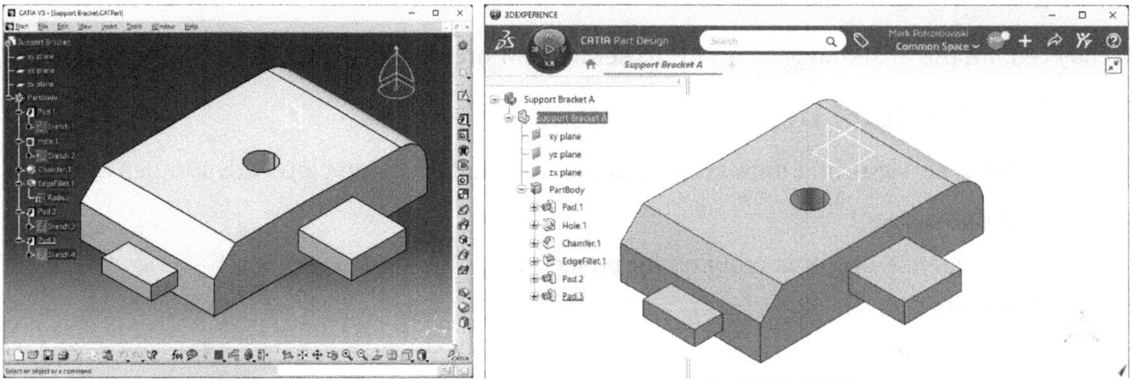

CATIA V5 ***3DEXPERIENCE***

Figure 1–5

1.2 Deployment and Licensing

The 3DEXPERIENCE platform can be integrated to an existing business model using the solution that best serves that business – using the Software-as-a-Service (SaaS), Platform-as-a-Service (PaaS), or Infrastructure-as-a-Service (IaaS) options.

On-Premise Platform Deployment

Any running of services and data storage are on local hardware. The basic requirements for on-premise installation are:

- License server
- Database software
- Webserver

It may require the assistance of a VAR to set up your on-premise 3DEXPERIENCE installation.

On-Cloud Platform Deployment

Any running of services and data storage are on the cloud. The on-cloud advantages are:

- Fast deployment
- Only a license server is required for on-cloud
- Simplicity
- Collaboration and connection
- Security and reliability
- Scalability

Licensing

Both the 3DEXPERIENCE platform and V5 use trigrams to denote licenses. In V5, each trigram represents a product or a package of products. For example, the MCE (Mechanical Product Creation) package contains PDG (Part Design 2), ASD (Assembly Design 2), GS1 (Generative Shape Design 1), and FM1 (Functional Molded Part).

V5 Licensing

In V5, configurations of licenses are purchases. For example, purchasing a CAC+FPE+HDX+MCE configuration would include these elements:

- CAC – Base V5 PLMExpress
- FPE – Fabricated Product Creation Package
- HDX – Mechanical Shape Design Package
- MCE – Mechanical Product Creation Package

Additional licenses are also available as add-ons and shareable products.

3DEXPERIENCE Platform Licensing

In the 3DEXPERIENCE platform, roles are purchased instead of configurations. The role includes a set of specific licenses that are typically used together for a specific job task. Several roles are shown in Figure 1–6.

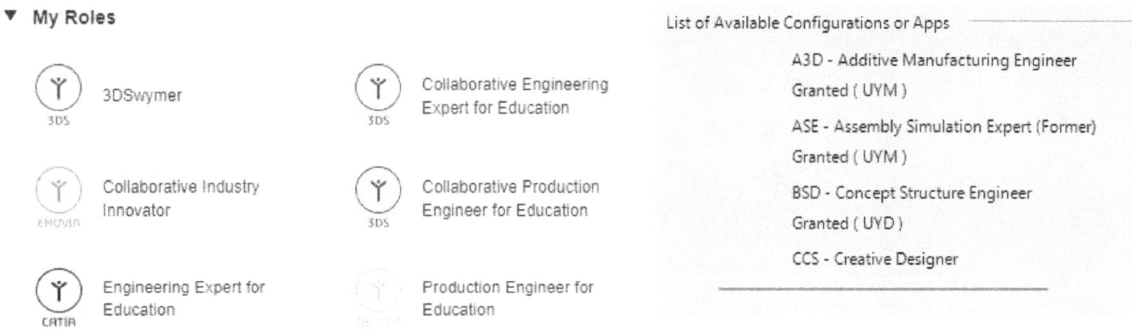

Figure 1–6

For example, the MDG (Mechanical Designer) role includes 40 different apps. These individual apps are still identified by their trigram.

Roles are available for:

- System architects
- Mechanical designers
- Creative designers
- Surface designers
- Decision makers

In the 3DEXPERIENCE platform, all licenses are named-user licenses, which means that administrators must assign these licenses to a specific person. A license may only be moved to another user after 30 days of inactivity.

1.3 3DEXPERIENCE Platform PLM Objects

Individual files are now referred to as *objects* and may contain other information than strictly file data. In general, these can be thought of as their V5 counterparts. There are equivalents for parts, products, and drawings. Many object types are available, as shown in Figure 1–7.

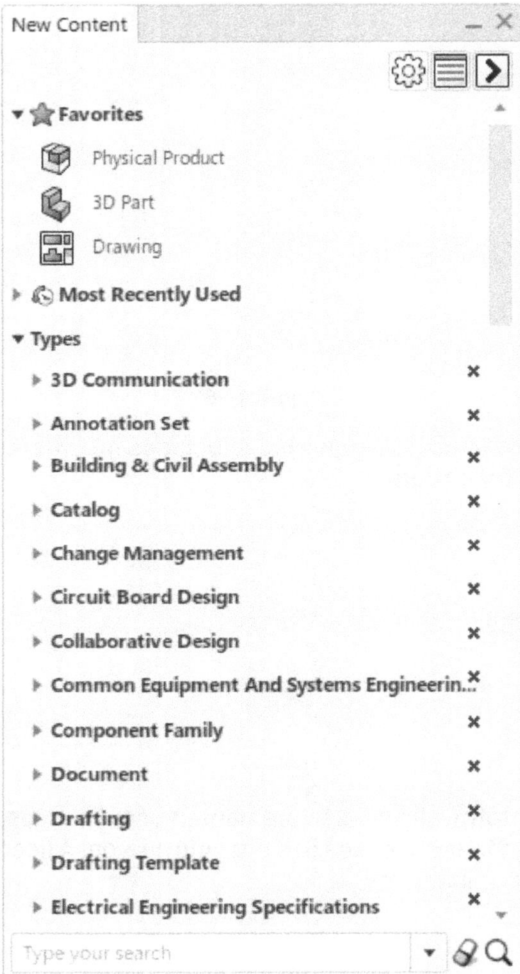

Figure 1–7

Products can be grouped into types. A product file is an assembly that contains representations. A representation is the 3D visualization of a model. It can be a 3D shape, which would be a V5 part or CGR (lightweight file). It can also be a drawing or other object that represents the model.

Product Structure

The following table illustrates how V5 objects have been simplified. The entities are now organized into basic categories of **product** and **representation**.

V5	3DEXPERIENCE	Category
Product	**Physical Product**	**Product**
Component		
Part Instance	**3D Part Instance**	**Representation**
Part Representation	**3D Shape Representation**	

The image shown in Figure 1–8 provides a comparison of the V5 and the 3DEXPERIENCE platform product structures.

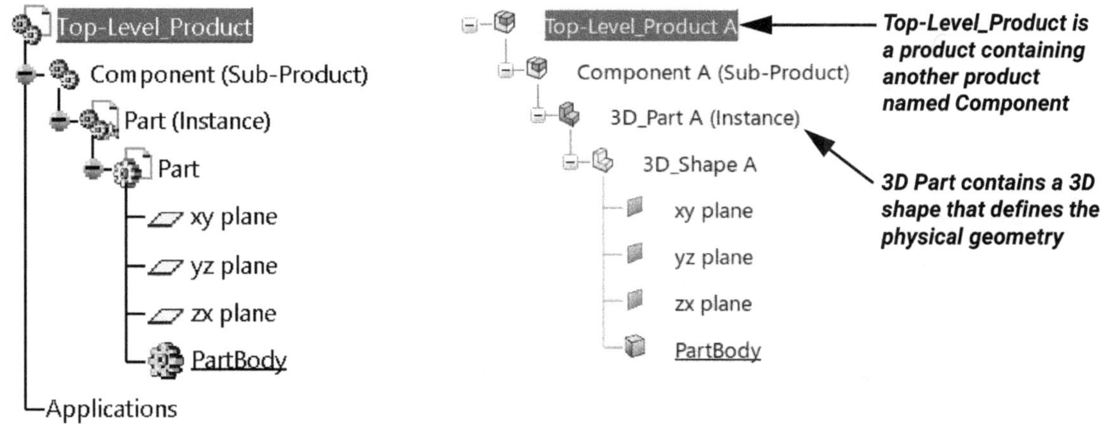

Figure 1–8

1.4 Launching the 3DEXPERIENCE Platform

The 3DEXPERIENCE platform infrastructure is organized around a centralized engineering database. This permits concurrent communication of the latest design data. As a result, the chance of using obsolete data is minimized for all participants with access to the system.

Connecting to the System

The centralized database structure requires that you log in to the system with the appropriate credentials to use the software. When you launch the 3DEXPERIENCE platform, the *Login | 3DEXPERIENCE ID* dialog box opens, as shown in Figure 1–9, in which you must enter your username and password. Your administrator must provide this information before you can use the 3DEXPERIENCE platform.

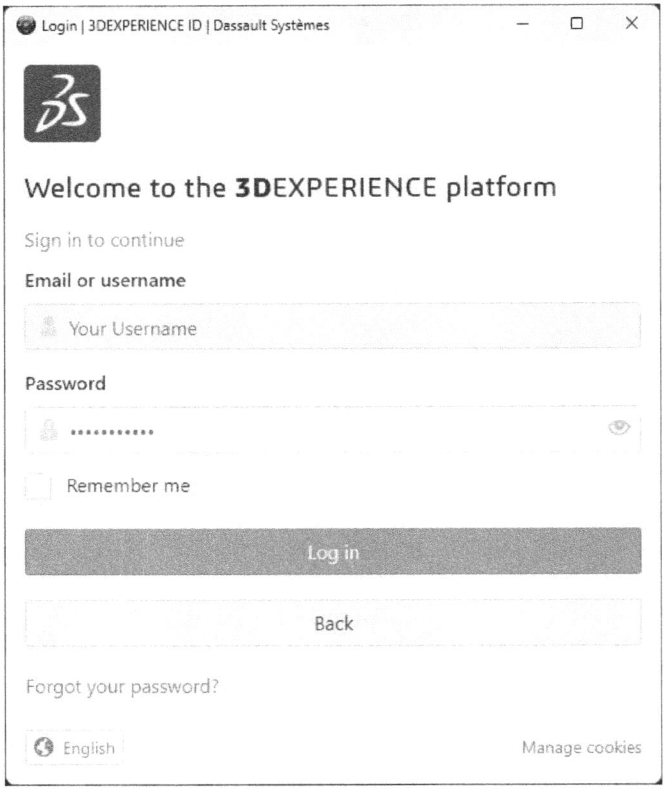

Figure 1–9

Platform Credentials

The *3DEXPERIENCE Platform* dialog box, shown in Figure 1–10, determines the specific location and type of data that you can pull from or push to the database by setting your credentials.

In the Rand 3D environment, the *Collaborative Space* is set to **Common Space** and the *Responsibility* is set to **Leader**, and they are limited to the specific collaborative space the user is working within. Access to these responsibility permissions is granted by an administrator. Generally, the *Responsibility* values available in the 3DEXPERIENCE platform include:

- **Public Reader:** "View Only & Information Set Public"
- **Reader:** "View Only & All Information"
- **Contributor:** "View Only & Evaluate Information"
- **Author:** "Edit Content"
- **Leader:** "Approve & Release"
- **Owner:** "Full Control/Admin of Collaborative Space"

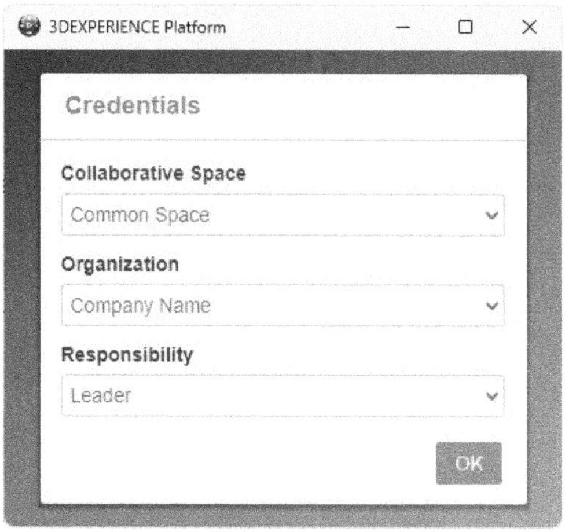

Figure 1–10

Note: *If you are not using this content in the Rand 3D environment, use the credentials, Collaborative Space, and Responsibility provided by your system administrator.*

1.5 Working with Models

Locating a Model

Models are located in the engineering database using the search bar, as shown in Figure 1–11.

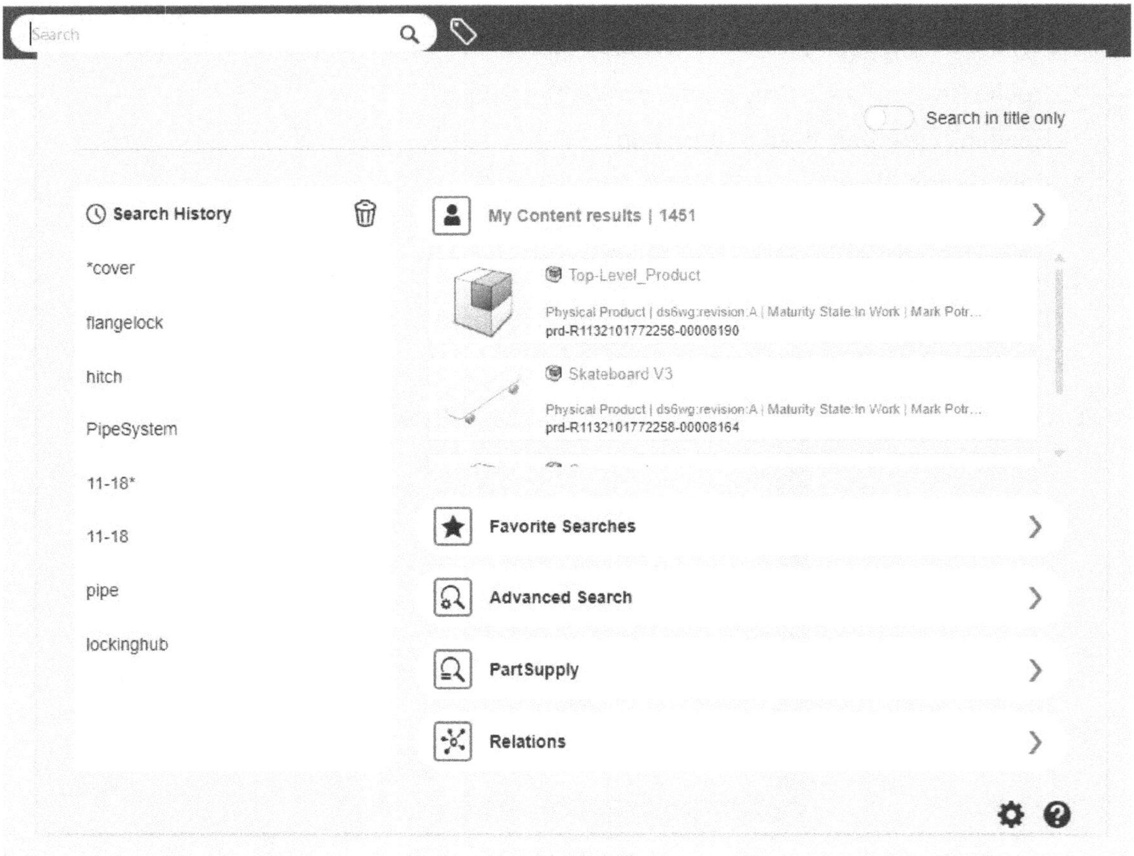

Figure 1–11

How To: Use the Search Bar

1. In the search bar, enter the filename or a portion of the filename. Using wildcards (*) is permitted.

2. Searches may be prefaced with the following to further filter the results:

Preface	Description
folder:	Root folder
prd:	Products
fav:	Favorite
prt:	Parts
rvw:	Review

3. Search results can be filtered using the **6W Tags** ( ), as shown in Figure 1–12.

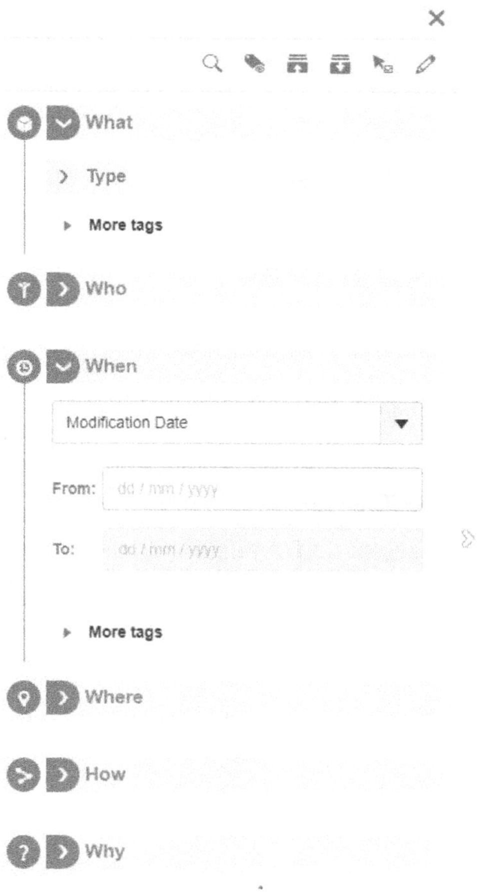

Figure 1–12

4. Open the file by double-clicking on it in the list. You can also right-click to access additional options, such as **Explore** or **Properties**, as shown in Figure 1–13.

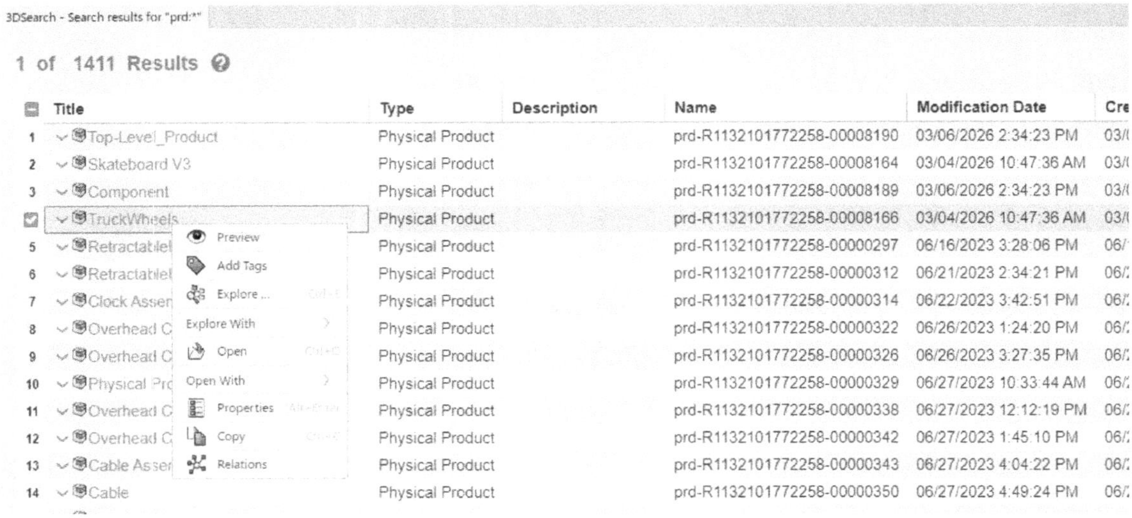

Figure 1–13

Importing a CATIA V5 Model

Standard CATIA files can be imported from your local file system.

How To: Import a CATIA V5 Model

1. In the Top Bar, click (Add/Create).
2. Click next to **Import** and select **CATIA File**.
3. Select the file(s) to import and click **Open**.

4. Select the import options shown in Figure 1–14.
5. Click **OK**.

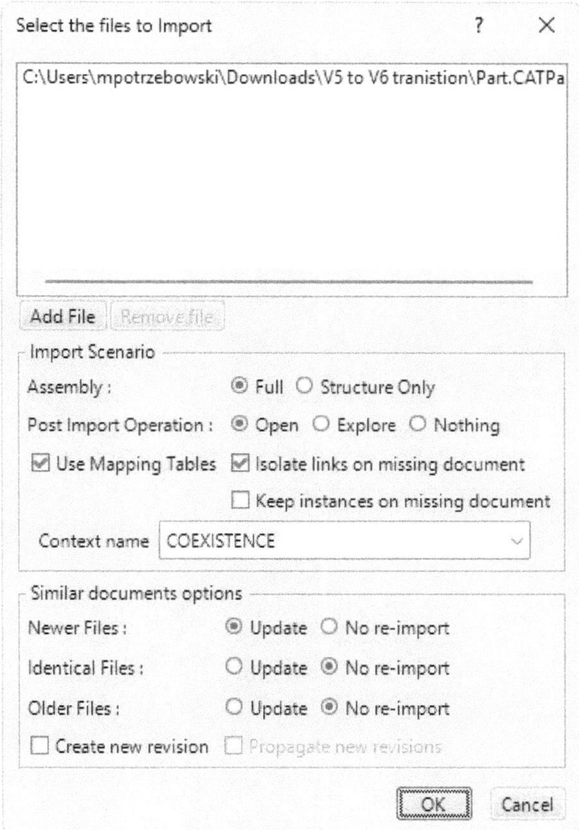

Figure 1–14

Importing a 3DXML File

3DXML is a proprietary format that facilitates transfer of CATIA files in a lightweight proprietary XML format. 3DXML can be in two formats: **With Authoring** (editable format) and **For Review** (non-editable). 3DXML files can be imported from you local file system.

How To: Import a 3DXML File

1. In the Top Bar, click (Add/Create).
2. Click **Import**.
3. Select the file to import.

4. Select the import options shown in Figure 1–15.
5. Click **OK**.

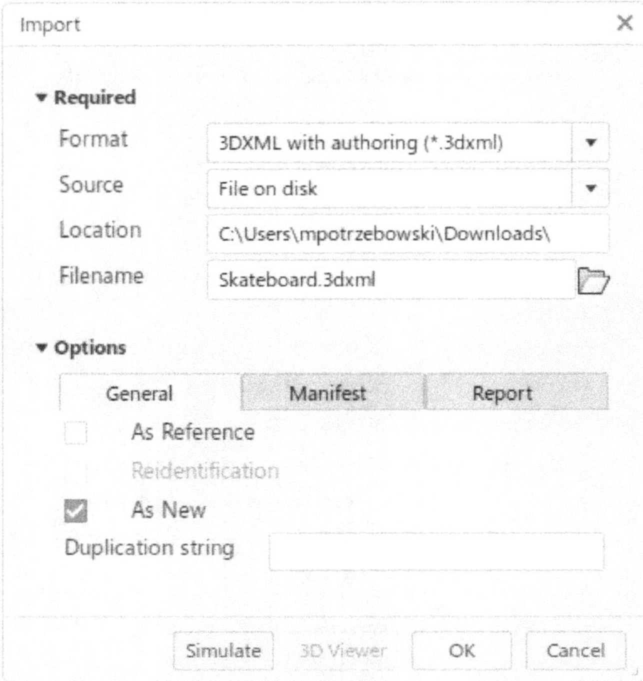

Figure 1–15

Imported objects will open in the Explore mode and will have to be opened to edit them.

Explore

Assemblies, folders, and other "container" type documents can be explored. This is similar to opening a folder in Windows. All the contents of the parent item will be listed. From there, selected sub-elements can be viewed or opened.

How To: Explore

1. Search and find an assembly or folder.
2. Right-click and select **Explore**.

Turntable

Particularly with large assemblies or folders, it may be useful to engage the turntable view. The turntable will show a 3D representation of the assembly, as shown in Figure 1–16.

Parts are visible based on tree expansion:

- If the tree is expanded and open, the part will be displayed in the turntable.
- If a particular branch of the tree is collapsed and not visible, then that part will not be displayed in the *3D* area.

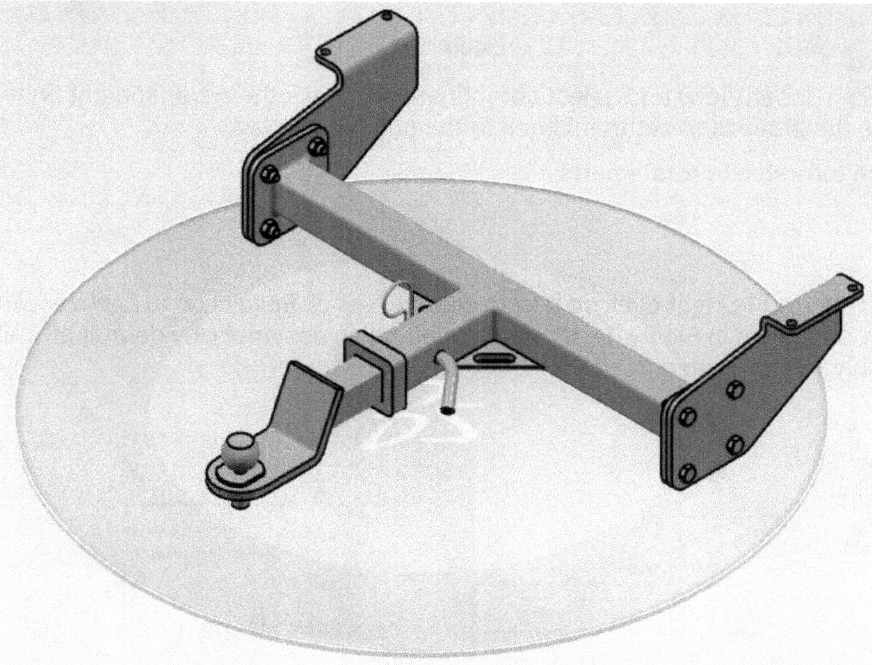

Figure 1–16

Essentially, the turntable is a large preview. To modify and analyze the parts, they will need to be opened.

How To: Use the Turntable

1. Find an assembly or folder and **Explore** it.
2. In the *View* tab of the Action Bar, click (Swap Turntable/In-place), or press <F9> to toggle the exploded turntable view.

3. Click (Text View) to display labels on parts, as shown in Figure 1–17.

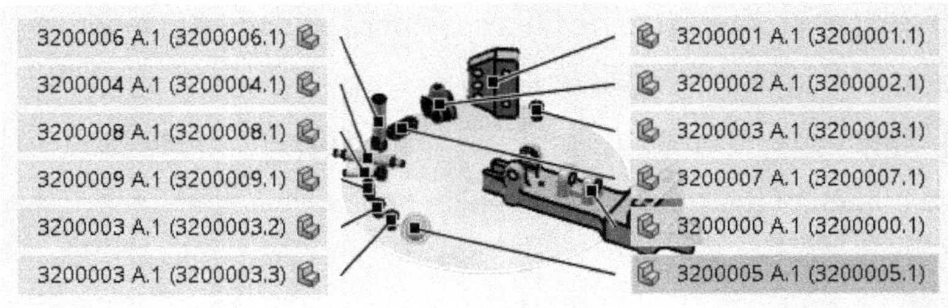

Figure 1–17

4. Click (Ghost View) and select components to make them transparent on the screen. Reverse the process to set them back to the original display.
5. Drag the turntable to rotate parts.

Open

Typically, to open a file, right-click on it from either a *Search Results* or an *Explorer* window, then select **Open**, as shown in Figure 1–18. When opening an assembly, by default all child parts of that assembly will be loaded.

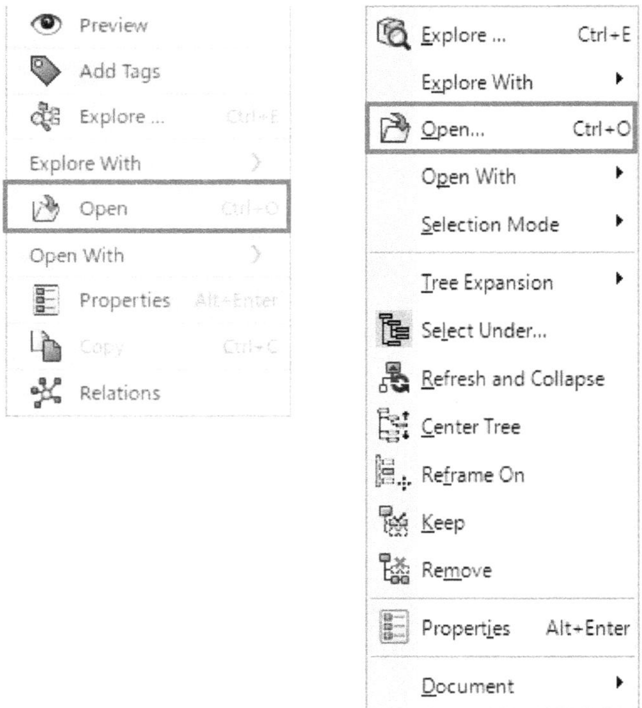

Figure 1–18

Open Advanced

Extra options are available when using **Open With**, as shown in Figure 1–19.

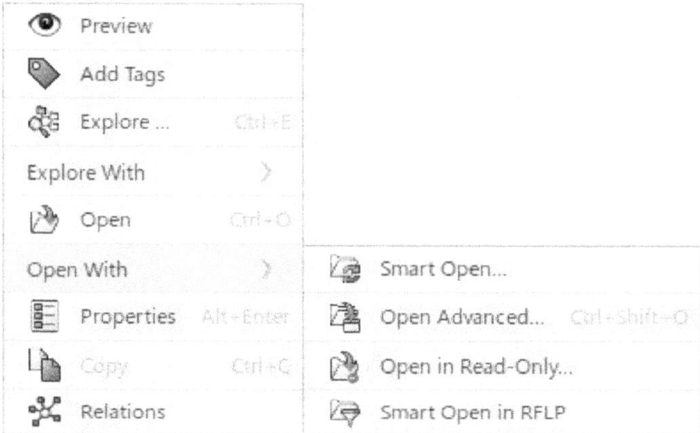

Figure 1–19

Open Advanced displays the *Open Advanced* dialog box, as shown in Figure 1–20.

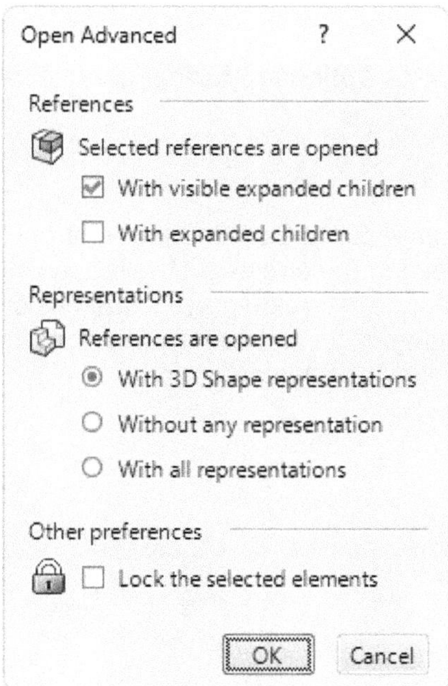

Figure 1–20

The advanced options are as follows:

Section	Description
References	**With visible expanded children** opens only the parts that are expanded in the tree. **With expanded children** opens all subparts of an assembly, regardless of the tree being expanded.
Representations	Select what type of references will be loaded.
Other preferences	Select to automatically lock (check out) the selected elements for modification.

Save

Due to the integration of 3DEXPERIENCE CATIA with a centralized file database, local file storage does not typically occur. Instead, files are stored in the engineering database for access by other team members or departments. File access is controlled by the database administrator or someone with the appropriate security access.

- Click (Share) and **Save**. The files will be saved to the database using the default settings.
- Click (Share)>**Save with Options** to further control the saving operation.

Save with Options

Save with Options is somewhat similar to Save Management in V5. Here the current status of the parts can be checked by viewing the circles on the left, as shown in Figure 1–21. Filters can be used to pick what types of parts are displayed, such as only showing modified items. If a part has been accidentally changed, it can be excluded from being saved. To make a copy of a part, there is **Save As New** as well as revision options.

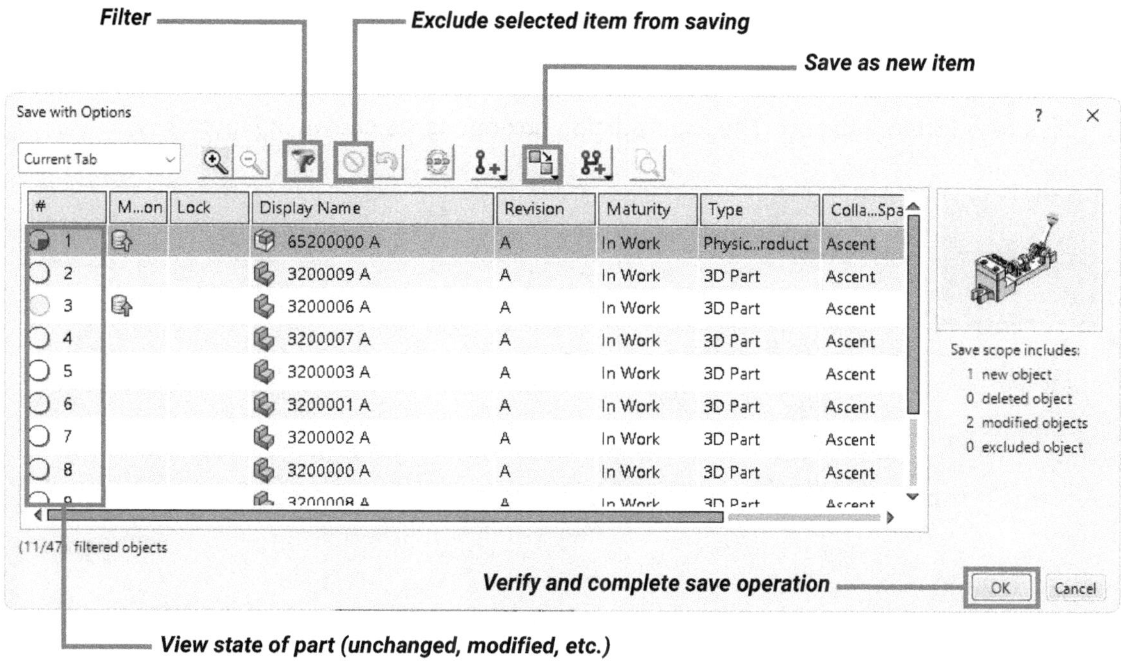

Figure 1–21

The current state of each item is shown by the color of the circle on the right, as shown in Figure 1–22. **New** is blue, **Modified** is yellow, **Not modified** is white, and **Modified and locked by others** is red.

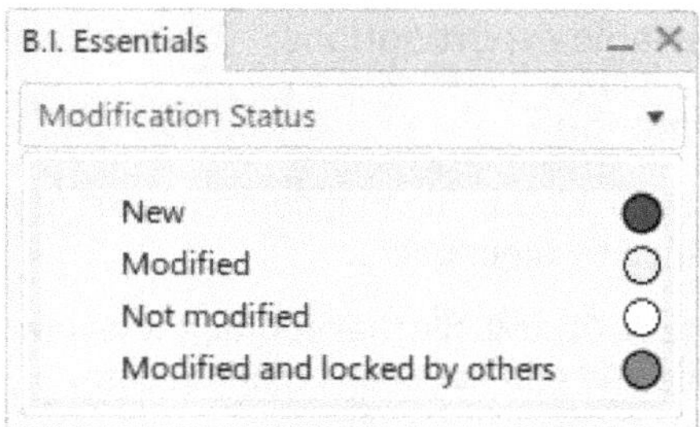

Figure 1–22

Export

Exporting will allow a file to be stored outside of the 3DEXPERIENCE platform vault in order to be shared with users of other systems.

How To: Export a File

1. Click (Share)>**Export**. The *Export* dialog box opens, as shown in Figure 1–23.

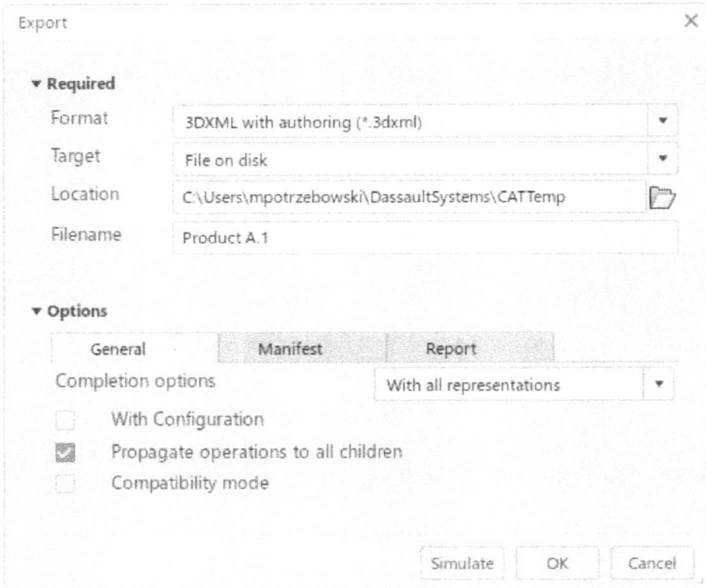

Figure 1–23

2. Select the *Format* drop-down list to change the file type of the exported file. The following table lists some of the available export options:

Option	Description
3DXML with authoring	Creates a 3DXML file that contains part feature data. This part can be modified by other users.
3DXML with review	Creates a 3DXML file that contains a review. Other users will be able to see the file and add notes and markup data.
CATIA file	Creates a file that will be compatible with CATIA V5.
IGES3D	Exports as a neutral .IGS file. Commonly used to transfer surface data between CAD programs.
STEP	Exports as a .STP file. Commonly used to transfer solid data between CAD programs.
STL	Exports a Stereo Lithography file. Typically used for 3D printing and rapid prototyping.

3. Select the location to save the file.
4. (Optional) Set exclusion options.

5. Click **OK**.

While saving, the *B.I. Essentials* window opens and color codes each part, as shown in Figure 1–24. **To be exported** is green, **To be excluded** is white, **To be delegated** is blue, and **To be waived** is cyan.

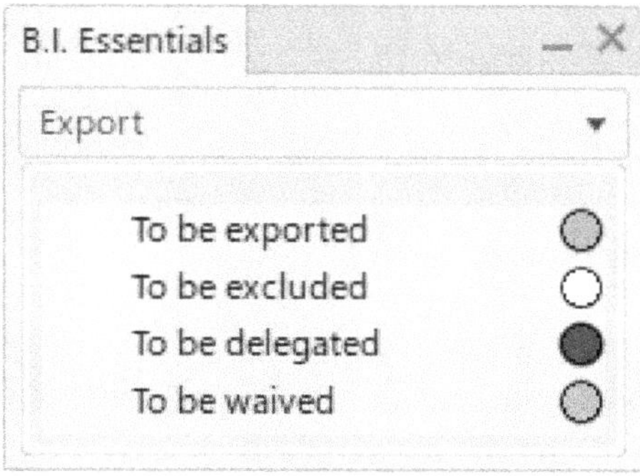

Figure 1–24

To exclude a part from being exported:

1. Select the part while the *Export* dialog box is open.
2. Click **Exclude** in the floating dialog menu, as shown in Figure 1–25.

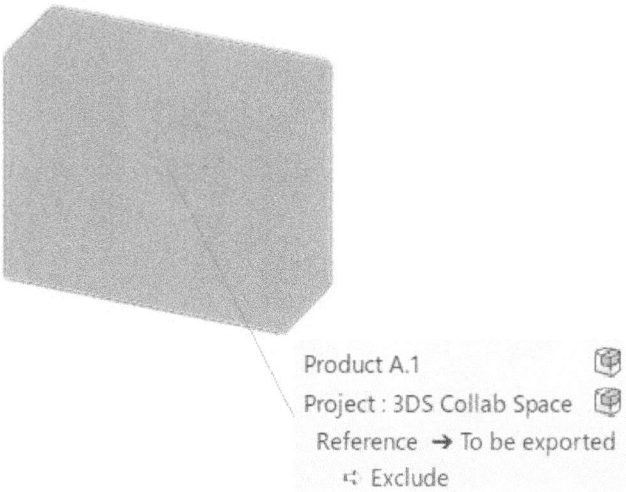

Figure 1–25

Note: *Excluding this way can only be done when using 3DXML as the output type.*

Practice 1a
Access the 3DEXPERIENCE Platform

Practice Objectives

- Log in to the 3DEXPERIENCE platform.
- Import a model.
- Make an edit to the model and save it.
- Open the revised model via search.

In this practice, you will log in to the 3DEXPERIENCE platform and import a model. You will change the geometry of a model and save it to the database, then reopen it using search.

Task 1: Launch the 3DEXPERIENCE platform.

1. Double-click the **3DEXPERIENCE R2026x** icon on the desktop, as shown in Figure 1–26.

Figure 1–26

Note: *The icon may very depending on implementation.*

2. In the *Login | 3DEXPERIENCE ID* dialog box (shown in Figure 1–27), enter the *Username* assigned by your administrator.

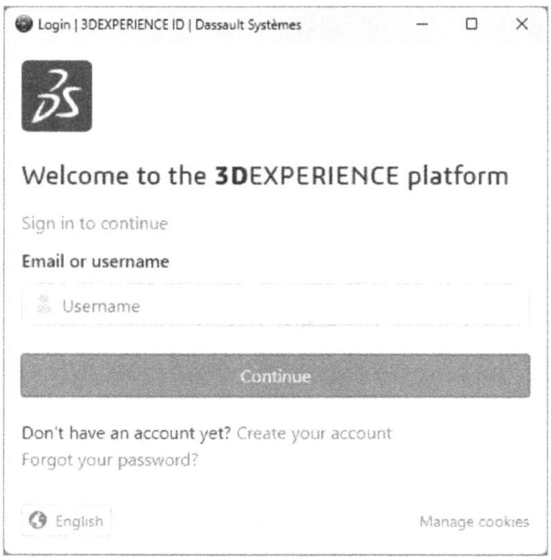

Figure 1–27

3. Click **Continue**.
4. Enter your *Password*, also given to you by your administrator.
5. Click **Log in**.
6. In the *3DEXPERIENCE Platform* dialog box, expand the *Collaborative Space* drop-down list and select **Common Space**, as shown in Figure 1–28. Click **OK**.

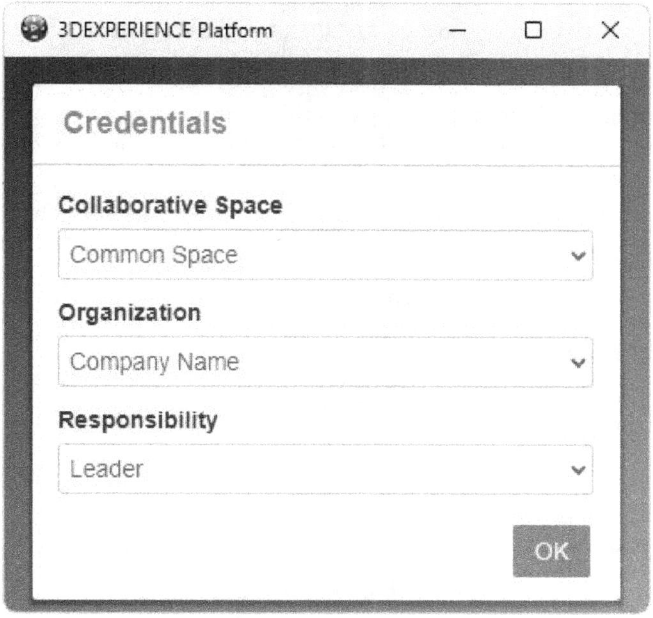

Figure 1–28

Note: *If you are not using this content in the Rand 3D environment, use the credentials, Collaborative Space, and Responsibility provided by your system administrator.*

7. If presented with the welcome screen (shown in Figure 1–29), navigate through it with the arrows on the sides or small circles at the bottom, then close it by clicking the **X** in the top-right corner.

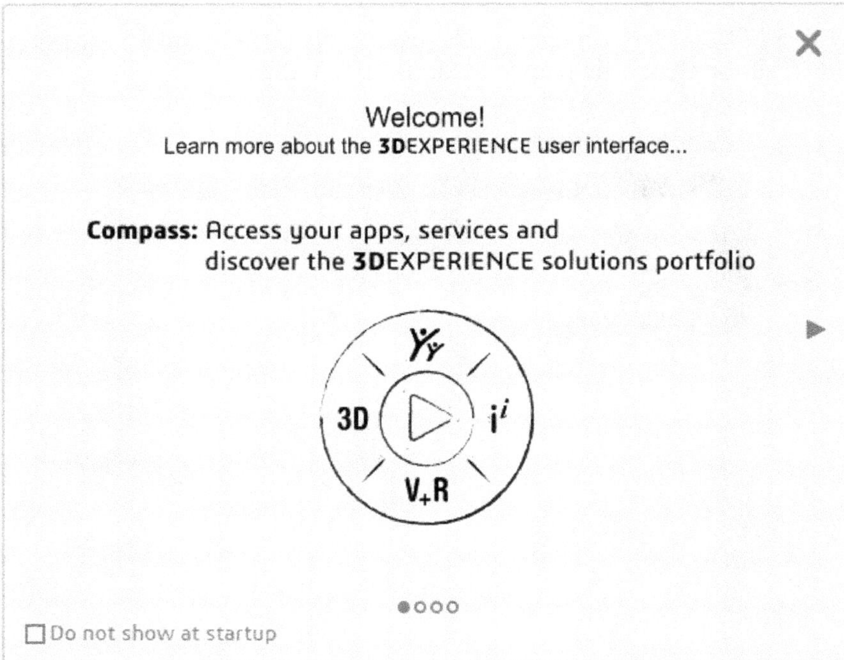

Figure 1–29

Task 2: Set the 3DEXPERIENCE platform to add your initials to new and imported objects.

1. In the Top Bar, click  (User Icon) and select **Preferences**, as shown in Figure 1–30. (The SS stands for *Student## Student##*; if using your own login, your first and last initals will be displayed here instead.)

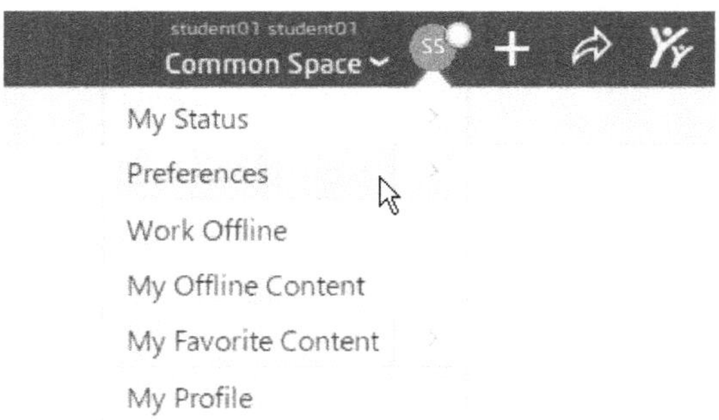

Figure 1–30

2. In the *Preferences* dialog box, select the *App Preferences* tab, as shown in Figure 1–31.
3. Expand **Social and Collaborative>Global Design Management** and select **Collaborative Lifecycle**, as shown in Figure 1–31.
4. In the *Identification* section, in the *Identification String* field, add your initials followed by an underscore, as shown in Figure 1–31.

   Note: *Alternatively, you can type* ***Identification String*** *into the search settings under the Preferences tab and let it find the field for you.*

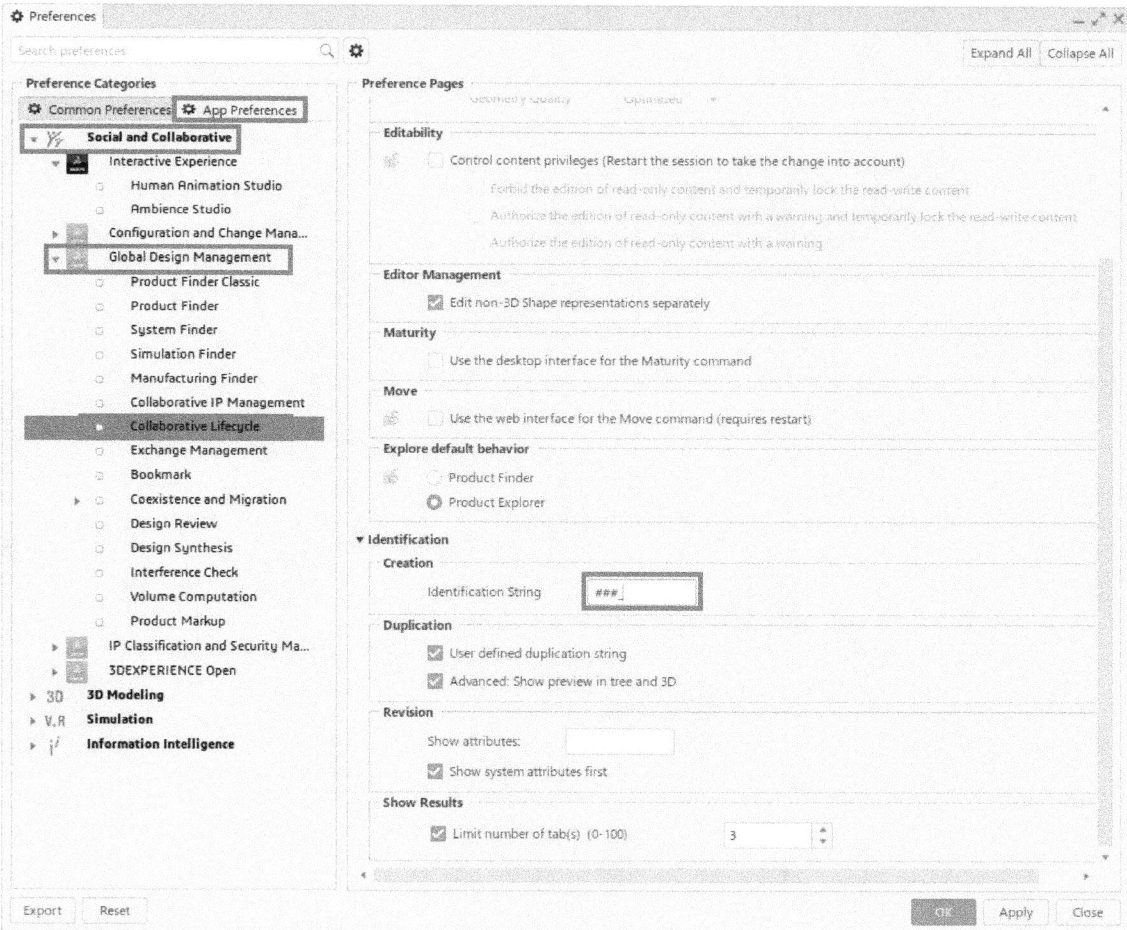

Figure 1–31

Note: *The images in this guide will not show initials preceding the names.*

5. Click **OK**.

Task 3: Import a CATIA part.

1. In the Top Bar, click  (Add/Create)>**Import**.
2. In the *Import* dialog box, click  (Open).
3. Navigate to the *3DEXPERIENCE Transition Practice Files* folder, select **Bore-Device-Assembled.3dxml**, and click **Open**.
4. Ensure that the settings in the *Import* dialog box match those shown in Figure 1–32.

   Note: *The Duplication string field will show your initials based on the preference setting you made in Task 2.*

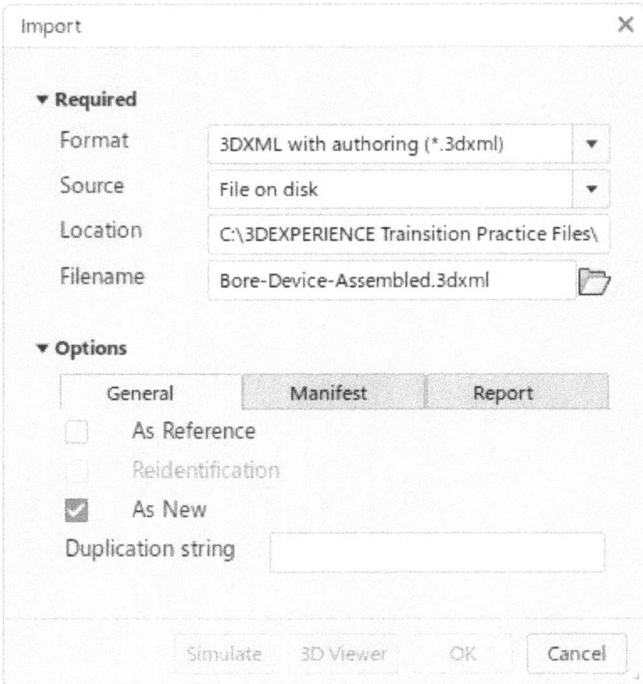

Figure 1–32

5. Click **OK**.
6. In the *Operation report* dialog box, click **OK**.

Task 4: Investigate the Explorer.

1. The model displays as shown in Figure 1–33.

   Note: *The initial display in the Explore view within the ENOVIA Product Finder app is a representation of the model, rather than the geometry.*

Figure 1–33

2. Expand the listing in the specification tree, as shown in Figure 1–34.

   Note: *You may need to click the arrow on the left side of the screen to see the specification tree the first time you open an object. Your objects will have your initials as a prefix.*

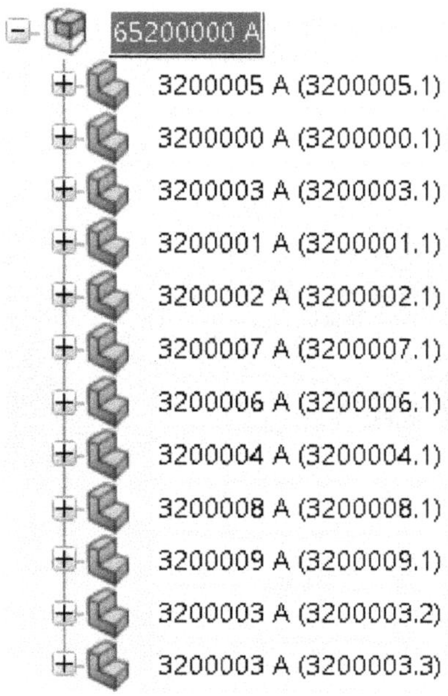

Figure 1–34

3. In the *View* tab of the Action Bar, click (Swap Turntable/In-place) until the assembly displays fully assembled, as shown in Figure 1–35.

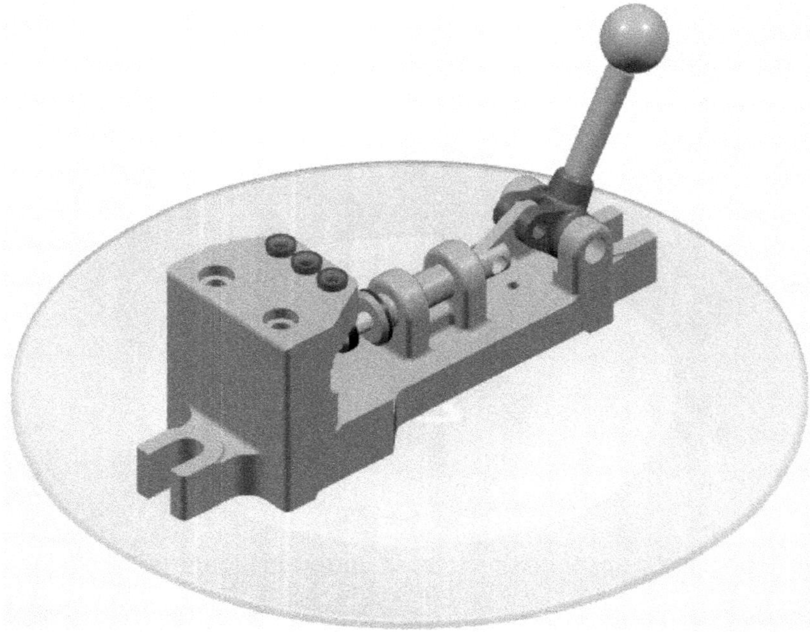

Figure 1–35

4. Click and drag the turntable to rotate the assembly, until it displays approximately as shown in Figure 1–36.

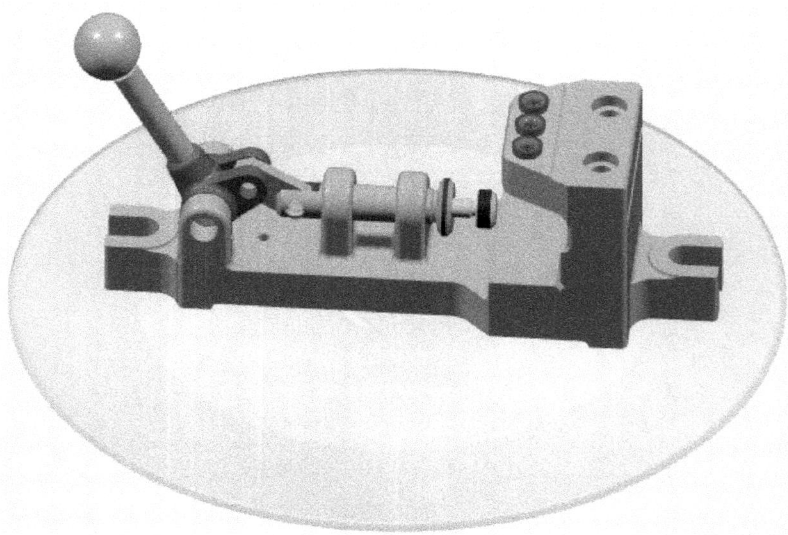

Figure 1–36

5. Click (Swap Turntable/In-place) to view the components, as shown in Figure 1–37.

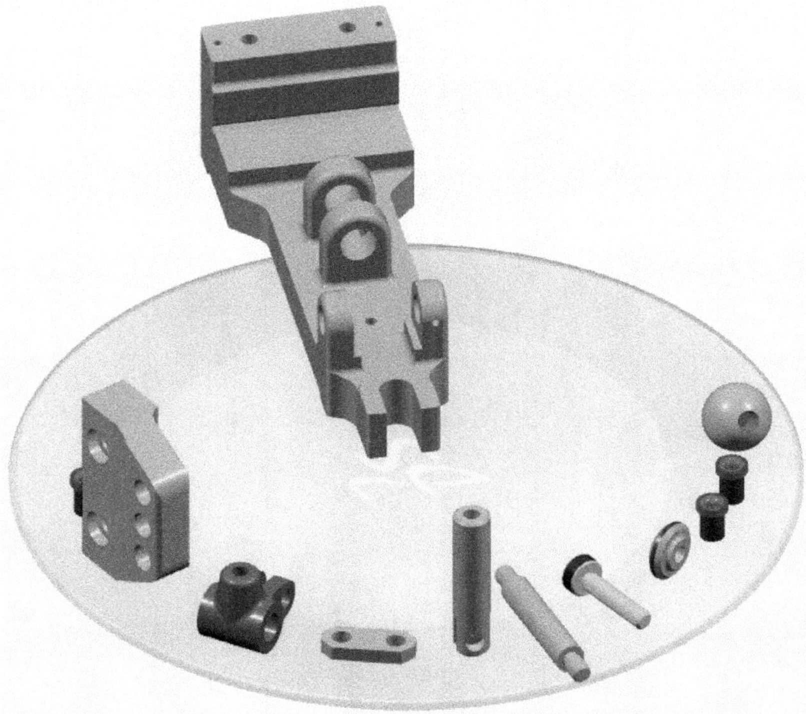

Figure 1–37

6. In the *View* tab, click (Text View) to view callouts of each component found in the assembly, as shown in Figure 1–38.

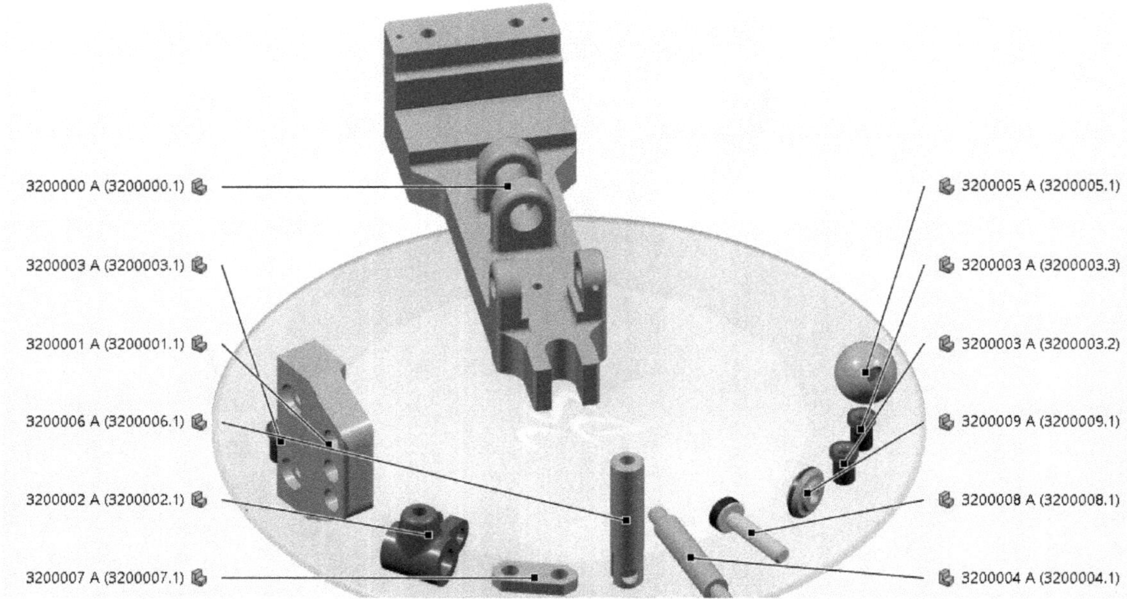

Figure 1–38

7. Select several text labels and note that as they are selected, the applicable model highlights both on screen and in the specification tree.

   Note: *Your objects will have your initials preceding their name. In the text and images in this content, the names will be shown without any prefixes.*

8. Click (Text View) to turn off the callouts.

9. Select the **3200001** component and in the *View* tab of the Action Bar, click (Ghost View). Note that the object is displayed transparently, as shown in Figure 1–39.

   Note: *Objects set to Ghost View will have next to them in the specification tree.*

   Edges have been turned off in the View Mode, otherwise the outline will still show.

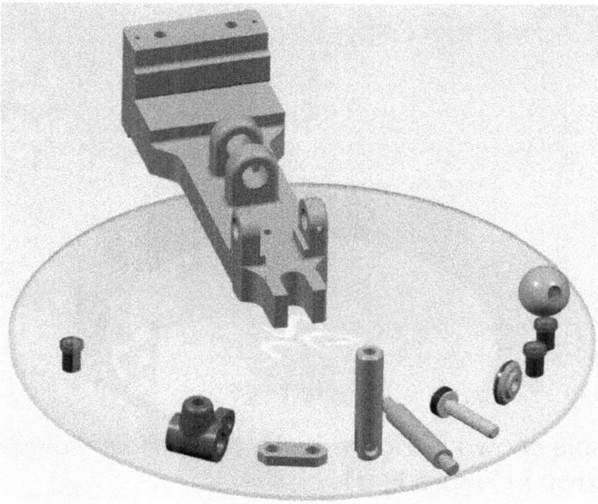

Figure 1–39

10. Select the **3200001** component again and click (Ghost View) to reset it to shaded.
11. Click (Swap Turntable/In-place) to view the assembled model.

Task 5: Open the assembly for editing.

1. In the specification tree, right-click on **65200000** and select **Open**.
2. In the Action Bar, select the *Product Modification* tab. This tab allows you to complete assembly-related tasks, such as assembling new components.
3. In the specification tree, right-click on **3200001** and select **3200001.1 object>Open in New App**.

   Note: *If you do not see the specification tree, click the arrow on the left side of the screen.*

4. The part opens in its own tab, as shown in Figure 1–40.

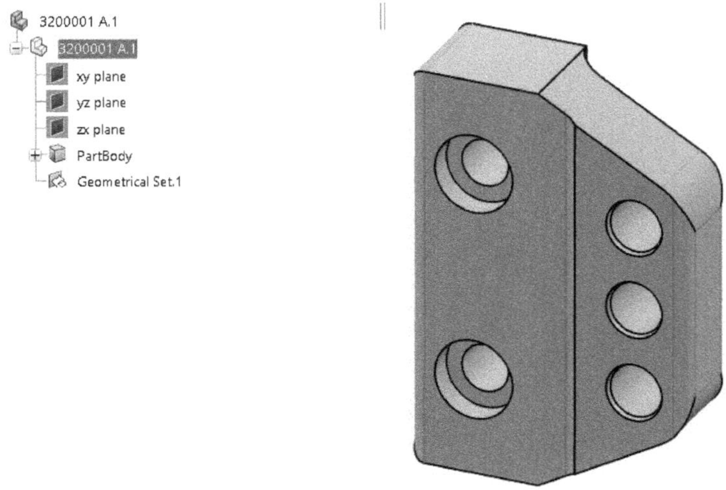

Figure 1–40

5. Double-click on the hole shown in Figure 1–41. In the *Hole* dialog box, change the *Main diameter* to **10**, as shown in Figure 1–41.

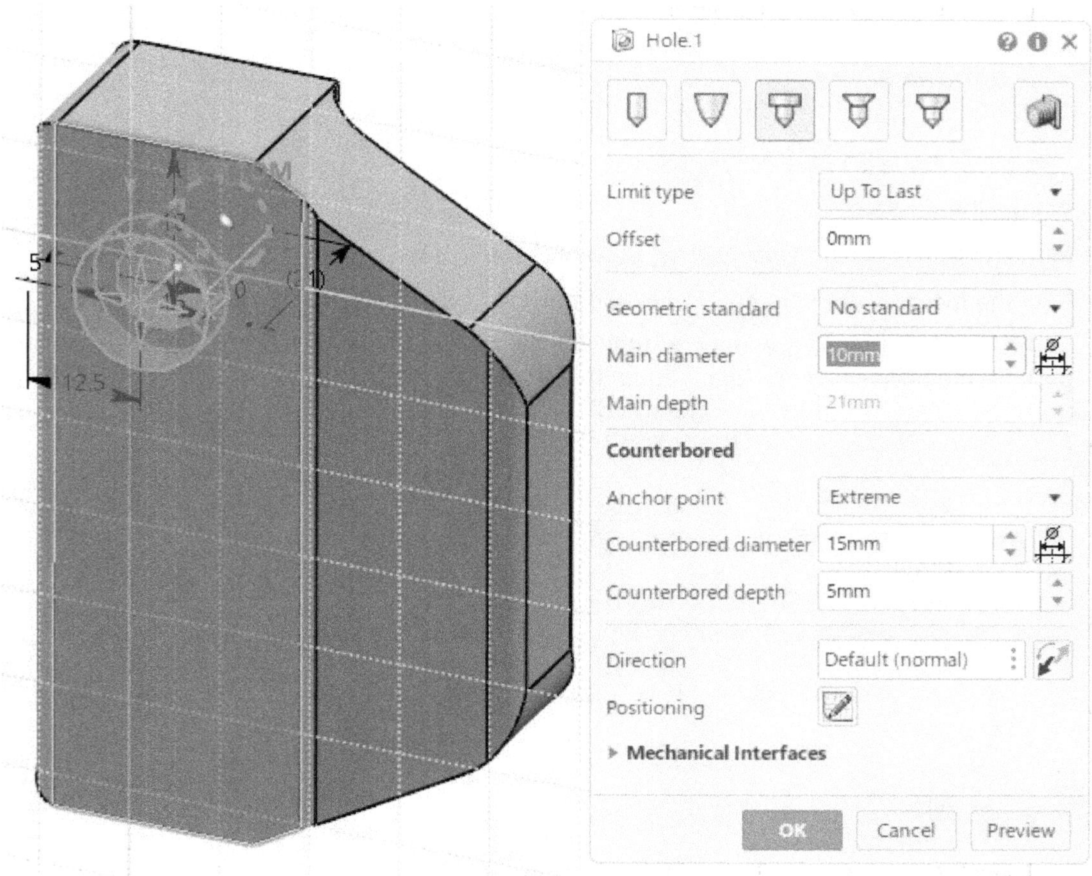

Figure 1–41

6. Click **OK**.
7. Close the *3200001* part tab.
8. In the Action Bar, click  (Update) to update the assembly.

Task 6: Save the assembly, then use the search bar to reopen it from the database.

1. In the Top Bar, click (Share)>**Save**.
2. Close all the open tabs.
3. In the search bar, type ***Your_Initials_652**** and press <Enter>.
4. Find the most recent version of the assembly, right-click, and select **Open**.
5. In the specification tree, expand **3200001** fully and double-click on **Hole.1** to activate the part, then double-click on **Hole.1** again to edit the feature. Note that the diameter is the updated 10mm, as shown in Figure 1–42.

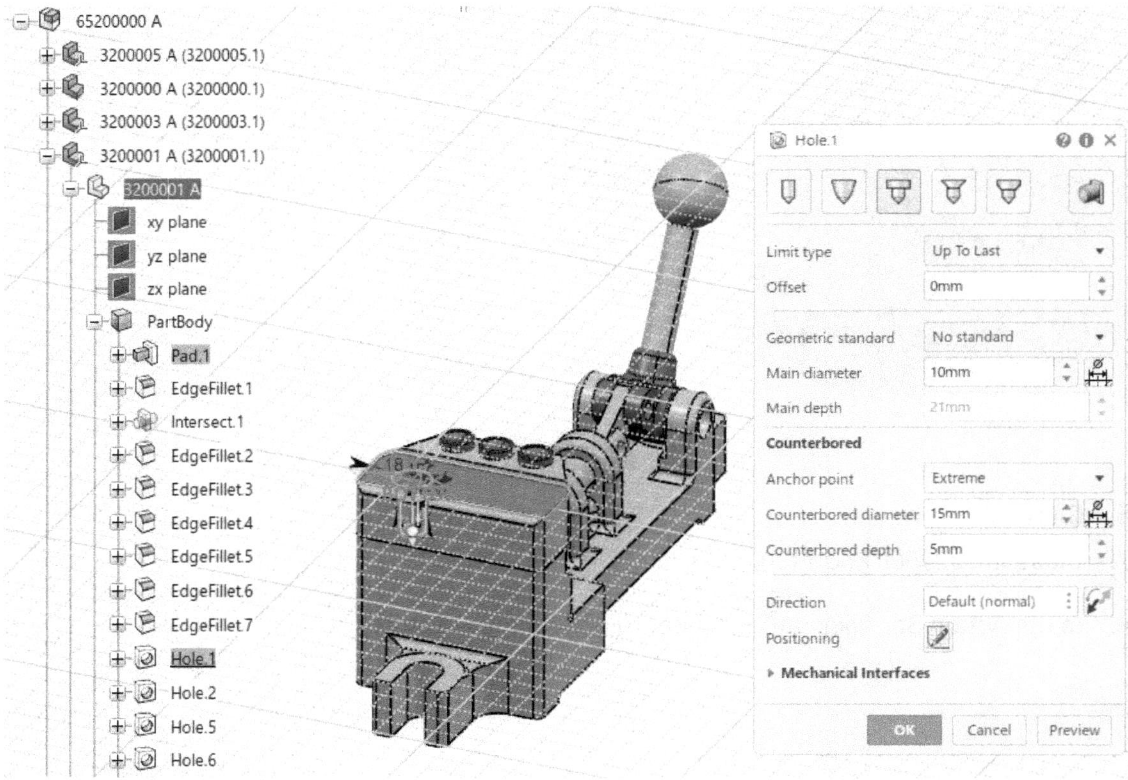

Figure 1–42

6. Click **Cancel** in the *Hole* dialog box.
7. Close the tab.

End of practice

Chapter 2

Getting Started with the 3DEXPERIENCE Platform

In this chapter, you are introduced to the 3DEXPERIENCE platform interface and will learn how to customize the Action Bar and apps to suit your preferences and requirements and to help you work more efficiently.

Learning Objectives

- Review the settings in the *Preferences* dialog box.
- Review the recommended settings for completing this guide.
- Learn how to manipulate the Action Bar to customize the interface and streamline your working environment.
- Customize the 3DEXPERIENCE platform to display your preferred apps.

2.1 User Interface

Welcome Screen

When you launch the 3DEXPERIENCE platform, you are presented with a welcome screen on a web page , as shown in Figure 2–1.

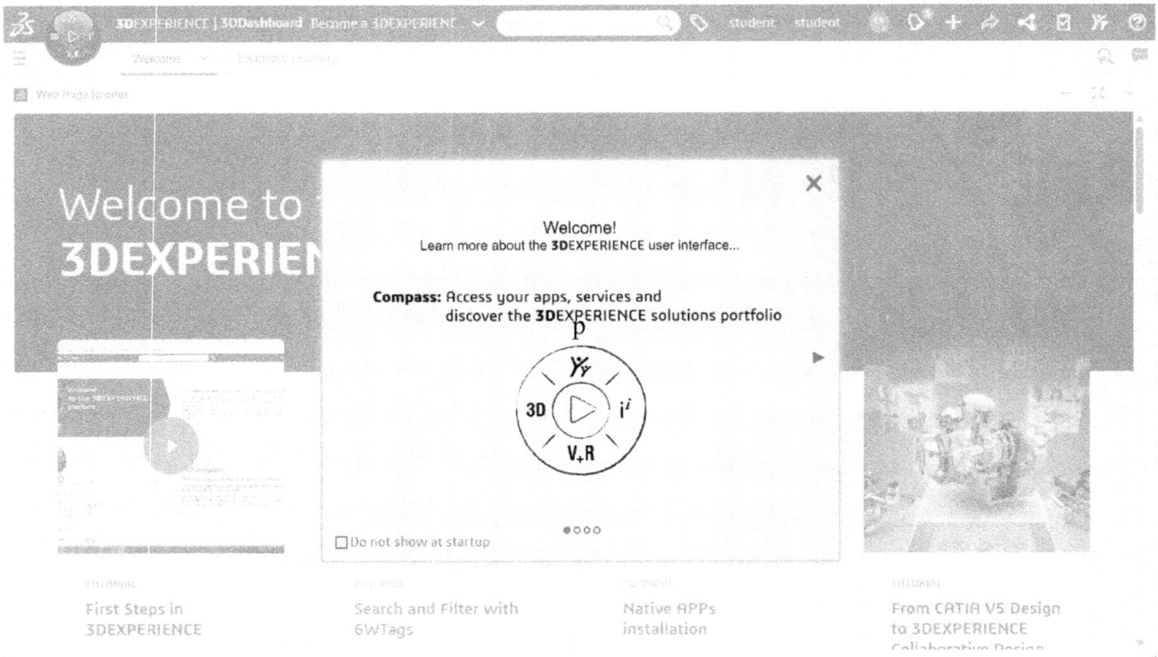

Figure 2–1

This welcome screen has multiple pages, accessed by the arrows on the side or the circular buttons at the bottom, as shown in Figure 2–2. The circular buttons allow you to move to a specific page.

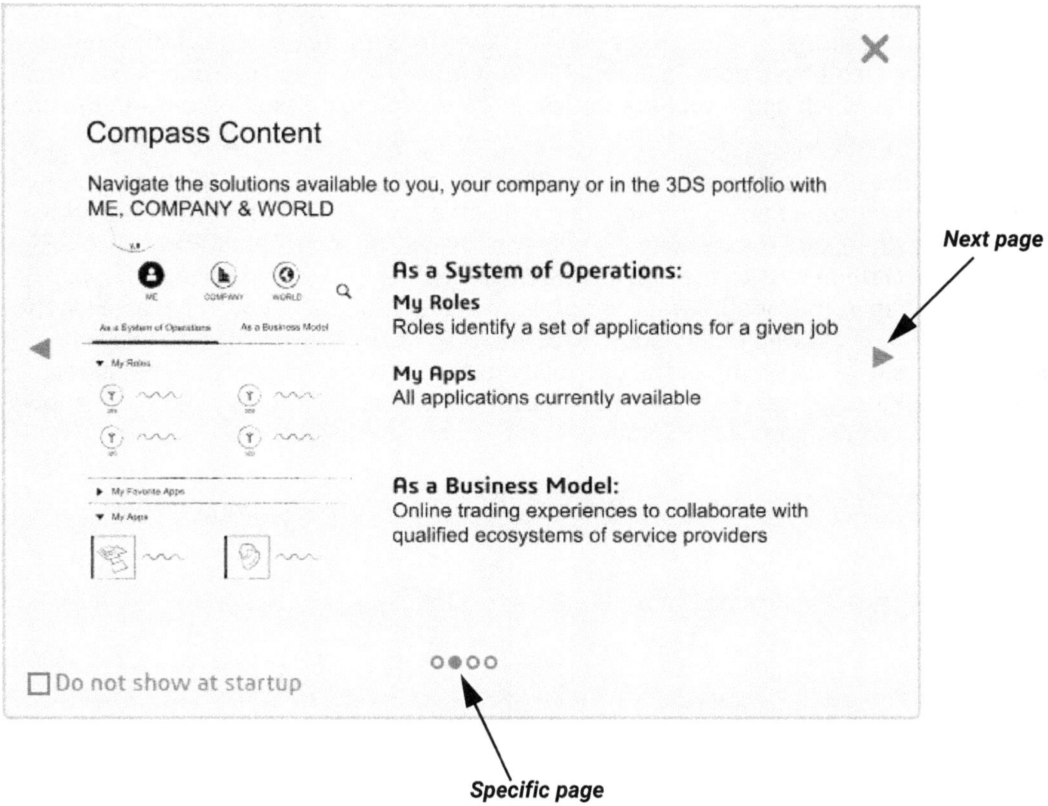

Figure 2–2

You can click through this welcome screen to discover the basics of the 3DEXPERIENCE platform user interface. If you do not want to see this screen when the 3DEXPERIENCE platform launches, select **Do not show at startup**.

Web vs. Desktop Apps

Once you log in to 3DEXPERIENCE CATIA, you are taken to a web page. Within 3DEXPERIENCE, there are apps for both desktop (installed and run on your computer) and web-based (run in a web browser) applications. The first page you are taken to is an area that can be customized to show many of the web-based apps (a.k.a. widgets). It is also where you can access the desktop apps. You can find which apps you have access to by selecting on the Compass in the upper-left corner of the screen.

The app icons have color and graphical indicators to help you understand the type of software they represent. Navy blue next to the app icon indicates it is a CATIA app (intended primarily for CAD modification), and once chosen, a new window will open for the 3DEXPERIENCE CATIA program. Orange next to the app indicates an ENOVIA (PLM management) app. Desktop apps open in the locally installed software and do not display with an arrow in the upper-right corner, while web-based apps (widgets) display an arrow and open in a web browser. Widgets give you some of the capability of the software quickly but are limited, whereas the desktop app can be slower but give more options. Examples of both are shown in Figure 2–3. Most of the apps used in this content will be desktop apps.

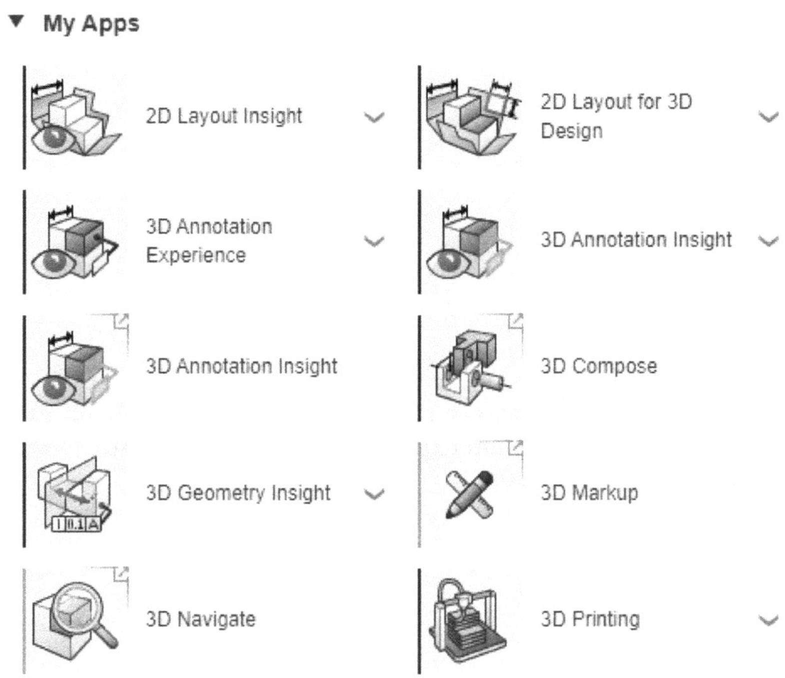

Figure 2–3

Screen Layout

When you open a model in 3DEXPERIENCE CATIA Part Design, the screen displays as shown in Figure 2–4. The major areas of the interface that are labeled are discussed in the following topics.

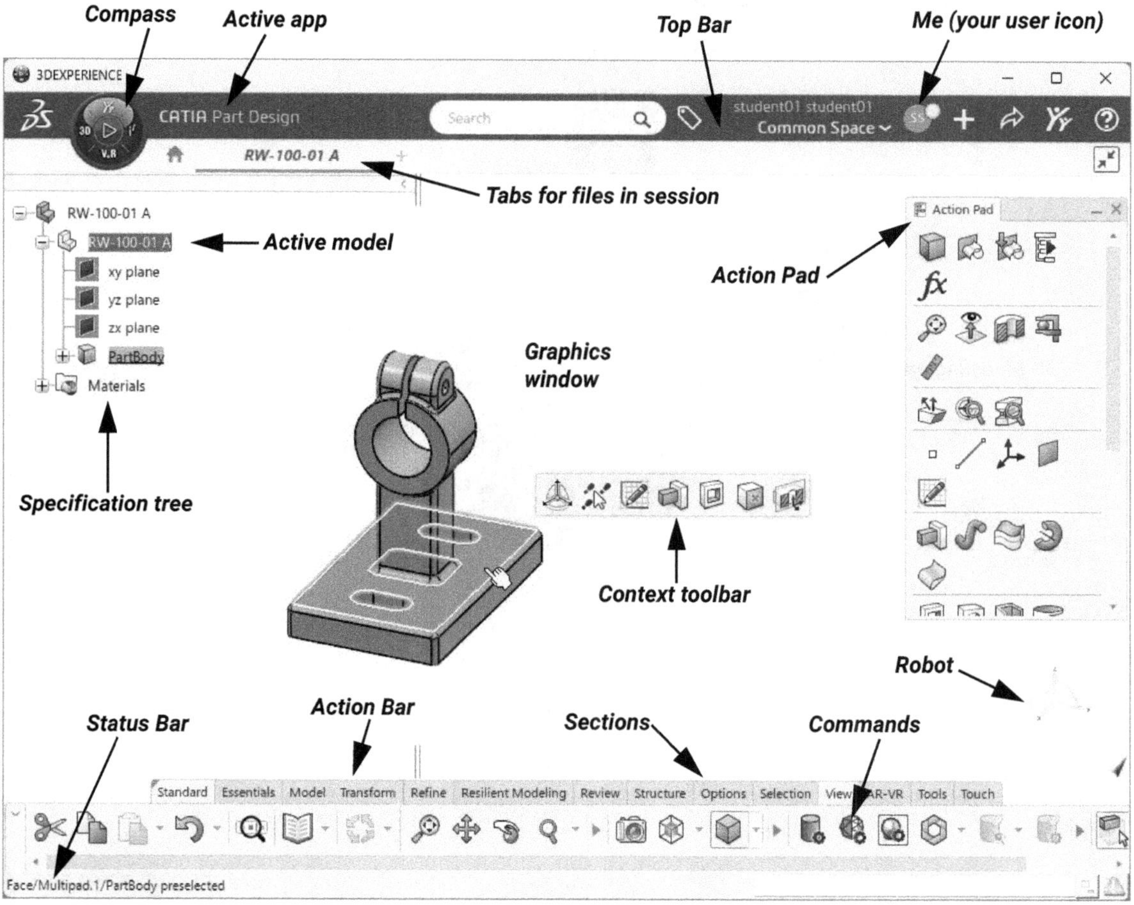

Figure 2–4

Commands

The primary way of interacting with the software is to select icons in the Action Bar, *Action Pad*, or context toolbar. You can customize the interface by arranging the location of the toolbars and selecting the icons to display.

Compass

The Compass enables you to access various apps. The Compass is broken into two fictional areas. The inner circle named the **Play** button and the outer ring named **Roles, Apps & Solutions portfolio**. The outer ring allows you to switch between roles and apps freely, while the **Play** button allows you to interact only with the applicable apps. Some of the major categories in the 3DEXPERIENCE platform system are shown in Figure 2–5.

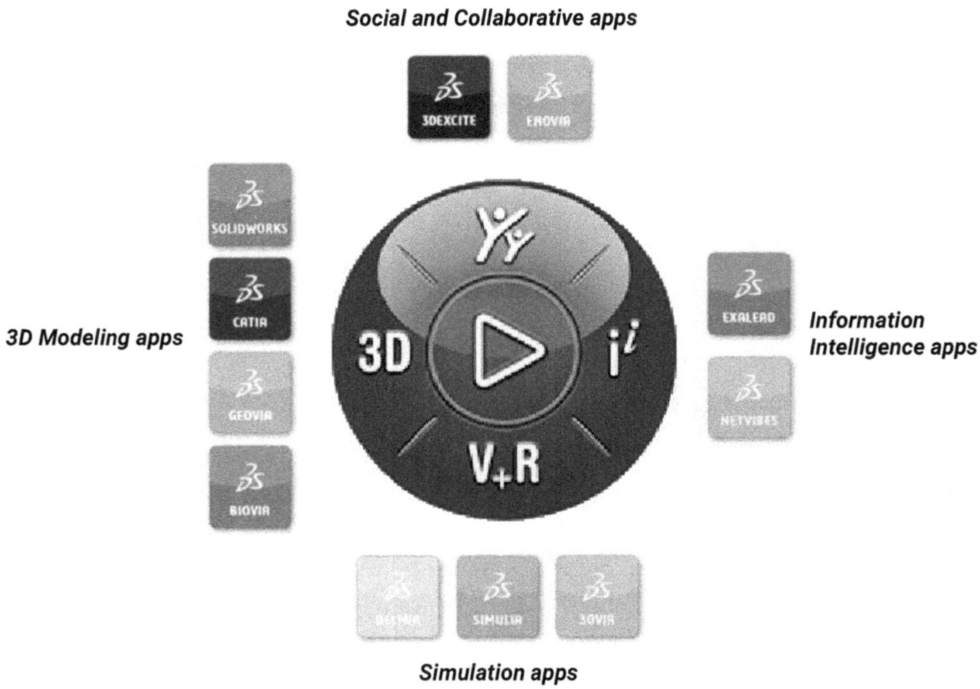

Figure 2–5

Search Bar

The search bar enables you to look up CATIA files within the engineering database. Searches can include wildcard (*) use (as shown in Figure 2–6) and can be refined in various ways.

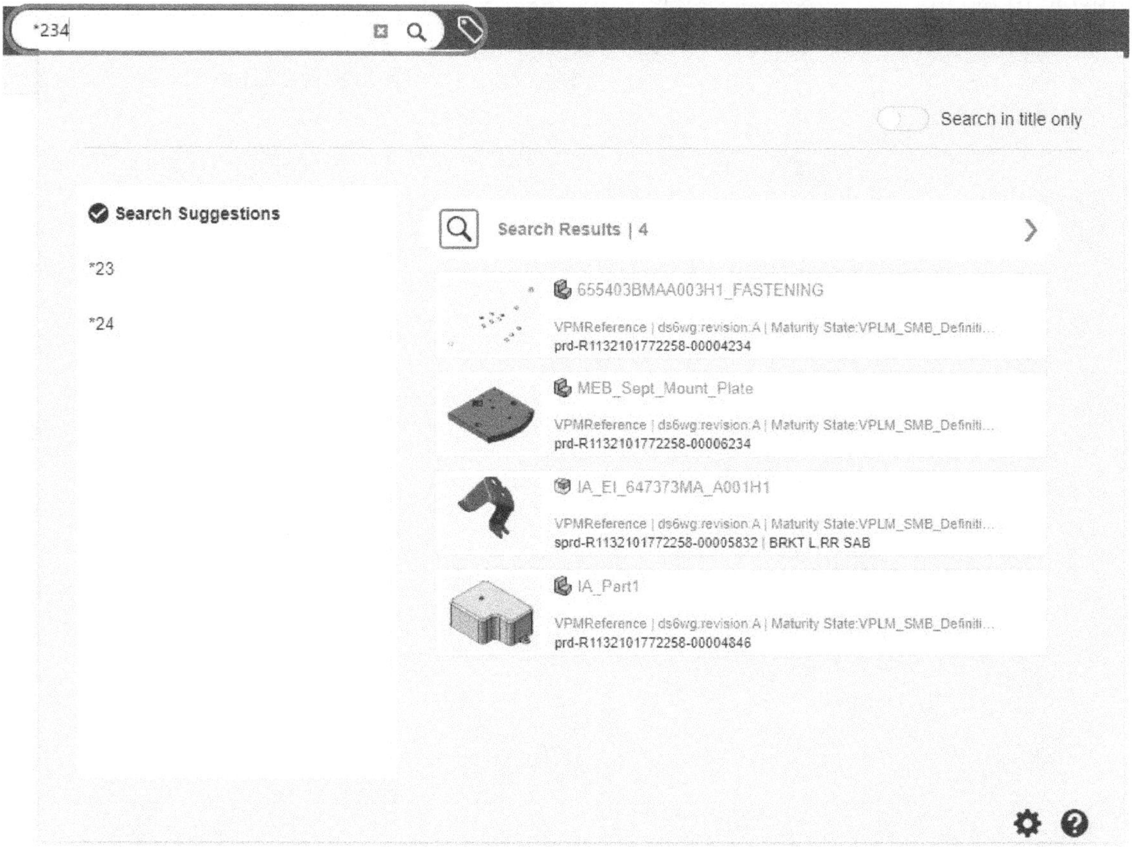

Figure 2–6

Specification Tree

The specification tree is available when working with parts, assemblies, and drawings. It displays a variety of information about the model and displays the features of the part in the order in which they were created, as shown in Figure 2–7. This provides quick access to parameters, functions, materials, and commonly used measurements.

> **Note:** *The specification tree can be quickly toggled on and off by pressing <F3>.*

Figure 2–7

Robot

The Robot is available for part and assembly models. It displays in the lower-right corner of the model window and can perform various functions, as shown in Figure 2–8. The Robot is used to:

- Freely rotate the model in all three directions.
- Rotate the model in a plane.
- Pan along one direction.
- Pan in a plane.
- View down an axis direction by selecting the X, Y, or Z letter. Selecting again flips the view in the opposite direction.

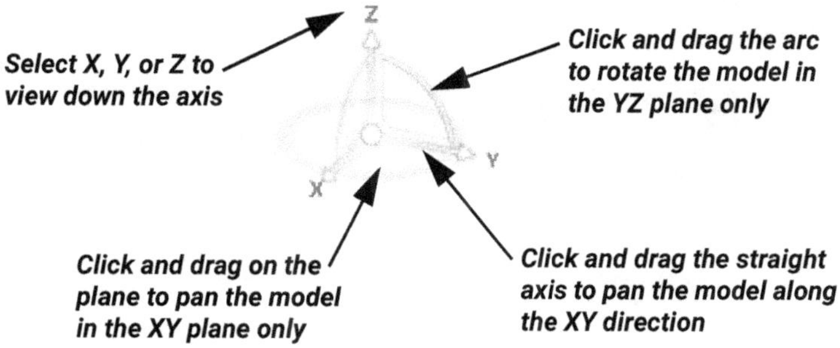

Figure 2–8

Tabs

Multiple objects can be open at the same time. Each object is presented in its own tab, and you can switch back and forth between objects simply by selecting the tab name. Tabs can also be subdivided into smaller windows called widgets, as shown in Figure 2–9.

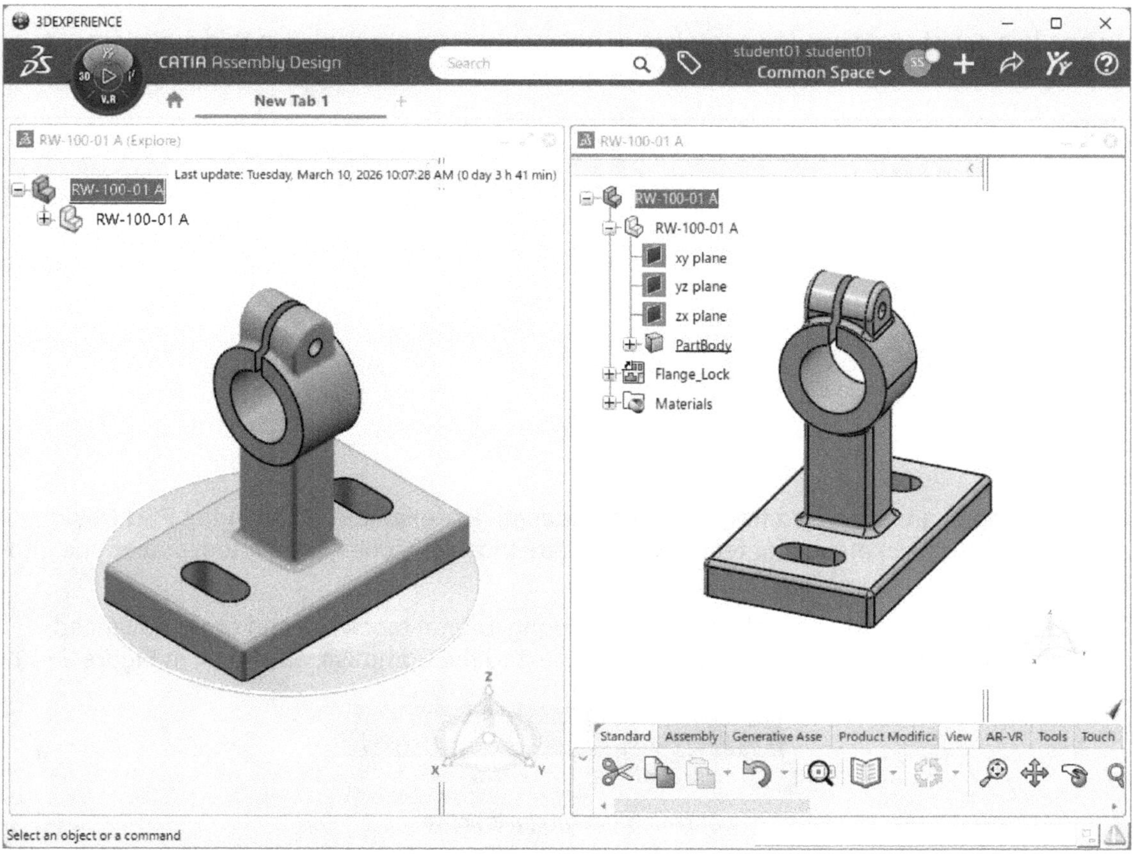

Figure 2–9

You can access options for controlling the display of widgets by right-clicking on the tab where they are stored, as shown in Figure 2–10.

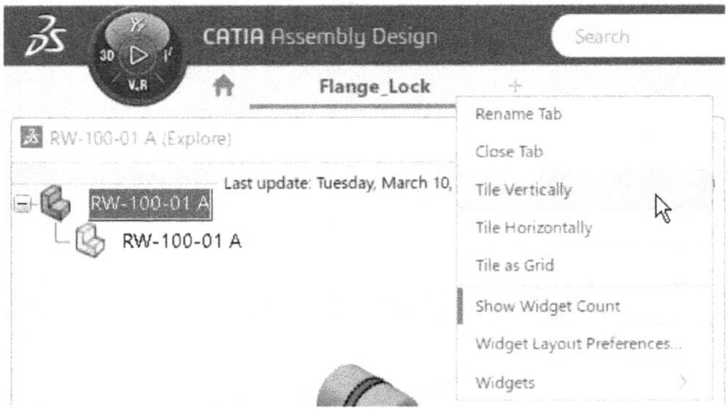

Figure 2–10

Apps

An app is a set of tools used to complete certain tasks. The apps used in this guide are as follows:

Icon	Workbench
	Part Design
	Drafting
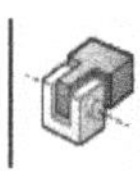	Assembly Design

Additional apps are accessed from within other apps. For example, when in the Part Design app, you will create sketches for features. To create those sketches, the system places you into the Sketcher app.

Other apps can be used for Analysis, Manufacturing, Digital Mock Up, and other advanced tasks. The name of the active app is displayed next to the Compass, as shown in Figure 2–11.

Assembly Design app is active

Figure 2–11

2.2 Action Bar Customization

Once an app is launched or a model or drawing is opened, the Action Bar displays at the bottom of the 3DEXPERIENCE platform window, as shown in Figure 2–12. The Action Bar is organized into sections, and each section has multiple commands.

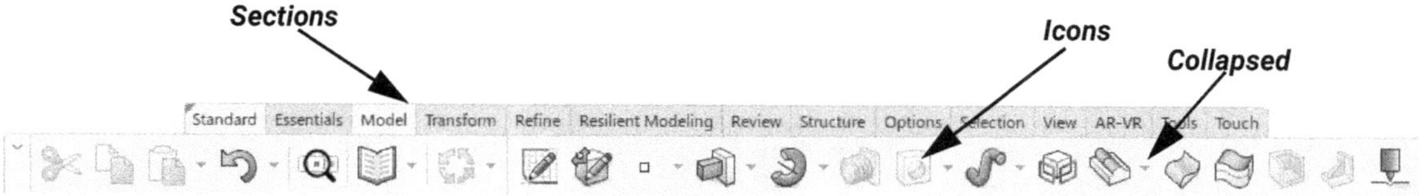

Figure 2–12

The default setting for the Action Bar is to display all the section names in dark gray, but with the name of the selected section displayed with a white background. Additionally, the icons display with their image, but no names. This display mode takes up the minimum amount of screen space, and if you hover your cursor over any of the sections or icons, a tooltip displays with the applicable name. However, until you are familiar with the modeling environment, you may want more information displayed.

You can right-click on the Action Bar and select **Display Icons and Text**. The Action Bar updates as shown in Figure 2–13. Note that the Action Bar now takes up considerably more space to account for the command names.

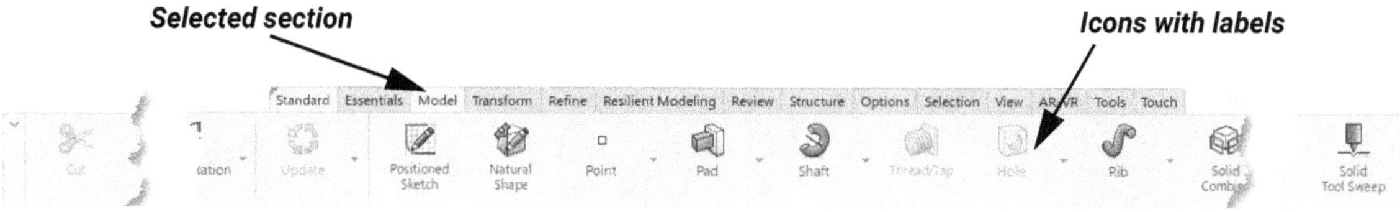

Figure 2–13

Add Commands

You can rearrange icons in the Action Bar by right-clicking on the Action Bar and selecting **Customize Mode**. When you do, if you right-click again anywhere on the Action Bar, you will see an expanded list of options, as shown in Figure 2–14.

> ***Note:*** *This list of options will vary depending on the location on the Action Bar where you right-clicked.*

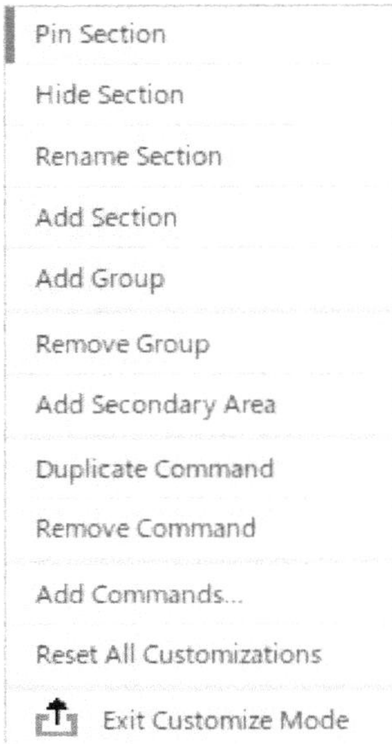

Figure 2–14

The list of options can include the following:

Command	Result
Pin Section	Constantly displays that sections commands while other sections are active.
Hide Section	Hides the currently active section
Rename Section	Renames the currently active section
Add Section	Adds a new empty section to the Action Bar that can be renamed and completely customized.
Add Group	Adds a group to the active section where new commands can be placed.
Remove Group	Removes the group that was right-clicked on.

Command	Result
Add Secondary Area	Adds a "hidden group" to the right of the group that was right-clicked on. Commands can be moved or added to this secondary area. The blue arrow indicating this secondary area can be clicked on to expand or collapse these commands from the display 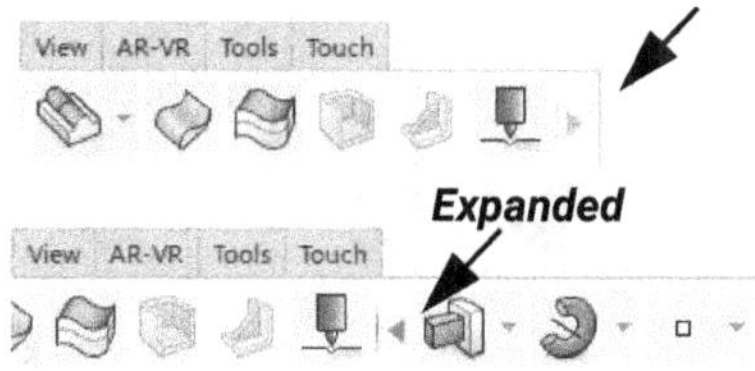
Duplicate Command	Creates a second command that can be moved to new location without moving original.
Add Commands	Opens the *Customize* dialog box, which lists all commands that can be added to the Action Bar.
Reset All Customizations	Returns the Action Bar back to its default settings.

To rearrange icons, simply drag them to the new location. When you release the mouse button, the icon will be moved to the location. In the example shown in Figure 2–15, the icon is moved from one location to another.

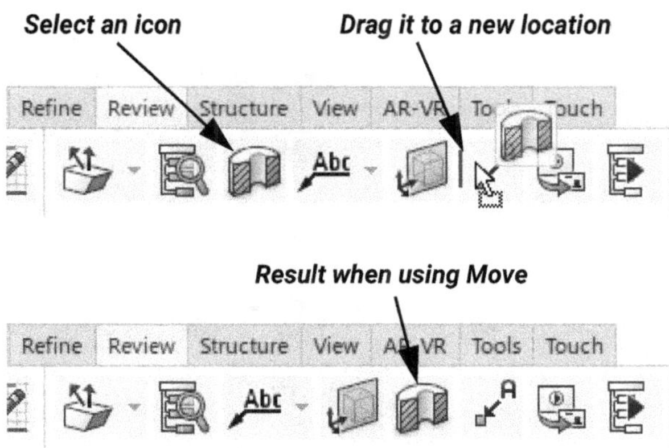

Figure 2–15

Expanding Flyouts

Some Action Bar icons contain flyouts, which display additional icons when selected. For example, the **Pad** feature icon in the *Model* section of the Action Bar contains a flyout, as shown in Figure 2–16.

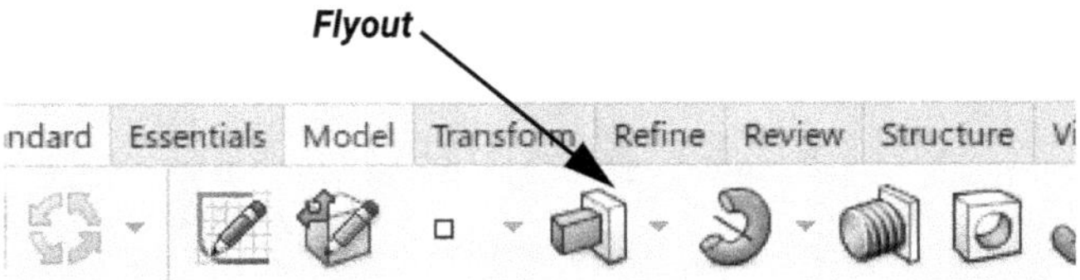

Figure 2–16

Note: Flyout options are grouped by type.

Clicking the flyout (the down arrow) displays the additional icons, as shown in Figure 2–17.

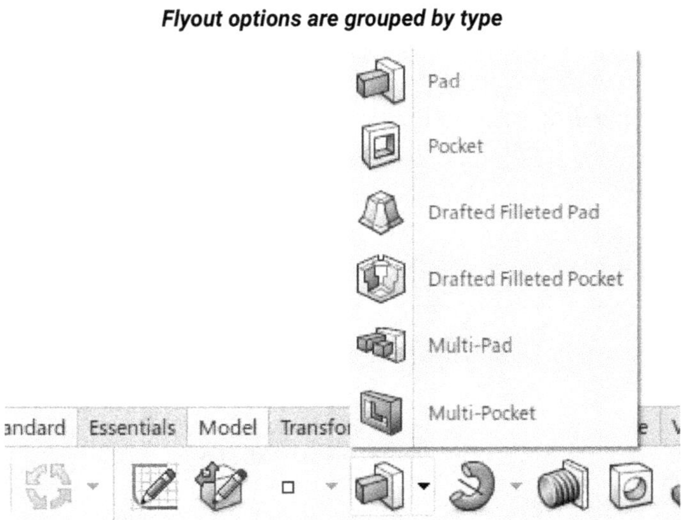

Figure 2–17

When rearranging icons in the Action Bar, you have to move or duplicate all options from the flyout. You cannot select individual options.

Another method for customizing the Action Bar is to select in the Top Bar, right-click, select **Display>Customize**, and select the *Sections* tab in the *Customize* dialog box, as shown in Figure 2–18.

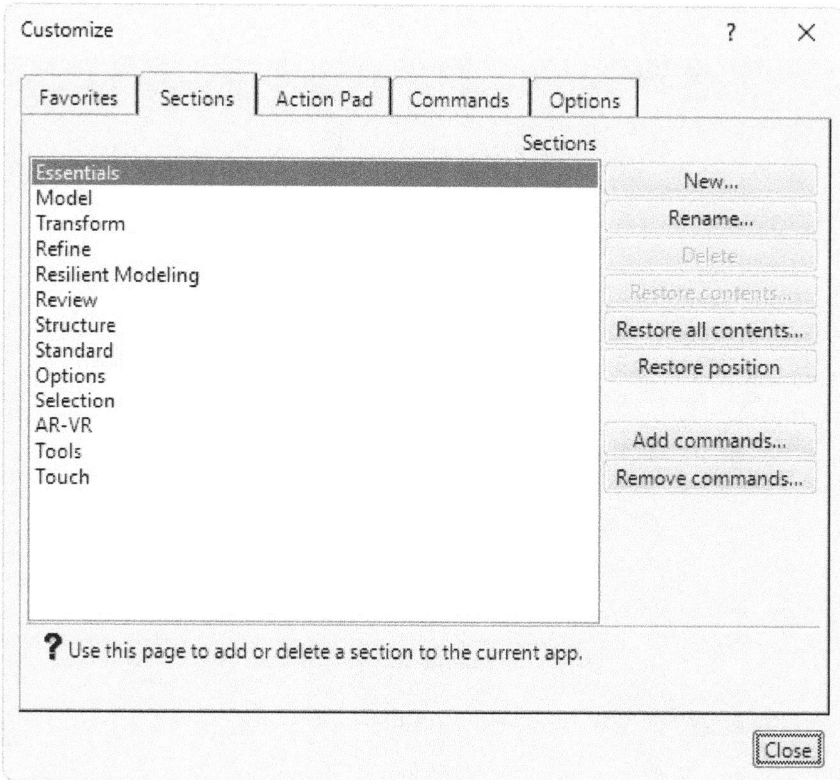

Figure 2–18

On this tab, you can create **New** Action Bar sections, **Rename** existing sections, or **Delete** custom sections you have added.

If you have added or removed commands, you can use the **Restore all contents** option to reset them. **Restore position** will reset the position of any sections you may have moved.

If you click **Add commands**, the *Commands list* dialog box opens, as shown in Figure 2–19, where you can select commands and add them to sections.

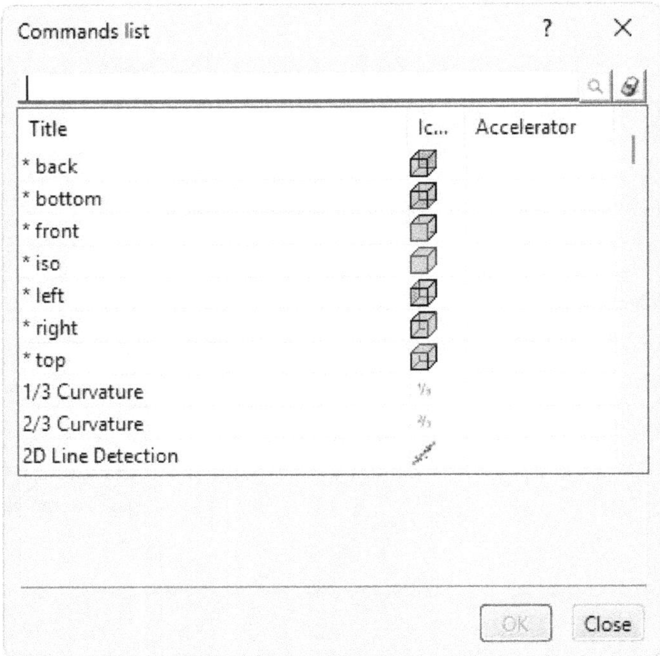

Figure 2–19

Remove commands allows you to remove commands from sections.

Pin/Unpin Sections

By default, when you navigate between sections of the Action Bar, the icons found in each section are displayed and the *Standard* section is pinned. You can set one or more sections to always display by right-clicking on the section name in the Action Bar and selecting **Pin Section**. The selected section will now be pinned and "permanently" displayed. To turn off a pinned section, right-click on the section's name and select **Pin Section** again.

Pinning a section has the following results:

- The pinned section title highlights in white with a blue triangle corner.
- If you select another section, the icons in the pinned section continue to display.

- The section displays in the sequence in which it originally exists. For example, if you pin the *Review* section, then select the *Model* section, the *Review* icons display as if added to the end of the *Model* section, as shown in Figure 2–20. Conversely, if you select the *Touch* section, the *Review* icons display as if added to the beginning of the Touch section.

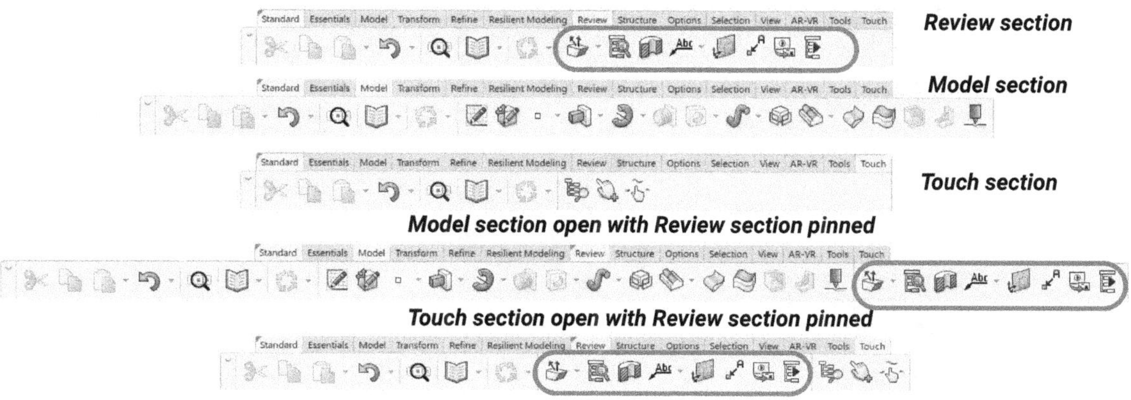

Figure 2–20

Action Pad

You can customize the commands found in the *Action Pad* (shown in Figure 2–21), which is opened by right-clicking in the modeling area and selecting **Display>Action Pad**.

Figure 2–21

In the Top Bar, right-click, select **Display>Customize**, and select the *Action Pad* tab in the *Customize* dialog box, as shown in Figure 2–22.

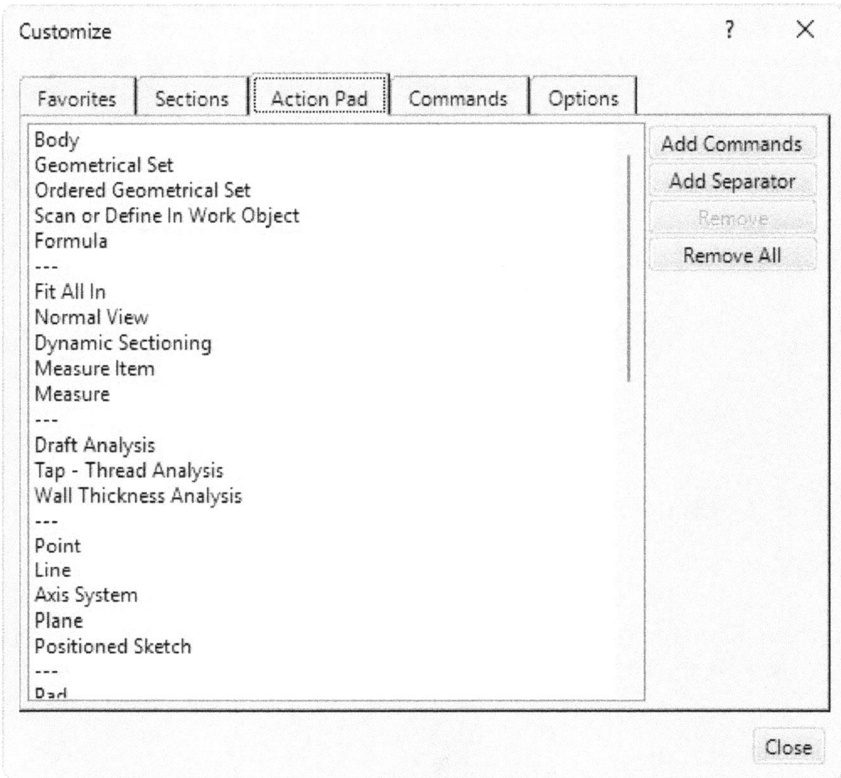

Figure 2–22

On this tab, you can add or remove commands and can create separators between groups of commands. You can also rearrange commands by dragging and dropping them in different locations in the list.

2.3 Color Scheme

You can customize the color scheme by right-clicking in the graphics area, selecting **Ambience**, and selecting one of the predefined schemes, as shown in Figure 2–23.

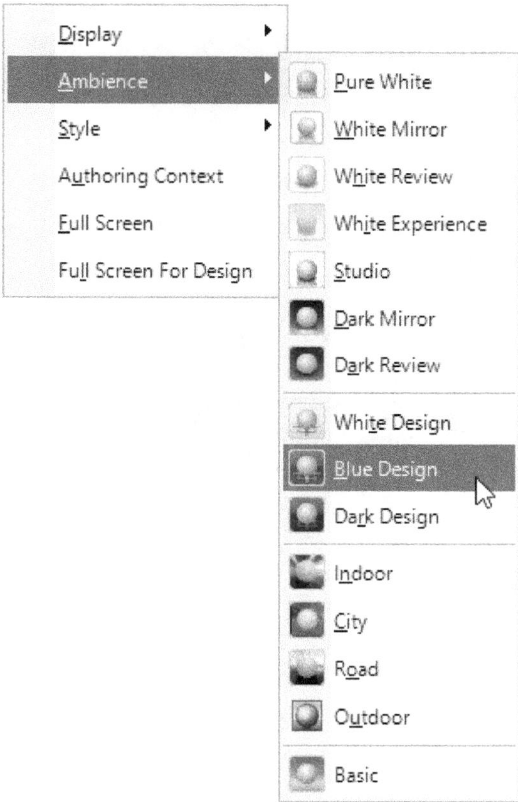

Figure 2–23

This content was developed using the **Basic** color scheme.

2.4 Favorite Apps

By default, when the 3DEXPERIENCE platform is started, you are in the basic 3DEXPERIENCE window, with no apps visible. To access the modeling apps, click the outer ring of the Compass, as shown in Figure 2–24.

Figure 2–24

The apps available under *My Favorite Apps* display, as shown in Figure 2–25. The *My Favorite Apps* section can be customized.

> **Note:** *The available apps on your system may differ from those shown, depending on how your system was set up and what licenses you have.*

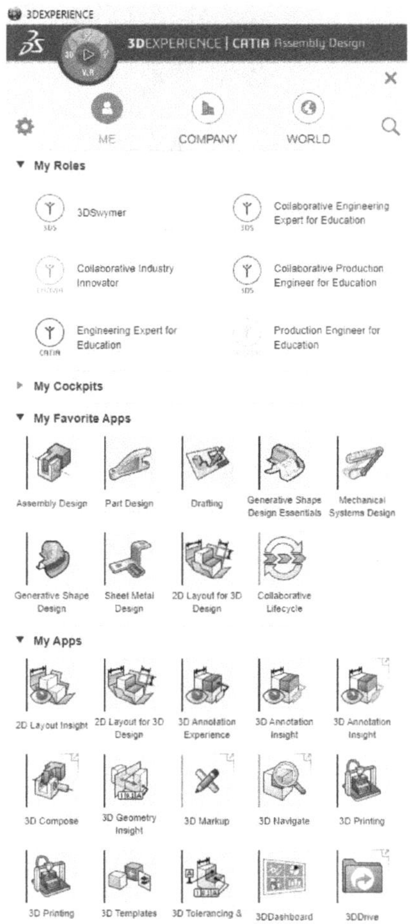

Figure 2–25

Customizing Favorites – Method 1

One way to customize your favorite apps is to move your cursor to the Top Bar, right-click, and select **Display>Customize**. In the *Customize* dialog box, select the *Favorites* tab, as shown in Figure 2–26.

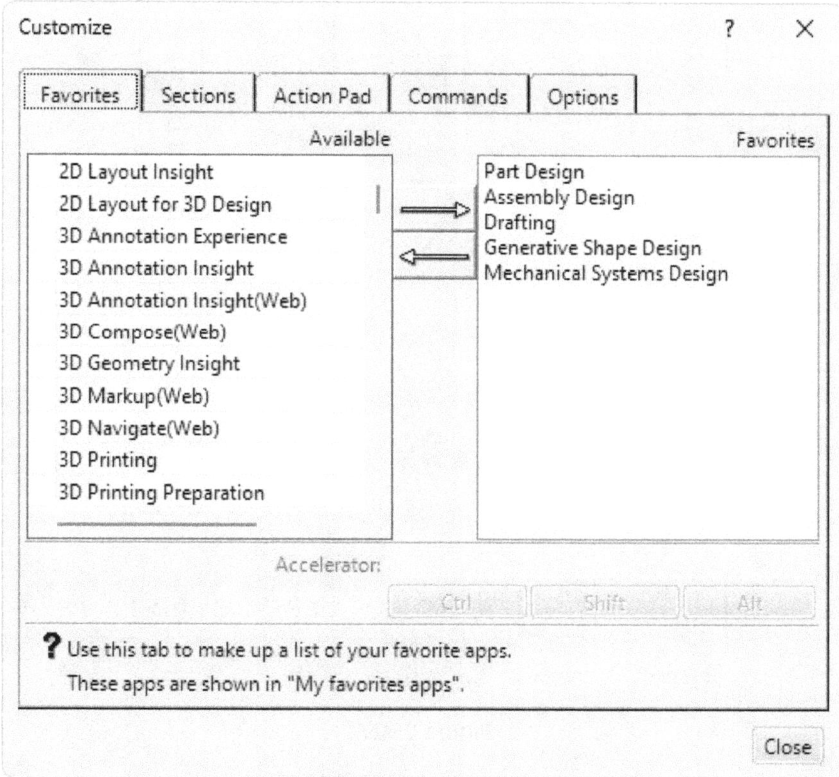

Figure 2–26

You can add or remove apps here by moving them between the *Available* and *Favorites* lists. To add an app to the *Favorites* list, select it in the *Available* list and click 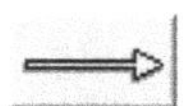. The app moves to the bottom of the *Favorites* list. Conversely, select an app in the *Favorites* list and click 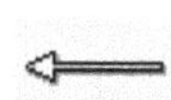 to move it to the *Available* list.

You can also rearrange the order in which your favorite apps are displayed by dragging and dropping them in the *Favorites* list.

Customizing Favorites – Method 2

A second method is to click outer ring of the Compass, then drag apps from the *My Apps* section and drop them into the *My Favorite Apps* section, as shown in Figure 2–27.

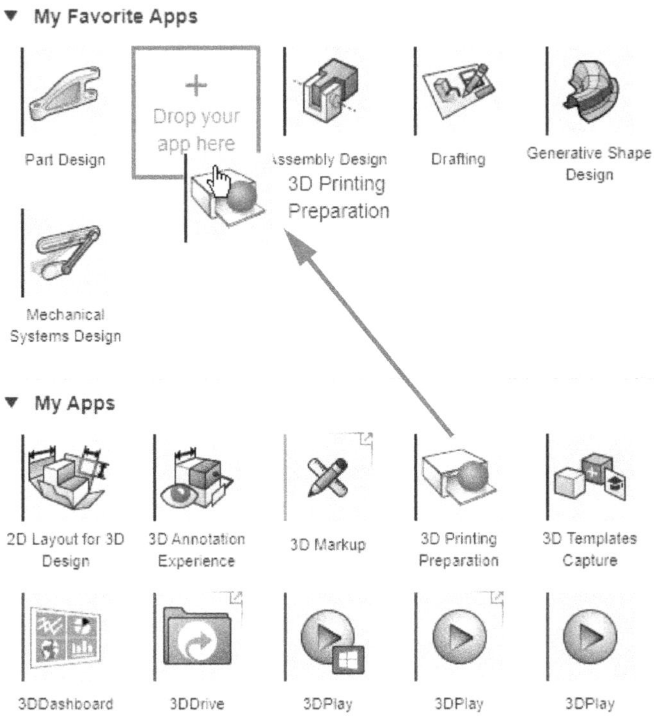

Figure 2–27

To remove an app from your favorites, drag and drop it to the location shown in Figure 2–28.

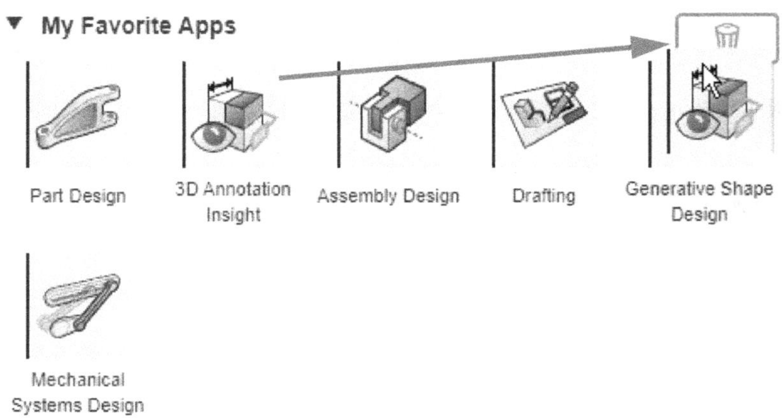

Figure 2–28

2.5 Preferences Dialog Box

When first started, the 3DEXPERIENCE platform uses a default set of configurations. These configurations include interface color scheme, model units, sketcher grid, spaceball configuration, and so on.

To open the *Preferences* dialog box, click your user icon in the top-right corner of the 3DEXPERIENCE window and select **Preferences**. The *Preferences* dialog box is used to customize the 3DEXPERIENCE platform options, as shown in Figure 2–29.

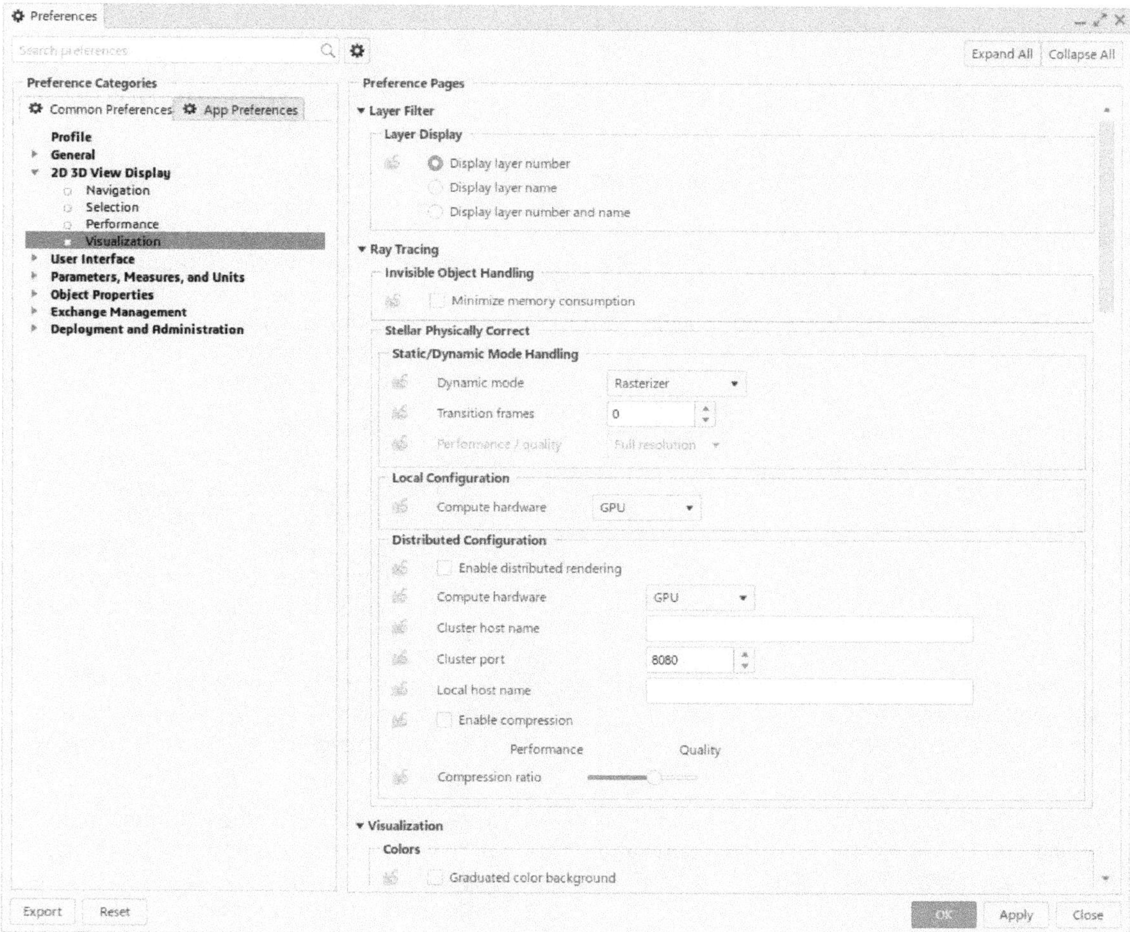

Figure 2–29

When setting the required options, the changes made are written to the files in the *CATSettings* folder.

Recommended Options

You should become familiar with the option menus to maximize efficiency within the CATIA environment. These options impact the results obtained when completing the practices available in this guide. The option menus are as follows:

Path	Option	Value
Common Preferences>General> Cache and Performance>PCS	**Undo Command**	The **Stack Size** option controls the number of undo operations that can be performed. Increasing this value also decreases CATIA performance, as the software must store more operation information. The maximum value is 99. It is recommended that you set this option to 15–20.
Common Preferences>User Interface>Tree>Tree Manipulation	**Zoom on Tree**	Disabling the **Tree zoom after clicking on any branch** option helps in working in the CATIA interface. Users often become confused when selecting a branch in the tree, which takes their focus off the model. With this option disabled, the tree can be zoomed by selecting the axis in the lower-right corner of the window.
Common Preferences>2D 3D View Display>Performance> Performance	**3D Accuracy**	These options control the quality of the model display in CATIA. A higher accuracy might result in an increase in system resource requirements. Proportional accuracy varies display quality relative to model size, while fixed accuracy does not. It is recommended that you set a *Proportional value* of **0.04**.
Common Preferences> Parameters, Measures, and Units>Parameters>Parameters & Relations	**Parameters Tree View**	These options control the display of parameter values and formulas in the tree. It is recommended that you select **Display values**.
Common Preferences> Parameters, Measures, and Units>Measures>Measure Tools	**Associativity**	These options control the automatic update of measurements in a part and product model. It is recommended that you enable **Automatic update in product**.

Path	Option	Value
Common Preferences>Object Properties>3D Shape>Display> Display	**Display In Tree**	These options control the display of model information in the tree. They include: • External references • Constraints • Parameters • Relations • Bodies under operations • Expand sketch-based feature nodes at creation It is recommended that you enable all of the options in this area.
Common Preferences>Object Properties>3D Shape> Infrastructure>3D Shape	**Hybrid Design**	Unless your company has standardized on the use of hybrid design, clear the **Enable hybrid design inside part bodies and bodies** option. Hybrid design changes the way wireframe and surface elements are stored in a part model and should not be enabled unless instructed by your CAD administrator.
App Preferences>3D Modeling> 3D Modeling Core>Sketcher> Sketcher	**Sketch Plane**	Disable the **Minimize viewpoint transformation** option so that the sketch orients correctly during creation.
App Preferences>3D Modeling> 3D Modeling Core>Sketcher> Sketcher	**Update**	Select **Generate update errors when the sketch is under-constrained** to have the software open an *Update Diagnosis* dialog box when exiting Sketcher with an under-constrained profile.
App Preferences>Social and Collaborative>Global Design Management/Collaborative Lifecycle>Identification	**Creation**	For the purposes of this guide, set the *Identification String* to your initials, followed by an underscore (for example, SEH_) so any new or imported objects are named with your initials as a prefix.

Practice 2a
Customization

Practice Objectives

- Set up favorite workbenches.
- Customize the on-screen toolbar display.
- Customize the CATIA configuration.

Task 1: Import a model.

1. In the Top Bar, click (Add/Create)>**Import**.
2. In the *Import* dialog box, click (Open).
3. Navigate to the *3DEXPERIENCE Transition Practice Files* folder, select **Flange_Lock_2.3dxml,** and click **Open**.
4. Ensure that the settings in the *Import* dialog box match those shown in Figure 2–30.

   Note: *The Duplication string field should show your initials due to the preference setting made in the first practice. The images in this content will not show the duplication string.*

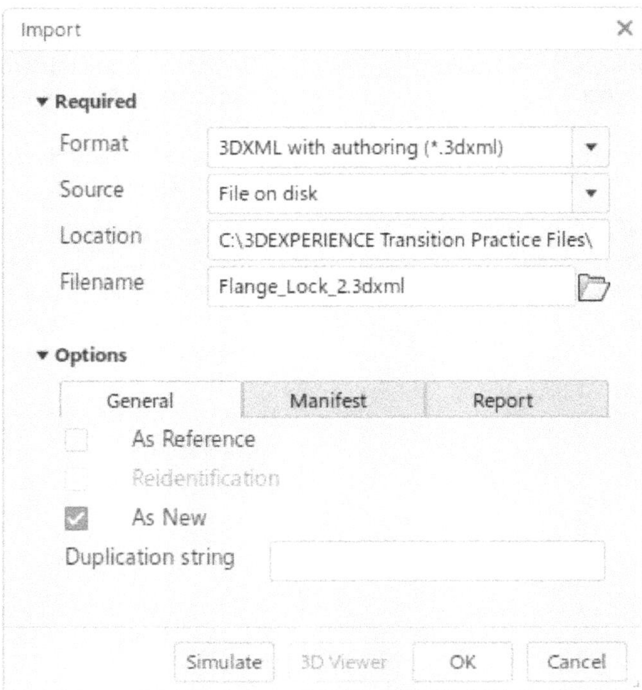

Figure 2–30

5. Click **OK**.
6. In the *Operation report* dialog box, click **OK**.
7. The model opens in Explore mode (in the ENOVIA Product Finder app), as shown in Figure 2–31.

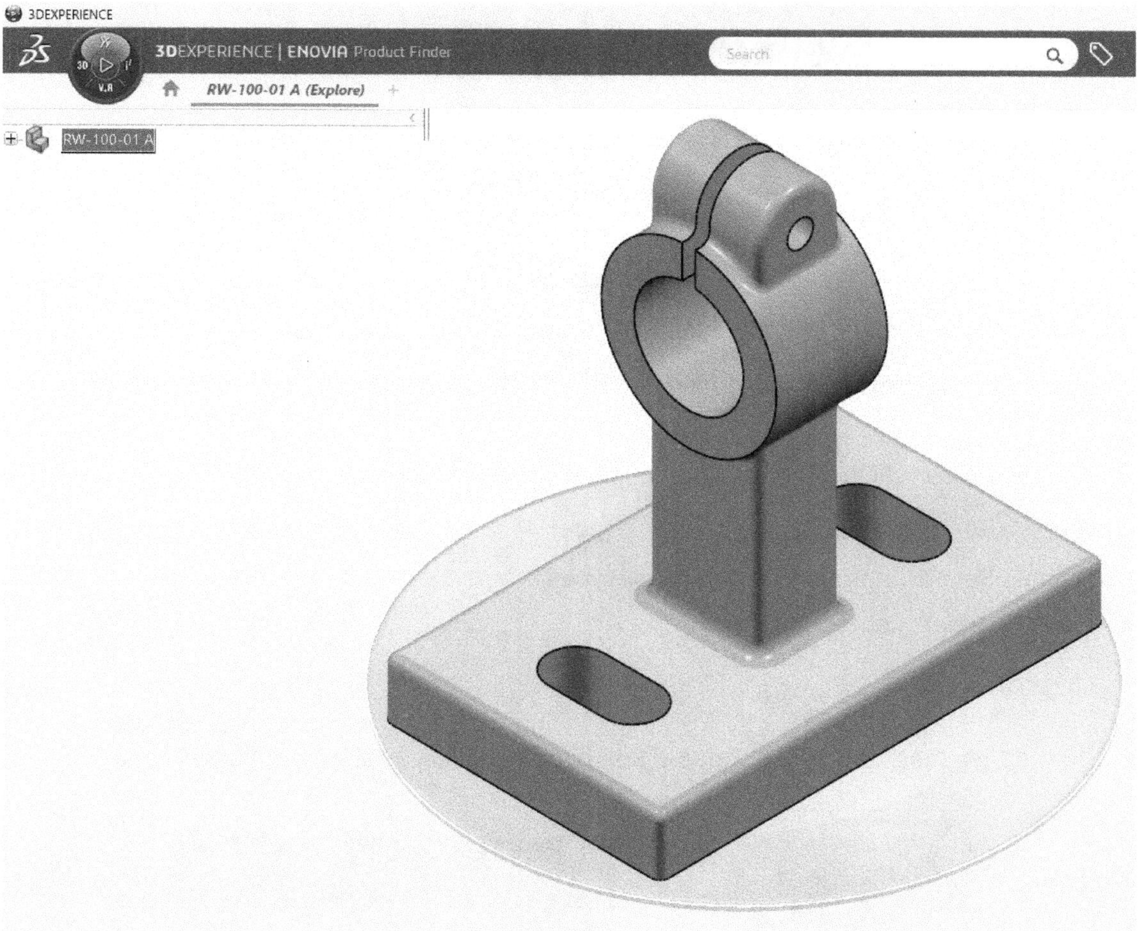

Figure 2–31

8. Right-click on **RW-100-01** in the specification tree and select **Open**.

9. The part opens for editing in a new tab. If the model opens in a widget panel instead of its own tab, in the upper-right corner of the widget window, click (Maximize), as shown in Figure 2–32.

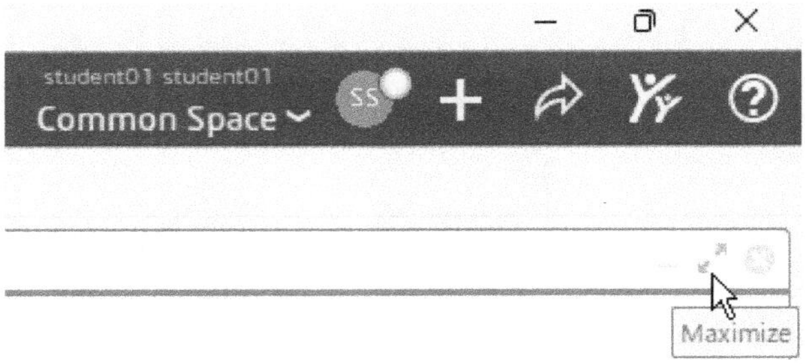

Figure 2–32

10. Close the *RW-100-01 (Explore)* tab.

Task 2: Ensure you are prompted for file attributes when creating new files.

1. In the Top Bar, click (Add/Create), then click **New Content**.
2. In the *New Content* window, click (Tools).
3. Enable **Set attributes at creation for all types**.
4. Close the *New Content* window.

Task 3: View favorite apps.

1. In the Compass, click **Roles, Apps & Solutions portfolio**, as shown in Figure 2–33.

Figure 2–33

2. Note the apps available under *My Favorite Apps*, as shown in Figure 2–34. Only the apps customized as favorite display here. If no customization has been done up to this point, the *My Favorite Apps* section may be empty.

   Note: *The apps available on your system will depend on your system setup and the licenses you have.*

Figure 2–34

3. To customize your favorite apps, move your cursor to the Top Bar, right-click, and select **Display>Customize**.

4. In the *Customize* dialog box, select the *Favorites* tab, as shown in Figure 2–35.

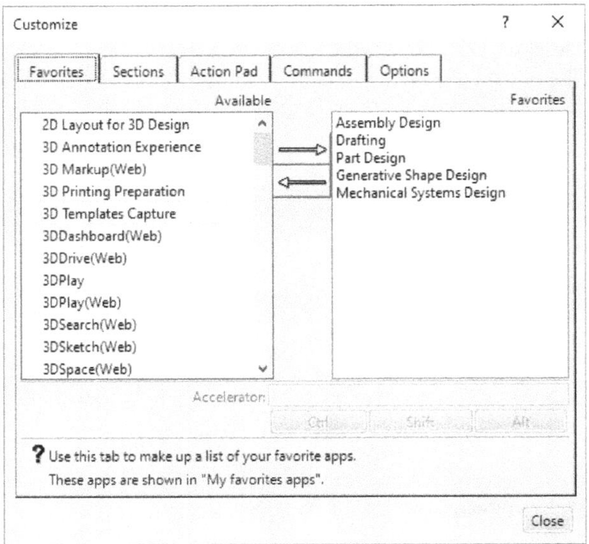

Figure 2–35

5. In the *Favorites* list on the right, remove Part Design by selecting **Part Design** and clicking 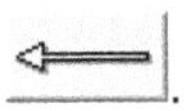.

6. Part Design moves to the *Available* list, as shown in Figure 2–36.

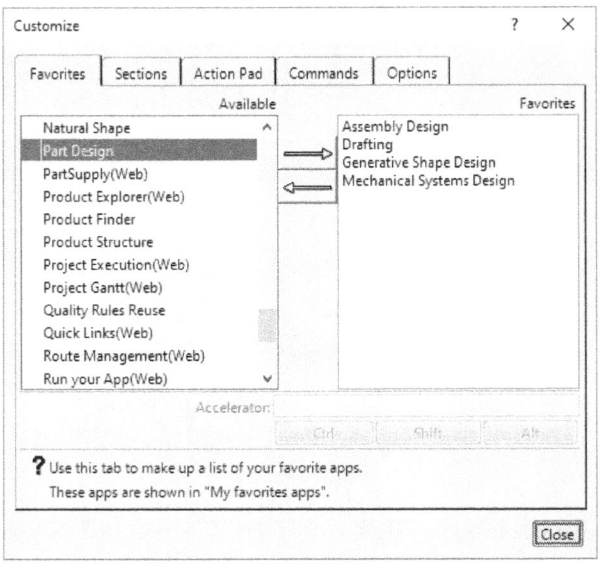

Figure 2–36

7. Close the *Customize* dialog box.

8. In the *3D Apps* area, expand *My Favorite Apps* (if necessary) and note that  (Part Design) has been removed, as shown in Figure 2–37.

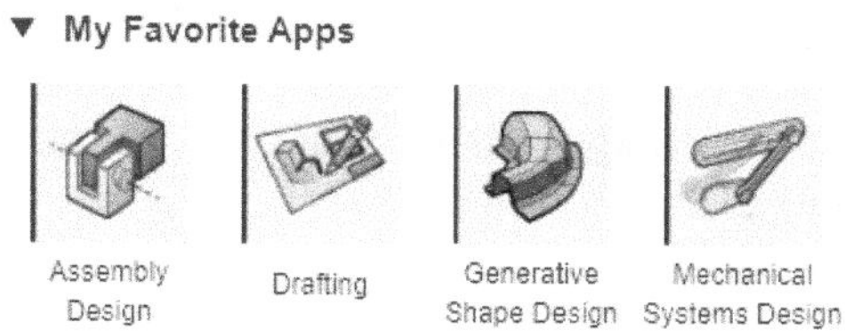

Figure 2–37

9. Add  (Part Design) back into the *My Favorite Apps* section by repeating Steps 3 to 7 but this time, select **Part Design** in the *Available* list and click 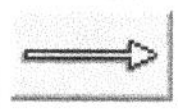.
10. In the *Customize* dialog box, click and drag **Part Design** to the top of the *Favorites* list (as shown in Figure 2–38), so it appears first in your list of apps.

    Note: *You can rearrange the order in which any apps appear by dragging them to the correct location.*

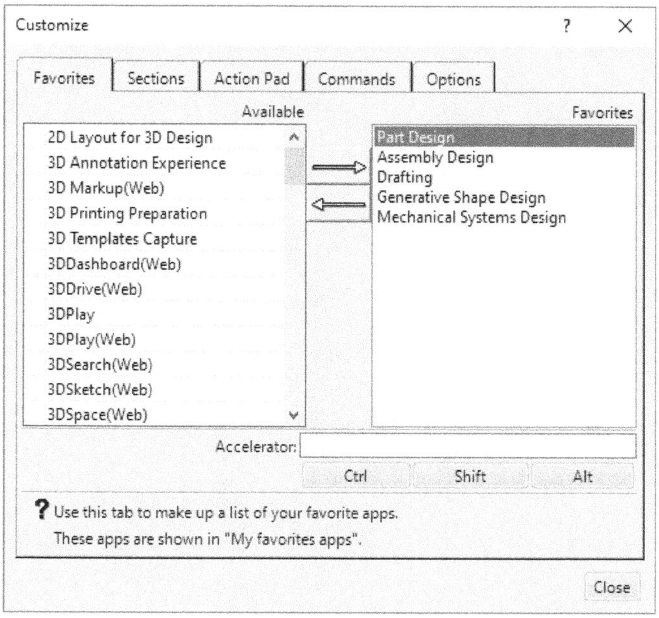

Figure 2–38

11. Close the *Customize* dialog box.

12. In the *3D Apps* area, expand *My Favorite Apps* (if necessary) and click (Drafting) to activate the Drafting app.
13. Click **OK** to accept the default *Drawing Title*. All of the Action Bar sections and icons update to drafting functions.
14. Select the *RW-100-01* tab to switch windows back to the **Flange_Lock** part. Note that all of the toolbar icons update to part design functions.
15. Click (Close) in the *Drawing Title* tab.
16. Double-click on the **RW-100-01** product at the top of the specification tree.
17. Note that the drawing is still referenced in the specification tree. This is because it is still in session. Right-click on the drawing and select **Unload**, as shown in Figure 2–39.

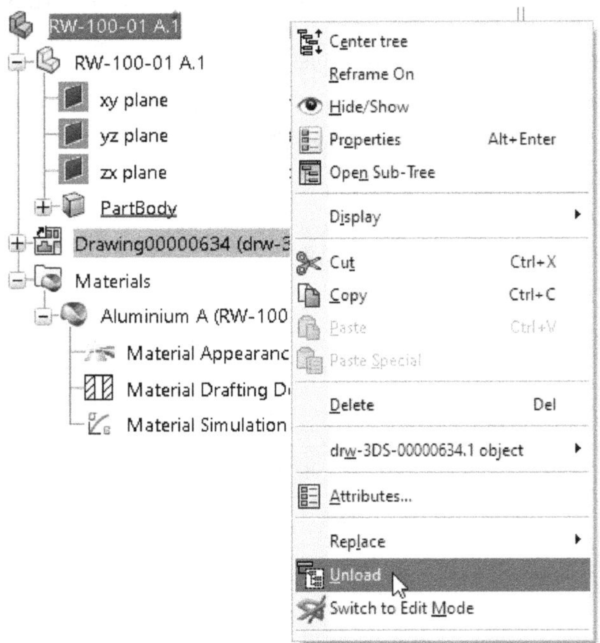

Figure 2–39

18. Click **Close** when prompted.

Task 4: Change the Action Bar display.

1. Note that, by default, the Action Bar displays with icons only for the selected section and with no labels for those icons. The *Assembly* section is shown in Figure 2–40.

Figure 2–40

2. Right-click on the Action Bar and select **Display Icons and Text**, as shown in Figure 2–41.

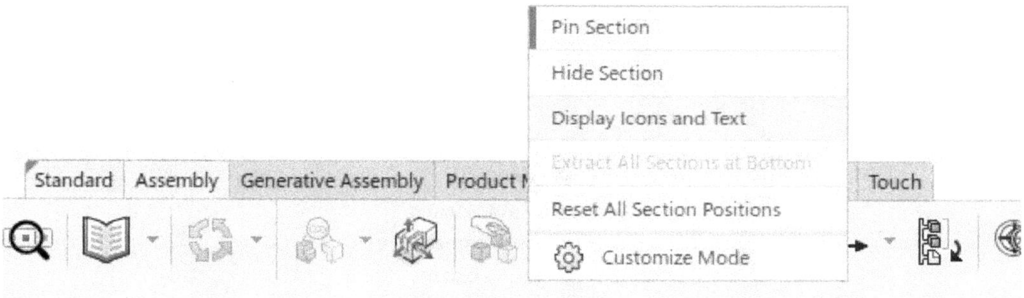

Figure 2–41

- The names for the icons display, as shown in Figure 2–42.

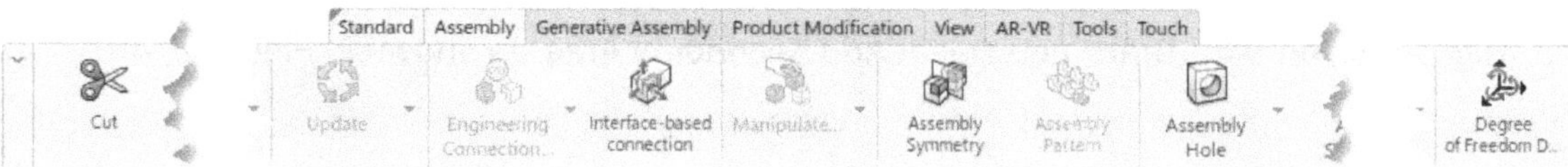

Figure 2–42

3. Right-click on the Action Bar and select **Display Icons Only** again to turn off the labels.

Task 5: Customize Action Bar icon positioning.

1. Double-click on **RW-100-01** at the part level (second level) of the specification tree to switch back to the **Part Design** app. The tree will display as shown in Figure 2–43.

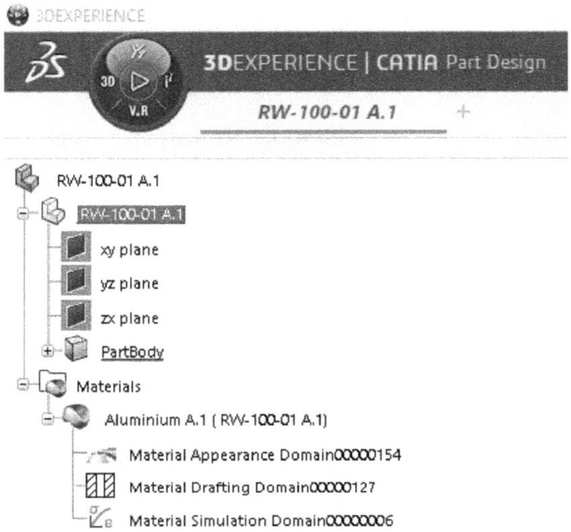

Figure 2–43

2. In the Action Bar, select the *Essentials* section if not already selected.
3. Right-click on the Action Bar and select **Customize Mode**.
4. Right-click on  (Draft) and select **Add Secondary Area**, as shown in Figure 2–44.

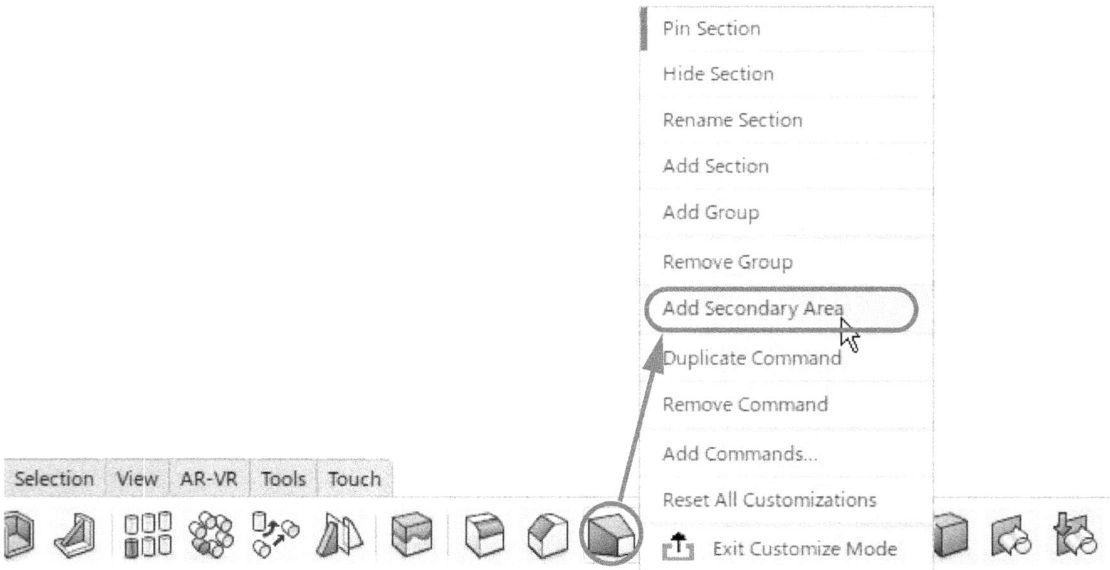

Figure 2–44

- This will create a new expandable/collapsible area to the right of **Draft**, as shown in Figure 2–45.

Figure 2–45

5. Select  (Edge Fillet) and drag it to the secondary area you just created. When a blue vertical bar appears (as shown in Figure 2–46), indicating the location where the icon will be placed, let go of the cursor.

Figure 2–46

- The **Edge Fillet** icon is relocated to the secondary area, as shown in Figure 2–47.

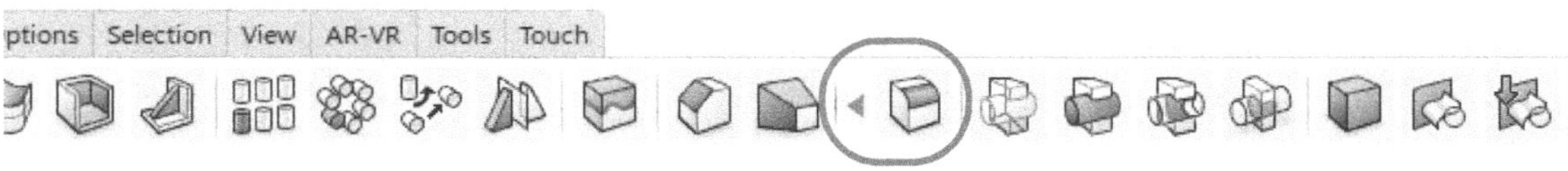

Figure 2–47

6. Repeat the previous step to move the  (Split) icon. The Action Bar updates as shown in Figure 2–48.

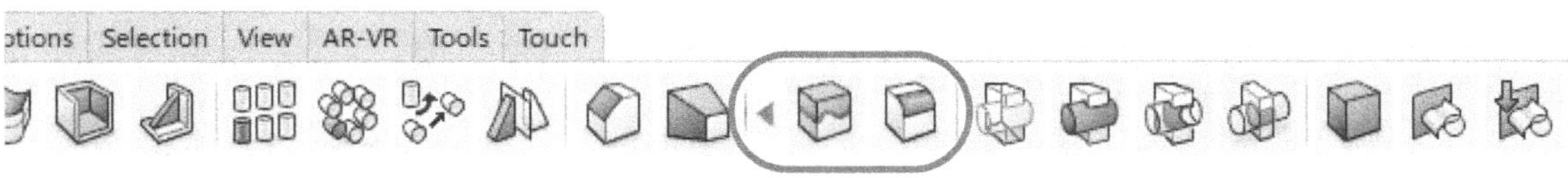

Figure 2–48

7. Right-click on the Action Bar and select  (Exit Customize Mode).

8. Note that the two icons can now be hidden in the Action Bar. Click (collapse) to collapse the group, as shown in Figure 2–49.

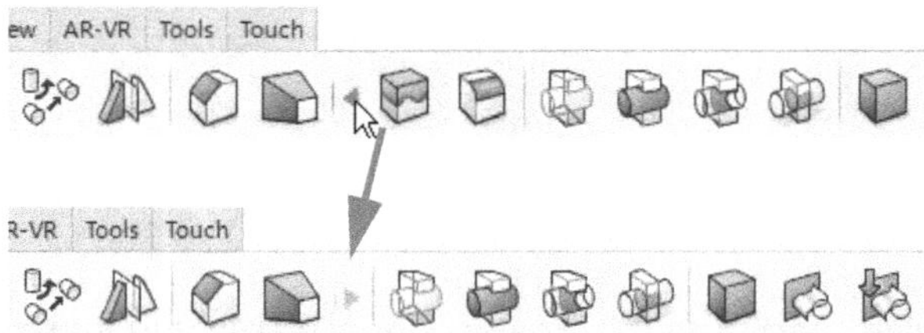

Figure 2–49

9. Click (Expand) to show the two icons again.

Task 6: Set the *Model* section of the Action Bar to always be visible.

1. In the Action Bar, select the *Model* section.
2. Right-click on the Action Bar and select **Pin Section**, as shown in Figure 2–50.

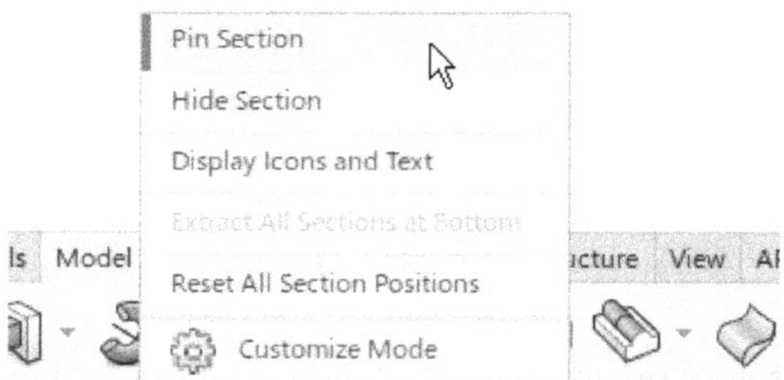

Figure 2–50

- Note that there is a blue triangle in the top-left corner of the *Model* section tab (as shown in Figure 2–51), indicating that it is pinned.

3. Select the *Refine* section. Note that the icons in the *Model* section are still visible, as shown in Figure 2–51.

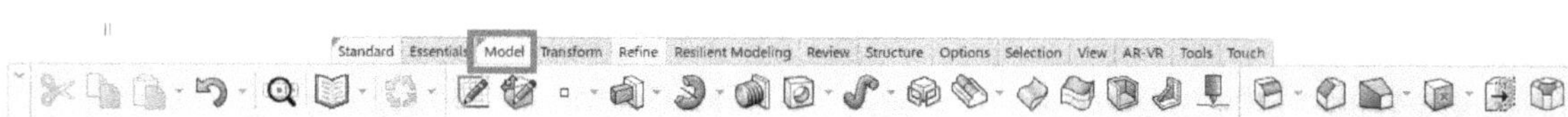

Figure 2–51

4. Select several other sections and note that the *Model* icons are always visible.
5. Right-click on the Action Bar and select **Customize Mode**.
6. Right-click on the Action Bar again and select **Reset All Customizations**. The Action Bar returns to the default setup.
7. Click **OK** to accept the reset.

IMPORTANT: The images going forward in this content will have the section labels on and the icon labels turned off to save space. You may want to leave the labels displayed until you begin to recognize the icons.

Task 7: Display the Action Bar.

1. Right-click in the graphics window and select **Display>Action Pad**. The *Action Pad* displays, as shown in Figure 2–52.

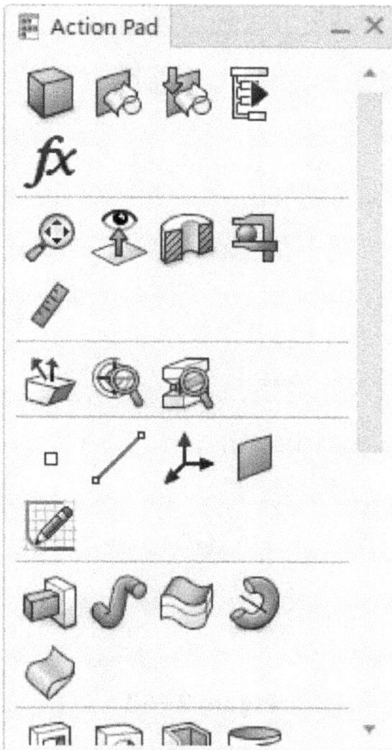

Figure 2–52

- The *Action Pad* will allow you to quickly access common commands quickly.

Task 8: Modify your CATIA settings.

In this task, you will begin modifying the options in CATIA to the recommended settings for the practice in this guide.

1. To modify the display performance of CATIA, select (User Icon)>**Preferences**.

2. Select **Common Preferences>2D 3D View Display>Performance** from the left side of the *Preferences* dialog box. Set the *3D Accuracy* to **Proportional**, with a value of **0.04**, as shown in Figure 2–53.

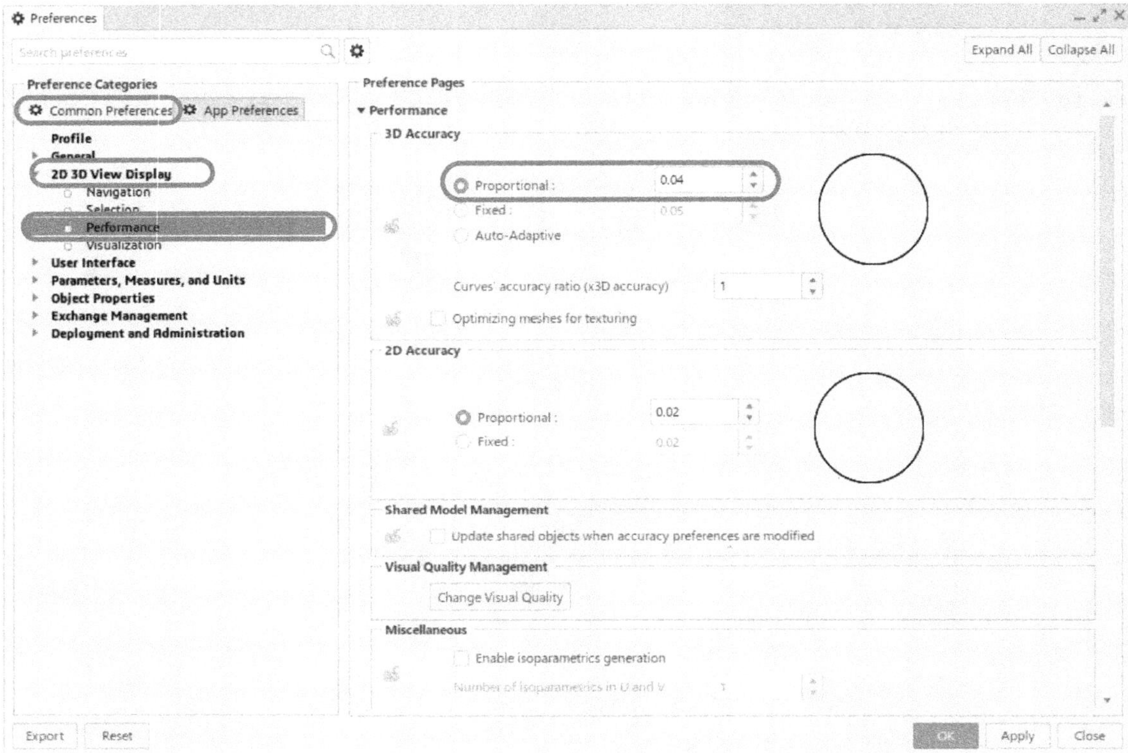

Figure 2–53

Task 9: Complete the CATIA settings modification.

1. Use the following information as a guide to complete the remaining configurations. All the configurations are done under  (User Icon)>**Preferences**.

Path	Option	Value
Common Preferences> General>Cache and Performance>PCS	**Undo Command**	The **Stack Size** option controls the number of undo operations that can be performed. Increasing this value also decreases CATIA performance, as the software must store more operation information. The maximum value is 99. It is recommended that you set this option to 15–20.

Path	Option	Value
Common Preferences> User Interface>Tree>Tree Manipulation	**Zoom on Tree**	Disabling the **Tree zoom after clicking on any branch** option helps in working in the CATIA interface. Users often become confused when selecting a branch in the tree, which takes their focus off the model. With this option disabled, the tree can be zoomed by selecting the axis in the lower-right corner of the window.
Common Preferences> Parameters, Measures, and Units>Parameters> Parameters & Relations	**Parameters Tree View**	These options control the display of parameter values and formulas in the tree. It is recommended that you select **Display values**.
Common Preferences> Parameters, Measures, and Units>Measures> Measure Tools	**Associativity**	These options control the automatic update of measurements in a part and product model. It is recommended that you enable **Automatic update in product**.
Common Preferences> Object Properties>3D Shape>Display>Display	**Display In Tree**	These options control the display of model information in the tree. They include: • External references • Constraints • Parameters • Relations • Bodies under operations • Expand sketch-based feature nodes at creation It is recommended that you enable all of the options in this area.
Common Preferences> Object Properties>3D Shape>Infrastructure>3D Shape	**Hybrid Design**	Unless your company has standardized on the use of hybrid design, clear the **Enable hybrid design inside part bodies and bodies** option. Hybrid design changes the way wireframe and surface elements are stored in a part model and should not be enabled unless instructed by your CAD administrator.
App Preferences>3D Modeling>3D Modeling Core>Sketcher>Sketcher	**Sketch Plane**	Disable the **Minimize viewpoint transformation** option so that the sketch orients correctly during creation.

End of practice

Chapter 3

Creating a New Part

In this chapter, you will learn how to create a new part in 3DEXPERIENCE. You will learn the methods for starting a new part model and creating geometry.

Learning Objectives

- Review the general steps for creating a new part.
- Create a sketch for the model profile.
- Understand methods for modifying the part.

3.1 Creating a New 3D Part

The 3DEXPERIENCE Part Design modeling engine is the same as CATIA V5, which ensures file compatibility so V5 data will be able to transfer to 3DEXPERIENCE without any issues. Because of this, most of the modeling commands are very similar and the overall approach to modeling is quite familiar, with a few differences.

There are three main ways to create a new 3D part:

- Use the Compass.
- Click **Add/Create** in the Top Bar.
- Add to an assembly (design in context).

Using the Compass to Create a New Part

Using the Compass to create a new part is very similar to using the Start menu in V5.

How To: Create a New Part Using the Compass

1. Click the outer ring of the Compass, as shown in Figure 3–1.

Figure 3–1

2. Select the app that you would like to use, such as **Part Design** or **Generative Shape Design**, as shown in Figure 3–2.

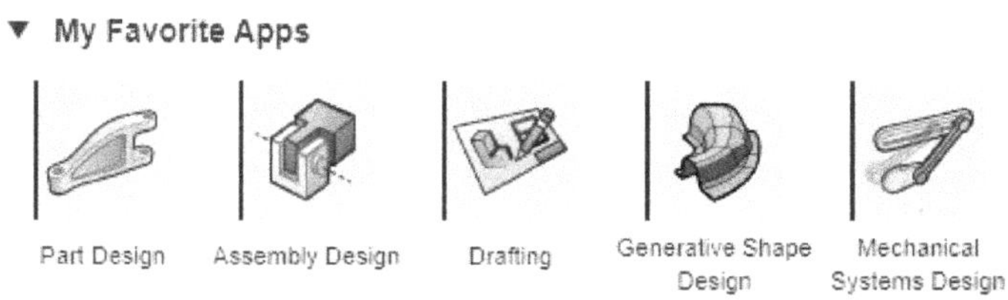

Figure 3–2

3. A part file is created when entering the app, as shown in Figure 3–3.

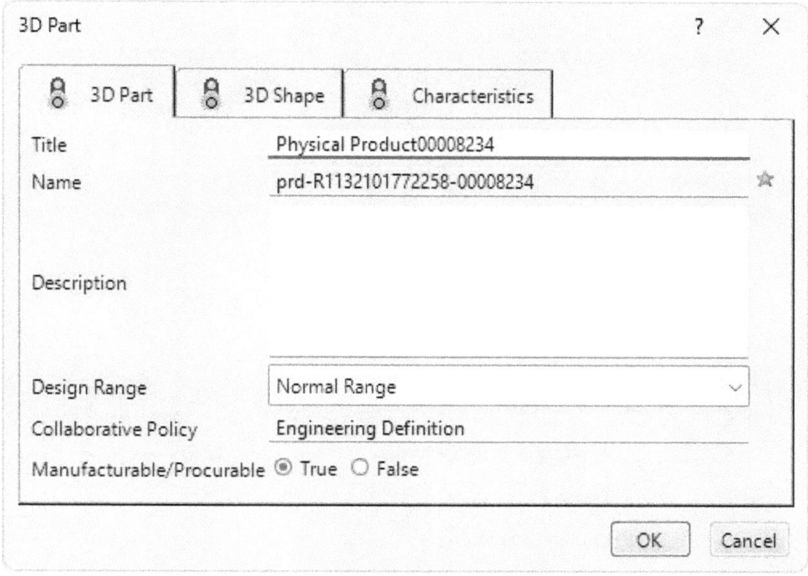

Figure 3–3

Using the Add Command

When you click the **Add/Create** icon, a drop-down list displays, and you can select to create a **Physical Product**, **3D Part**, or **Drawing** directly, as shown in Figure 3–4.

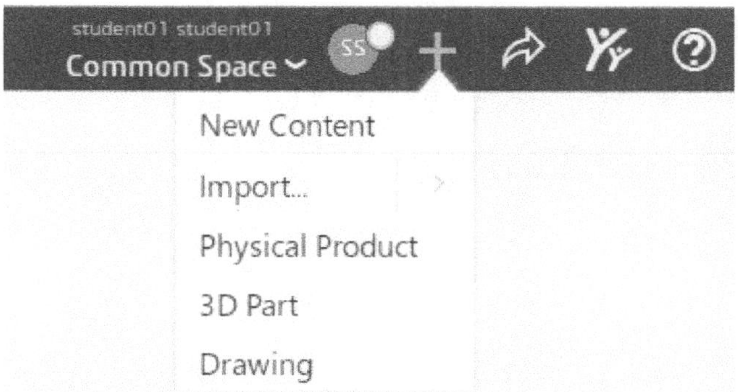

Figure 3–4

If you select **New Content**, all other 3DEXPERIENCE platform objects can be created, as shown in Figure 3–5.

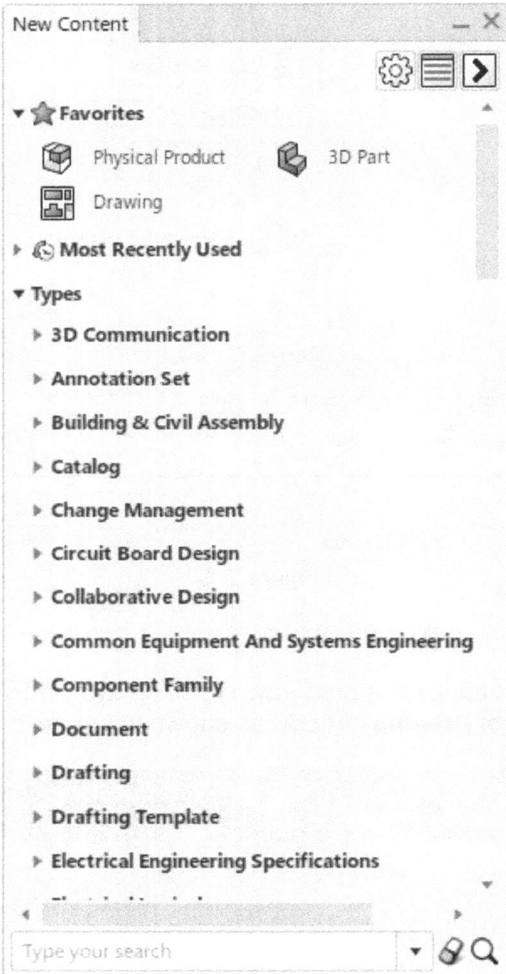

Figure 3–5

Build a New Part in an Assembly (Design in Context)

This, too, is similar to adding a new part in an assembly in V5. However, there is a small change to the terminology.

To add a part, right-click on the product and select **Insert>3D Part**, as shown in Figure 3–6. Keep in mind that a 3D part is specifically a 3D shape that contains a product that will only hold a shape file. This is analogous to a V5 instance.

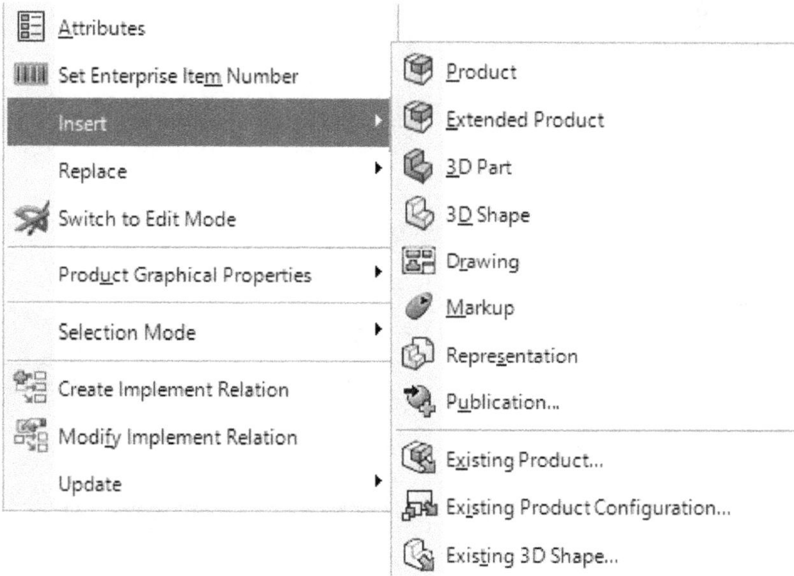

Figure 3–6

3.2 New Part Dialog Box

The new part dialog box has extra options compared to V5. There are two *Titles* – one for the *3D Part* and one for the *3D Shape*, as shown in Figure 3–7. These would correlate to the part instance and reference, in V5 terminology.

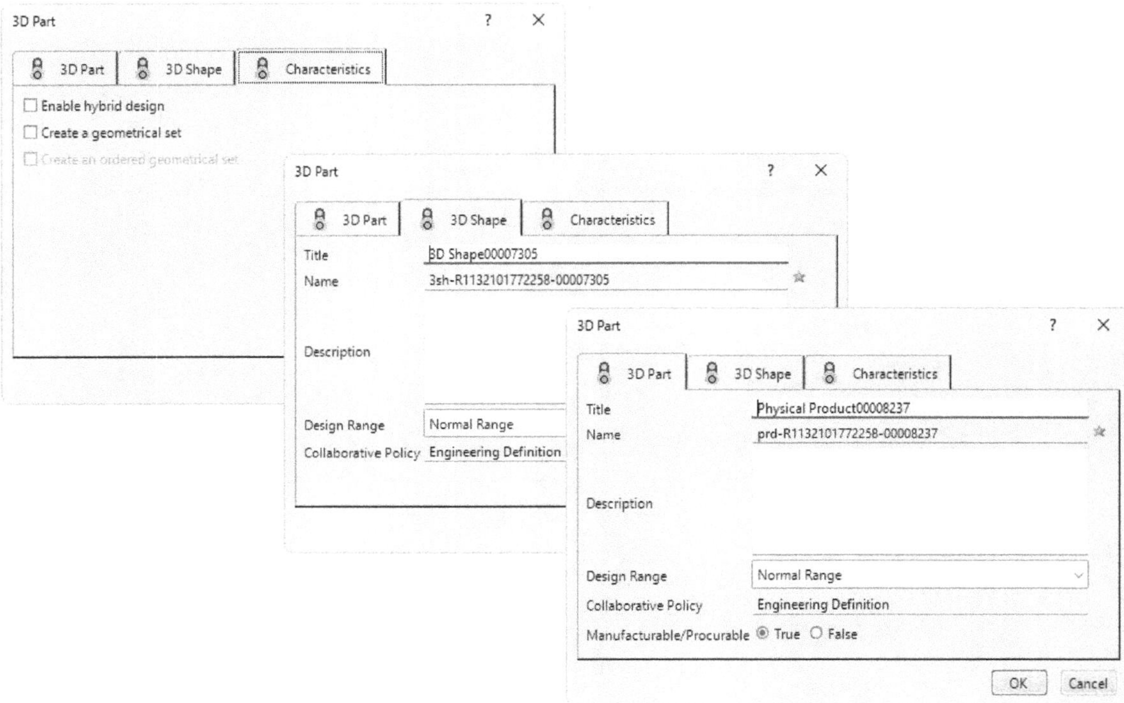

Figure 3–7

In titling the part and shape, you can see how they would appear in the tree, as shown in Figure 3–8. The 3D part is a container that will contain reference information (such as position in an assembly, reviews, or drawing) for that part. The 3D shape will be the 3D model and contain 3D features, such as pads, pockets, extrudes, joins, etc.

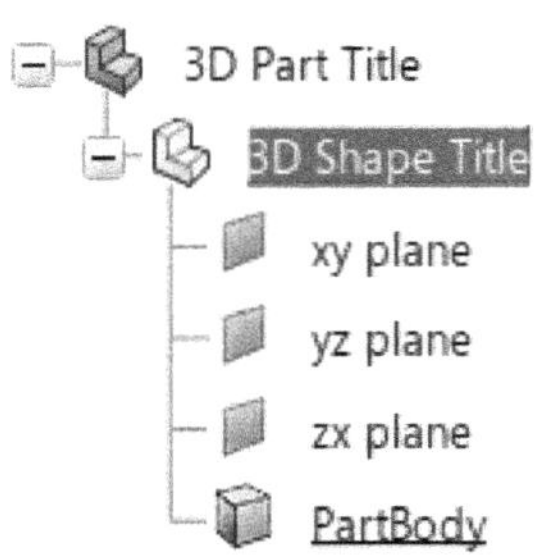

Figure 3–8

3.3 Using Commands

Commands are found in the Action Bar at the bottom of the screen, as shown in Figure 3–9.

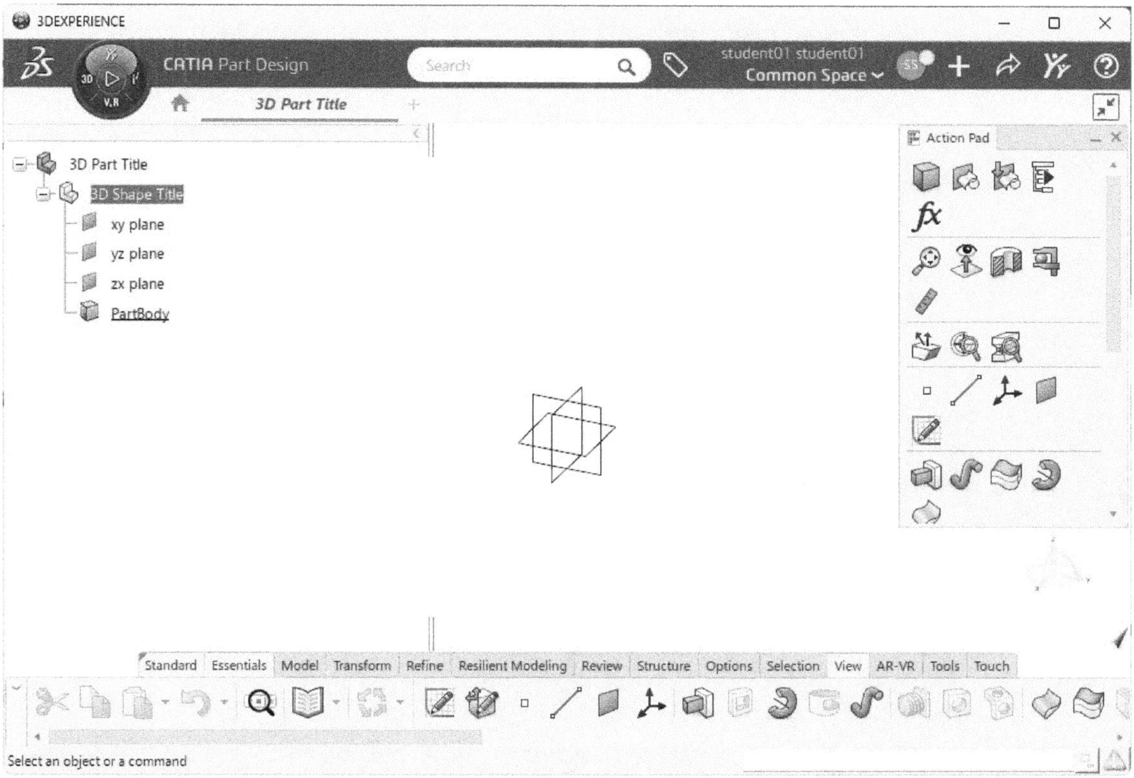

Figure 3–9

Generally, CATIA applications will also have an *Action Pad* on the right that provides easy access to commonly used commands. Also, there are now context-sensitive commands, which appear when clicking items, showing available actions.

For example, the following are methods to create a sketch.

How To: Use the Action Bar or Action Pad to Create a Sketch

1. Click  (Positioned Sketch). There is no longer an icon for a non-positioned sketch.

2. The *Sketch Positioning* dialog box displays, as shown in Figure 3–10. If (Smart Positioning) is selected, choosing a plane will automatically enter the sketch workbench using a preset orientation. This is similar to V5's standard sketch.

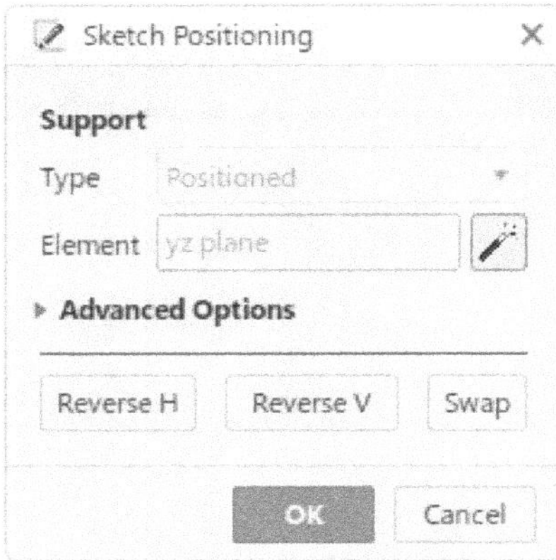

Figure 3–10

3. Disable (Smart Positioning) to allow user input for the supports within the *Sketch Positioning* options.

4. Select **Advanced Options** to expand the dialog box and display all the *Sketch Positioning* options available, as shown in Figure 3–11.

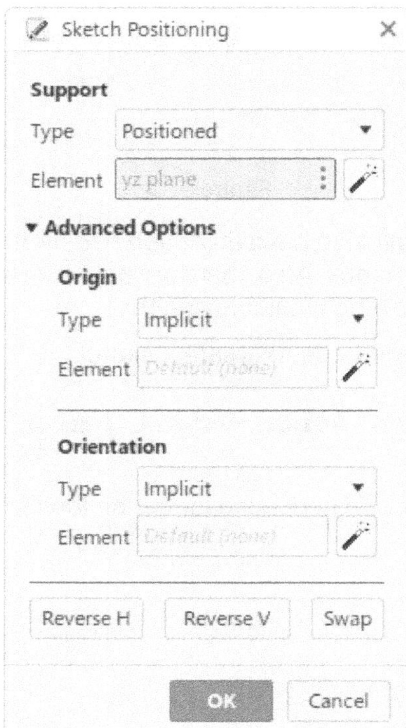

Figure 3–11

How To: Create a Sketch with the Context Options

1. Select a plane.
2. The sketch command will become available in a floating toolbar near the mouse, as shown in Figure 3–12.

Figure 3–12

3. Click  (Quick Sketch). There will be no positioning options if the sketch is created in this manner.

3.4 Sketching Geometry

Sketch geometry is nearly identical to V5. The commands are now located in the Action Bar and have been regrouped. Icons have been slightly adjusted to accommodate larger screens and to improve detail. Additionally, sketch geometry and modification can now be performed through the context menus. Also, it is possible now to directly create text in Sketcher.

How To: Create Sketch Geometry Contextually

1. Pick an existing geometry as a reference element, as shown in Figure 3–13.

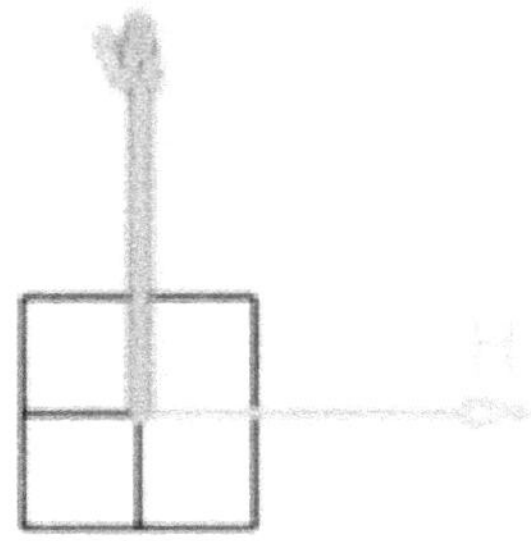

Figure 3–13

2. Commands will appear near the mouse cursor, as shown in Figure 3–14.

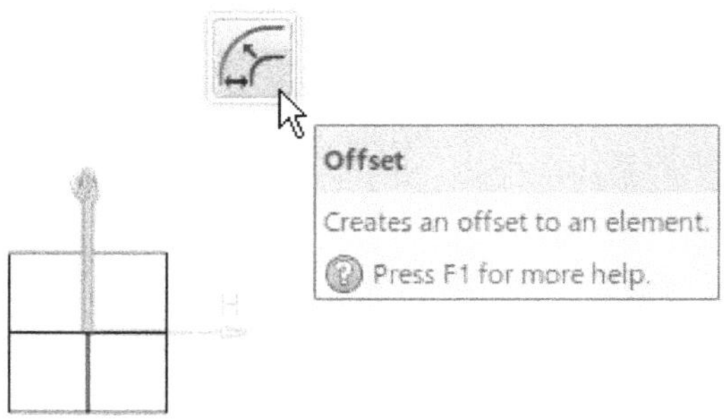

Figure 3–14

3. Select the desired geometry and build as usual, as shown in Figure 3–15.

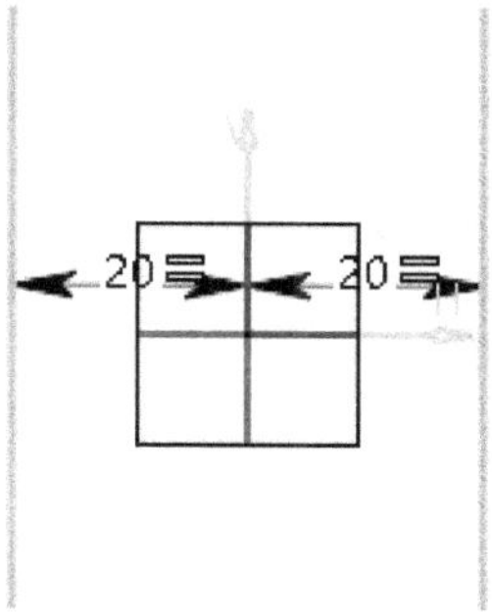

Figure 3–15

How To: Create Text in Sketcher

Text can be written directly inside of Sketcher.

1. In the *Sketch* section of the Action Bar, click (Text).
2. The *Text Creation* dialog box will open. Type in the desired text and set font and spacing options, as shown in Figure 3–16.

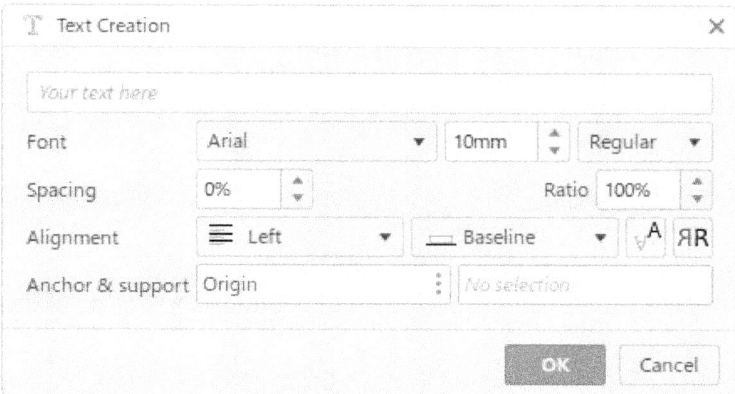

Figure 3–16

3. Click a location in the sketch and the text will move to that area, as shown in Figure 3–17.

Figure 3–17

4. Click **OK** to complete text creation.

Sketch Constraints

Sketch constraints are generally similar to their V5 counterparts. As with most of the 3DEXPERIENCE Part Design commands, they can be built using the Action Bar, *Action Pad*, or contextually. Using the Action Bar or *Action Pad* to access the commands is nearly identical to V5. A nice quality-of-life improvement is that values for dimensions can now be entered directly after creating the constraints.

How To: Create Constraints Using the Constraint Command

1. Click or double-click on (Constraint).
2. Select a single or multiple elements, as shown in Figure 3–18.

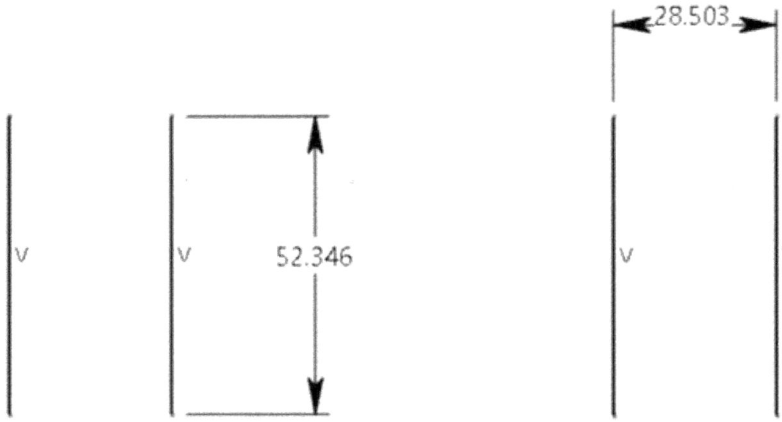

Single element *Multiple elements*

Figure 3–18

3. (Optional) Pick extra constraint options from the context toolbar, as shown in Figure 3–19.

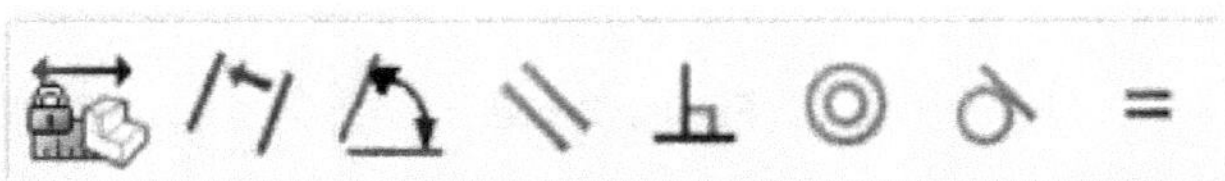

Figure 3–19

- Alternatively, right-click and pick a specific constraint, as shown in Figure 3–20.

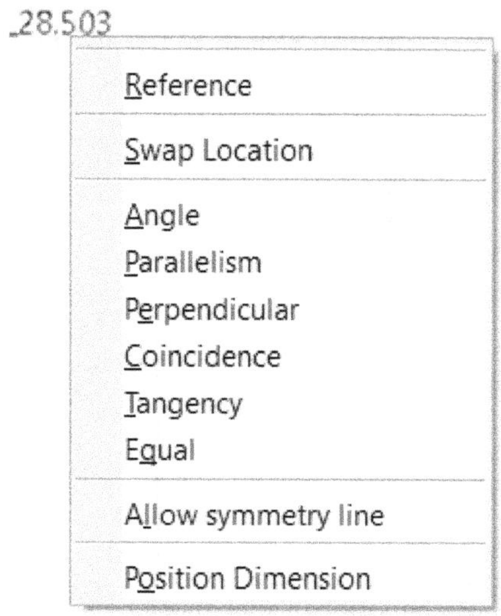

Figure 3–20

4. Click in the background to complete the command.
5. If creating a dimension, key in the value, as shown in Figure 3–21.

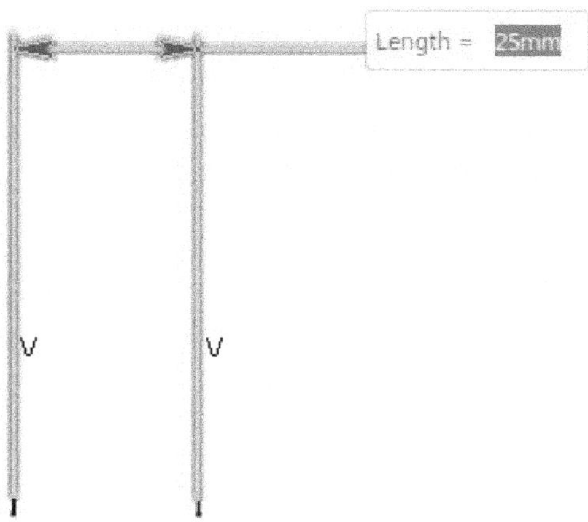

Figure 3–21

How To: Create Constraints Using the Context Toolbar

1. Click the desired geometry or geometries (hold <Ctrl> to select multiple objects, if needed), as shown in Figure 3–22.

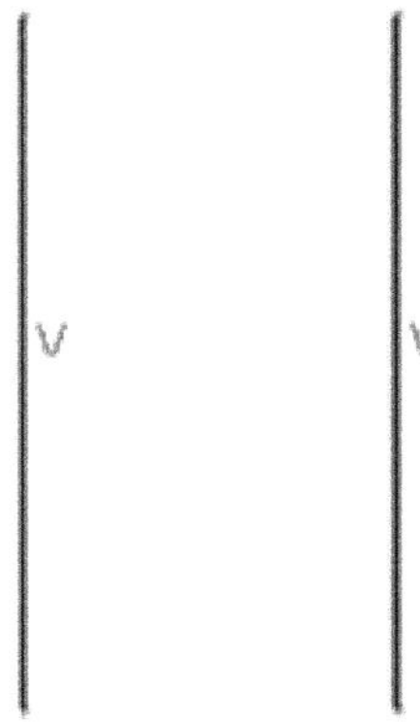

Figure 3–22

2. Select  (Constraint) from the context toolbar, as shown in Figure 3–23.

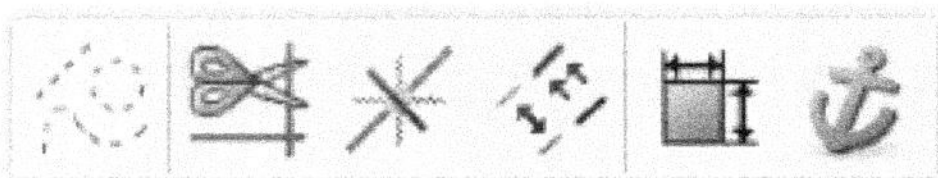

Figure 3–23

3. Depending on selections, there may be a sub menu (as shown in Figure 3–24) to select particular constraints. If needed, select a constraint.

Figure 3–24

4. Click in the background.

How To: Exit the Sketch

1. To exit Sketcher, click  (Exit App) in the Action Bar, as shown in Figure 3–25.

Figure 3–25

3.5 Feature Creation

3D features can be created almost identically to the commands in V5. There are several new context-sensitive ways to create features as well. 3D feature commands, such as **Pad**, **Pocket**, **Extrude**, **Revolve**, etc., can be activated from the context menu. The Robot can also be used to create and modify 3D features, using a relatively free-form approach. This works well with "dumb" models that have no feature history.

Using Commands

To create a 3D feature, select the command and the references, or vice versa. This is the standard approach and will display a dialog box with information about the feature in a similar fashion to V5.

How To: Create a 3D Feature Using a Command

1. Click the reference item, as shown in Figure 3–26.

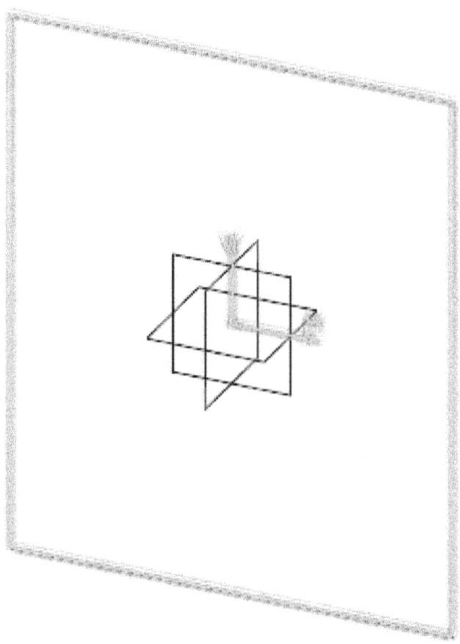

Figure 3–26

2. Select the command. In this example,  (Pad) is selected.

3. Enter the size and other information in the dialog box, as shown in Figure 3–27.

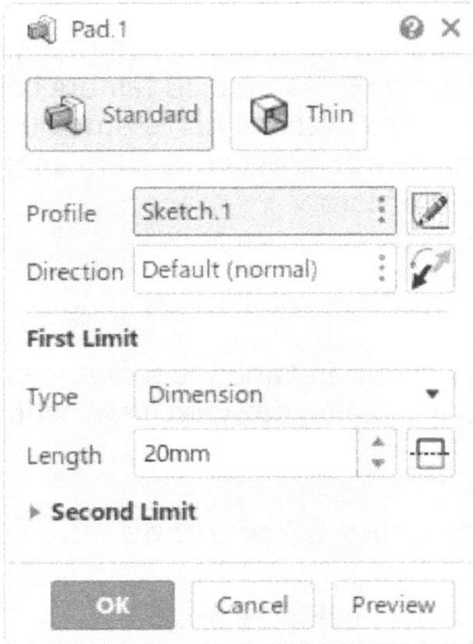

Figure 3–27

4. Click **OK** to complete the feature. The completed feature displays, as shown in Figure 3–28.

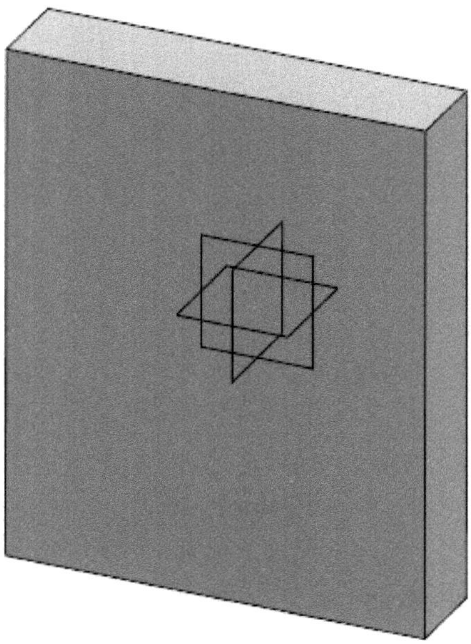

Figure 3–28

Using Commands via Context Toolbar

If a 3D feature is built using the context menus, then the feature creation dialog box will not open by default. It is still accessible by double-clicking on the item during feature creation.

How To: Create a Feature Using the Context Menu

1. Click the reference item.
2. Select the command (in this case, **Pad**) in the context toolbar, as shown in Figure 3–29.

Figure 3–29

3. Drag the arrow or click the number to enter a precise value, as shown in Figure 3–30. Hold <Ctrl> while dragging to create a symmetrical (mirrored extent) feature.

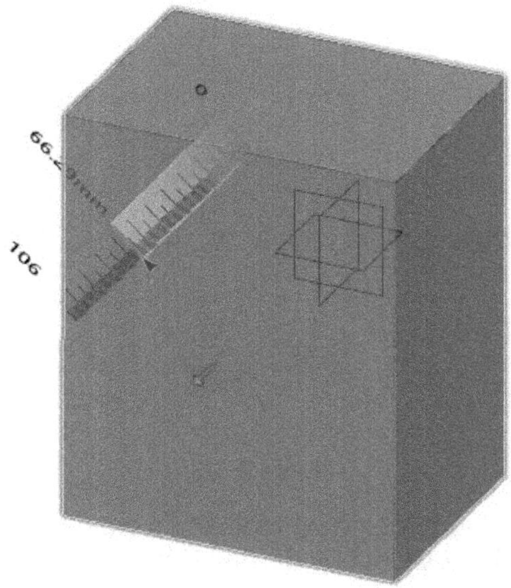

Figure 3–30

4. The cursor will have a checkmark. Click in the background to complete the feature.

Using the Robot to Create Shapes

The Robot (compass in V5) can also be used to build and modify 3D shapes.

How To: Create a Feature Using the Robot

1. Select a profile, as shown in Figure 3–31.

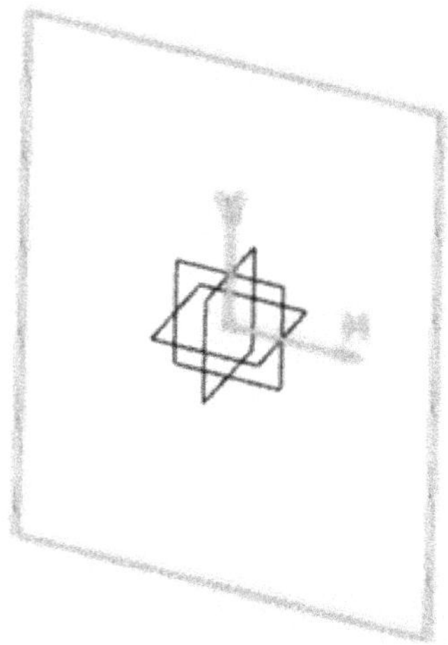

Figure 3–31

2. Click  (Use Robot) in the context toolbar, as shown in Figure 3–32.

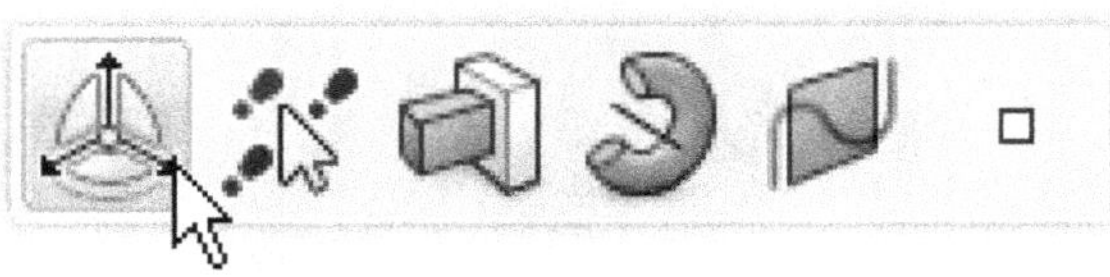

Figure 3–32

3. Robot options appear in another context toolbar. To create a 3D shape from a sketch, select **Create Features Mode**, **Global Mode**, and **Upper Dimension**.

Icon Set	Command	Results
	**Create Features Mode**	Adds a feature to the selected geometry.
	Move Features Mode	Translates or rotates the selected geometry using Robot.

Icon Set	Command	Results
	**Global Mode**	Affects entire connected part.
	Local Mode	Affects only selected face and associated geometry.
	**Upper Dimension**	Used to create a new 3D shape.
	Same Dimension	Used to replicate an existing shape.

4. Drag the Robot to generate geometry, as shown in Figure 3–33. In **Part Design**, dragging in a single direction will generate a pad feature. Rotating the part will generate a shaft. In **Generative Shape Design**, doing the same will generate an extrude or revolve, respectively.

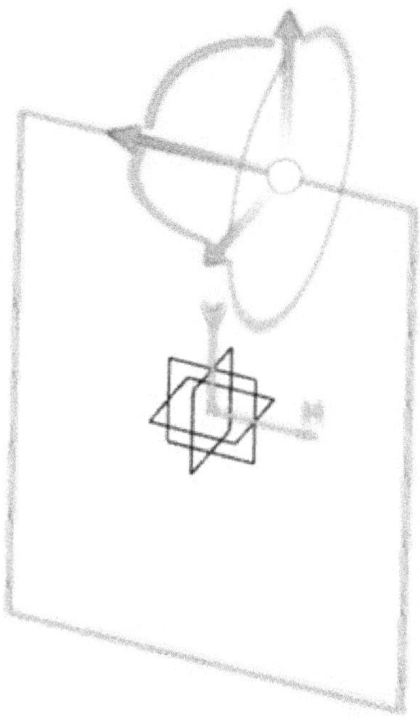

Figure 3–33

5. After initially dragging the Robot, a ruler will open displaying the current size of the feature. Click the value to modify it. The arrow can be dragged to targeted faces and planes to snap the new shape to it. Holding <Ctrl> will create a symmetrical (mirrored) element, as shown in Figure 3–34.

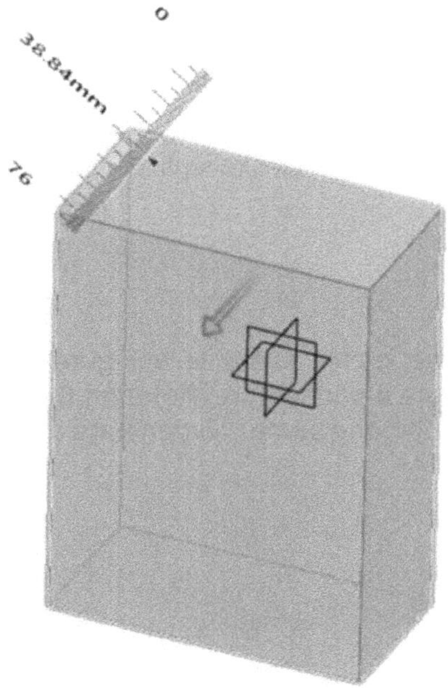

Figure 3–34

6. Click in the background to finish creation of the feature.

3.6 Part Modification

Modifying parts can be exactly like V5 (double-click anything to change it) or the Robot and context menus can be used for a more direct approach to modification.

Double-Click

Just like in V5, double-click on a feature, dimension, or almost any other item that is listed in the tree to modify it. The modification box will open and changes can be made from there.

Using the Robot for Modification

The Robot can be used to tweak parts and features in a variety of ways. In general, it can be used to adjust faces to new lengths and new angles. Items can be copied and moved. Patterns can be created. Features can be set to use the same dimensions and values.

How To: Translate and Rotate Faces Using the Robot

1. Click the face to be modified, as shown in Figure 3–35.

Figure 3–35

2. Click  (Use Robot) in the context toolbar.

3. Verify the Robot settings in the context toolbar (shown in Figure 3–36). Typically, **Create Features Mode** and **Local Mode** will be used to modify the part.

Figure 3–36

4. Translate and rotate the Robot until the face is in the desired position, as shown in Figure 3–37.

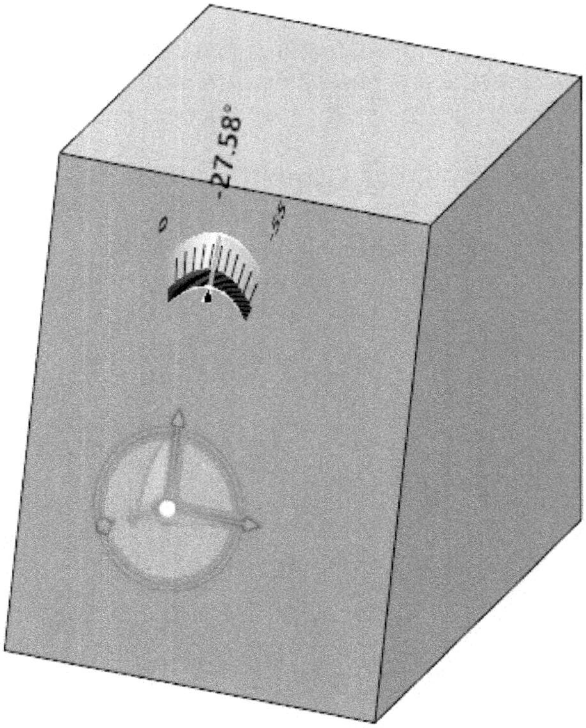

Figure 3–37

5. Click in the background to complete the change.

How To: Reuse Feature Specifications

1. Select a dress-up feature, such as a hole, fillet, or chamfer, as shown in Figure 3–38.

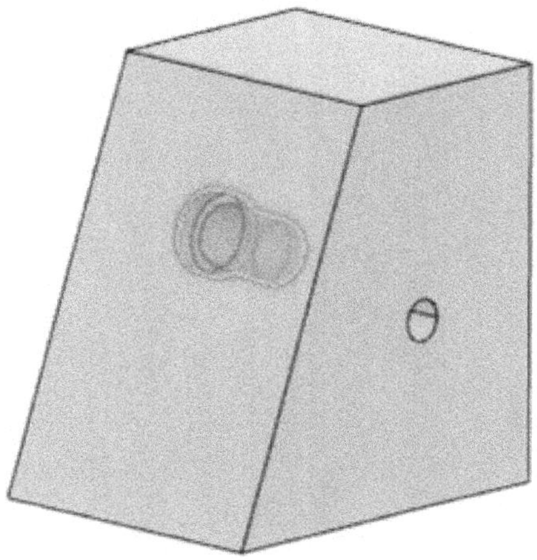

Figure 3–38

2. In the context toolbar, click **Semantic Painter**, as shown in Figure 3–39.

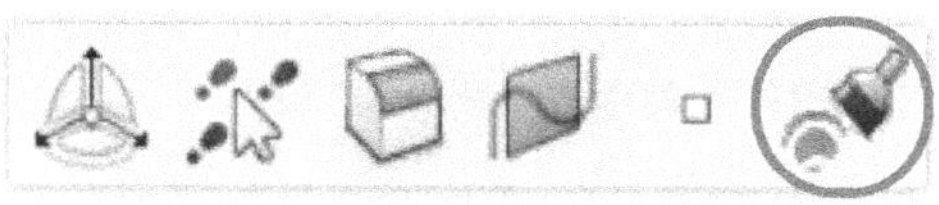

Figure 3–39

3. Select the target feature to *paint*, as shown in Figure 3–40.

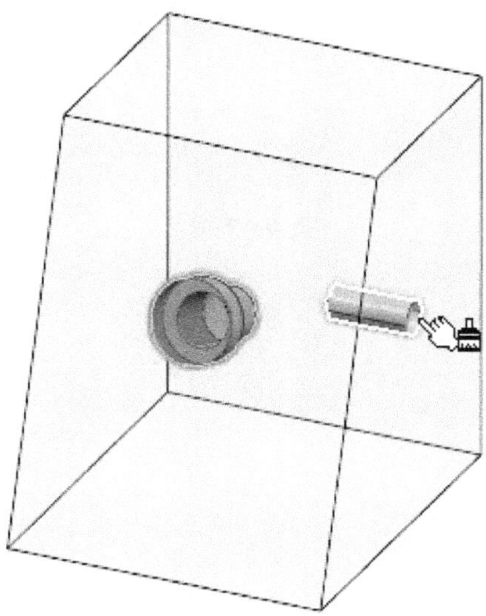

Figure 3–40

4. The targeted feature will now use the size and values of the original feature, as shown in Figure 3–41.

Figure 3–41

How To: Duplicate and Pattern Items with the Robot

1. Select the feature you want to duplicate. A hole was selected in this example.
2. Click  (Use Robot) in the context toolbar.
3. Set the Robot context menu to **Create Features Mode**, **Global Mode**, and **Same Dimension**, as shown in Figure 3–42.

Figure 3–42

4. Drag the selected item (in this case, a hole) along an axis while holding <Ctrl>, as shown in Figure 3–43.

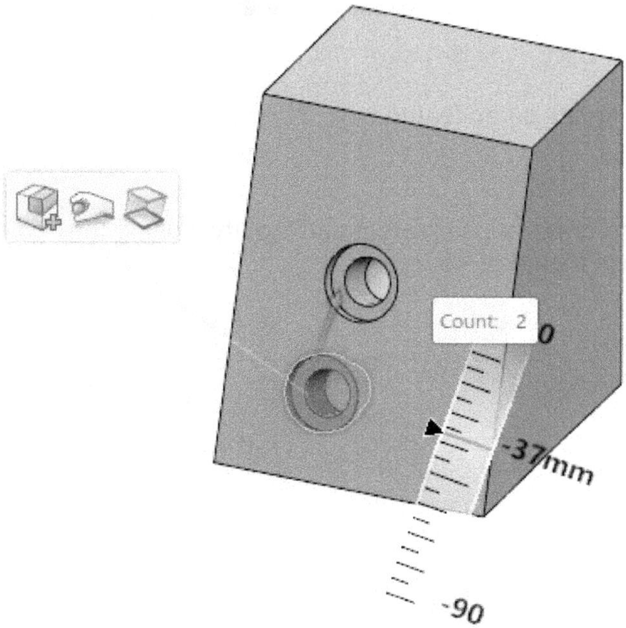

Figure 3–43

5. Enter the number of items in the *Count* field.
6. Click in the background to finish the pattern, as shown in Figure 3–44.

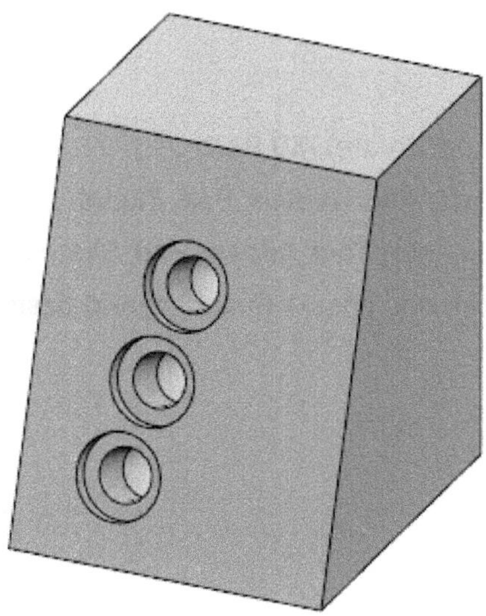

Figure 3–44

Practice 3a
Create a New Part

Practice Objectives

- Create a sketch to create a pad feature.
- Modify a pad feature.

In this practice, you will create a pad feature and modify it using the *Pad* dialog box. You will create the part shown in Figure 3–45.

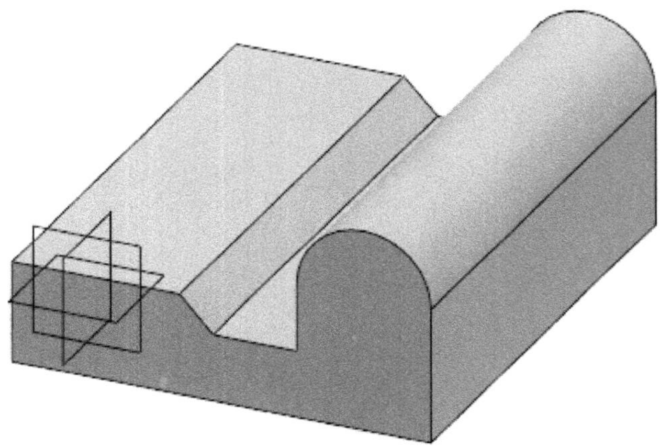

Figure 3–45

Task 1: Create a new part.

1. In the Top Bar, click  (Add/Create)>**3D Part**.
2. In the *3D Part* dialog box, enter ***Your_Initials*_Pad_Sketch** as the *Title*.
3. Select the *3D Shape* tab and enter ***Your_Initials*_Pad_Sketch** as the *Title*.
4. Select the *Characteristics* tab and ensure **Enable hybrid design** is disabled.
5. Click **OK**.

6. In the graphics window, select the **YZ plane**, as shown in Figure 3–46.

Figure 3–46

7. In the context toolbar, click (Sketch).

Task 2: Sketch the profile.

1. Sketch and constrain the part profile, as shown in Figure 3–47.
   - 50 (1.969 in)
   - 60 (2.362 in)
   - 25 (4.921 in)
   - 125 (4.921 in)
   - 20 (0.787 in)
   - 45 (1.772 in)

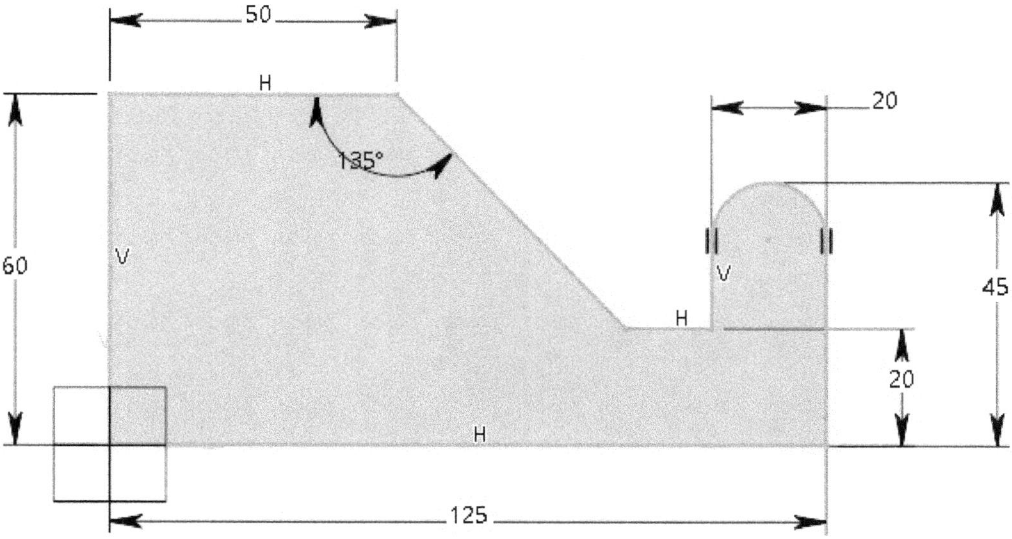

Figure 3–47

2. In the *Standard* section of the Action Bar, click (Exit App) to exit the Sketch application.

Task 3: Create a pad feature from the sketch.

1. With the sketch highlighted, in the *Model* section of the Action Bar, click (Pad).
2. The *Pad* dialog box opens and the geometry previews, as shown in Figure 3–48.

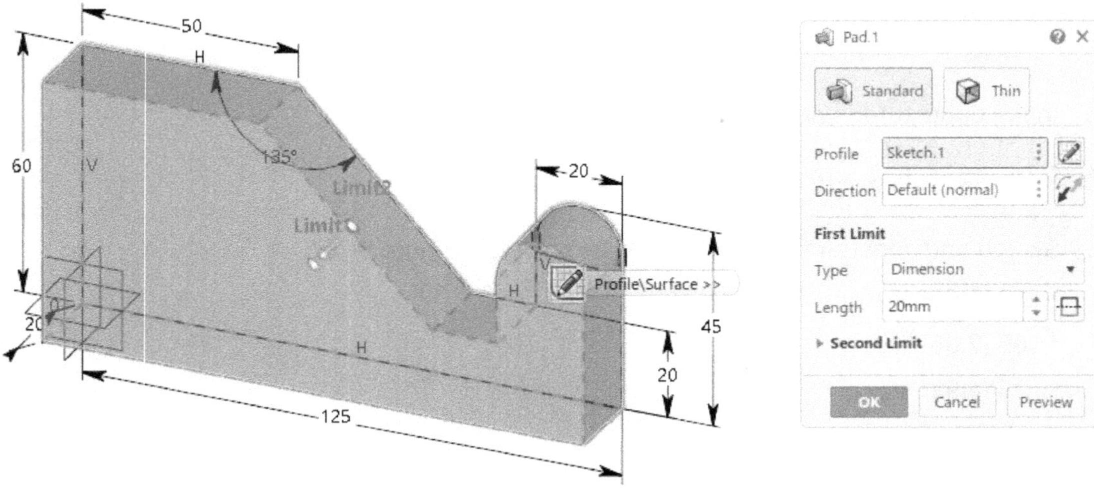

Figure 3–48

3. In the *Length* field, enter **75** (2.953 in).
4. Click **OK** to complete the feature. The resulting geometry displays as shown in Figure 3–49.

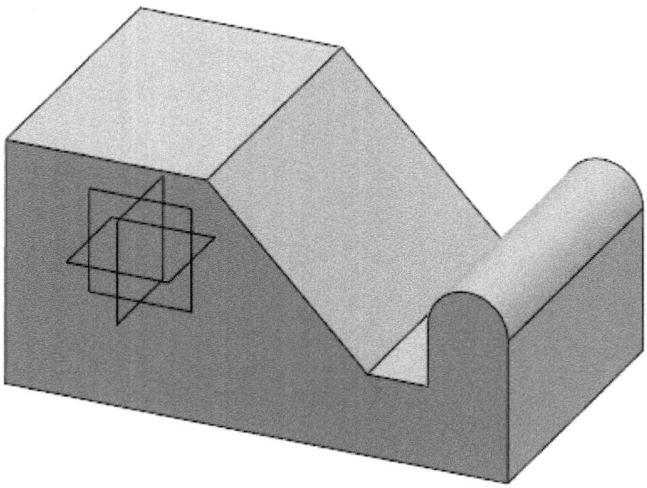

Figure 3–49

Task 4: Make dimensional changes to the pad feature.

1. Double-click on any face of the pad feature. The *Pad* dialog box also opens.
2. Double-click on the **60** (2.362 in) dimension (shown in Figure 3–50) to open the *Constraint* dialog box. Change the value to **30** (1.181 in) and click **OK**.

   Note: *You can press <Enter> instead of clicking* ***OK****.*

3. Repeat this process to change the **20** (0.787 in) dimension to **40** (1.575 in) and the **45** (1.772 in) dimension to **60** (2.362 in).

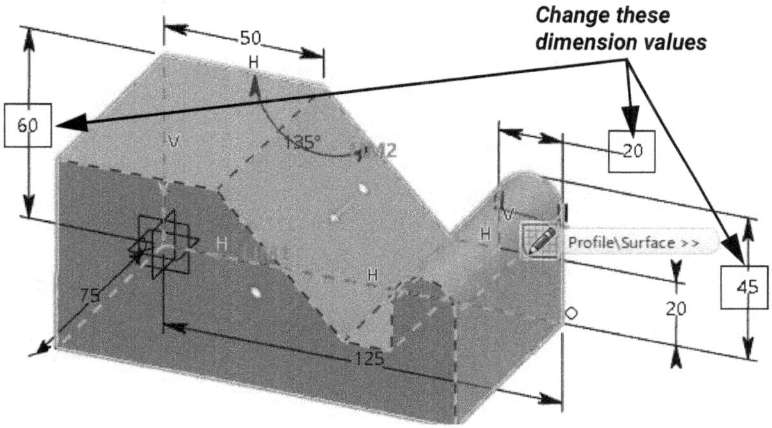

Figure 3–50

4. Click **OK** in the *Pad* dialog box to complete the dimensional changes and update the geometry. The resulting geometry displays as shown in Figure 3–51.

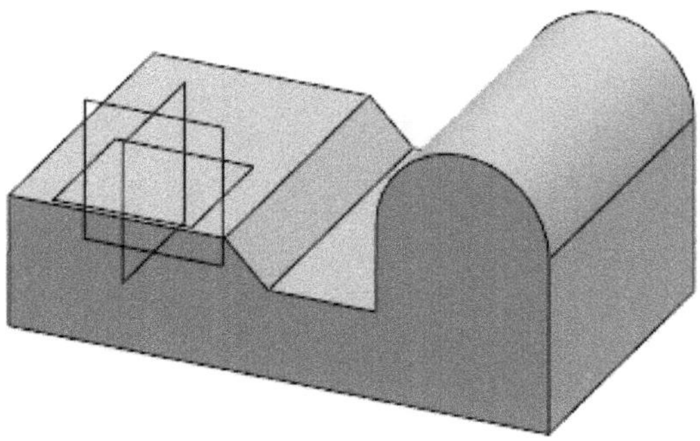

Figure 3–51

Task 5: Change the attributes of the feature.

1. Double-click on the pad feature again to open the *Pad* dialog box.
2. Select the (Mirrored extent) option. The software previews the geometry in wireframe, as shown in Figure 3–52. The geometry is symmetrical about the sketch and has a total length of 150 (5.906 in).

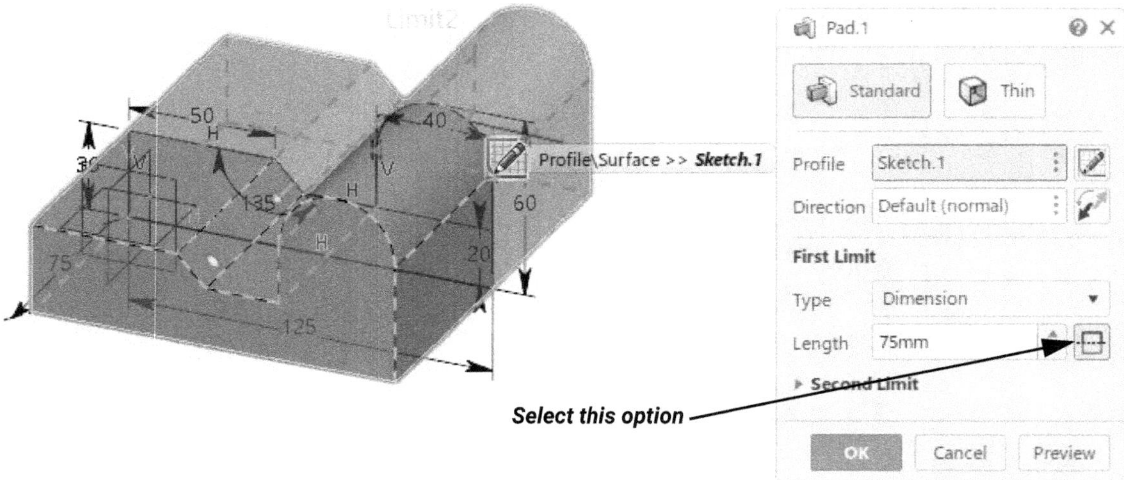

Figure 3–52

3. Clear the (Mirrored extent) option.
4. In the *First Limit* area, enter **50** (1.969 in) for the *Length*.

5. Click the arrow next to **Second Limit** to expand it. In the *Second Limit* area, enter **100** (3.937 in) for the *Length*. Click **Preview** and the resulting geometry displays, as shown in Figure 3–53.

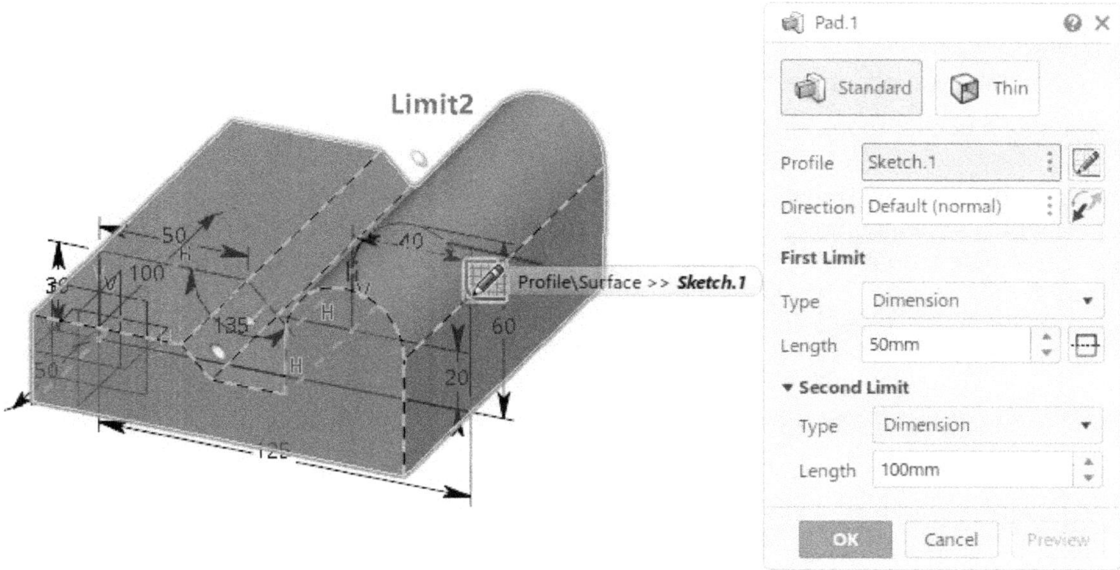

Figure 3–53

6. Click **OK** in the *Pad* dialog box to complete the change and update the geometry.

Task 6: Save the part and close the window.

1. In the Top Bar, click  (Share)>**Save** to save the part.
2. Close the *Pad_Sketch A.1* tab.

End of practice

Practice 3b
Create Pocket Features

Practice Objectives

- Create a sketch to create a pocket feature.
- Modify a pocket feature.

In this practice, you will create and modify three pocket features. The first feature will represent a hole with a keyway groove to accept a shaft. The second feature will create a cylindrical elongated hole cutout on the flange of the part. The completed model is shown in Figure 3–54.

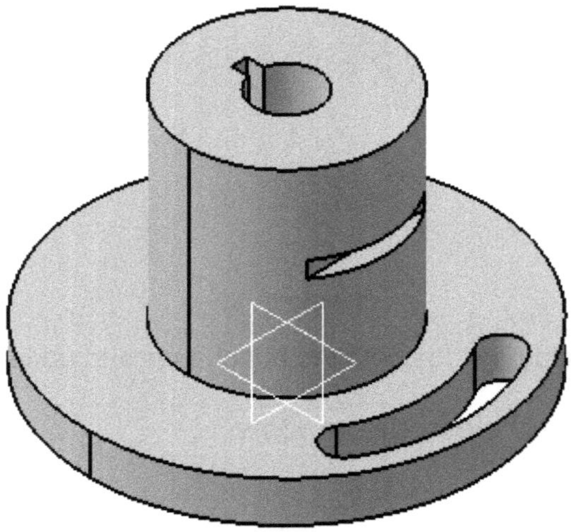

Figure 3–54

Task 1: Open a model and create a profile on the top of it.

1. In the Top Bar, click (Add/Create)>**Import**.
2. In the *Import* dialog box, click (Open).
3. Navigate to the *3DEXPERIENCE Transition Practice Files* folder, select **Pockets.3dxml,** and click **Open**.
4. Click **OK** in the *Import* dialog box.
5. Click **OK** in the *Operation Report* dialog box.
6. You are currently in Explore mode. Right-click on **Pockets** in the specification tree and select **Open**.

7. Select the top cylindrical face of the model and click  (Sketch) in the context toolbar, as shown in Figure 3–55.

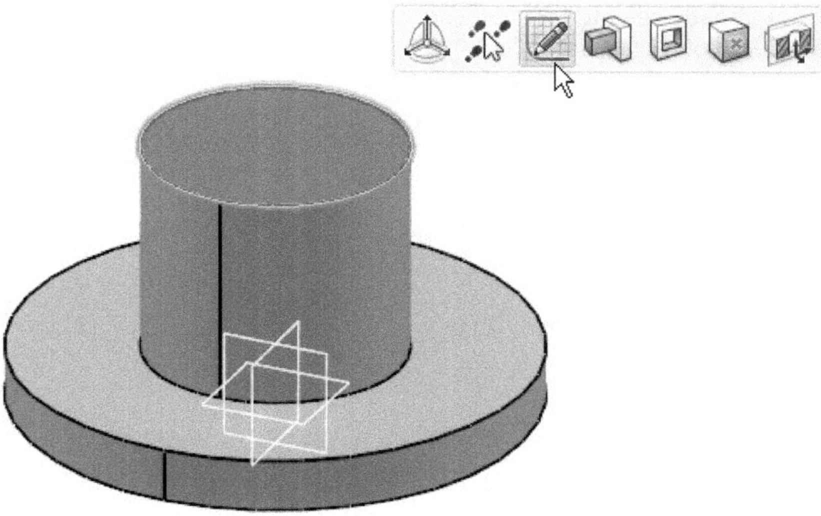

Figure 3–55

8. Sketch the profile as shown in Figure 3–56. Note that the arc is concentric with the cylindrical face and the keyway geometry is symmetrical about the vertical axis.
   - 4 (0.157 in)
   - 8 (0.315 in)
   - 12 (0.472 in)

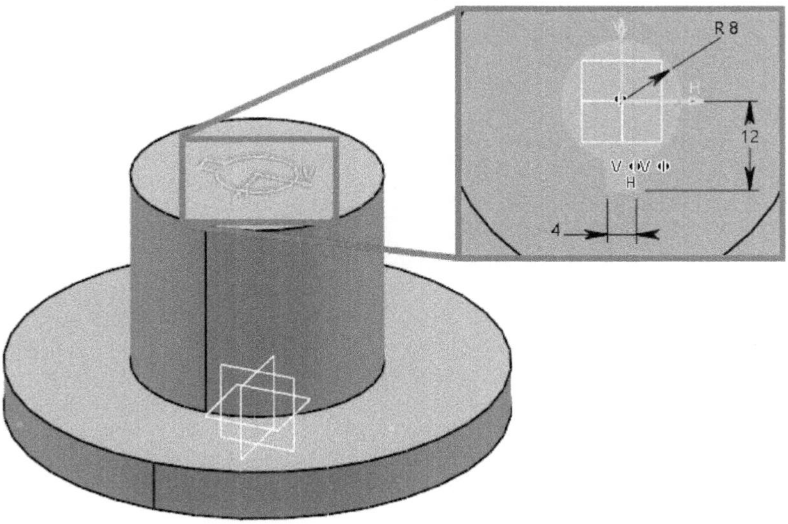

Figure 3–56

9. In the Action Bar, click (Exit App) to complete the sketch.

10. In the *Essentials* section of the Action Bar, click (Pocket) and select the sketch just created, if not already selected. The *Pocket* dialog box opens, as shown in Figure 3–57, indicating a *Depth* of **33** (1.299 in).

    Note: *The initial depth value can vary.*

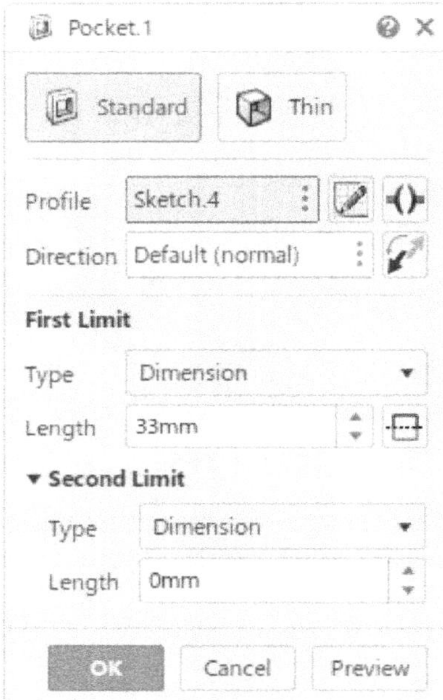

Figure 3–57

11. Verify that the arrow indicating direction points down into the part. Also confirm that the arrow indicating the material side points toward the inside of the profile, as shown in Figure 3–58.

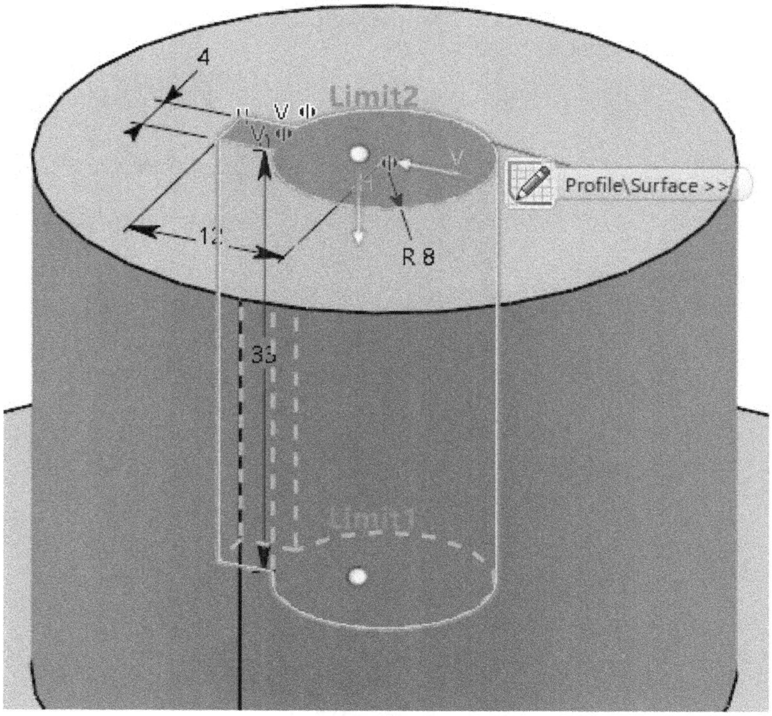

Figure 3–58

12. Enter a depth of **40** (1.575 in) and click **OK**. The completed pocket feature displays as shown in Figure 3–59.

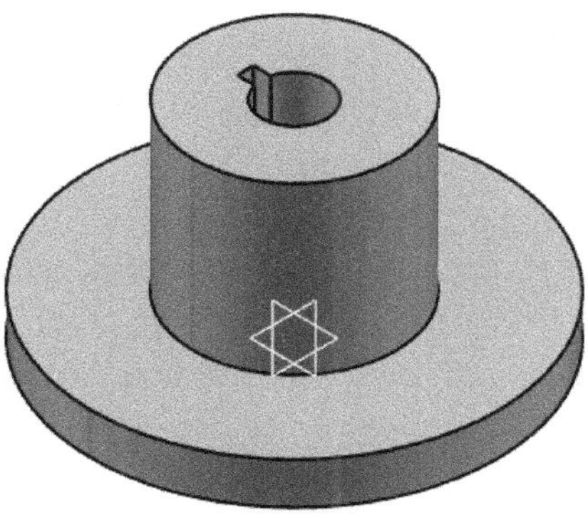

Figure 3–59

Task 2: Modify the pocket feature.

In this task, you will carry out a design change on the model. You will modify the depth of the cutout so that it will always extend up to the top face of the flange. This is done by modifying the depth options for the pocket feature.

1. Locate the pocket feature in the specification tree and double-click on it to open the *Pocket* dialog box.
2. In the *First Limit* area, set *Type* to **Up to plane** and select the face shown in Figure 3–60.

   Note: *Since the section does not entirely intersect the selected face, the* ***Up to surface*** *option cannot be used.*

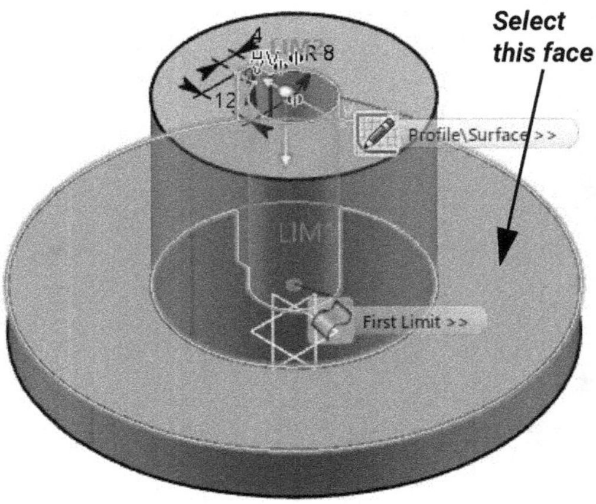

Figure 3–60

3. Click **OK** to complete the modification.
4. In the *View* section of the Action Bar, click  (View Modes) to display the *View Modes* window.
5. Click  (Shading With Edges and Hidden Edges) from the top of the window to review the depth of the feature.
6. Modify the depth of **Pad.1** from *40* (1.575 in) to **50** (1.969 in). Review the model to verify that the pocket feature is reacting correctly (depth should still run to the previously selected surface).
7. Once complete, return the model to the  (Shading With Sharp and Smooth Edges) display and close the *View Modes* window.

Task 3: Create a second pocket feature.

1. Select the face of the model shown in Figure 3–61 and click (Sketch).

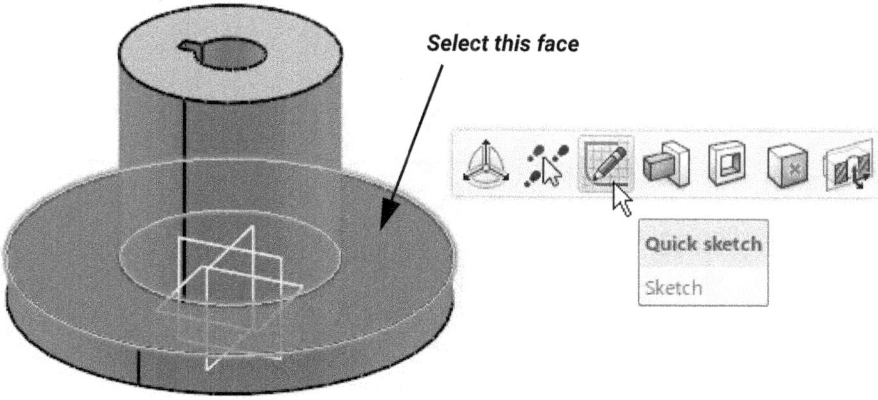

Figure 3–61

2. Sketch the profile as shown in Figure 3–62, using (Cylindrical Elongated Hole). To create the angle dimension, create two construction lines that are symmetrical about the vertical (**V**) axis and pass through the center of each arc.
   - 5 (0.197 in)
   - 40 (1.575 in)

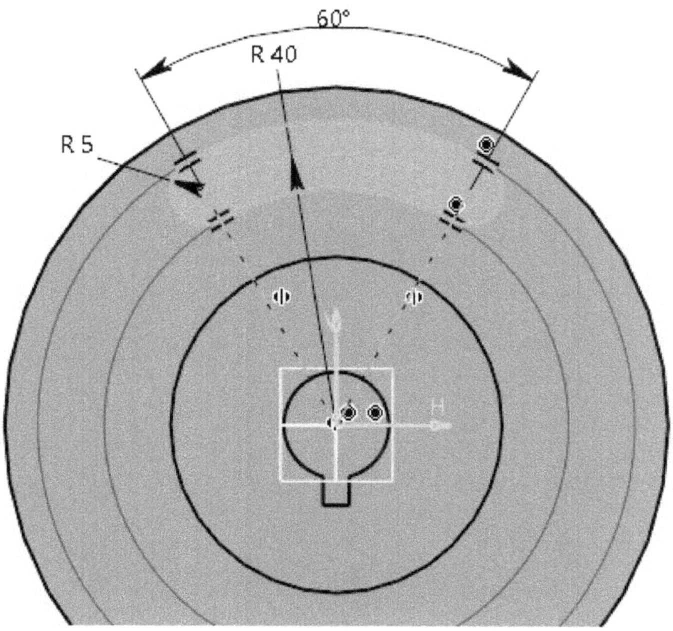

Figure 3–62

3. In the Action Bar, click (Exit App) to complete the sketch.

4. In the *Essentials* section of the Action Bar, click (Pocket) and select the sketch just created, if not already selected. Define the depth using the **Up to last** option. The completed feature displays as shown in Figure 3–63.

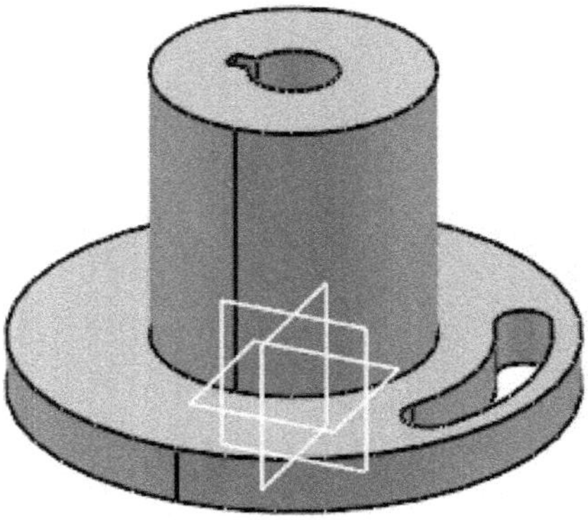

Figure 3–63

Task 4: Create a pocket using two limits.

In this task, you will sketch a profile for a pocket feature on the YZ plane. Then, you will create a pocket feature that cuts material from both sides of the sketch plane.

1. Create a sketch on the **YZ plane**. Sketch the profile as shown in Figure 3–64.
   - 4 (0.157 in)
   - 10 (0.394 in)
   - 20 (0.787 in
   - 40 (1.575 in)

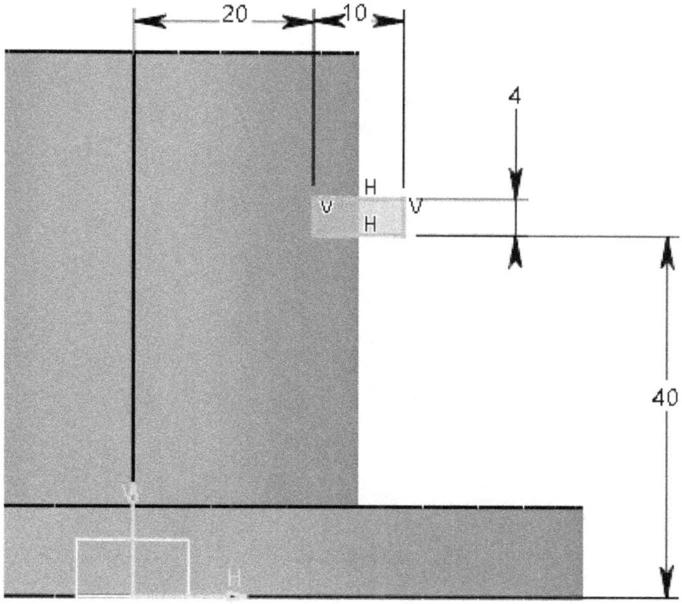

Figure 3–64

2. In the Action Bar, click (Exit App) to complete the sketch.
3. In the *Essentials* section of the Action Bar, click (Pocket) and select the sketch just created, if not already selected.
4. In the *First Limit* area, set the *Type* to **Up to last**.
5. Expand the arrow next to **Second Limit** if needed, and in the *Second Limit* area, set *Type* to **Up to last**.

6. Click **OK** to complete the feature. The model displays as shown in Figure 3–65.

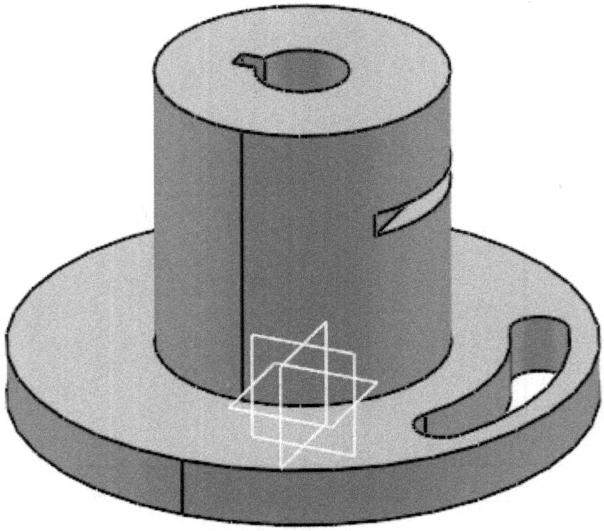

Figure 3–65

Task 5: Use the Robot to duplicate the pocket just created.

1. Select the pocket you just created, then click (Use Robot) in the context toolbar, as shown in Figure 3–66.

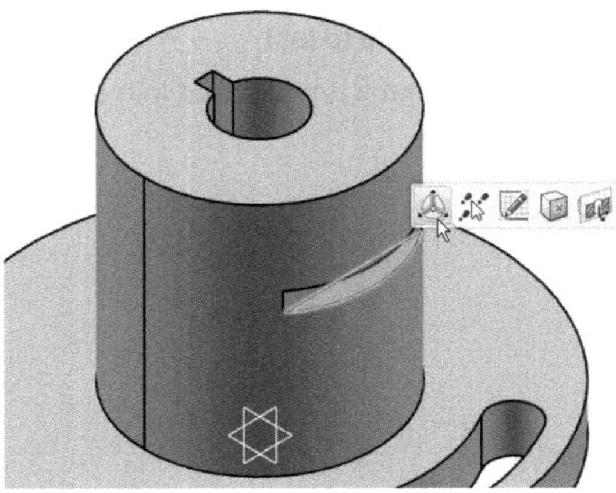

Figure 3–66

2. Ensure that the secondary context toolbar that opens has the options shown in Figure 3–67 enabled.

Figure 3–67

3. Select the axis running parallel to the axis of the cylinder, then hold <Ctrl> and drag down until the scale displays **12**, as shown in Figure 3–68.

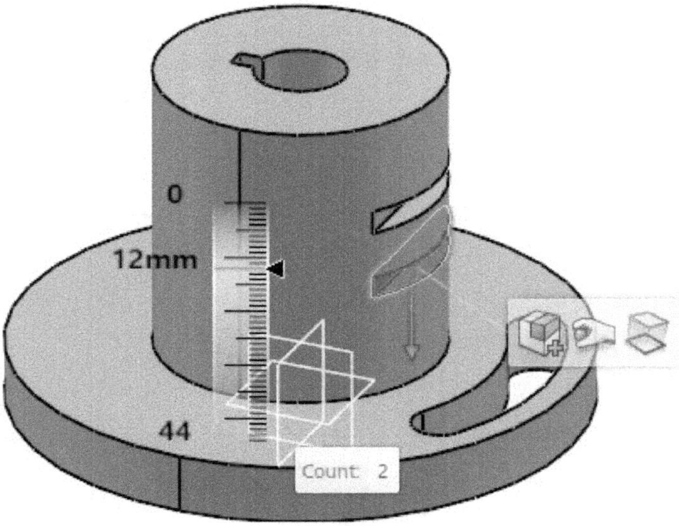

Figure 3–68

4. Edit the *Count* to **3** and click on the screen to complete the pattern.

5. In the specification tree, double-click on **RectPattern.1**. The *RectPattern* dialog box opens, as shown in Figure 3–69.
   - Note the number of instances and spacing values. Also note that the *Reference element* is listed as **RobotDirection**.

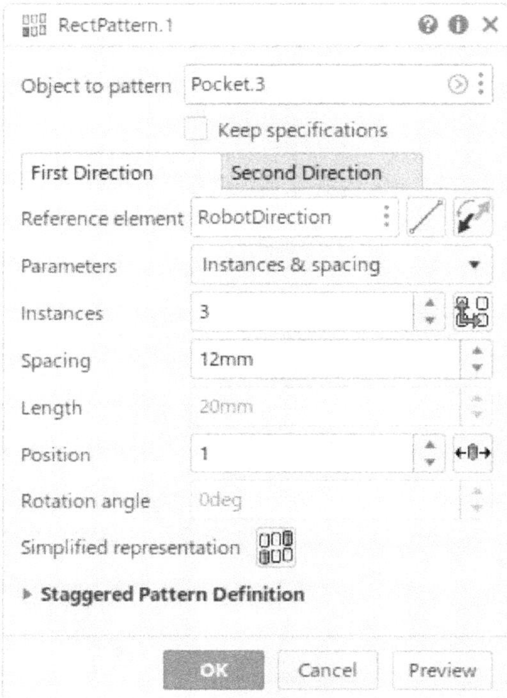

Figure 3–69

6. In the Top Bar, click (Share)>**Save** to save the part.
7. Close the *Pocket A.1* tab.

End of practice

Chapter

4

Lifecycle Management

This chapter teaches you how to use lifecycle management tools within the 3DEXPERIENCE platform interface. Lifecycle management tools enable you to track modifications and lifecycle status changes and to generate design alternatives made to a component.

Learning Objective

- Use lifecycle management tools.

4.1 Using Lifecycle Management

Lifecycle management encompasses management of the phases of design data from concept to release through obsolescence. Lifecycle management functionality in the 3DEXPERIENCE platform enables you to control:

- File access
- The ability to add design modifications
- Engineering change versioning

Lifecycle management tools also enable you to generate 3D part and product files with a different name to enable exploration of design variants.

Lifecycle Management Tools

Lifecycle management tools can be accessed by clicking **3D** in the Compass and selecting  (Collaborative Lifecycle). The Action Bar updates to provide access to the *Lifecycle* and *Collaboration* sections, as shown in Figure 4–1.

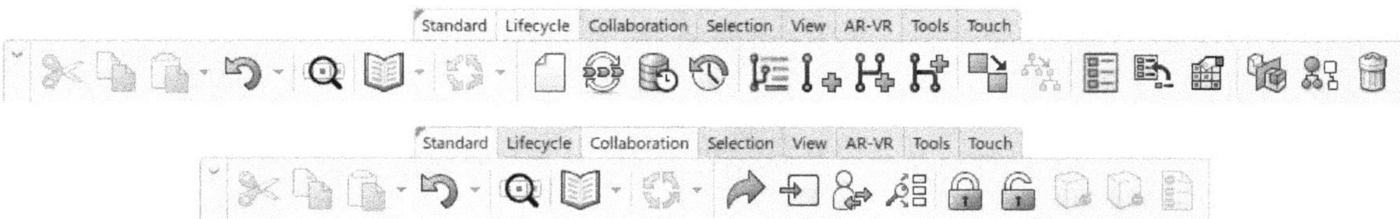

Figure 4–1

Some of the key tools are listed in the following table:

Icon	Option	Description
	**Maturity**	Controls the data lifecycle status. Five maturity states are available: **IN_WORK**, **RELEASED**, **FROZEN**, **REMOVED**, and **OBSOLETE**.
	**New Minor Revision**	Creates a new minor revision of an object (e.g., A.1 becomes A.2).
	**New Revision**	Creates a new revision of an object (e.g., A.1 becomes B.1).
	**New Revision From**	Creates a new revision of an assembly by integrating changes from another assembly.

Icon	Option	Description
	New Branch	Creates new content from existing content while maintaining a link to the original (e.g., P1.A1 becomes P2.A1).
	Iterations	Replaces objects with previous iterations, if enabled by an administrator.
	Delete	Enables deletion of part references and representations from the database. Requires sufficient security access and should be used with caution as it results in a permanent deletion and cannot be undone.
	Revisions	Explore revisions, duplicates, and evolutions of the selected object.
	Lock	Locks files and prevents other users from propagating (saving) modifications to locked items in the database.
	Unlock	Unlocks files and enables other users to propagate (save) modifications to previously locked items in the database.
	Change Owner	Enables object ownership to be transferred to another user working on the same project in the same company. Object ownership rights are required for transferring to another user.

Maturity

Maturity sets the state of the part at its current revision level. There are five options: **Private** (Draft), **In Work**, **Frozen**, **Released**, and **Obsolete**, as shown in Figure 4–2.

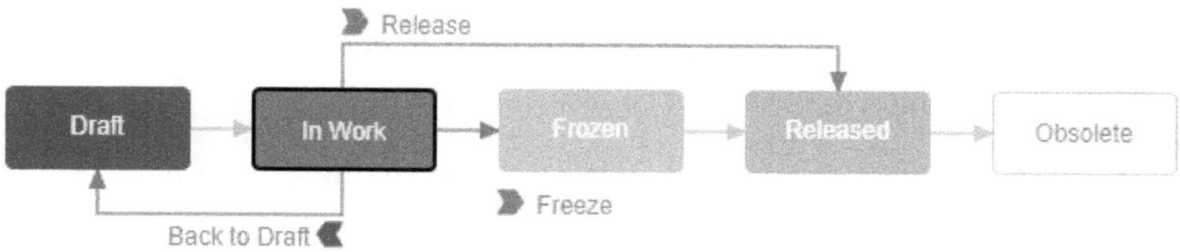

Figure 4–2

A Private part may be transferred to In Work. An In Work part can be demoted to Private, promoted to Frozen, or directly promoted to Released. A Frozen part may be demoted back to In Work or promoted to Released. A Released part can no longer be demoted.

When a part is marked Released, it can no longer be modified. A new version will have to made in order to change the part.

How To: Change Maturity

Use the following steps to change the maturity of an in-session object:

1. Select the component(s) in the product specification tree.
2. Click (Maturity) in the *Lifecycle* section of the Action Bar.
3. The *Maturity* dialog box will open with the available options displayed as blue interactive text along with a flow chart graphic.
4. Select the text of the maturity level option you wish to set the object to.

Minor Revisions

A minor revision is a change that does not affect the form, function, or fit of a part. Therefore, the part is interoperable with other minor revisions. For example, the thickness of a wall of a part may be thinned for cost savings, but the part is otherwise functionally the same.

By default, minor revisions are not allowed unless enabled by an administrator.

Minor revisions will show as a number at the end of a part name, as shown in Figure 4–3.

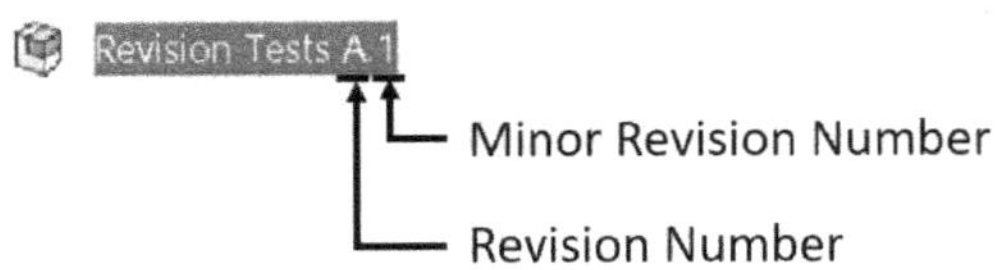

Figure 4–3

How To: Create a Minor Revision

Use the following steps to create a new minor revision of an object:

1. Select the component(s) in the product specification tree.
2. Click (New Minor Revision) in the *Lifecycle* section of the Action Bar.
3. Click **OK** to finalize the creation of the new revision and close the dialog box.

New Revisions

A new revision usually involves a change to the form, fit, or function of a part. For example, a hole for a bolt may be moved to a more structurally sound location on the part. Because the hole has now moved, this part is no longer interchangeable with other revisions. This is still considered the same part and will still have the same identifiers, such as the same part number, name, or title.

How To: Create a New Revision

Use the following steps to create a new revision of an object:

1. Select the component(s) in the product specification tree.
2. Click (New Revision) in the *Lifecycle* section of the Action Bar.
3. Click **OK** to finalize the creation of the new revision and close the dialog box.

New Revision From

This command is used for a separate group to make a change, then later reintegrate it. For example, a supplier company may need to create their own revision of the data, work on it, then reapply their changes to the OEM's data.

New Branch

A branch is very similar to a revision, but with one major difference: the identifier of the part is changed. For example, a new part may need to be built from an old one, but the new part will have a different part name and number. However, the history of the model will still show its ties to the original part.

How To: Create a New Branch

Use the following steps to create an new branch of an object:

1. Select the component(s) in the product specification tree.
2. Click (New Branch) in the *Lifecycle* section of the Action Bar.
3. Click **OK** to finalize the creation of the new revision and close the dialog box.

Iterations

If enabled by administration, an iteration of the file is stored every time the file is saved. This command allows you to compare and revert to previous iterations of a part.

Delete

This command will remove the selected data from the database. Caution is needed as this is permanent.

Revisions

Click (Revisions) to display a chart, as shown in Figure 4–4, that shows previous revisions of the current model and to show how the current revision is related to other revisions.

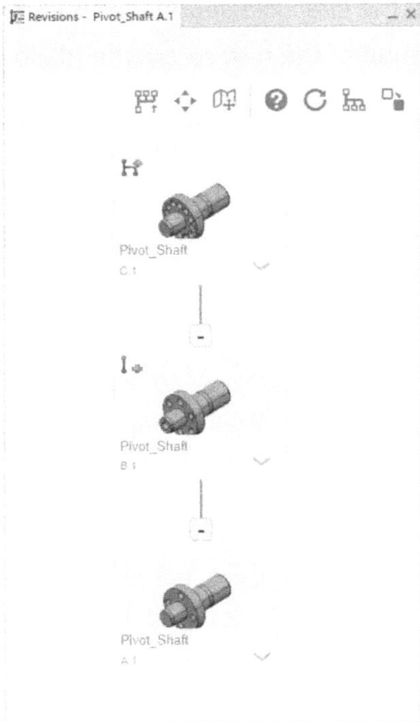

Figure 4–4

Replacing Parts

Once variations of a particular component have been created and saved, **Replace** can be used to quickly explore various design alternatives.

How To: Replace a Part

Use the following steps to replace an assembled component with a similar component:

1. Select the component to be replaced.
2. Right-click on the component to replace. Select **Replace>Replace by Existing** (or **Replace by Latest Revision** or **Replace by Revision**) in the context menu.

3. If using **Replace by Existing**, use **Search** to identify the component and select the replacement component from the results listing. If using **Replace by Revision**, select the replacing version from the *Select a version* dialog box. **Replace by Latest Revision** uses the newest revision. The system updates the assembly once a component has been replaced.

Assembly constraints do not have to be redefined when replacing a component that has been created using **New Revision**. Any child components of the replaced component automatically reference the replacement components.

New Revision combined with **Replace Component** enables efficient design changes and exploration of the *what if* scenarios typical of an early prototype environment.

4.2 Managing Rights and Ownerships

Lock

To help collaborate with other users, you may want to use (Lock) to lock access to a certain file so that others will not be able to save over your data. Locking a file is similar to "checking out" from a database. When you have locked a file, other users are prevented from making changes to the shape and writing over it. Some actions, such as creating revisions, are still permitted.

When a file is locked, a green key will appear in the icon, as shown in Figure 4–5, indicating that you are currently the user with save access to this file.

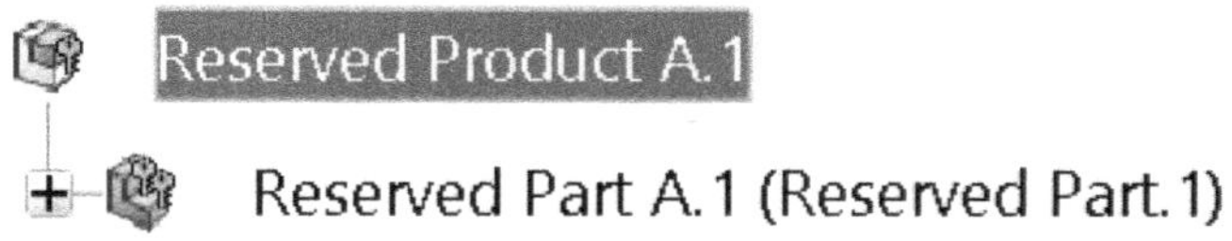

Figure 4–5

For parts in an assembly, there are two potential keys. The upper one is the "instance," which controls the position of the item in the assembly. The lower key is the "reference" and refers to the shape data of the part.

Data locked by other users will display red locks instead of green keys, as shown in Figure 4–6.

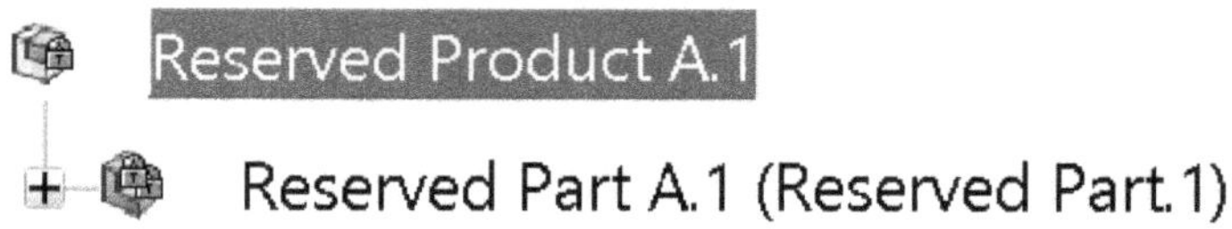

Figure 4–6

Unlock

If you have locked a file and wish to make it available for others to modify, use (Unlock) to unlock it. This is a "check in" process.

Transfer Ownership

Certain user roles may be placed into groups that have access to specific sets of data. For example, the design group may be allowed to modify the product, while the test group is not. Instead, the test group creates and modifies the jigs and fixtures they use to help with testing.

If a user of different group needs access to modify an item that they typically cannot, the ownership must be transferred to them. It could be that a designer wants to allow the test group to make changes to a specific part, and they could transfer the ownership to the test group.

How To: Transfer Ownership

1. Select the items to be transferred.
2. Click  (Change Ownership) in the *Collaboration* section of the Action Bar.
3. Find the user that this data will be transferred to by using the search located in the Top Bar, as shown in Figure 4–7.

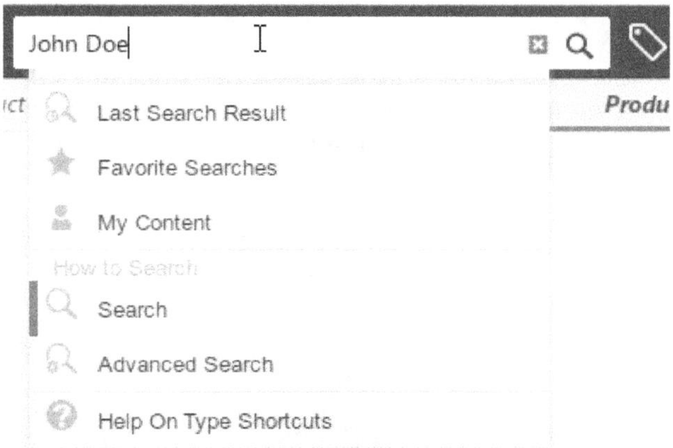

Figure 4–7

4. Click **OK** to complete the action.

Practice 4a
Lifecycle Management

Practice Objectives

- Change product maturity.
- Create a new major version.
- Replace a component.

In this practice, you will modify an assembly so that it displays as shown in Figure 4–8. You will change file maturity, create a new major version of a 3D part, and modify it. You will then replace the original component with the modified component.

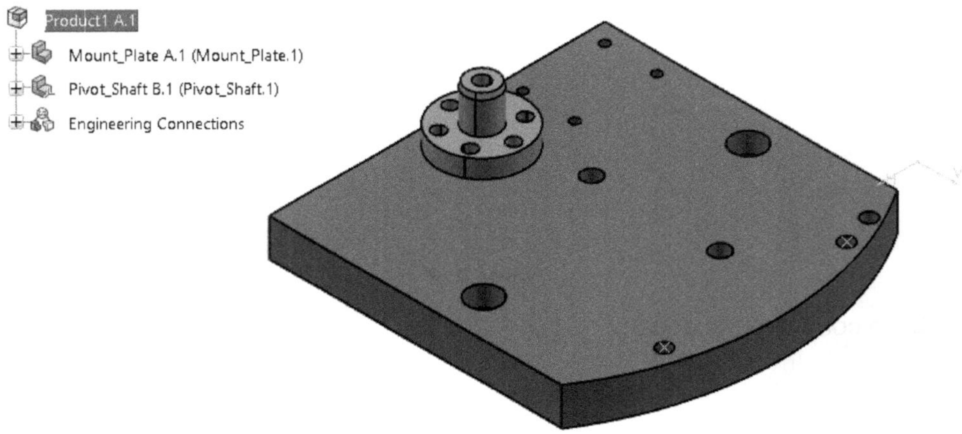

Figure 4–8

Task 1: Import the fixture assembly.

1. In the Top Bar, click (Add/Create)>**Import**.
2. In the *Import* dialog box, click (Open).
3. Navigate to the *3DEXPERIENCE Transition Practice Files* folder, select **Fixture.3dxml,** and click **Open**.
4. Ensure the settings in the *Import* dialog box match those shown in Figure 4–9.

   Note: *The Duplication string field should show your initials due to the preference setting made in the first practice.*

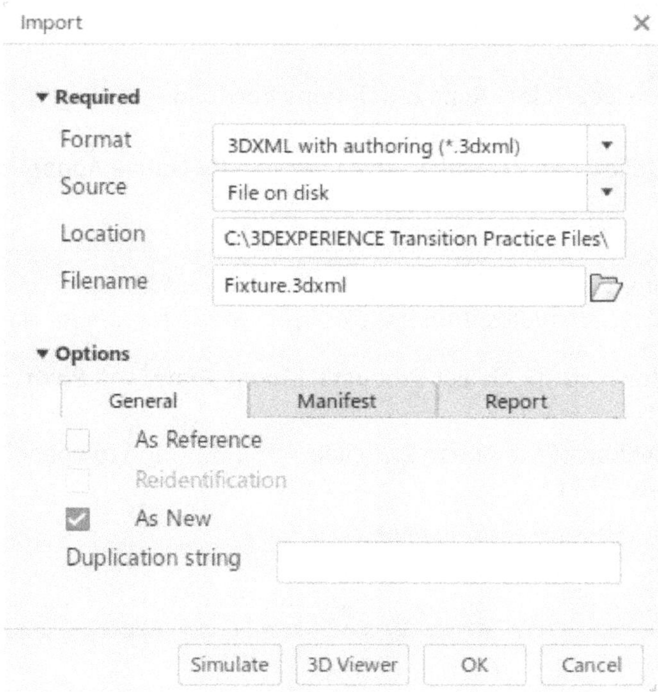

Figure 4–9

5. Click **OK**.
6. Click **OK** in the *Operation Report* dialog box.
7. **Product1** will be shown in the tree, but no geometry will display. Expand **Product1** in the tree to load the geometry into the display.
8. Right-click on **Product1** in the specification tree and select **Open**.
9. In the *View* section of the Action Bar, set the view to (* iso). If necessary, click (Fit All In). The assembly displays as shown in Figure 4–10.

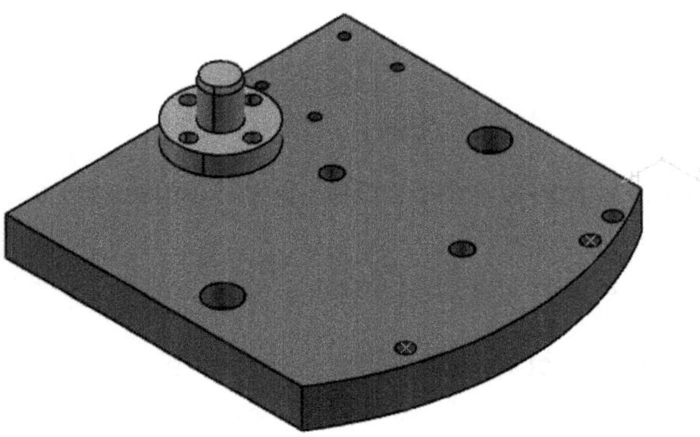

Figure 4–10

Task 2: Identify the maturity level of the product and components.

1. In the Compass, select **Roles, Apps & Solutions portfolio**.

2. In the apps area, click (Collaborative Lifecycle for Native Apps).

   Note: *Do not click (Collaborative Lifecycle for Dashboard), as this will open a browser window for your 3DDashboard. Note that the small arrow in the upper-right corner of the icon differentiates it from the Collaborative Lifecycle for Native Apps icon.*

3. Press and hold down <Ctrl>. Select **Product1**, **Mount_Plate**, and **Pivot_Shaft** from the specification tree.
4. In the *Lifecycle* section of the Action Bar, click (Maturity) to open the *Maturity* window, as shown in Figure 4–11.

   Note: *The current Maturity Status is* ***In Work****.*

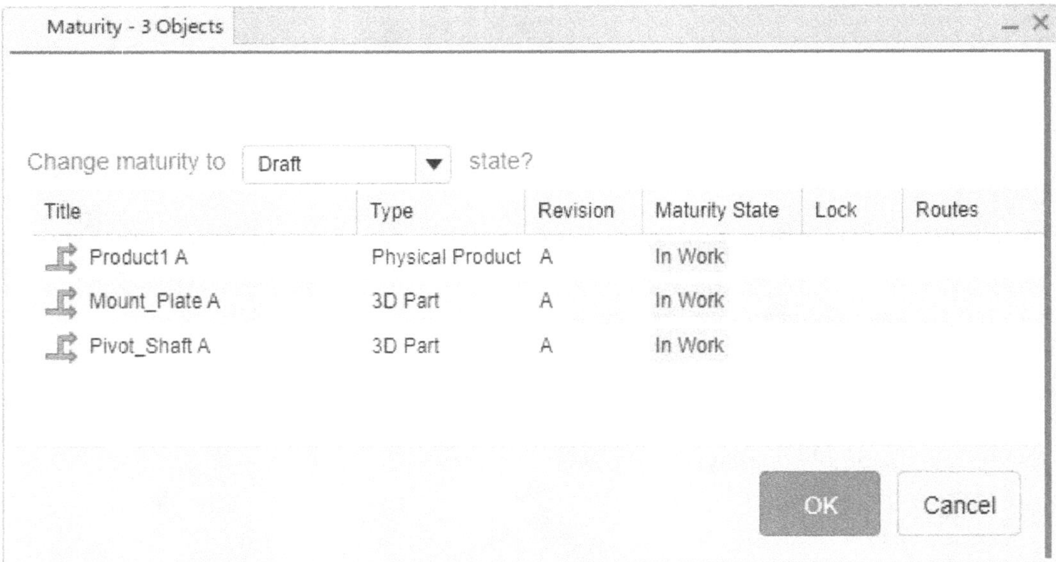

Figure 4–11

5. Click **Cancel** to close the window without changing the maturity status for any of the selected items.
6. Click on the screen to clear any selected items.
7. Click (Maturity) and select **Mount_Plate** in the specification tree.
8. In the *Maturity* window, click **Release**, as shown in Figure 4–12. The window will disappear when complete.

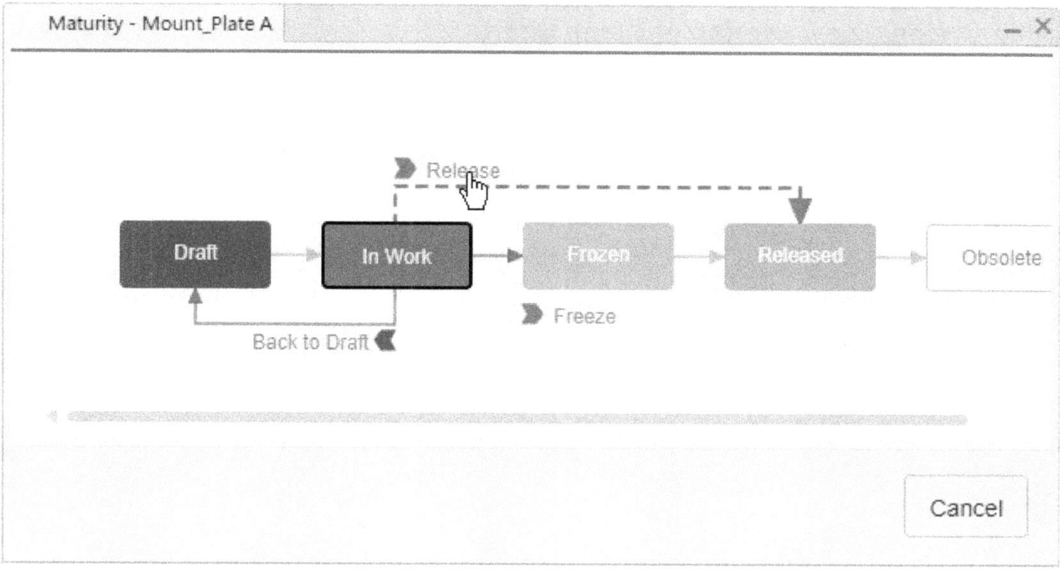

Figure 4–12

__Note:__ Changing the Maturity to __Released__ makes the data visible in the database for project members with Viewer level access.

Task 3: Reserve a component.

1. Click on the screen to clear any selected items.
2. In the *Collaboration* section of the Action Bar, click (Lock) and select **Pivot_Shaft** in the specification tree.
3. In the *Lock* dialog box, select the **Instance** and **Reference** options, as shown in Figure 4–13. Locking both options prevents modification of either of the 3D part or 3D shape (geometry) levels by another user.

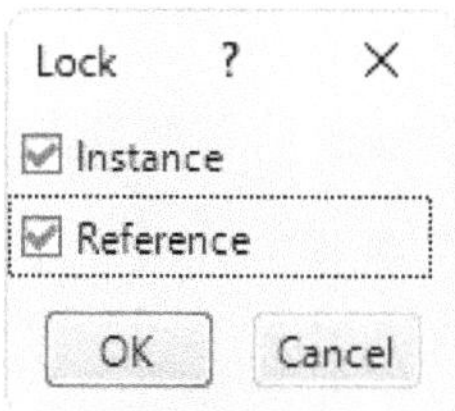

Figure 4–13

4. Click **OK**. The specification tree icon for **Pivot_Shaft** updates to reflect the locked status ( ).

Task 4: Create a new version of Pivot_Shaft.

1. In the *Lifecycle* section of the Action Bar, click (New Revision).
2. The *New Revision* dialog box displays, as shown in Figure 4–14. If it does not display, ensure that the **Pivot_Shaft** was still selected from Task 3.

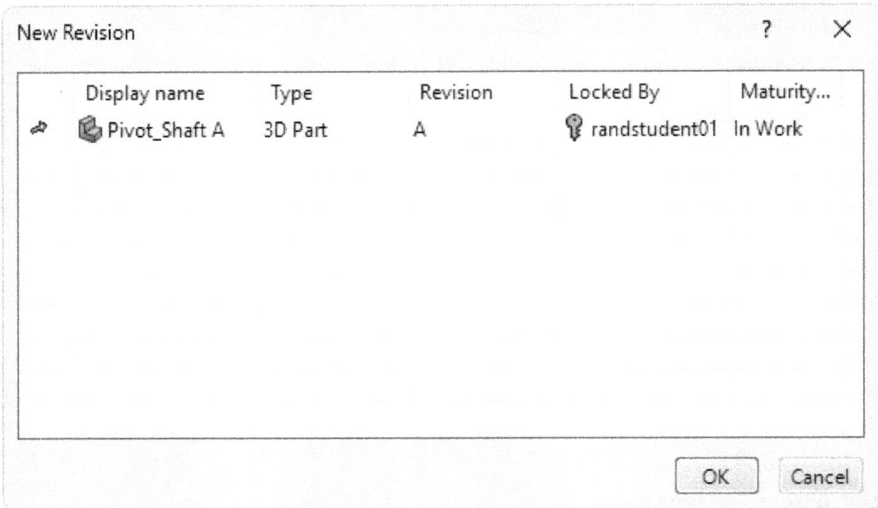

Figure 4–14

3. Click **OK**.
4. The **Pivot_Shaft B.1** model opens in a new tab.

Task 5: Develop an alternate design for Pivot_Shaft.

1. Modify the number of instances in the circular pattern from *4* to **[6]**.

2. Create an **8mm Hole** feature through the entire part, concentric to the part axis, as shown in Figure 4–15.

Figure 4–15

3. Save the changes and close the *Pivot_Shaft B* tab.

Task 6: Replace a component.

1. Right-click on **Pivot_Shaft** in the specification tree and select **Replace>Replace by Revision**, as shown in Figure 4–16.

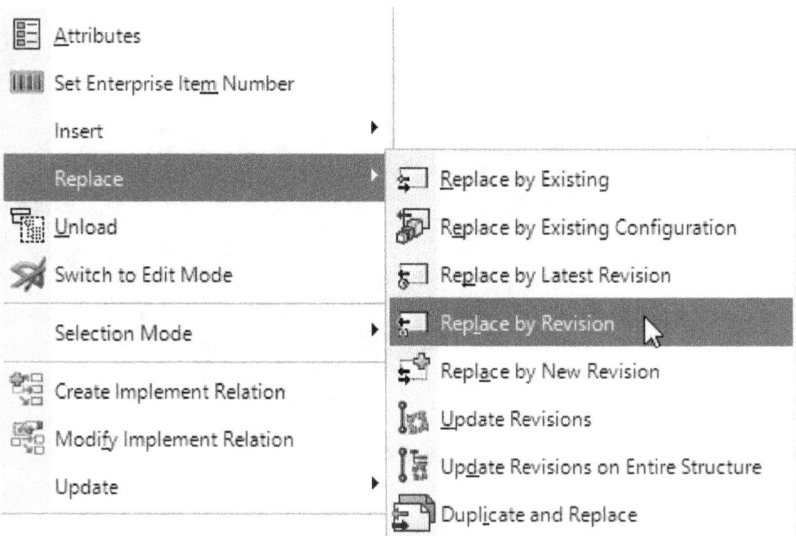

Figure 4–16

2. The *Revision Selector* window lists all of the files created using the **New Revision** command, as shown in Figure 4–17.

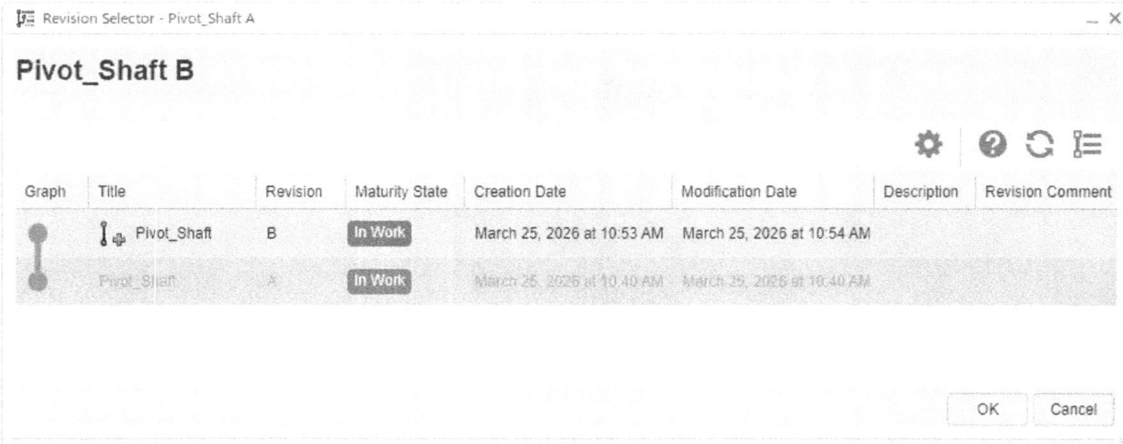

Figure 4–17

3. Select **Revision B** and click **OK**.
4. The product and specification tree should now display **Pivot_Shaft B**, as shown in Figure 4–18.

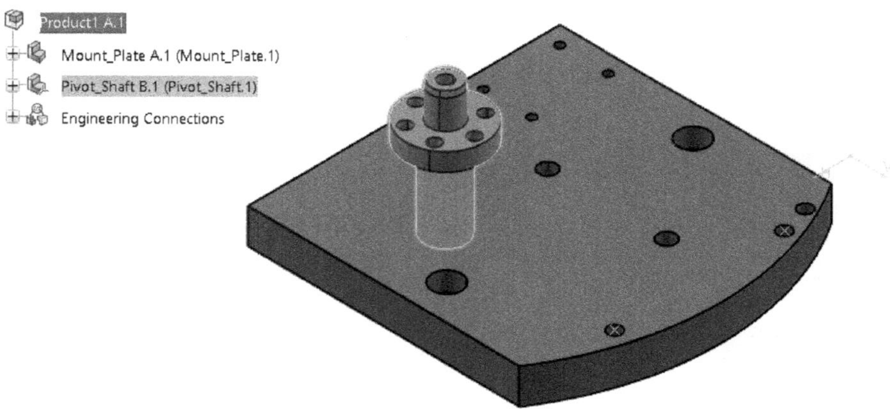

Figure 4–18

5. Save the product and close the tabs.

   Note: *Within 3DEXPERIENCE, the ability to use major and minor revisions can be customized by your administrator. So while this example shows major revisions (A, B, C, D, etc.), minor revisions can also be controlled in a similar manor (A.1, A.2, B.1, B.2, etc.).*

End of practice

Chapter 5

Engineering Connections and Constraints

This chapter covers how to activate the Assembly Design app and access assembly-specific options. It also guides you through the process of creating an assembly and describes the available assembly constraints.

Learning Objectives

- Learn the various engineering connection types.
- Learn how to start a new product.
- Understand how to add additional components to an assembly.

5.1 Engineering Connections Overview

Engineering connections are defined as the type of motion created between two parts and the group of constraints that define it. The type of engineering connection that is created is based on the type of constraints applied between parts, 3D shapes, or products. For example:

- A coincidence constraint between axes
- A contact constraint between planar faces

These two assembly constraints would result in a revolute engineering connection. Engineering connections are very similar to kinematic joints in CATIA V5.

When using the  (Engineering Connection) option, a connection type can be chosen to define the desired type of connection (as shown in Figure 5–1), then a template can be used (as shown in Figure 5–2) to quickly pick from a predefined group of constraints that best fit the design intent of that engineering connection.

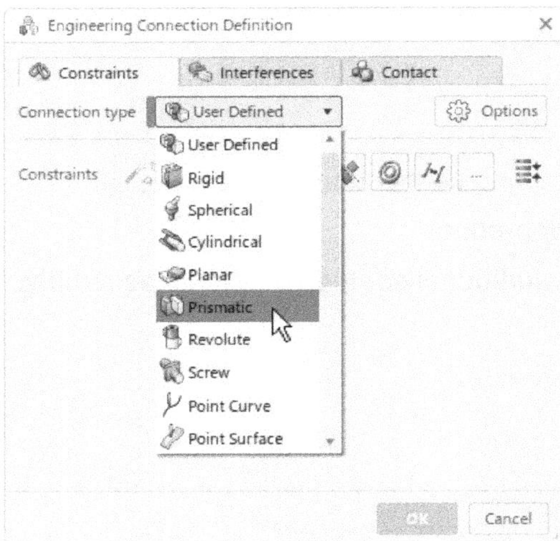

Figure 5–1

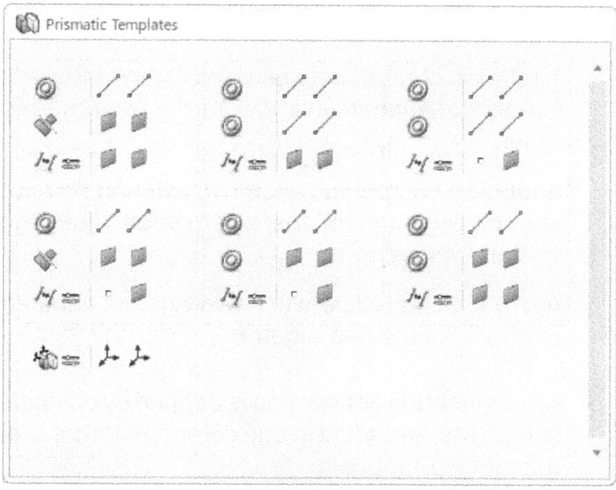

Figure 5–2

The available engineering connections are described in the following table:

Icon	Name	Description
	**User-Defined**	A combination of constraints, which is incompatible with the predefined engineering connection types.
	**Rigid**	Welds components together.
	**Spherical**	Point-Point constraint enabling free rotation about the common points.
	**Cylindrical**	Axis-Axis/Line-Line constraint permitting relative motion along the constrained entities.
	**Planar**	Plane-Plane constraint permitting sliding and rotation relative to the constrained entities.
	**Prismatic**	A constraint group permitting relative translation along a single degree of freedom.
	**Revolute**	A constraint group permitting one degree of rotational freedom.
	**Screw**	A constraint that combines rotational and translational motion, allowing for one motion to drive the other.
	**Point Curve**	A constraint permitting a point to be constrained to a linear or non-linear curve.
	**Point Surface**	A constraint permitting a point to be constrained to planar or non-planar surface.

Icon	Name	Description
	**Gear**	A relation created between two existing Revolute engineering connections, where a ratio links the two together. Driving one affects the other.
	**Rack**	A relation created between two existing Revolute and Prismatic engineering connections, where a ratio links the two together. Driving one affects the other.
	**Cable**	A relation created between two existing engineering connections where a ratio links the two together.
	**Universal**	An engineering connection is defined by coincidence constraint between two points, and a line in one component that is coincident with a plane in the other component.
	**Roll Curve**	An engineering connection that allows one curve to roll tangent relative to another curve. The rotation of the first curve defines the distance along the second curve. Example: A wheel rolling along a path.
	**Slide Curve**	An engineering connection that allows one curve to slide tangent relative to another curve. The rotation of one curve does not directly affect the position of the other curve. Example: A cam follower.
	**Fix**	An engineering connection that locks a component from moving relative to a reference when updating. There are four types of fix constraints with the difference between them being what is referenced.
	**Free**	An engineering connection that measures one part or two parts in relation to one another.
	**Symmetry**	An engineering connection that allows two components to be symmetrical relative to a symmetry plane.
	**Projection**	A constraint permitting an axis to be constrained to a point on a surface.

The available constraints that are used to create the engineering connections are described in the following table. These are the individual rules that define how an engineering connection works.

Icon	Name	Description
	Contact	A constraint between two surfaces that maintains an offset of 0.
	Coincidence	A constraint between two geometric elements allowing them to have the same location and orientation.
	Offset	A constraint that controls a distance between two planar or curved faces.
Fix		
	Fix	Locks the component in its current position in space relative to another component. Supports other constraints.
	Fix in Space	Locks the component to the assembly's origin. Can stand alone as a constraint.
	Fix Together	Selected components (two or more) act as one rigid object. Moving one moves all. Does not over constrain the assembly when other constraints already exist.
	Fix Together Relatively	Only works when two selected components act as one rigid object. If a third object is added, CATIA automatically converts the constraint to Fix Together.
Angle		
	Angle	Creates an angle value between two planar surfaces or linear objects. Locks the angle.
	Parallelism	Creates an parallel condition between two planar surfaces or linear objects.
	Perpendicularity	Creates a perpendicular condition between two planar surfaces or linear objects.
	Hinge	Creates one rotational degree of freedom about a shared axis. Allows rotation about an axis and is not locked.
Curve		
	Curvilinear Distance	Defines and controls the distance between two points following along a curve.
	Roll	Defines a curve rolling tangent along another curve. The rotation of the first curve defines the distance along the second curve. Example: A wheel rolling down a path.
	Slide	Defines a curve sliding tangent along another curve. The rotation of one curve does not directly affect the position of the other curve. Example: A cam follower.

Icon	Name	Description
Axis-Based		
	Planar	Creates a Planar constraint only using axis systems as references.
	Prismatic	Creates a Prismatic constraint only using axis systems as references.
	Cylindrical	Creates a Cylindrical constraint only using axis systems as references.
	Revolute	Creates a Revolute constraint only using axis systems as references.
	Spherical	Creates a Spherical constraint only using axis systems as references.
	Universal	Creates a Universal constraint only using axis systems as references.
Advanced		
	Symmetry	Defines components so their position is symmetrical with respect to a symmetry plane.
	Compound	Defines a relationship between two engineering connections to control an angle or distance.
	Projection	Positions a component by projecting a point onto a plane, line, or surface.
	Tangency	Defines two geometrical objects to share a tangent direction at their point of contact.

A comparison of what constraints looked like in CATIA V5 and what engineering connections look like in 3DEXPERIENCE Assembly Design is shown in Figure 5–3.

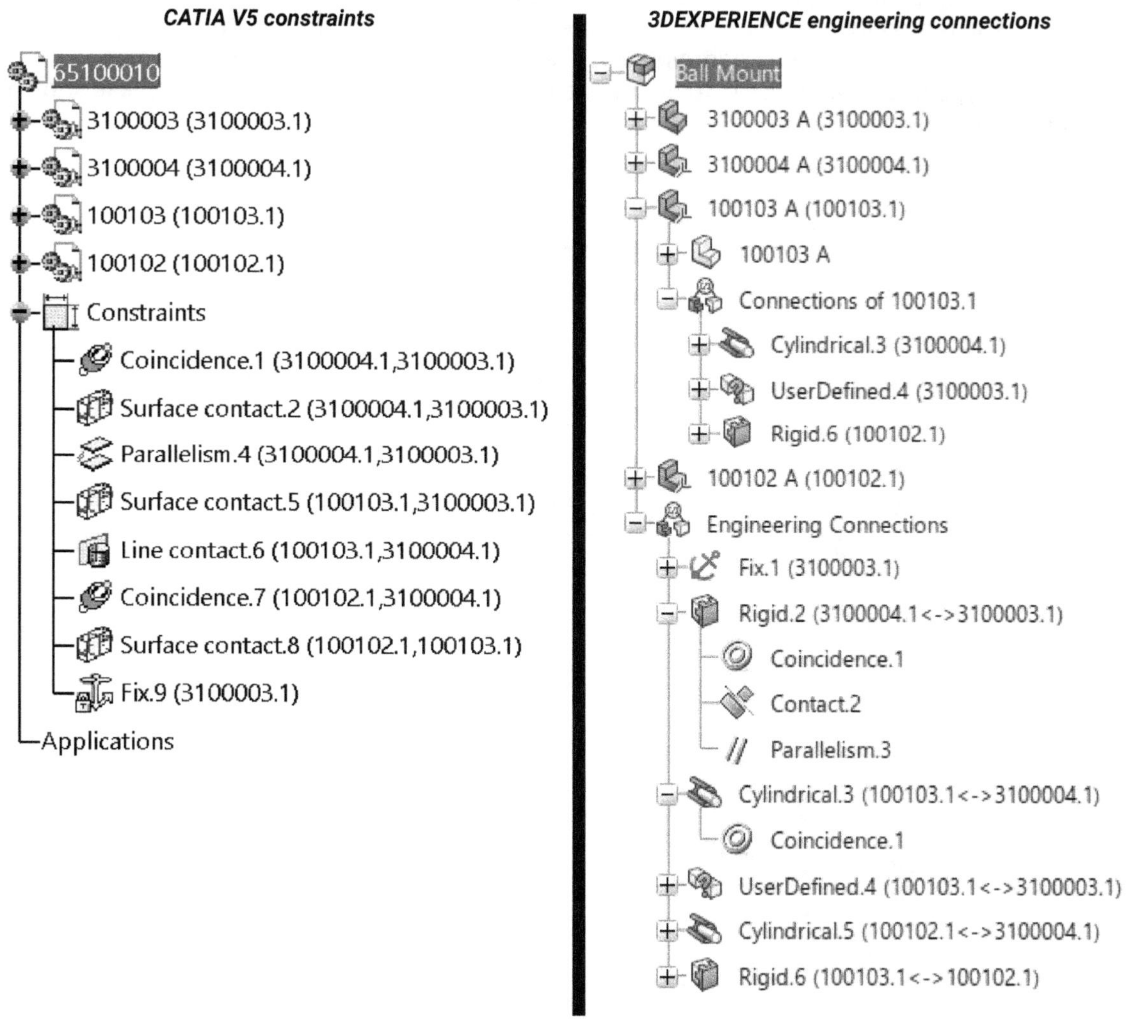

Figure 5–3

Engineering connections can be applied to a product (or assembly) using the (Assembly Design) app. This app is for the design of assemblies in conjunction with the Part Design and Drafting apps.

When an engineering connection is being created, red and green indicators show if appropriate supports have been chosen for each constraint or connection type itself. If red is indicated, either a support is missing or a support was selected that does not work in that specific situation. The red connection type basically means something is wrong with the engineering connection and an issue needs addressed. A green indicator means the constraint or connection type has what it needs to define the engineering connection. An example is shown in Figure 5–4.

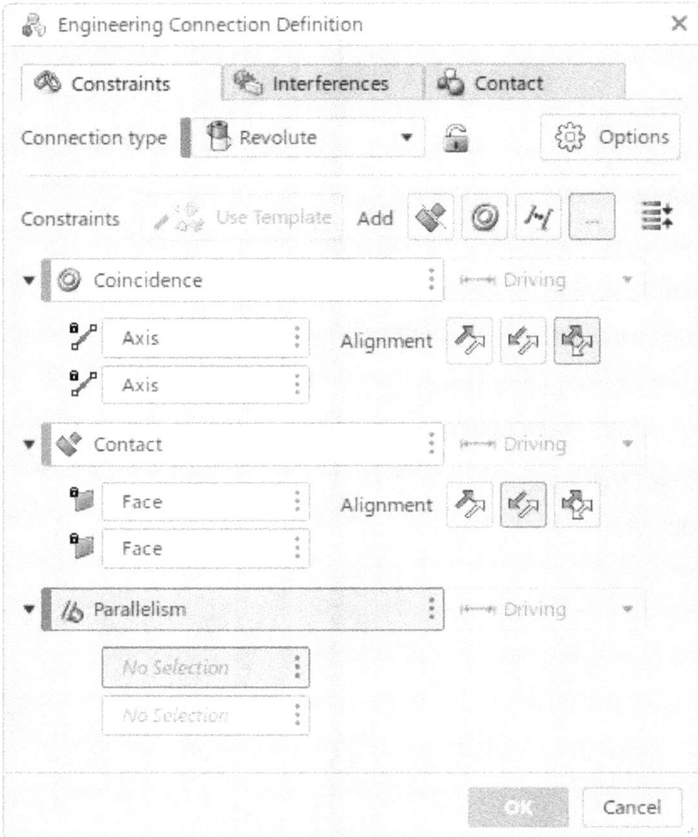

Figure 5–4

5.2 Starting a New Product

A new product can be created in two ways:

- In the Compass (shown in Figure 5–5), click the **Outer Ring**, then select (Assembly Design). Fill in the applicable information in the *Physical Product* dialog box.

Figure 5–5

- Select (Add/Create)>**Physical Product** in the Top Bar. Fill in the applicable information in the *Physical Product* dialog box.

In either case, the *Physical Product* dialog box displays, as shown in Figure 5–6. When the 3DEXPERIENCE platform creates a new product, a generic name and identifier are assigned to it. You can change the *Title* and add a *Description*, as well as set other options.

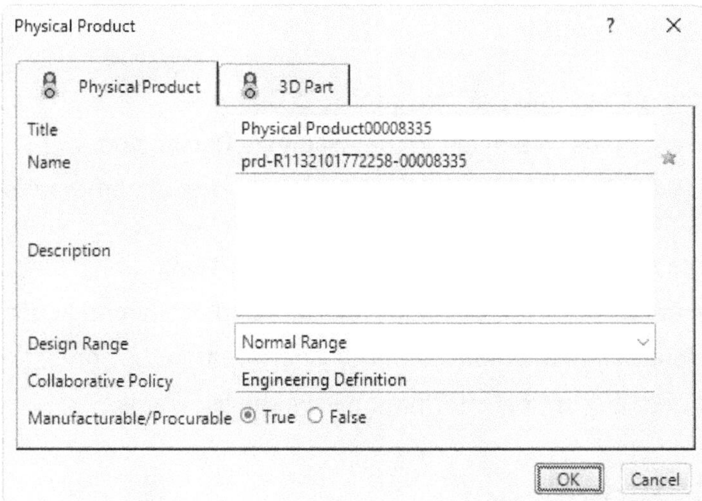

Figure 5–6

The *3D Part* tab, shown in Figure 5–7, enables you to also create a new part model as the first component in the assembly.

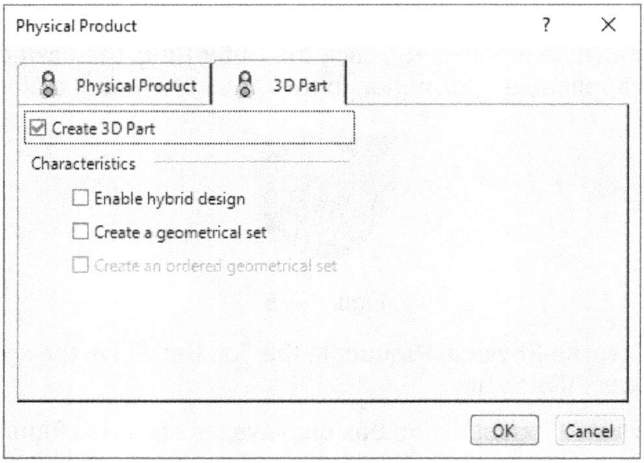

Figure 5–7

How To: Create an Assembly

The steps for creating an assembly is very similar to CATIA V5.

1. Create a new product file by activating the **Assembly Design** app.
2. In the *Physical Product* dialog box, modify the desired product properties (e.g., *Title*, *Version Comments*, and *Description*).
3. Add components to the assembly using the assembly tools.
4. Position components using the Compass and/or using engineering connections.
5. Add assembly features to the model or modify parts within the context of the assembly.
6. Analyze and extract any critical information from the assembly.

Adding Components

A component is an object that is added into an assembly. Components can be added to an assembly using the same methods as CATIA V5. The following table describes some of the icons found in the *Product Modification* section of the Action Bar:

Icon	Option	Description
	**Product**	Creates a new subassembly within the top-level assembly with its own product file.
	**3D Part**	Creates a new 3D part within the top-level assembly containing a 3D shape.

Icon	Option	Description
	**3D Shape**	Creates a new 3D shape within the top-level assembly without the creation of a 3D part.
	**Existing Product**	Adds a product or 3D part to the assembly whose file already exists within the engineering database.

You can also right-click on the product and select **Insert**, as shown in Figure 5–8.

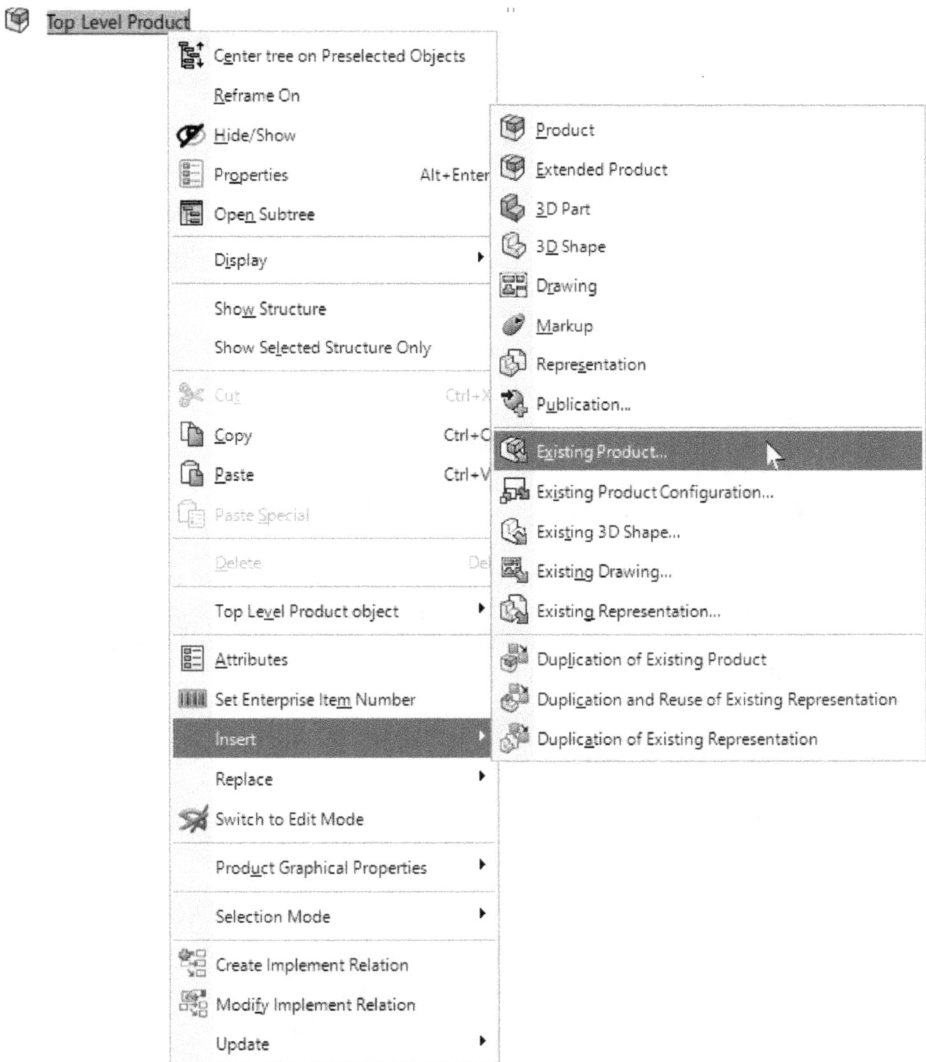

Figure 5–8

When adding in multiple existing components, <Ctrl> and <Shift> can be used.

Product Structure

The product structure is very similar to CATIA V5. The active level is highlighted in blue and operations are performed on the active level. A new level can be activated by double-clicking on that level. An example of a product specification tree with the top-level product activated is shown in Figure 5–9.

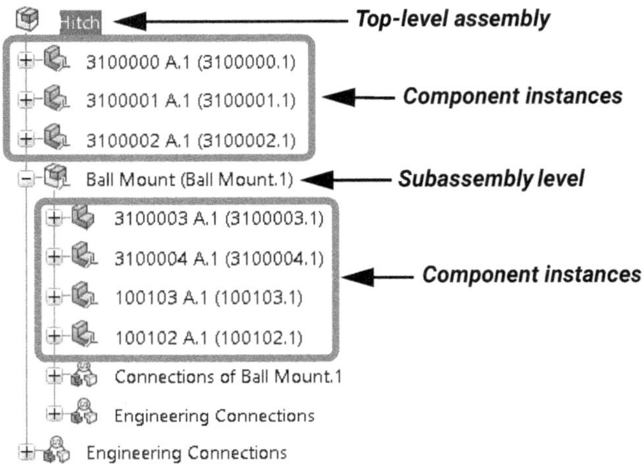

Figure 5–9

Moving and Manipulating Components

Components can be moved and manipulated using the Robot just like using the compass in CATIA V5. The Robot can be snapped onto components and the edges and arcs can be used to translate and rotate the component. When the Robot is snapped onto a component, the Robot will turn orange in color, as shown in Figure 5–10.

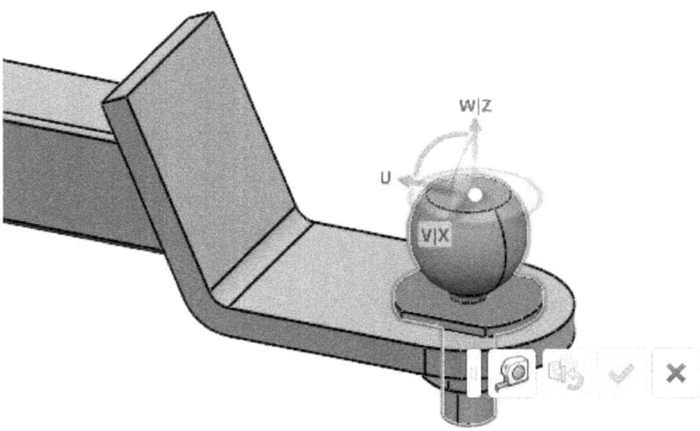

Figure 5–10

5.3 Applying Engineering Connections

Engineering connections can be found in the *Assembly* section of the Action Bar, as shown in Figure 5–11.

Commonly Used Tools

The *Assembly* section of the Action Bar is shown in Figure 5–11. This toolbar is available in the **Assembly Design** app, and controls how new components are added to the assembly. The same tools are available in the **Insert** context menus, as previously shown.

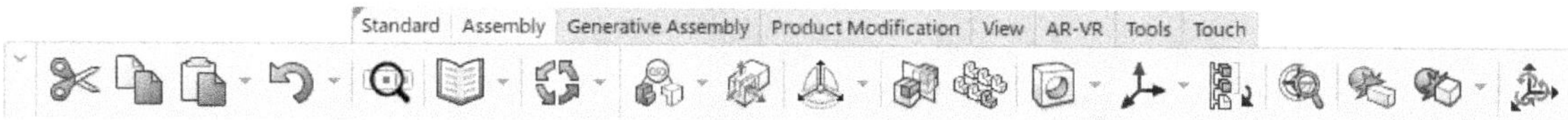

Figure 5–11

The  (Engineering Connection) option controls the relative position of components in the assembly.

There are three methods that can be used to create engineering connections.

- In the *Engineering Connection Definition* dialog box, select the constraints you wish to use from the *Add* area, as shown in Figure 5–12. Constraints will be placed in the engineering connection, waiting for you to select on the needed supports for each. The engineering connection will automatically set the connection type to an acceptable value, or CATIA will define the engineering connection as **User Defined**.

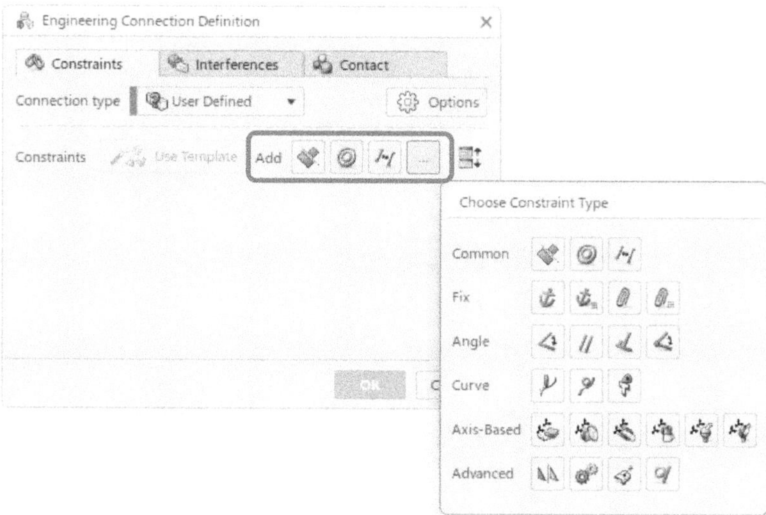

Figure 5–12

- Use the *Connection type* drop-down list in the *Engineering Connection Definition* dialog box, as shown in Figure 5–13, to select the type of connection that you want created. A template window will appear with different options for the type constraint groups that can be used to create the desired engineering connection, then you will select the geometry needed for each constraint.

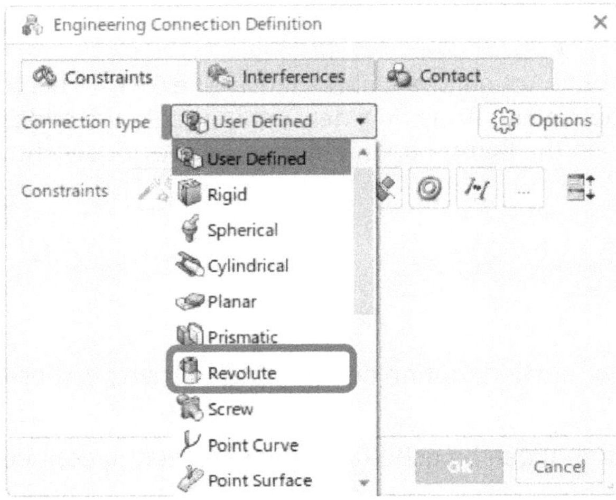

Figure 5–13

- Engineering connections can be quickly selected from a fly-out arrow under the standard **Engineering Connection** icon in the Action Bar, as shown in Figure 5–14. While this can be a faster way to pick a specific type of engineering connection, not all options will be available.

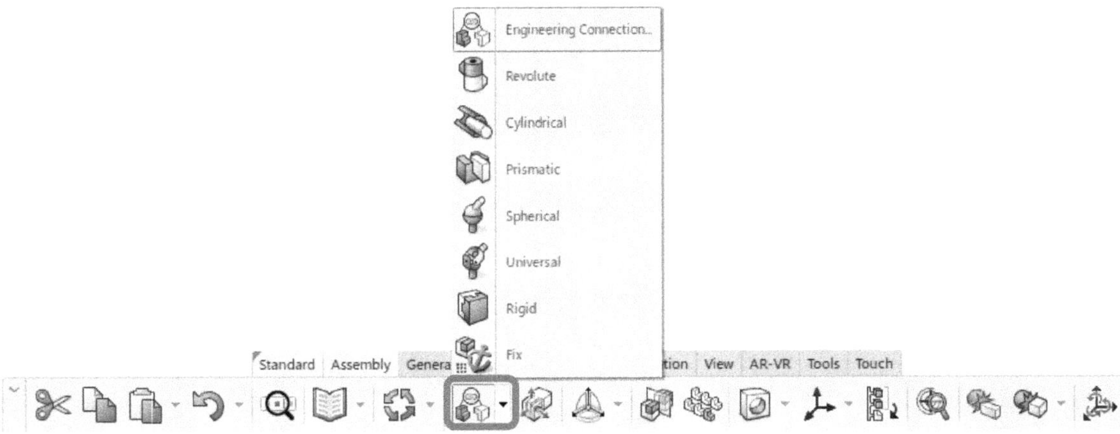

Figure 5–14

Practice 5a
Create Assemblies I

Practice Objectives

- Change product properties.
- Move components with the Robot.
- Apply assembly engineering connections.

In this practice, you will create a new ball mount assembly, as shown in Figure 5–15. You will use constraints to assemble the four components of the assembly. The ball mount assembly that you create is a subassembly of a larger assembly.

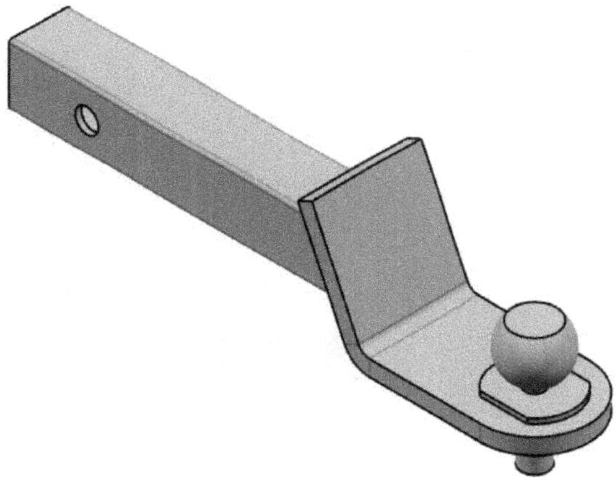

Figure 5–15

Task 1: Import components.

1. Import **Creating_Assemblies_I.3dxml**. A folder is imported containing the models needed for this practice. Expand the folders until the geometry is displayed, as shown in Figure 5–16.

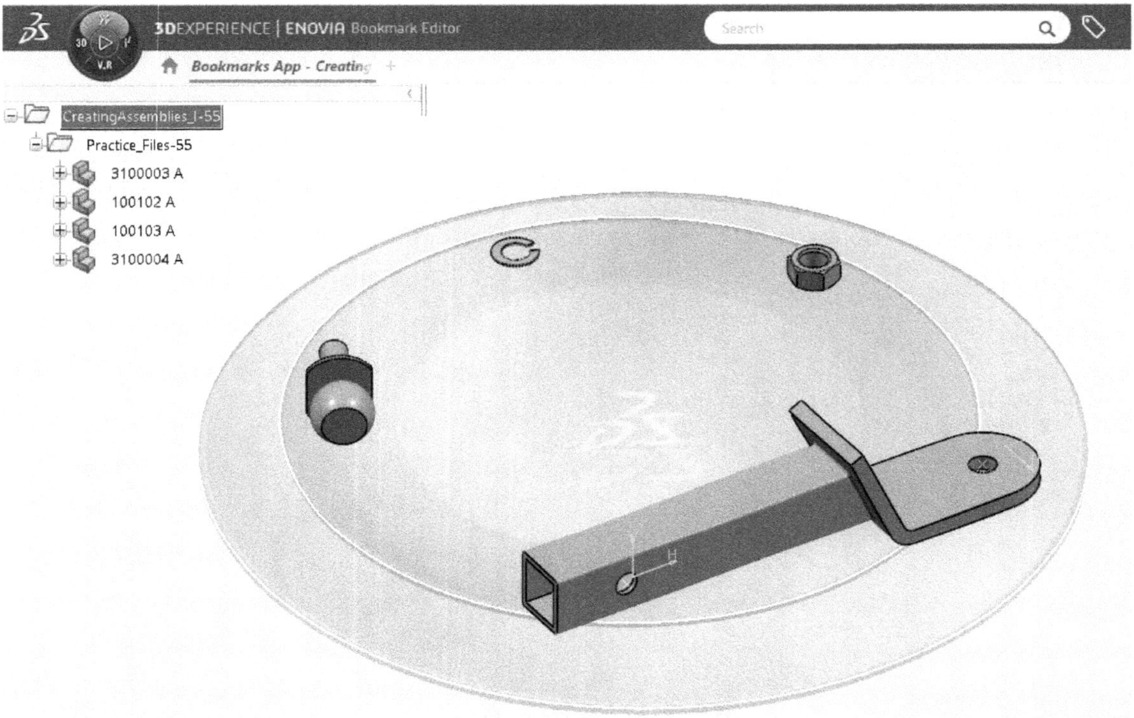

Figure 5–16

Task 2: Create a new product file.

1. In the Top Bar, select (Add/Create)>**Physical Product**.
2. In the *Physical Product* dialog box, type ***Your_Initials*_Ball Mount** in the *Title* field.
3. In the *Description* field, type **Ball Mount for Hitch**.
4. Click **OK**.

Task 3: Assemble the first component and fix it.

1. Ensure that you are in the **Assembly Design** app.You can check this by looking at the top of the screen next to the Compass. The app should read **3DEXPERIENCE | CATIA Assembly Design**. If not, switch to **Assembly Design** using the Compass.
2. Right-click on the top-level assembly (**Ball_Mount**) in the specification tree and select **Insert>Existing Product**, as shown in Figure 5–17.

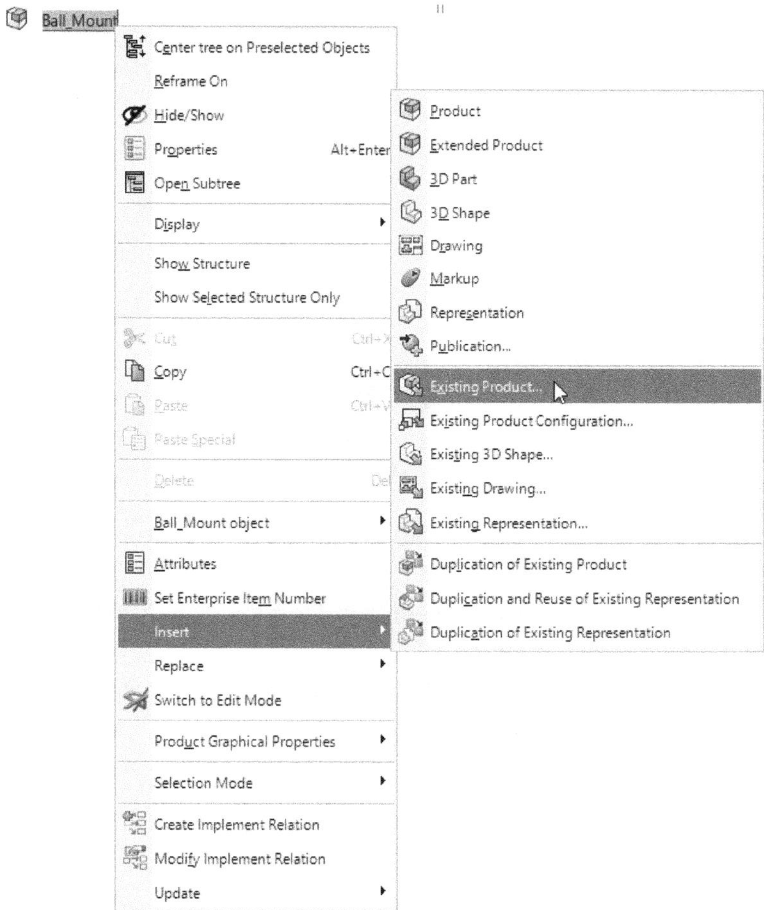

Figure 5–17

3. Select the *Bookmarks app - CreatingAssemblies_I* tab and select **3100003** (Mount) in the specification tree.
4. The system returns you to the *Ball Mount* assembly tab. Click on the screen to temporarily place the component. The component needs to be fixed.
5. Select the component on screen or in the specification tree and select  (Fix in Space) from the context toolbar.

6. This component is now fixed. Note the *Engineering Connections* section in the specification tree, as shown in Figure 5–18.

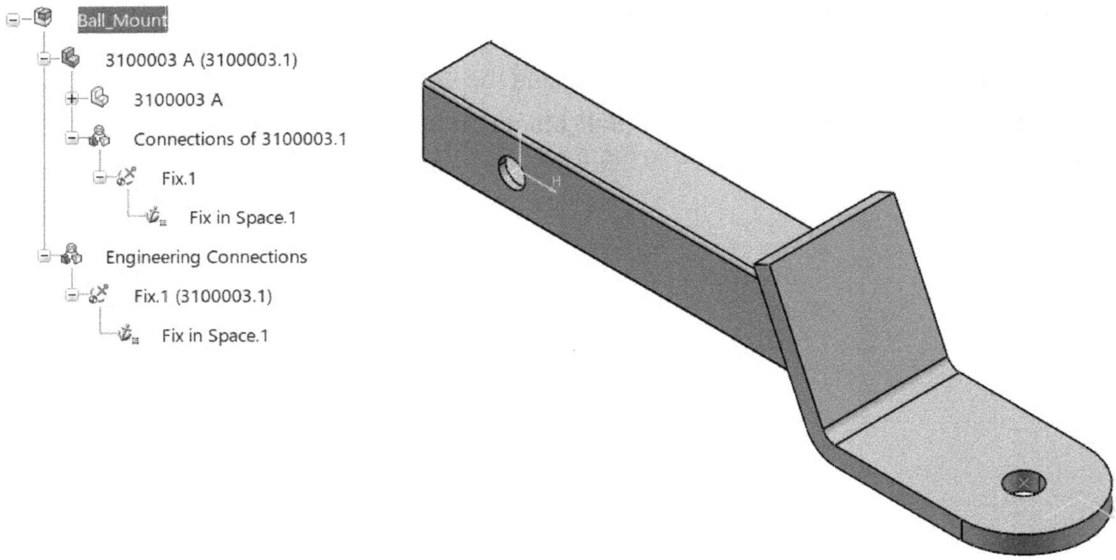

Figure 5–18

Task 4: Add the second component in a free position.

1. Bring another component into the assembly. Select **Ball_Mount** in the specification tree, right-click, and select **Insert>Existing Product**.
2. Select the *Bookmarks app - CreatingAssemblies_I* tab and select **3100004** (Ball) in the specification tree.

Note that the **3100004** (Ball) part is brought into the assembly and placed in the default position, so it intersects the **3100003** (Mount) component.

3. To view the **3100004** (Ball) geometry, the part needs to be moved away from the fixed assembly. Drag the **U** axis of the Robot on the **3100004** (Ball) part, as shown in Figure 5–19.

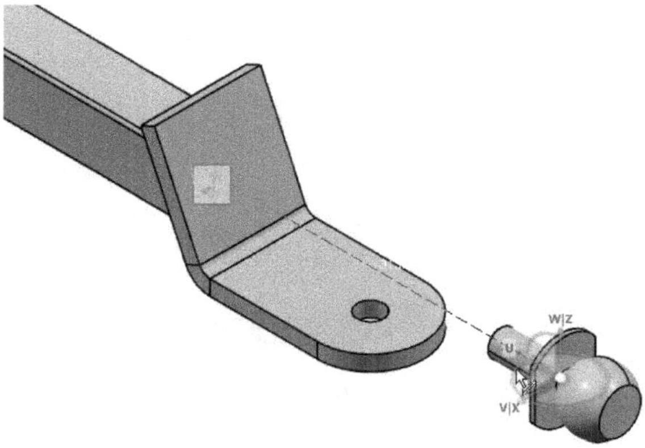

Figure 5–19

Task 5: Constrain the 3100004 (Ball) part.

1. Click on the screen to temporarily place the component.

2. In the *Assembly* section of the Action Bar, click (Engineering Connection). The *Engineering Connection Definition* dialog box will open.

3. In the *Add* area, click (Coincidence) to add it, as shown in Figure 5–20.

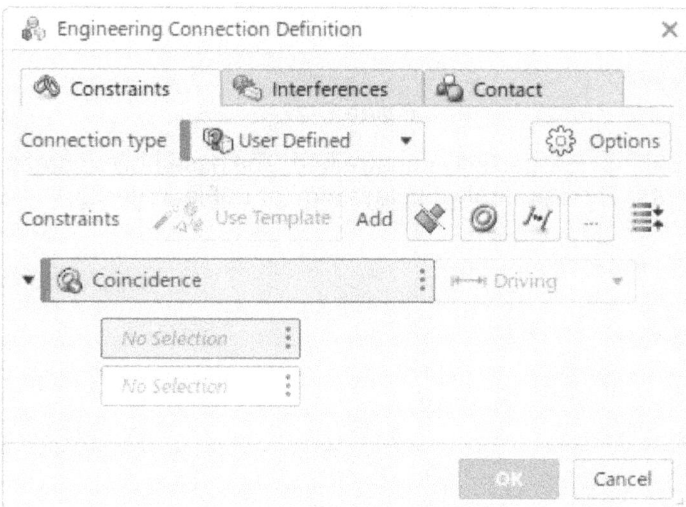

Figure 5–20

4. Select the axis of the **3100004** (Ball) stem by selecting the cylindrical surface, as shown in Figure 5–21. You might need to zoom in to the part.

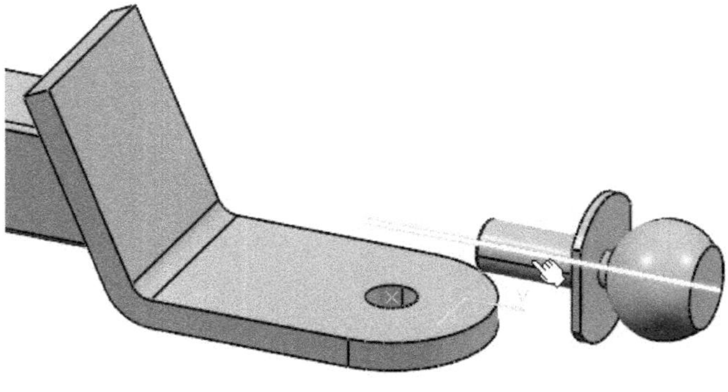

Figure 5–21

5. Select the axis on the **3100003** (Mount) part by selecting the inner cylindrical surface of the hole, as shown in Figure 5–22.

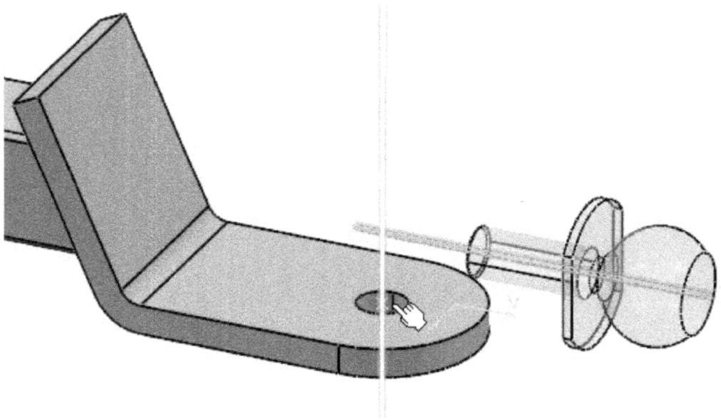

Figure 5–22

6. Part **3100004** (Ball) is now partially constrained. The assembly updates the position of all of the components. The assembly displays similar to Figure 5–23.

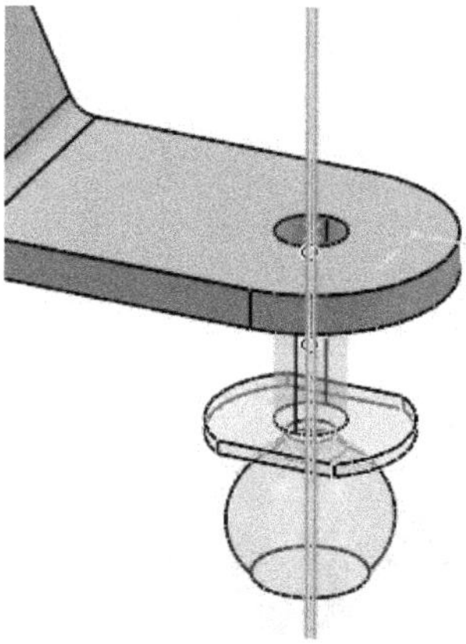

Figure 5–23

There is a good chance that the **3100004** (Ball) part is upside down, as shown above in Figure 5–23.

7. If the **3100004** (Ball) part is upside down, for the *Coincidence* constraint, select (Opposite) to set the *Alignment*. This will flip the **3100004** (Ball) part 180 degrees.

8. In the *Engineering Connection Definition* dialog box, click (Contact) to add it, as shown in Figure 5–24.

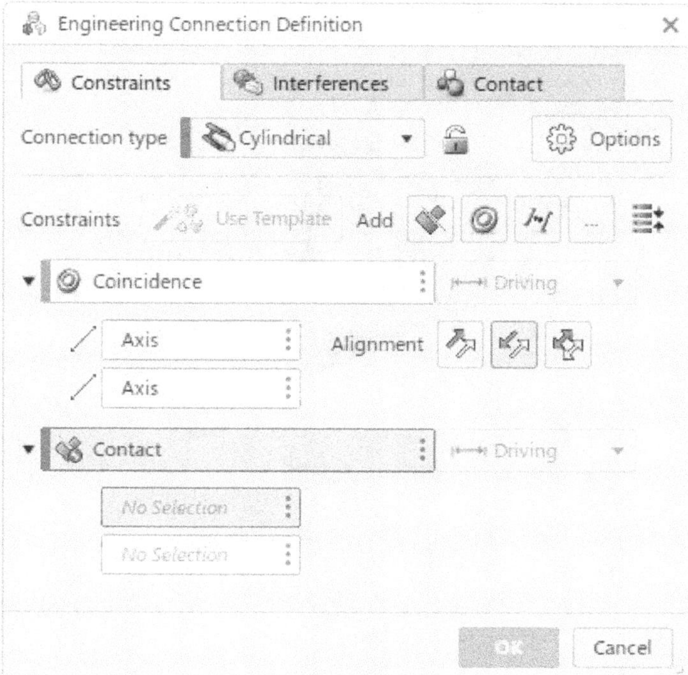

Figure 5–24

9. Select the bottom face of the **3100004** (Ball) part, as shown in Figure 5–25.

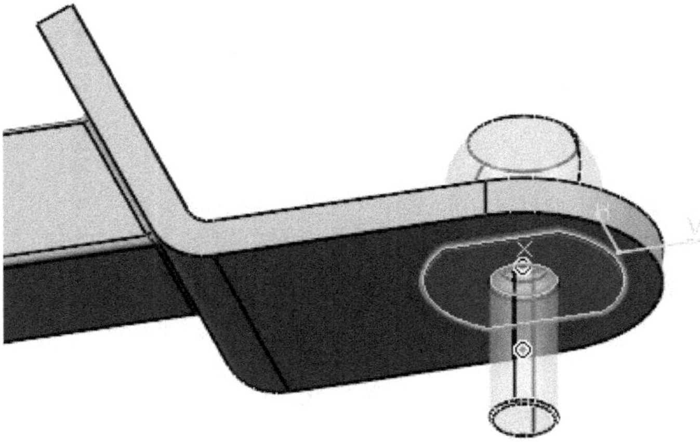

Figure 5–25

10. Select the top face of the **3100003** (Base) part, as shown in Figure 5–26.

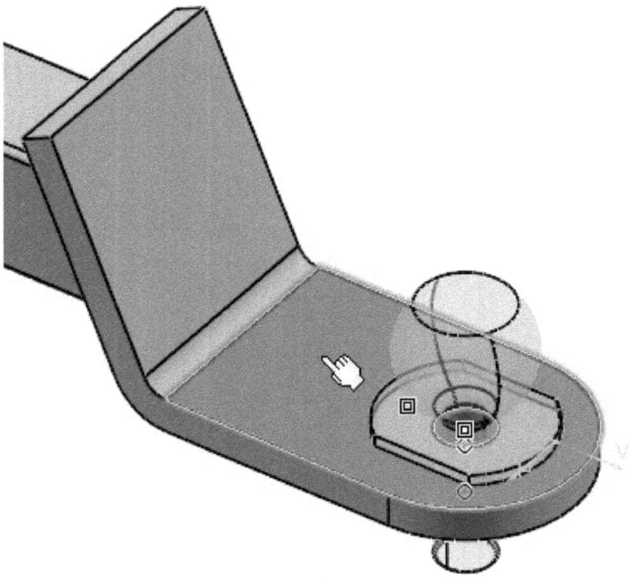

Figure 5–26

The **3100004** (Ball) part still has one degree of freedom; it is free to rotate to any angle with respect to the axis of the hole it is placed in. The next step will control the remaining degree of freedom.

11. In the *Add* area of the *Engineering Connection Definition* dialog box, click (Show All Constants). The *Choose Constraint Type* window appears.

12. Select (Parallelism). The *Engineering Connection Definition* dialog box updates, as shown in Figure 5–27.

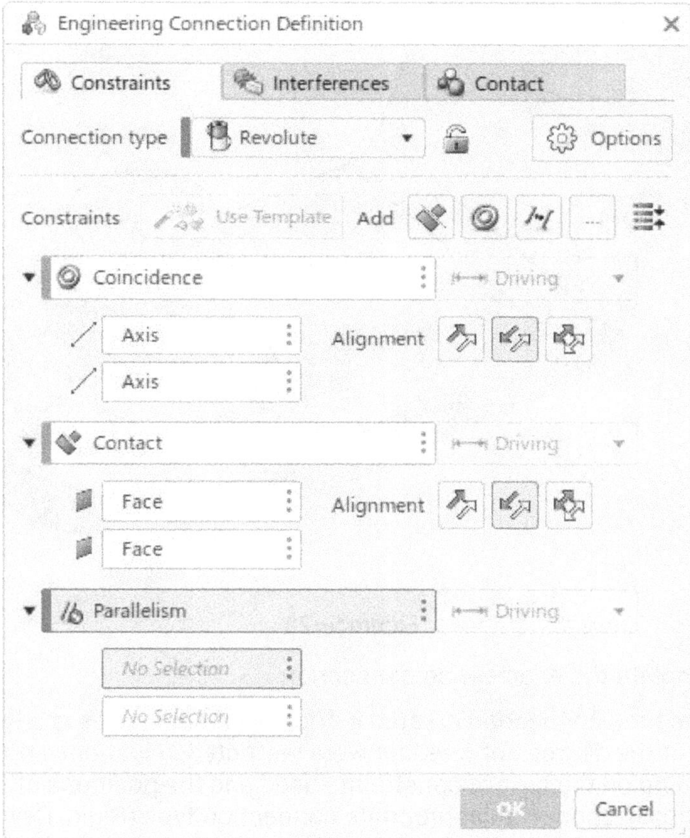

Figure 5–27

13. Select the two faces shown in Figure 5–28 to be used as references for the *Parallelism* constraint.

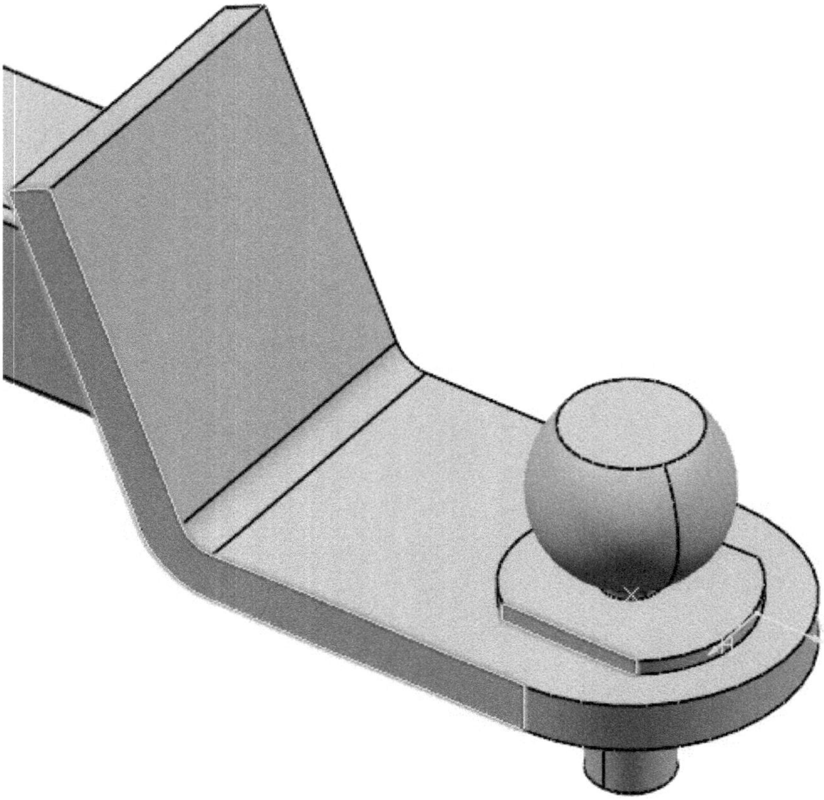

Figure 5–28

14. Click **OK** to complete the engineering connection.

Note that the engineering connection created in the specification tree is a **Rigid Constraint**. This is because all of the degrees of freedom were restricted in just one engineering connection. Depending on the type of constraints used and the positions of those constraints, CATIA will automatically choose an appropriate connection type (Rigid, Revolute, Cylindrical, etc.). CATIA also allows the user to reverse this process and start with choosing a *Connection type*, and it will auto populate the constraints needed to build that engineering connection. Either method is acceptable.

15. A dialog box reporting *Undefined Interference Specifications* will open, as shown in Figure 5–29. Click **No** to omit creation of the interference specification.

    ***Note:** To avoid seeing this warning, disable **Check interferences at validation** under **Me>Preferences>App Preferences>3D Modeling>Mechanical Systems>Assembly Design>Engineering Connections>Interferences**.*

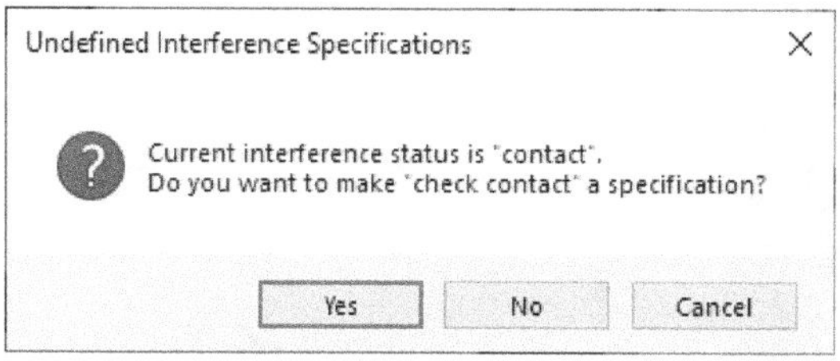

Figure 5–29

16. The components are now fully constrained and display as shown in Figure 5–30.

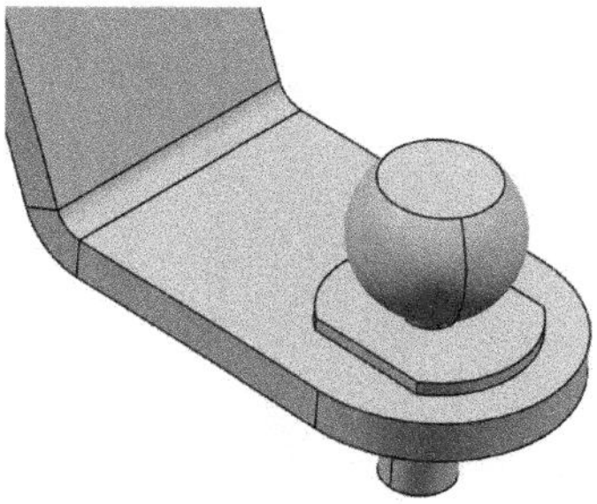

Figure 5–30

Task 6: Assemble the washer.

1. Right-click on **Ball_Mount** and select **Insert>Existing Product**.
2. Select the *Bookmarks App - CreatingAssemblies_I* tab and select **100103** (Washer) in the specification tree.
3. The system switches back to the *Ball Mount* tab.

4. Use the Robot axes to move the **100103** (Washer) part to a position clear of the product (as shown in Figure 5–31), then left-click on the screen to temporarily locate the washer.

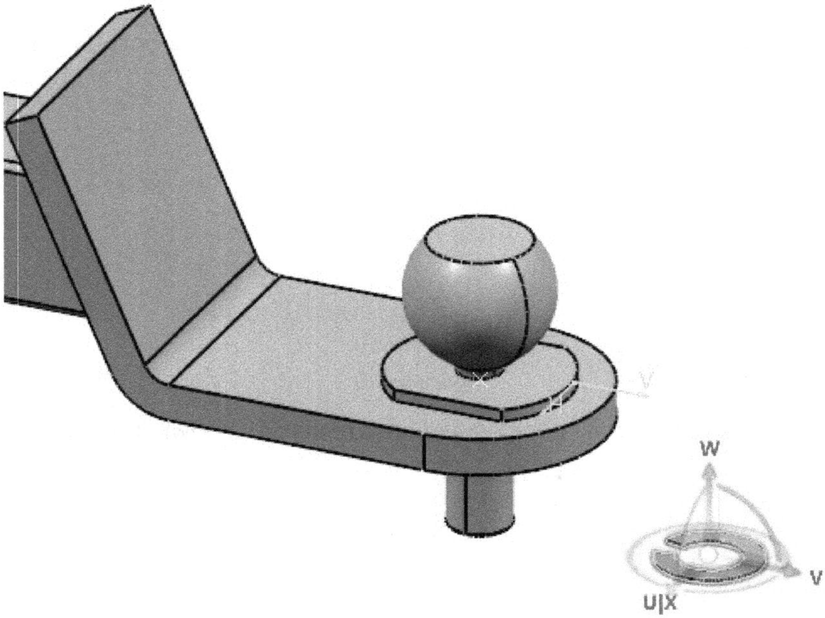

Figure 5–31

5. In the *Assembly* section of the Action Bar, click (Engineering Connection).
6. In the *Add* area of the *Engineering Connection Definition* dialog box, click (Coincidence) to add it, as shown in Figure 5–32.

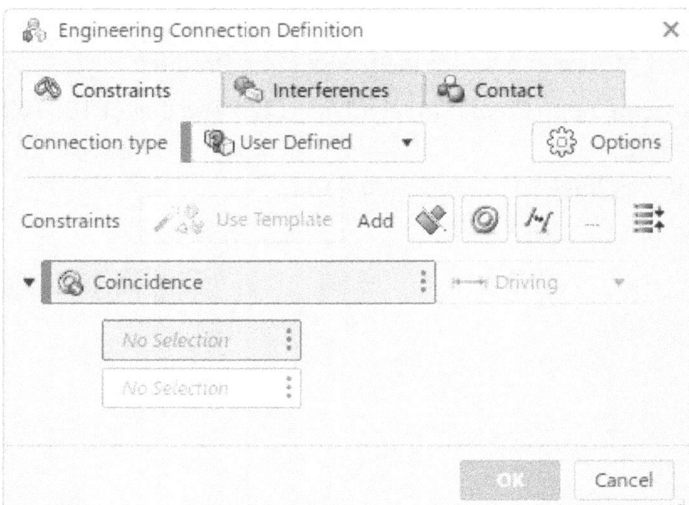

Figure 5–32

7. Select the inside curved surface of the **100103** (Washer) part, as shown in Figure 5–33.

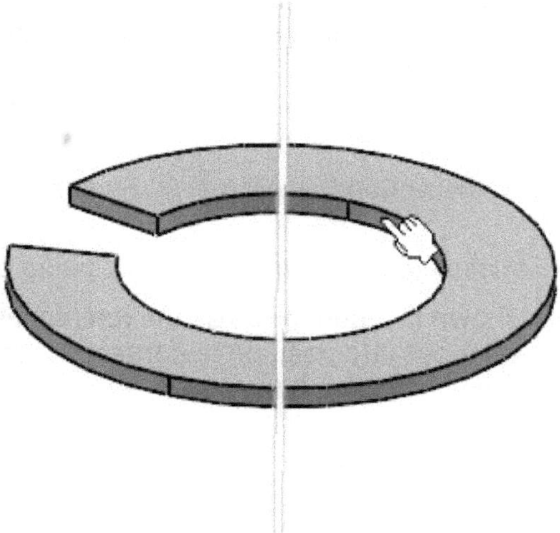

Figure 5–33

8. Select the curved surface of the shaft of the **3100004** (Ball) part, as shown in Figure 5–34. The parts will align so the hole is centered on the shaft.

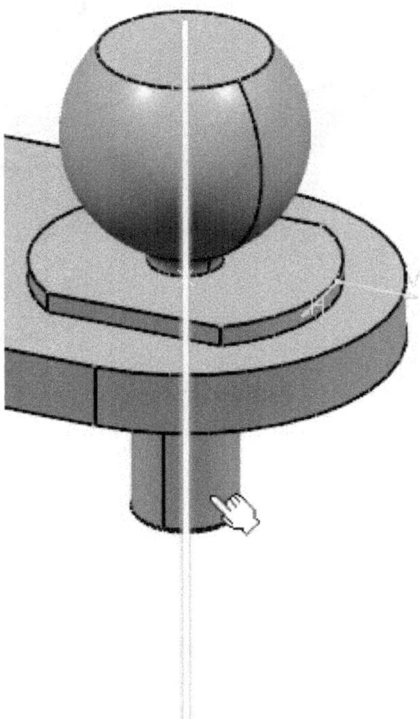

Figure 5–34

9. Click **OK** to complete the engineering connection.

10. In the *Undefined Interference Specifications* dialog box, click **No**.

An engineering connection can only be created between two components at a time. That means all constraints in the engineering connection can only reference a total of two parts. Any remaining degrees of freedom will have to be controlled by separate engineering connections. In this example, that means the two remaining DOF that will pair the **100103** (Washer) with the **3100003** (Mount) component.

11. In the *Assembly* section of the Action Bar, click (Engineering Connection).
12. In the *Add* area of the *Engineering Connection Definition* dialog box, click (Contact).
13. Select the two surfaces shown in Figure 5–35 as the references for the contact constraint. The washer will move into position to contact the mount part. Leave the *Engineering Connection Definition* dialog box open.

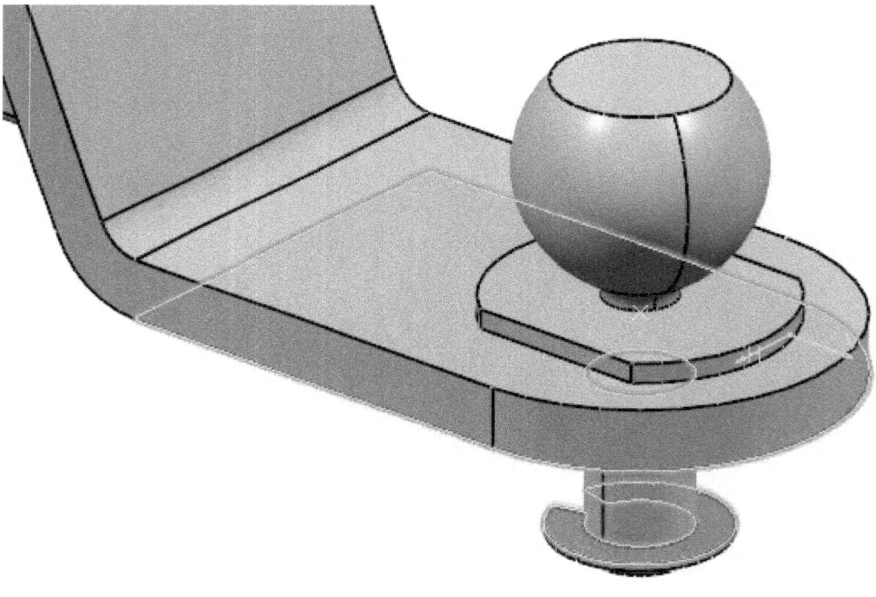

Figure 5–35

14. In the *Add* area of the *Engineering Connection Definition* dialog box, click (Show All Constants). The *Choose Constraint Type* window appears.

15. Select (Parallelism). The *Engineering Connection Definition* dialog box updates, as shown in Figure 5–36.

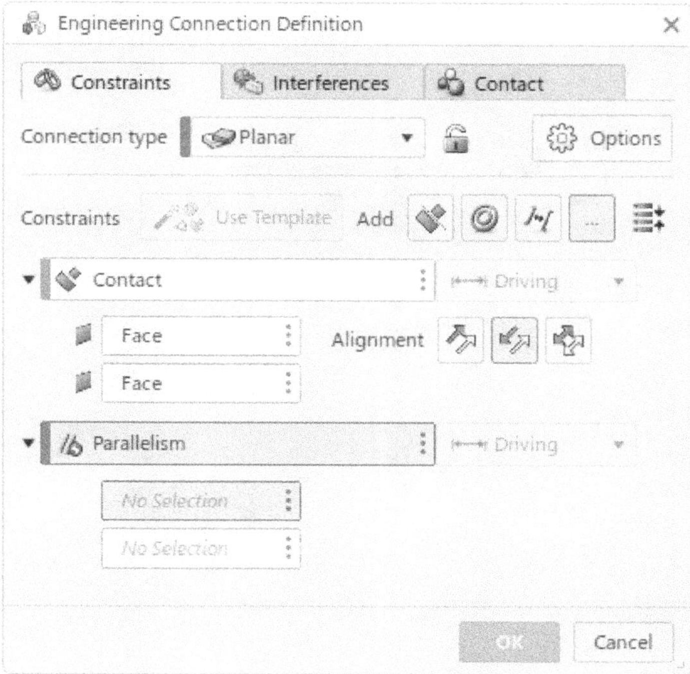

Figure 5–36

16. Select the **YZ Plane(s)** in both the **100103** (Washer) and **3100003** (Mount) parts. The fastest way to do this is to select the planes from the specification tree, as shown in Figure 5–37.

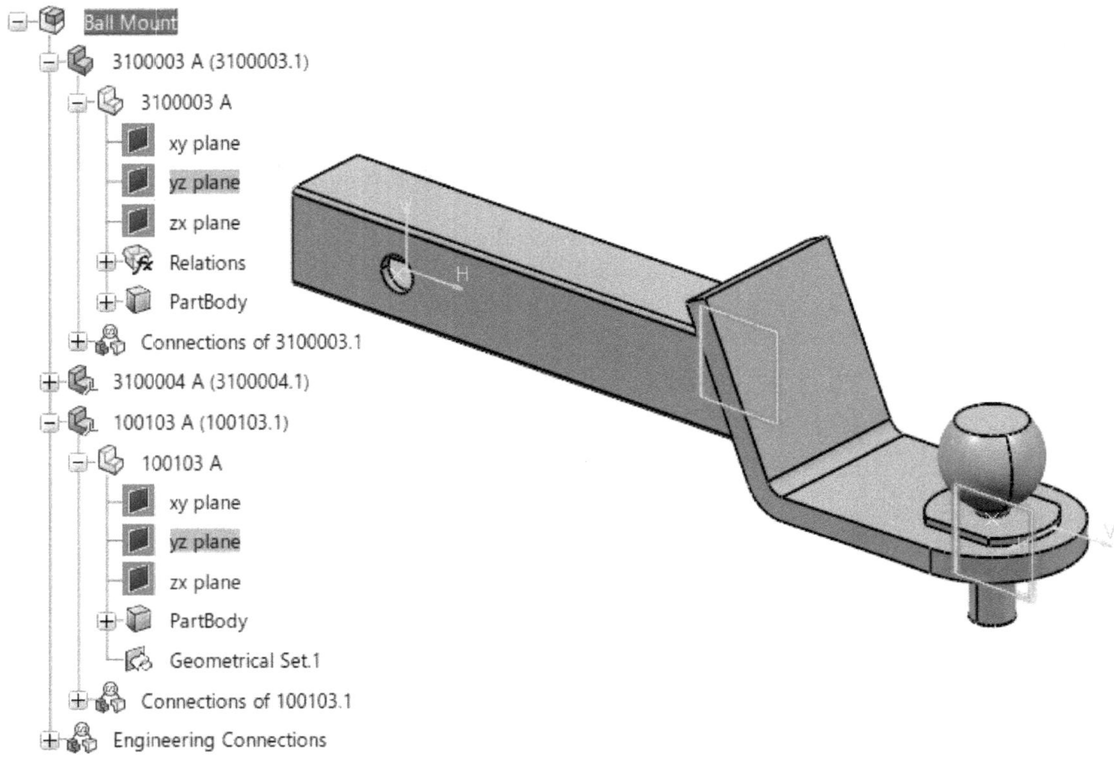

Figure 5–37

17. Click **OK** to complete the engineering connection.
18. In the *Undefined Interference Specifications* dialog box, click **No**.
19. To update the position of the components, click (Update).

Task 7: Add the nut component.

1. Right-click on **Ball_Mount** and select **Insert>Existing Product**.
2. Select the *Bookmarks app - CreatingAssemblies_I* tab and select **100102** (Nut) in the specification tree.
3. The system switches back to the *Ball Mount* tab.

4. Use the Robot to drag the nut away from the rest of the assembly, then click to place the new component in open space, as shown in Figure 5–38.

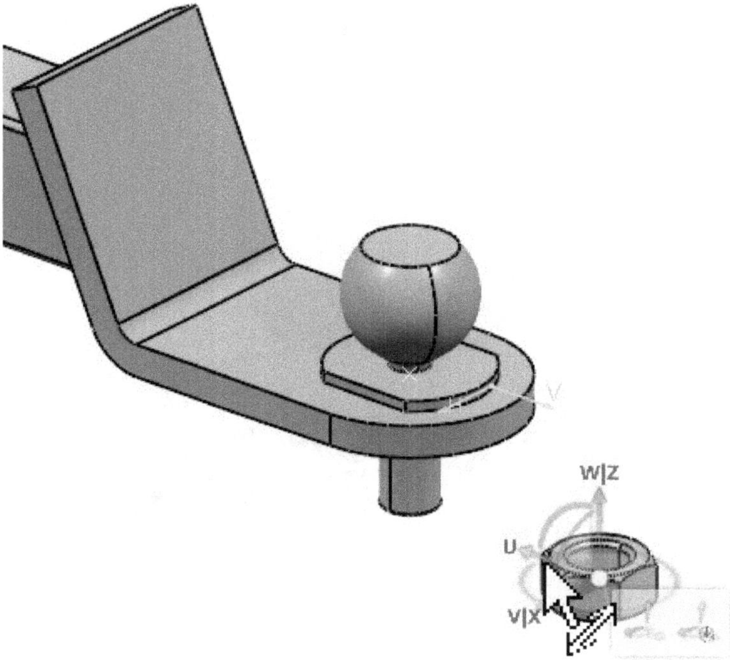

Figure 5–38

5. Click  (Engineering Connection).

6. In the *Engineering Connection Definition* dialog box, create a coincidence constraint to align the axis of the hole with the axis of the shaft, as shown in Figure 5–39.

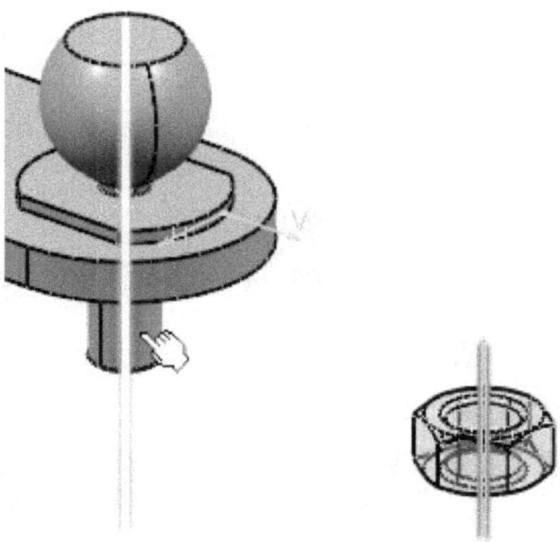

Figure 5–39

7. Click **OK** to finalize the engineering connection.

8. In the *Undefined Interference Specifications* dialog box, click **No**.
9. Click (Engineering Connection) and create a contact constraint between the two surfaces shown in Figure 5–40. Leave the *Engineering Connection Definition* dialog box open.

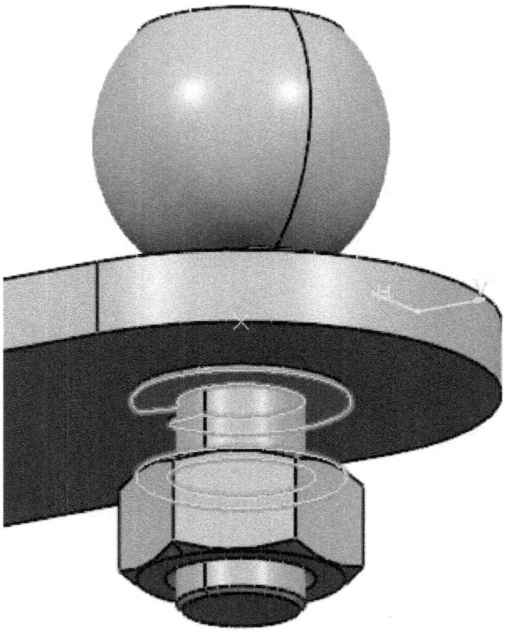

Figure 5–40

10. The nut still has a degree of freedom to rotate about the coincident axis. Click (Show All Constants) and select (Fix Together). This will add a *Fix Together* constraint to the engineering connection.
11. Select both the **100103** (Washer) and **100102** (Nut) parts to rigidly group the parts together.
12. Click **OK** to finalize the engineering connection.
13. In the *Undefined Interference Specifications* dialog box, click **No**.
14. Click (Update) to ensure all components and engineering connections are updated.
15. Save the assembly and close all tabs.

End of practice

Practice 5b
Create Assemblies II

Practice Objectives

- Apply engineering connections.
- Insert a subassembly.

In this practice, you will create the assembly shown in Figure 5–41. This assembly will consist of various parts and the subassembly that you created in a previous practice.

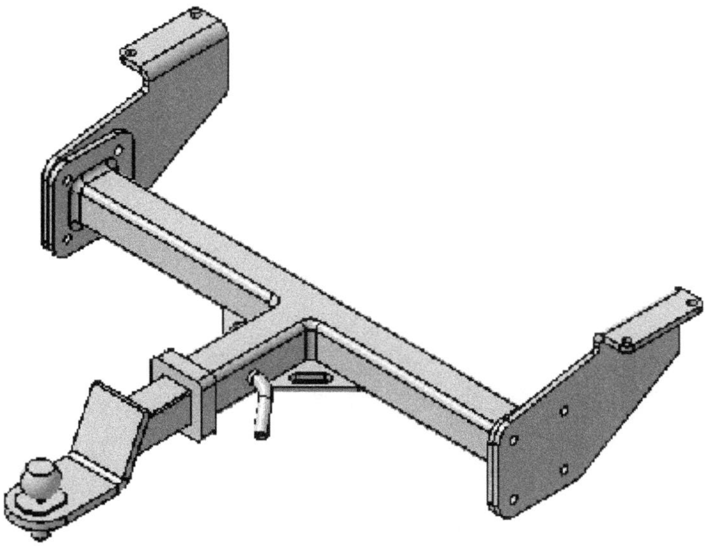

Figure 5–41

Task 1: Create a new product file.

1. Import **Creating_Assemblies_II.3dxml**.
2. In the Top Bar, select  (Add/Create)>**Physical Product**.
3. In the *Physical Product* dialog box, type ***Your_Initials*_Hitch** in the *Title* field.
4. In the *Description* field, type **Main Hitch Assembly**.
5. Click **OK**.

Task 2: Assemble the first component and fix it.

1. Right-click on the top-level assembly (Hitch) in the specification tree and select **Insert>Existing Product**.
2. Select the *Bookmarks app - Creating_Assemblies_II* tab and select **3100000** (T-Support) in the specification tree. The window will automatically switch back to the Hitch Assembly window.
3. Select **3100000** (T-Support) in the Hitch specification tree and click (Fix in Space) from the context toolbar. This component is now fixed.

Note that the *Engineering Connections* section now exists in the specification tree.

Task 3: Assemble the braces.

1. Insert the **3100001** (Left-Brace) component into **Hitch** using the same method as in Task 2, Steps 1 and 2.
2. Use the Robot to drag and rotate the model into the approximate orientation shown in Figure 5–42. Use the arrows to drag translation and the arcs to drag rotation.

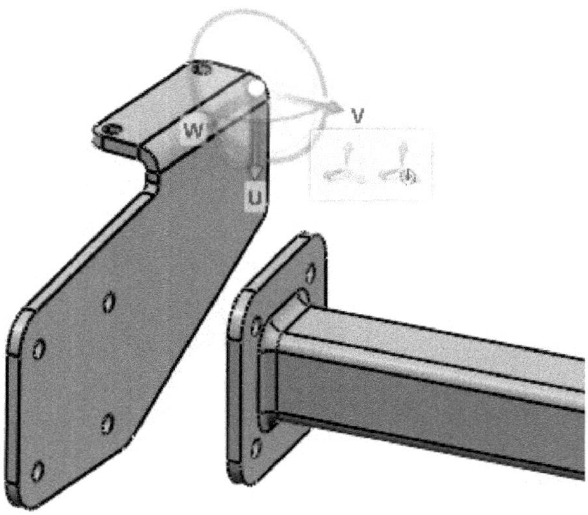

Figure 5–42

3. Click on the screen to temporarily place the component.
4. Create an engineering connection and set the *Connection type* to **Revolute**. The *Revolute Templates* window appears.

5. Select the *Constrain* options shown in Figure 5–43. This will populate the engineering connection with three empty constraints.

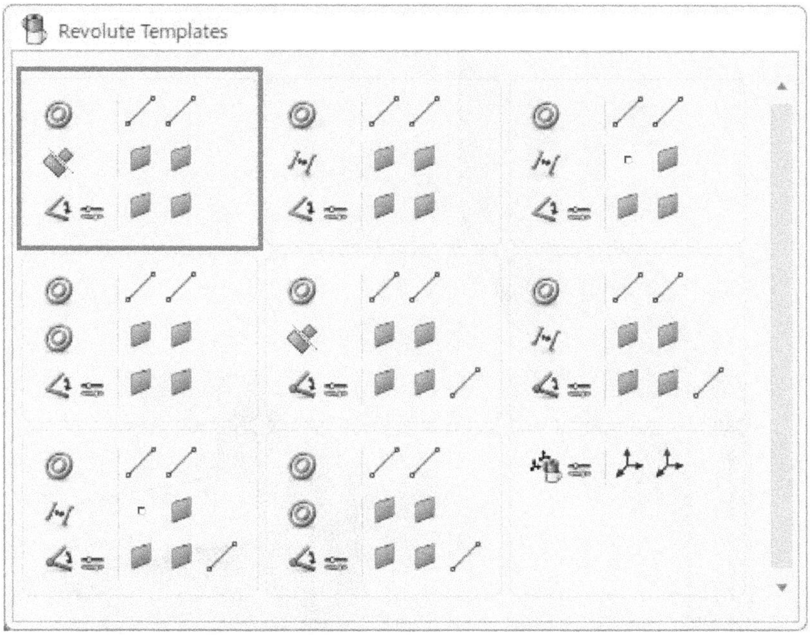

Figure 5–43

In the previous exercise, engineering connections were defined by creating constraints individually, and then by interpreting the type of constraints used, the engineering connection changed to the correct connection type. In this task, you are doing the opposite by first selecting the *Connection type*. You will then be given options for what constraints can be used to create the chosen connection type. Once the template is chosen, three empty constraints are created and it is up to the user to define the supports for each constraint.

6. To create the coincident constraint, select the upper-left hole in the **3100001** (LeftBrace) part and the upper-left hole in the **3100000** (T-Support) part, as shown in Figure 5–44.

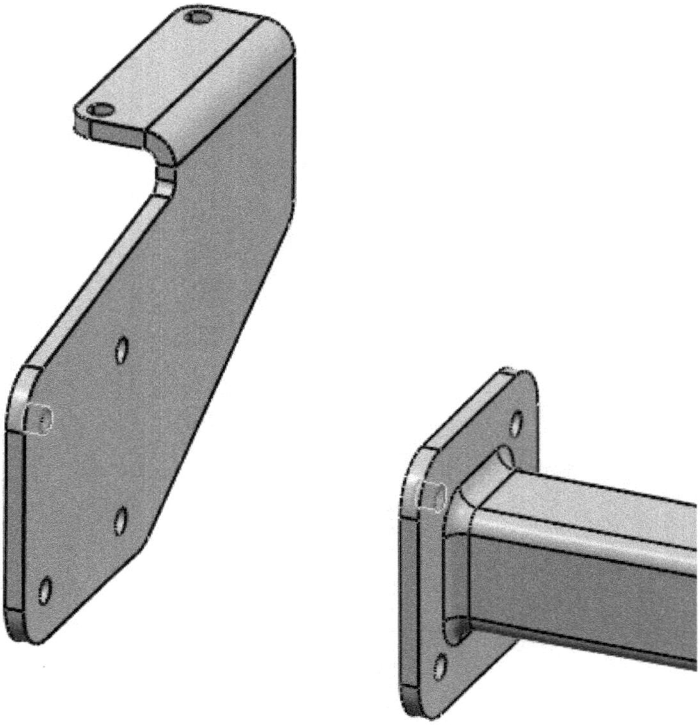

Figure 5–44

7. To create the contact constraint, select the right surface on the **3100001** (LeftBrace) part and the left surface on the **3100000** (T-Support) part, as shown in Figure 5–45.

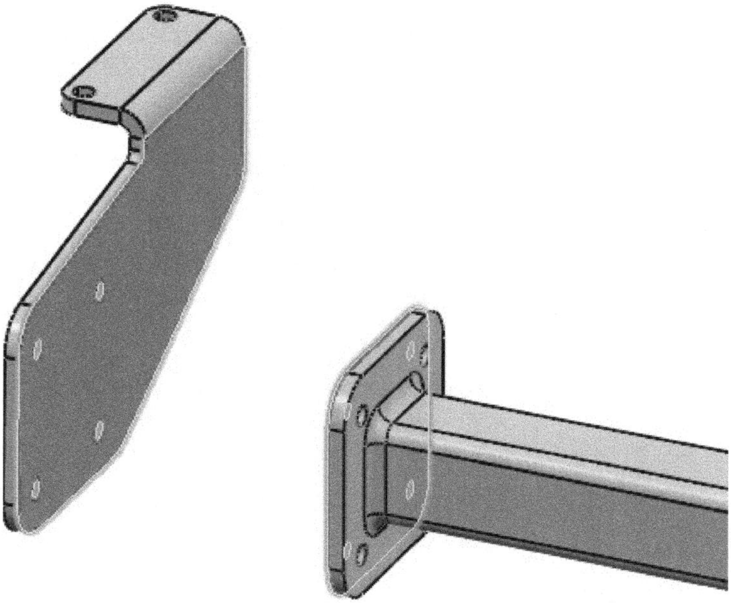

Figure 5–45

8. To create the angle constraint, select the front surface of the **3100001** (LeftBrace) part and the front surface on the **3100000** (T-Support) part, as shown in Figure 5–46.

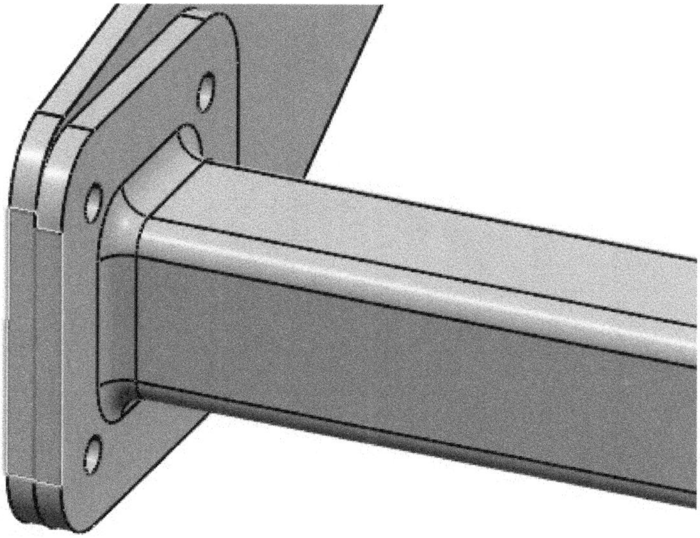

Figure 5–46

The *Angle* value that is created will be based off the position of the part when it was moved using the Robot earlier. While the supports are correct, you will now change the angle constraint to a parallel constraint because it better fits the design intent.

9. Right-click on the field that says **Angle** and select **Change type>Angle>Parallelism**. This will use the same inputs but swap the *Angle* constraint to a *Parallelism* constraint.
10. Click **OK** to finalize the engineering connection.
11. An *Invalid Engineering Connection configuration* dialog box appears because the *Revolute* connection type that was selected earlier no longer works with the parallel constraint. Select **Edit Connection** to make changes to the previous engineering connection.
12. In the *Connection type* field, change **Revolute** to **Rigid**. Note that the red indicator turns green. This is because the system sees this selection as acceptable.
13. Click **OK** to finalize the engineering connection.
14. In the *Undefined Interference Specifications* dialog box, click **No**.
15. Click  (Update) to ensure the components and engineering connections are updated.
16. Assemble **3100002** (Right-Brace) using the steps described in this task. The assembly should display as shown in Figure 5–47.

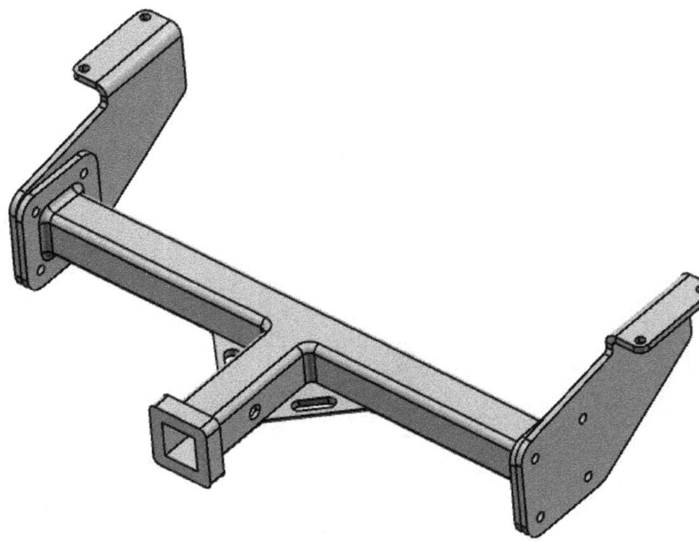

Figure 5–47

Task 4: Assemble the Ball_Mount subassembly.

1. Insert the **65100010** (Ball Mount) assembly into **Hitch** by right-clicking on **Hitch** and selecting **Insert>Existing Product**.
2. Select the *Bookmarks app - Creating_Assemblies_II* tab and select **65100010** (Ball Mount).

3. Drag the **65100010** (Ball Mount) assembly away from the model and use the Robot to manipulate the sub-assembly into a similar position as the one shown in Figure 5–48. Click to drop it into the product.

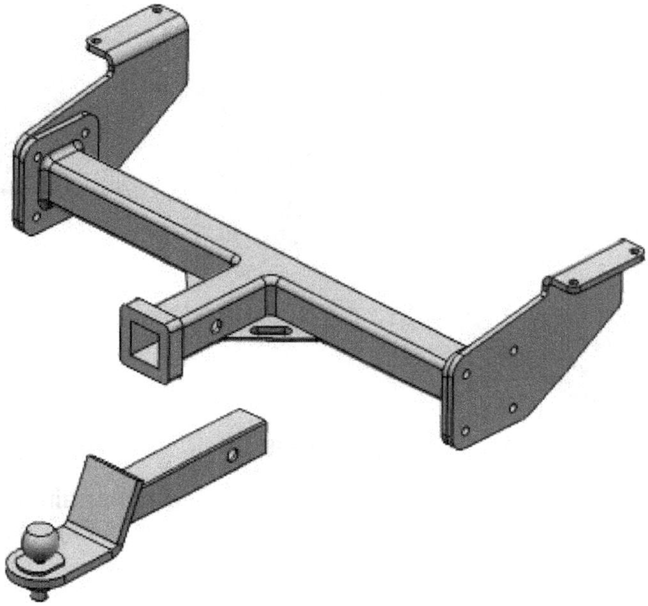

Figure 5–48

4. Create an engineering connection and insert a coincidence constraint between the axes, as shown in Figure 5–49. The assembly updates automatically.

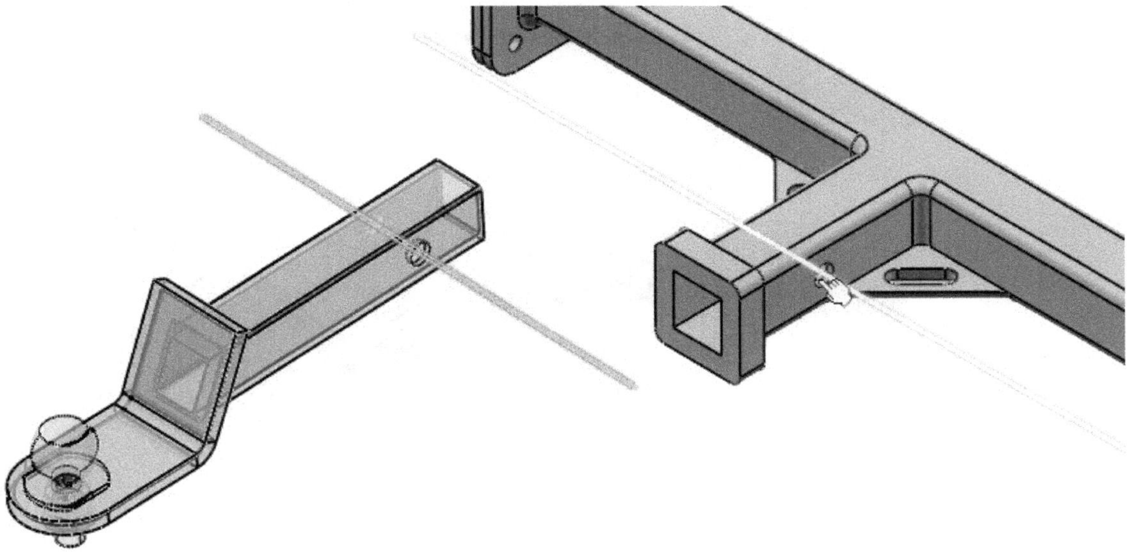

Figure 5–49

5. Within the same engineering connection, insert an offset constraint between **65100010** (Ball Mount) and **3100000** (T-Support), as shown in Figure 5–50. Set the *offset value* to **[0.4]**.

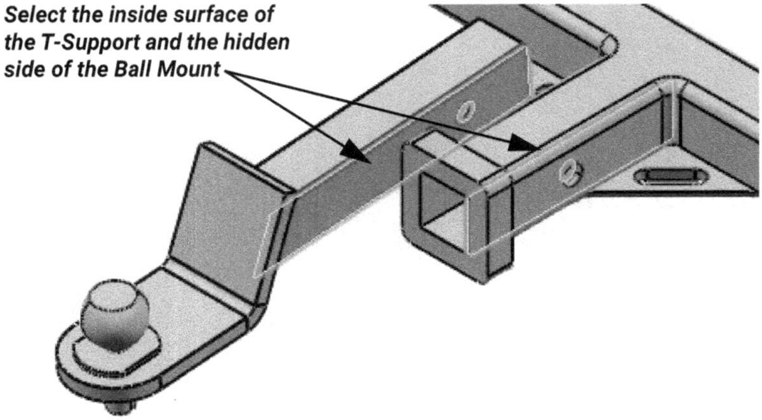

Figure 5–50

6. Within the same engineering connection, insert a parallel constraint between **65100010** (Ball Mount) and **3100000** (T-Support), as shown in Figure 5–51.

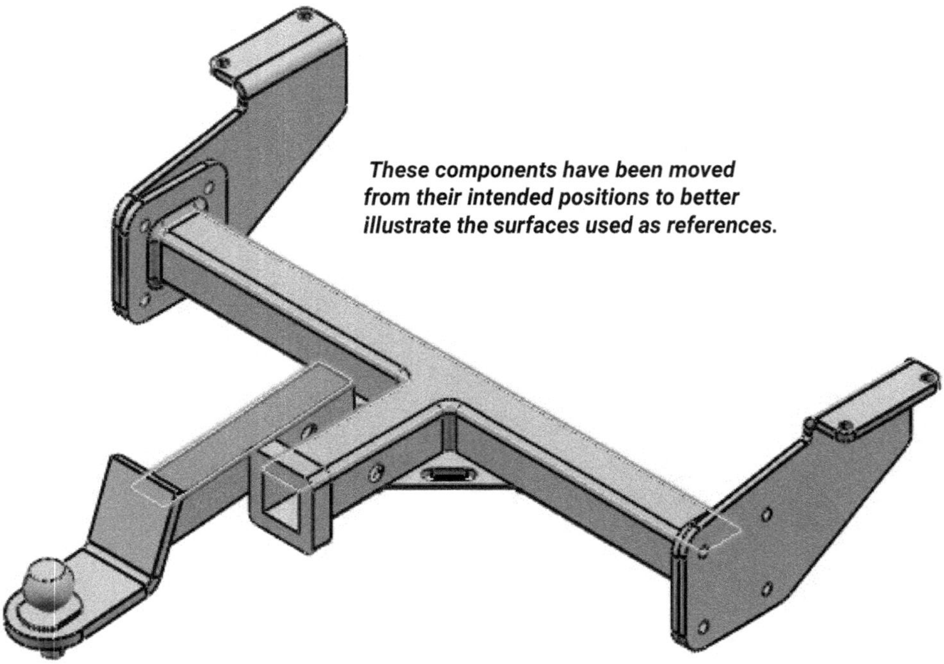

Figure 5–51

7. Click **OK** to finalize the engineering connection and close the dialog box.

8. In the *Undefined Interference Specifications* dialog box, click **No**.

9. Click  (Update) to ensure the components and engineering connections are updated. The model displays as shown in Figure 5–52.

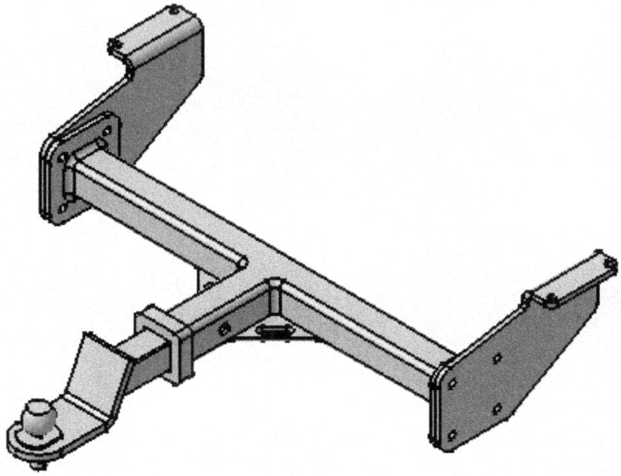

Figure 5–52

Task 5: Assemble the pin.

1. Insert **3100005** (Pin) into **Hitch** by right-clicking on **Hitch** and selecting **Insert>Existing Product**.

2. Drag the pin away from the model and use the Robot to manipulate the component into a similar position as the one shown in Figure 5–53. Click to drop it into the product.

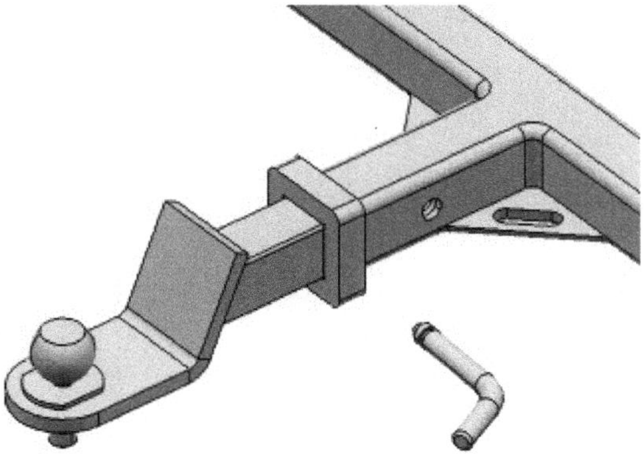

Figure 5–53

3. Create an engineering connection and insert a coincidence constraint between the hole of **3100000** (T-Support) and the axis of **3100005** (Pin), as shown in Figure 5–54.

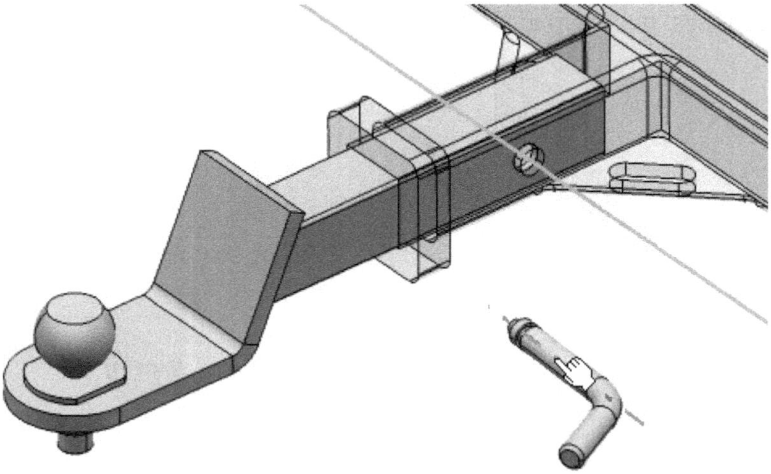

Figure 5–54

4. In the active *Engineering Connection Definition* dialog box, insert an offset constraint and select the face of the **3100005** (Pin) part shown in Figure 5–55.

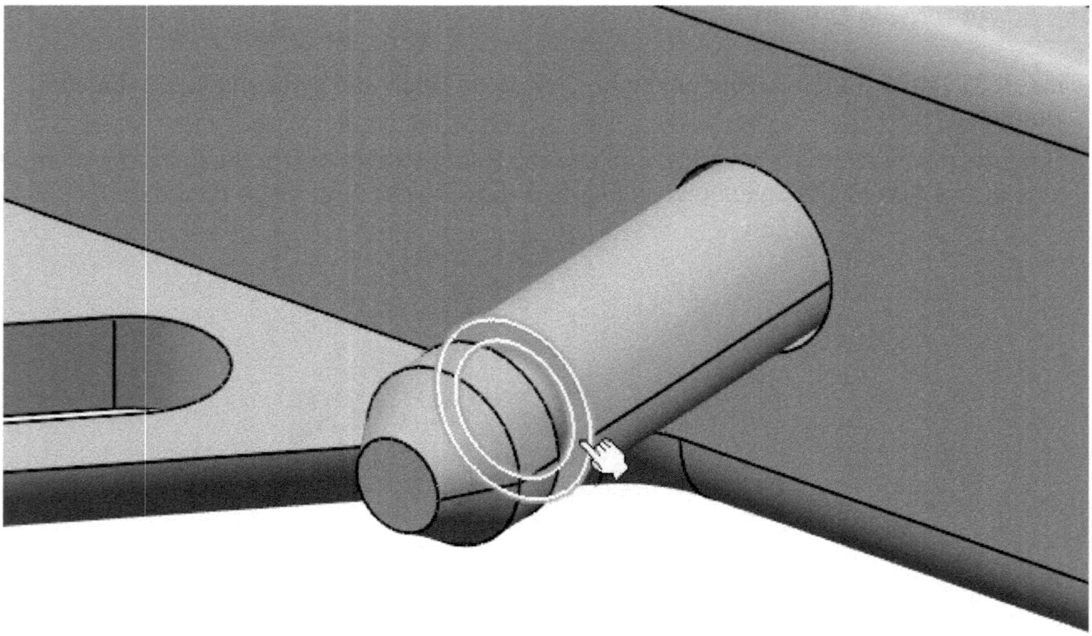

Figure 5–55

5. Select the face of the **3100000** (T-Support) part shown in Figure 5–56. Set the *offset distance* to **[0]**.

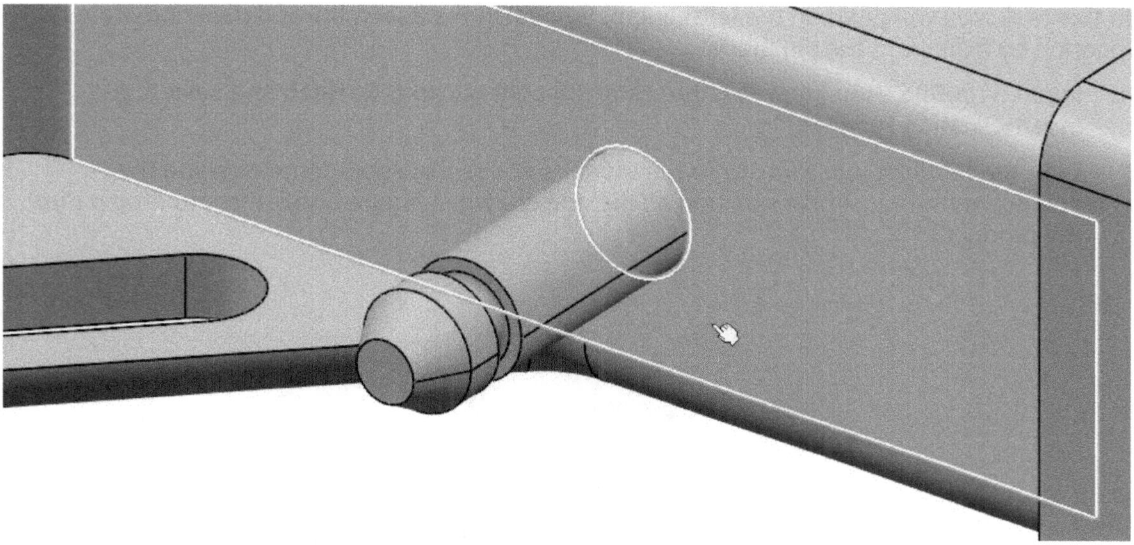

Figure 5–56

6. Update the assembly. The model displays as shown in Figure 5–57.

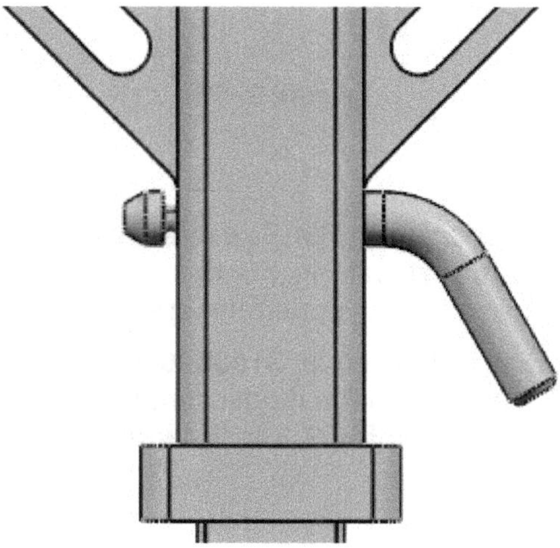

Figure 5–57

Task 6: Assemble the retaining pin.

In this task, you will position the retaining pin model in the assembly and then constrain its location by fixing it to the pin model.

1. Insert **3100006** (Retaining Pin) into **Hitch** by right-clicking on **Hitch** and selecting **Insert>Existing Product**.
2. Drag the retaining pin away from the model and use the Robot to manipulate the component into a similar position as the one shown in Figure 5–58. Click to drop it into the product.

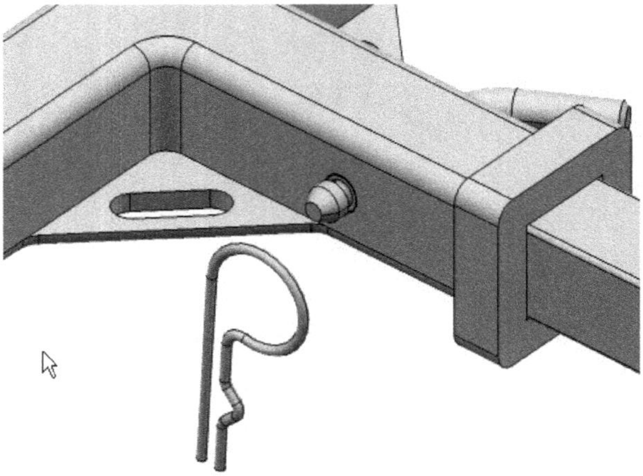

Figure 5–58

Design Considerations

Note the curved geometry of the **Retaining Pin**. Few references can be selected from the model to position it relative to the **T-Support** and **Pin**. For this reason, reference elements have been added to the model that will assist during constraint creation.

3. Show the **RefGeom** geometrical set under **3100006** (Retaining Pin) and **3100005** (Pin) in the specification tree. The **Retaining Pin** model contains two reference planes and a reference point, as shown in Figure 5–59. The **Pin** model contains a reference plane located at the center of the groove.

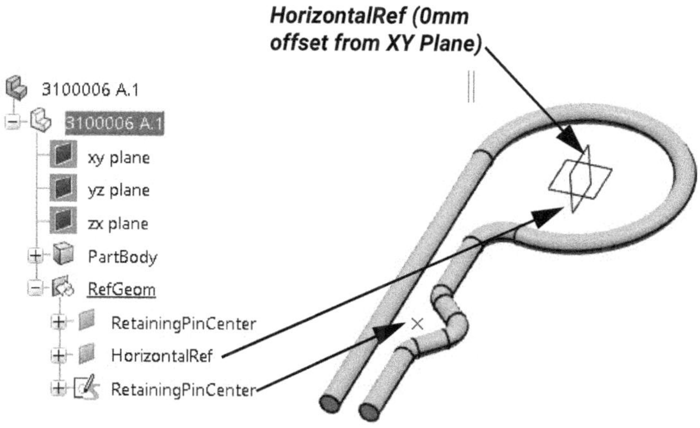

Figure 5–59

4. Using two engineering connections, insert the constraints listed in the table below using Figure 5–60 as a guide. The parallelism constraint will require its own engineering connection due to referencing the **T-Support**. Modify the alignment directions of the parallelism constraint to match the orientation of the **Retaining Pin** shown in Figure 5–60.

No.	Constraint	Reference 1	Reference 2
1	Coincident	Axis of Pin	RetainingPinCenter (sketched point) of Retaining Pin
2	Offset (0mm)	GrooveCenter (plane) of Pin	RetainingPinCenter (plane) of Retaining Pin
3	Parallelism	Face of T-Support	HorizontalRef (plane) of Retaining Pin

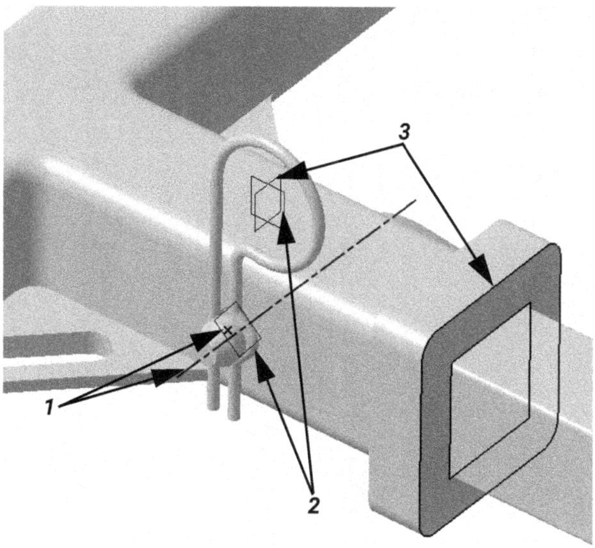

Figure 5–60

5. Update the assembly and hide **RefGeom** from **Retaining Pin**. The completed model displays as shown in Figure 5–61.

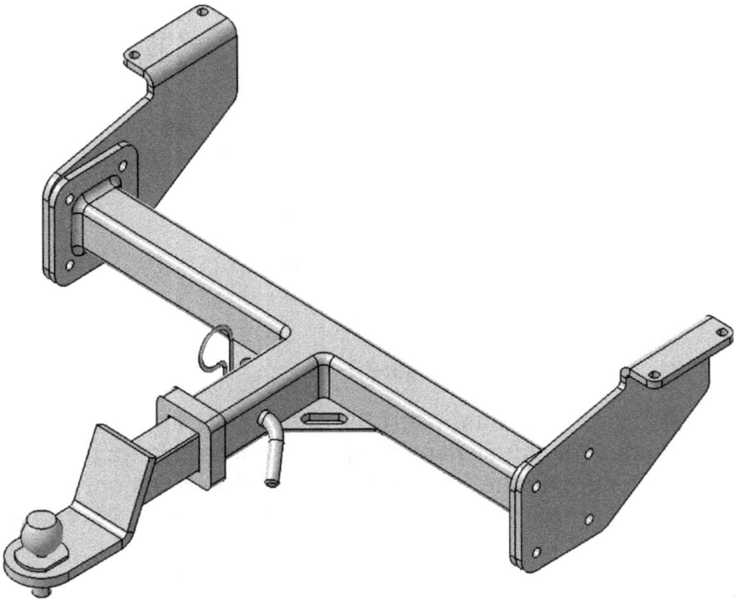

Figure 5–61

6. Save the assembly and close all tabs.

End of practice

Chapter 6

Weight Definition and Distribution

In the 3DEXPERIENCE platform, you can define both the weight and the weight distribution in an assembly. This chapter covers how to apply material properties to assign or calculate component weight.

Learning Objectives

- Apply material to a model.
- Declare or calculate weight.
- Calculate weight distribution.

6.1 Applying Materials

To assist in the generation of relevant mass properties measurements, materials can be applied to parts and assemblies.

Applying Materials to Components

Materials can be applied to the components of an assembly at the 3D part level within the **Assembly Design** app.

How To: Apply a Material to a Component

1. In the *Tools* section of the Action Bar, click (Material Browser) to open the *Material Browser* window (shown in Figure 6–1). If you know the name of the material, you can instead search for it directly in the *Search* field at the top of the 3DEXPERIENCE window.

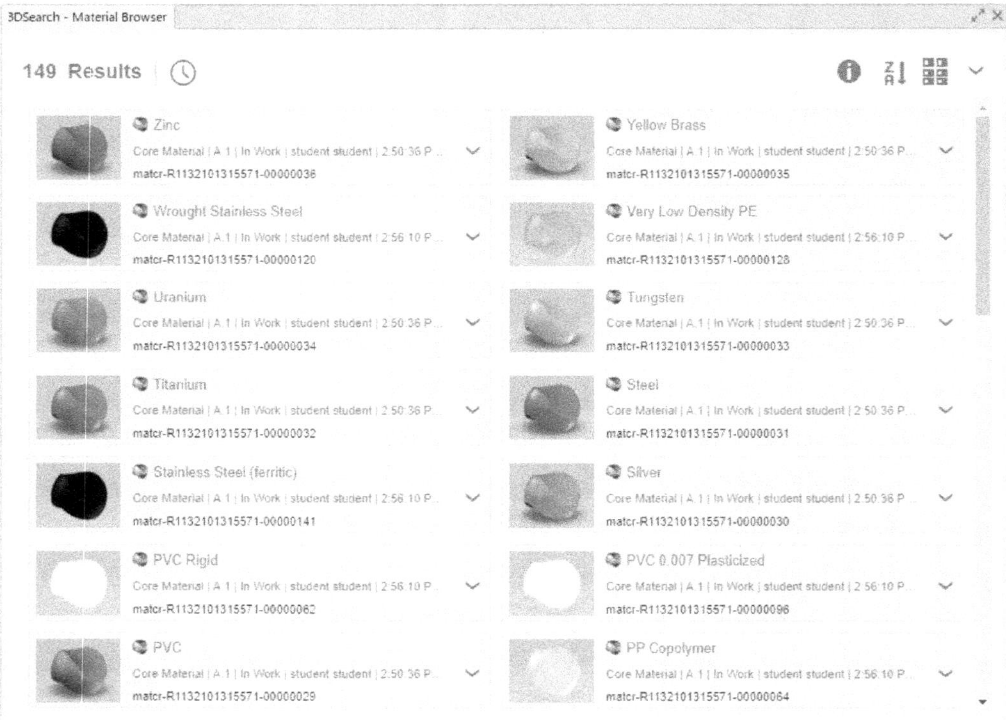

Figure 6–1

2. The view can be changed between *Thumbnail*, *Textual Title*, *Title*, and *Datagrid* using the icon in the upper-right corner of the *Material Browser*, as shown in Figure 6–2.

Figure 6–2

3. Right-click on the material in the *Material Browser* and select **Apply**, as shown in Figure 6–3.

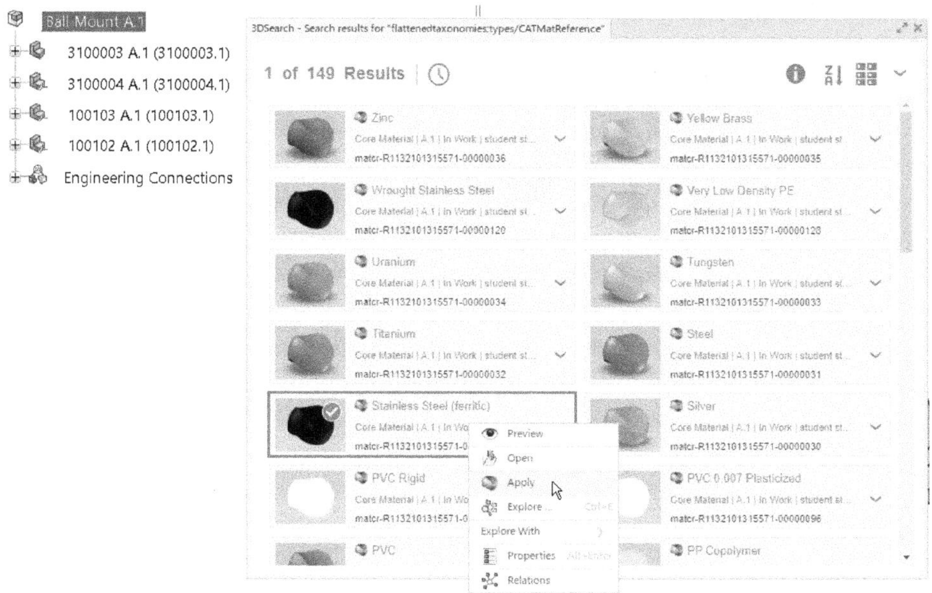

Figure 6–3

4. In the specification tree, select the specific component(s) to apply the material to.

5. Click (Exit Context Menu), as shown in Figure 6–4.

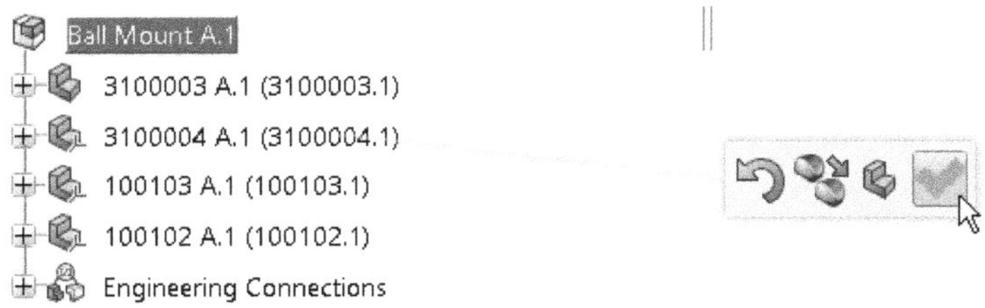

Figure 6–4

When this is done, the system considers each component's material property when performing related calculations.

Applying Material to Parts

You can also apply a material to a part in the **Part Design** app.

How To: Apply a Material to a Part

1. Activate the model at the 3D shape level, as shown in Figure 6–5.

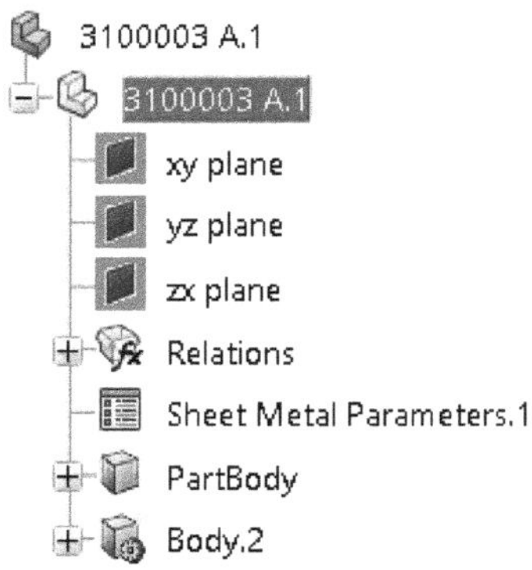

Figure 6–5

2. In the *Tools* section of the Action Bar, click (Material Browser).
3. Select a material in the *Materials Browser* window, right-click, and select **Apply**, then select the 3D shape.

4. The material is listed in the specification tree, as shown in Figure 6–6. All properties for the selected material are defined for the model to which the material is applied.

   Note: *The material has a set of properties that apply to three domains: Rendering (Appearance), Drafting, and Analysis (Simulation).*

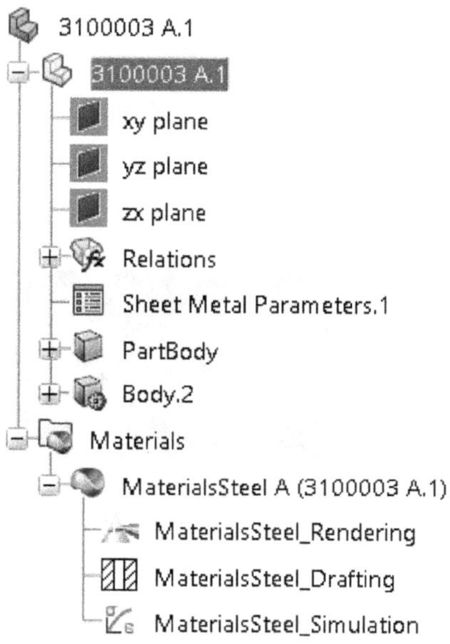

Figure 6–6

Viewing the Material in the Model

The model can also be viewed with the material rendering applied. In the *View* section of the Action Bar, click  (View Modes) and then click  (Shading With Material) to apply the material rendering to a model.

Changing Material Appearance

After a material is applied, you can change its properties. Double-click on the **Material Rendering** domain and the *Material Definition: Appearance Domain* dialog box opens, as shown in Figure 6–7. Here you can edit the appearance by changing the *Base Color*, *Roughness*, *Transparency*, and so on.

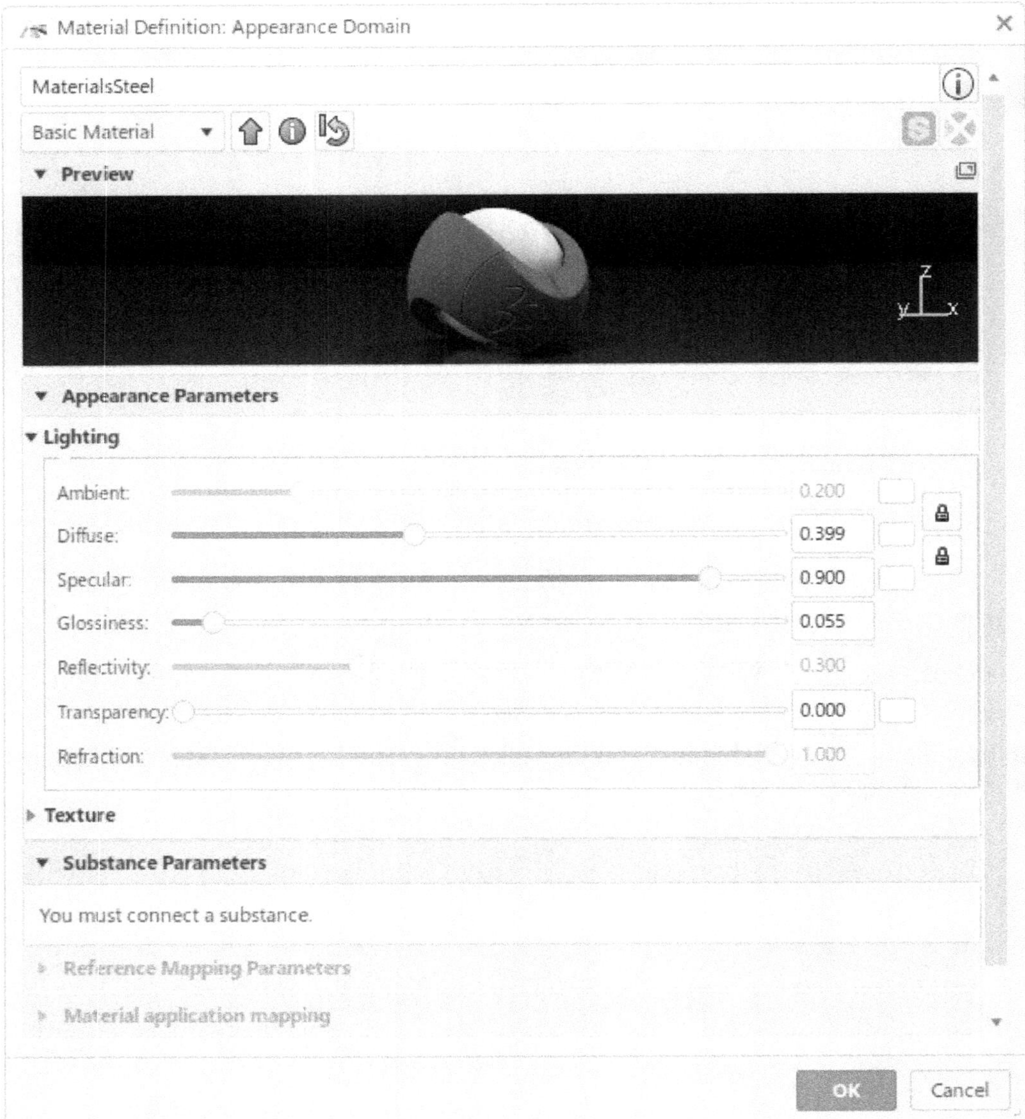

Figure 6–7

6.2 Weight Definition

The **Weight Definition** tool is used to check, calculate, or declare the weight of a part based on its geometry and/or material. This tool is part of the *B.I. Essentials* tools, which are accessed by clicking (B.I. Essentials) in the *Tools* tab of the Action Bar. In the *B.I Essentials* dialog box, expand the *Choose information to reveal* drop-down list and select **Weight Definition**, as shown in Figure 6–8.

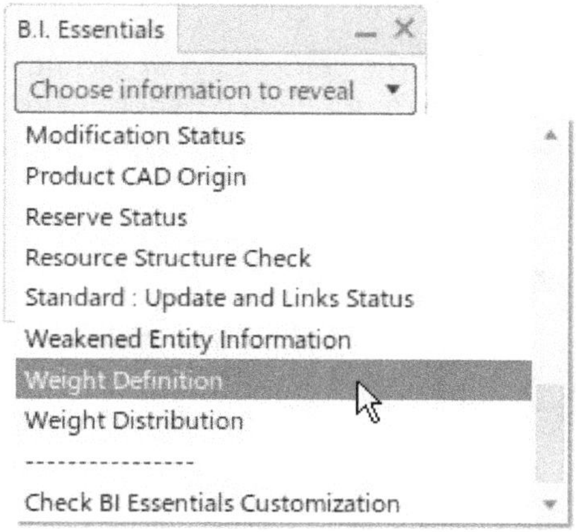

Figure 6–8

The **Weight Definition** tool uses color coding to indicate the status of each component, as shown in Figure 6–9.

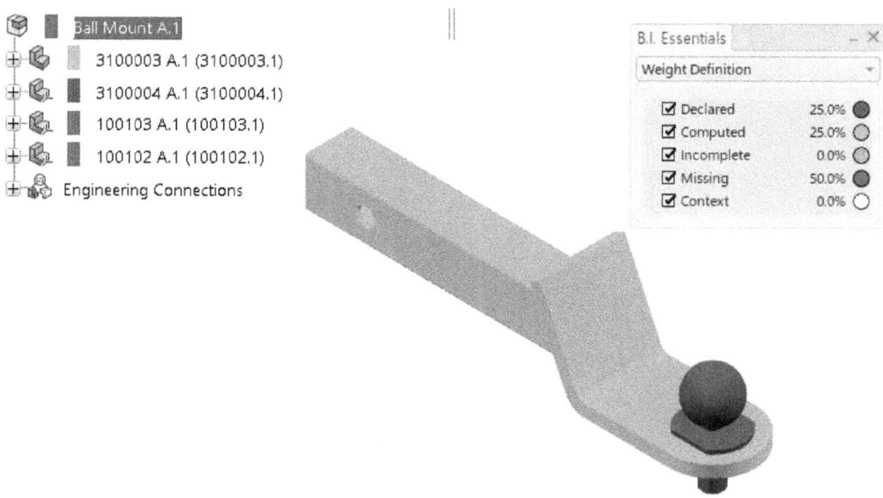

Figure 6–9

The color coding is broken into 5 categories:

- **Declared (Blue):** Weight is declared manually through the **Weight Definition** tool.
- **Computed (Green):** Weight is computed automatically using the geometry and material properties.
- **Incomplete (Orange):** Weight is partially defined.
- **Missing (Red):** No weight is assigned or calculated.
- **Context (Transparent White):** The assembly as a whole, or elements not taken into account for the weight computation.

The *B.I. Essentials* dialog box indicates the percentage of components falling into each category. You can select any category (or multiple categories) in the *B.I. Essentials* dialog box and the system will remove any components in that category from display, setting the color to transparent, as shown in Figure 6–10.

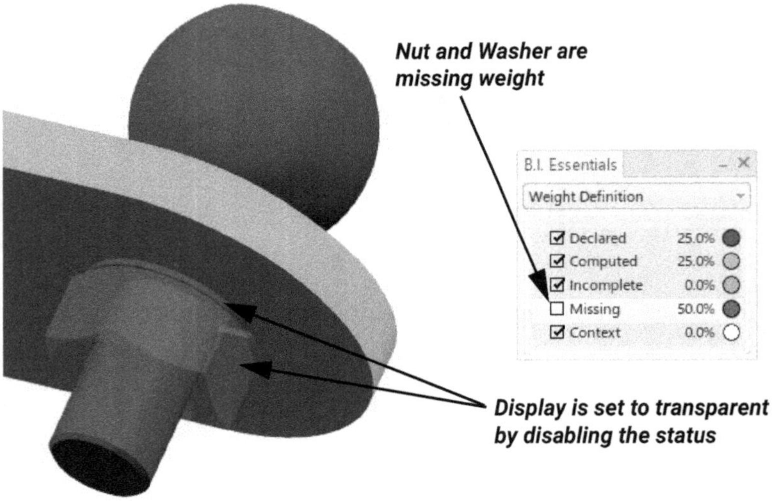

Figure 6–10

Weight Attributes Table

Clicking a component opens a set of hyperlinks on the screen related to declaring or computing the weight. The links displayed depend on the current status of the component. For example, if a component already has a calculated weight, the links are as shown in Figure 6–11.

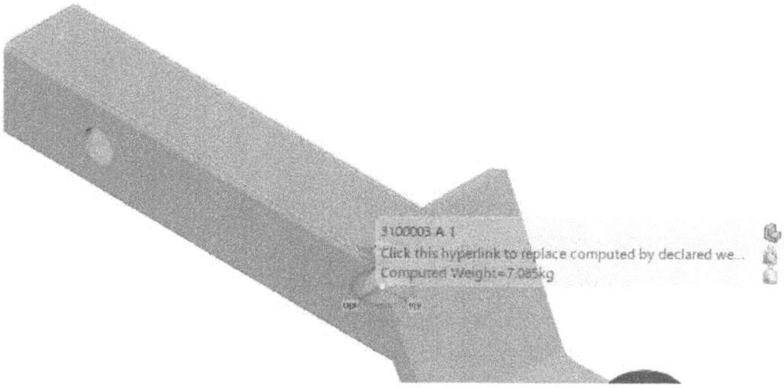

Figure 6–11

Clicking the links will open the *Weight Attributes* table for the component, as shown in Figure 6–12.

#	Attribute	Value
1	Weight [Tolerance]	7.085kg [6.731kg .. 7.439kg]
2	CoG along X [Tolerance]	5.118e-008mm [-22.67mm .. 22.67mm]
3	CoG along Y [Tolerance]	-21.309mm [-43.98mm .. 1.361mm]
4	CoG along Z [Tolerance]	-9.142mm [-31.813mm .. 13.528mm]
5	CoG Tolerance (±)	22.67mm
6	Volume	9.014e-004m3
7	Moment Ixx / G	0.106kgxm2
8	Moment Iyy / G	0.008kgxm2
9	Moment Izz / G	0.105kgxm2
10	Product of Inertia Ixy / G	3.231e-027kgxm2
11	Product of Inertia Ixz / G	0kgxm2
12	Product of Inertia Iyz / G	-0.011kgxm2
13	Mean Density	7860kg_m3
14	Include in ...ht Synthesis	Yes
15	Comment	

Figure 6–12

The weight will be listed in the *Weight* field. For components that do not have a calculated weight, you can declare a weight. This is particularly useful for purchased parts, where you may want to use the manufacturer's declared weight, rather than calculating it from your model.

6.3 Weight Distribution

To calculate the weight distribution, access the *B.I. Essentials* tools by clicking (B.I. Essentials) in the *Tools* tab of the Action Bar. In the *B.I. Essentials* dialog box, select **Weight Distribution**, as shown in Figure 6–13.

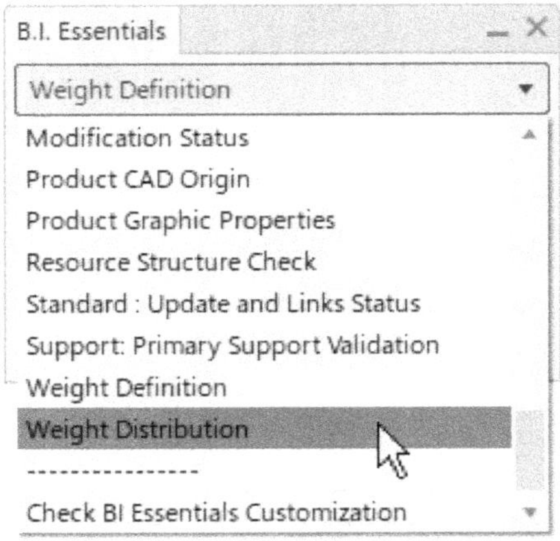

Figure 6–13

The **Weight Distribution** tool uses color coding to review components according to their weight, as shown in Figure 6–14.

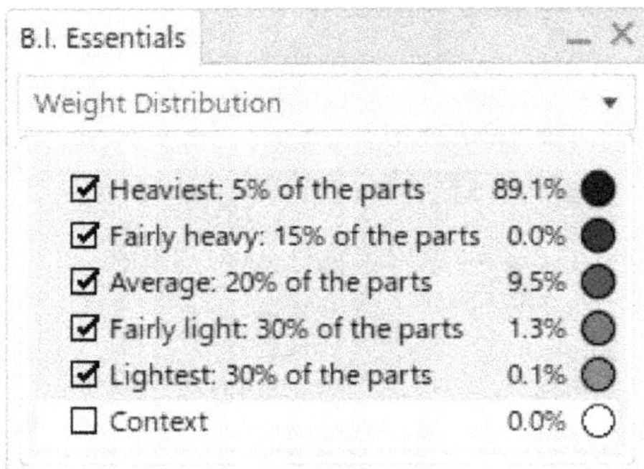

Figure 6–14

The **Weight Distribution** tool provides insights into your model weight so you can make informed decisions about adjusting components or materials.

Practice 6a
Weight Calculations

Practice Objectives

- Assign material.
- Calculate weight.
- Assign weight.
- Analyze the weight distribution.

In this practice, you will assign material to a model to calculate its weight. You will also assign weight using the *B.I. Essentials* tool, and will analyze the overall weight distribution.

Task 1: Import Ball_Mount_Weight and review how it is assembled.

1. Import **Ball_Mount_Weight.3dxml**.
2. Right-click on **Ball Mount** and select **Open**.
3. Set the view orientation to (* iso), and if necessary, click (Fit All In). The part displays as shown in Figure 6–15.

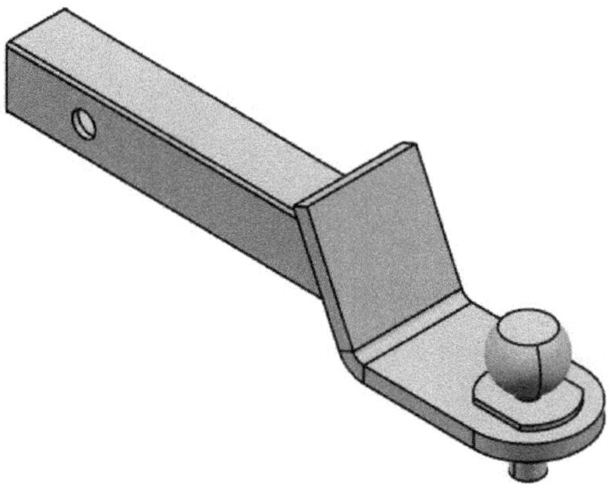

Figure 6–15

Task 2: Review the weight of the assembly components.

1. In the *Tools* section of the Action Bar, click (B.I. Essentials).

2. In the *Choose information to reveal* drop-down list, select **Weight Definition**, as shown in Figure 6–16.

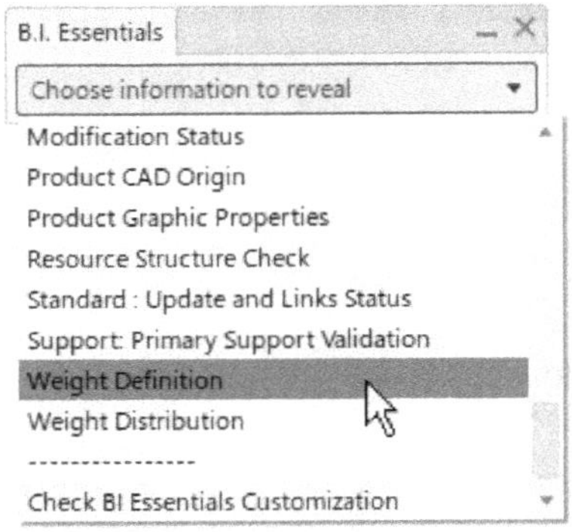

Figure 6–16

3. The model, *B.I. Essentials* dialog box, and specification tree all update to show the components with weight assigned, calculated, and so on, as shown in Figure 6–17.

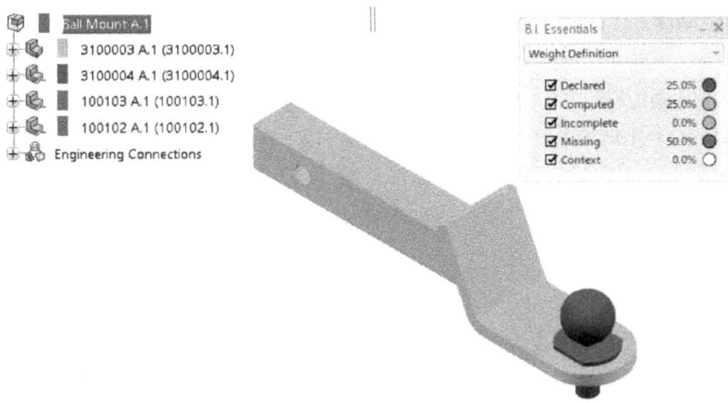

Figure 6–17

4. Select the ball part and note it has an assigned weight of 0.5kg, as shown in Figure 6–18.

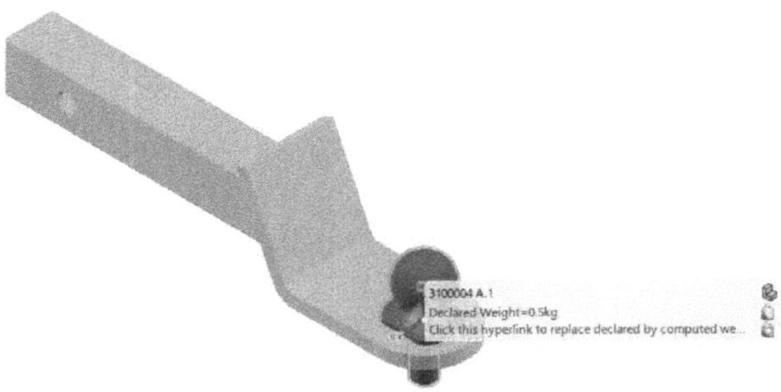

Figure 6–18

5. Close the *B.I. Essentials* dialog box.

Task 3: Assign a material to the ball part, then calculate the weight.

1. In the *Tools* section of the Action Bar, click (Material Browser) to open the material library.
2. With the *Material Browser* window open, search for the material named **MaterialsSteel**.
3. Once located, right-click on the line titled **MaterialsSteel** and select **Apply**.
4. Select **3100004** in the specification tree.
5. Click (Close) in the context toolbar.
6. With the ball part still selected, click (B.I. Essentials) in the *Tools* section of the Action Bar.
7. A window appears next to the selected part. Click the hyperlink **Click this link to replace declared weight with computed**.
8. In the *Weight Attributes* table, click (Update), as shown in Figure 6–19.

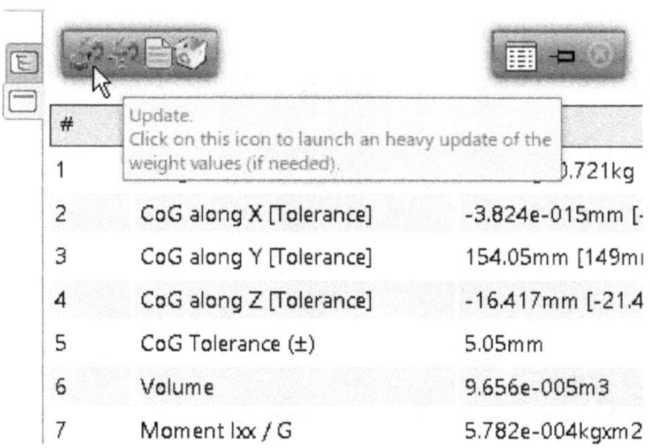

Figure 6–19

9. Close the *Weight Attributes* table and click on the screen.

10. Note that there are now only two **Missing** weights, as shown in Figure 6–20.

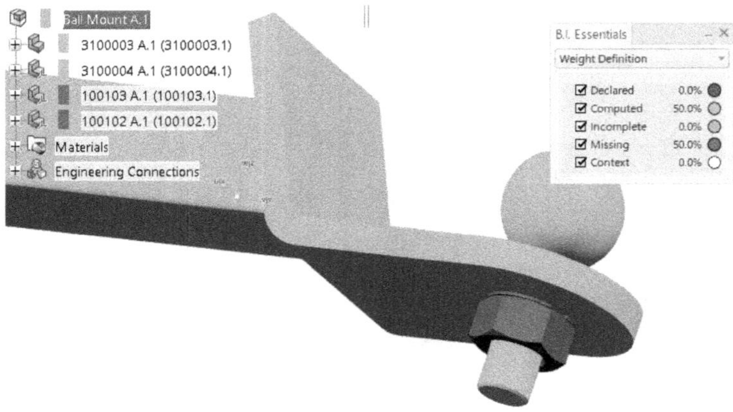

Figure 6–20

Task 4: Assign weight for the nut and washer.

1. Select the washer on the screen.
2. Click the **Click this hyperlink to declare a weight on this element** link, as shown in Figure 6–21.

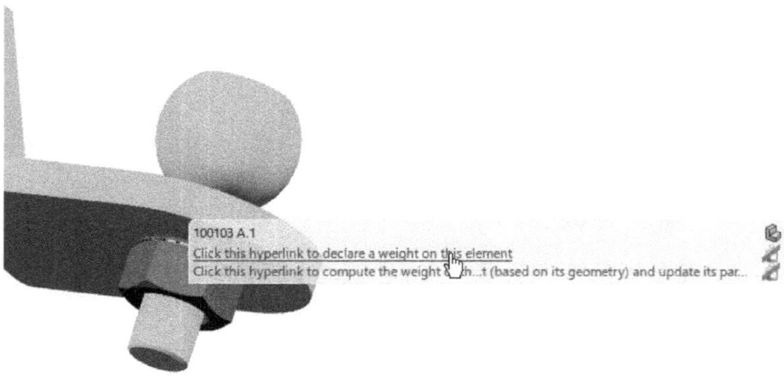

Figure 6–21

3. In the *Weight Attributes* table, enter **0.0075kg** for the weight, and in the *Comments* field, enter **Weight entered from supplier catalog**.
4. Close the *Weight Attributes* table.
5. Select the nut and use the same process followed for the washer, but enter a weight of **0.1kg**.

6. Close the *Weight Attributes* table and click on the screen. Note that there are no longer any **Missing** weights, as shown in Figure 6–22.

Figure 6–22

Task 5: Review the weight distribution.

1. In the *B.I. Essentials* dialog box, select **Weight Distribution** from the drop-down list, as shown in Figure 6–23.

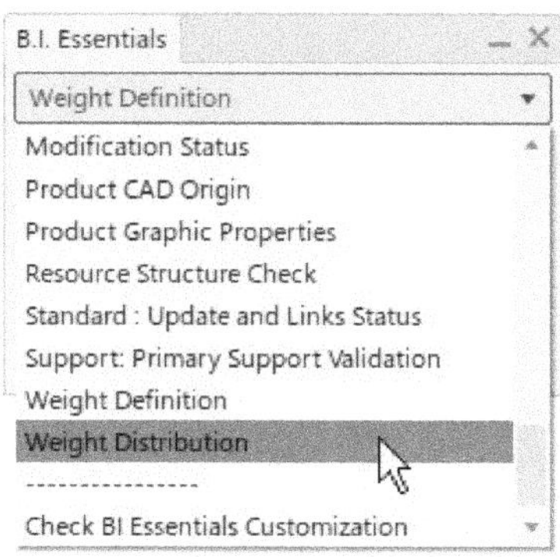

Figure 6–23

2. The model and *B.I. Essentials* dialog box display as shown in Figure 6–24.

   Note: *As you would expect, the majority of the weight of this product (89%) comes from the slide component.*

Figure 6–24

3. Save the assembly and close all tabs.

End of practice

Chapter 7

Working with Skeleton Models

Skeleton models are part files that only contain surfaces and reference geometry. Skeleton models help maintain the design intent of a model by including all of the vital volume requirements of components in a product. When using the top-down design method, skeletons are an intricate step.

Learning Objectives

- Understand the use of skeleton models.
- Understand how contextual design is used to create part geometry in the context of an assembly model.
- Use publications to identify and select elements to be externally referenced.
- Use skeleton models to share parameters between assemblies and components.
- Create a skeleton.

7.1 Publications

A publication is an organizational and reference management tool that is used to identify and select elements to be externally referenced. When an element is published, it is added to a new *Publications* branch in the specification tree and can be renamed so that it can be easily identified and selected by other designers.

For example, the dashboard surface of an automobile has been published in the **DashSkel** component shown in Figure 7–1. This publication is then externally referenced by any of the dashboard components, such as the HVAC vent bezel or the storage compartment lid, to define their shape.

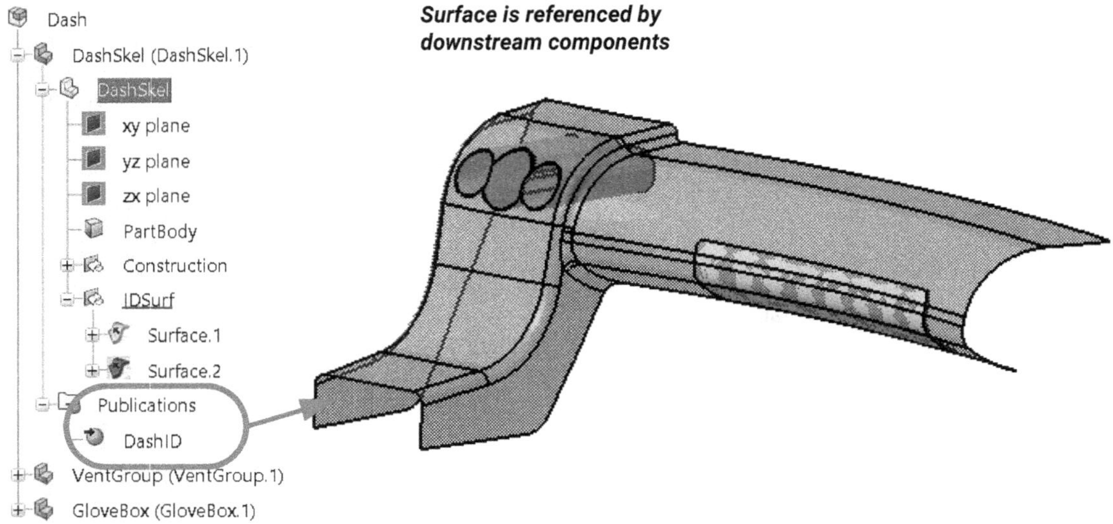

Figure 7–1

Creating this contextual link between elements ensures that the shapes of the dashboard components always match the defined design intent of the published surface. The use of publications in performing this operation acts as a controlling mechanism that defines the geometry that can be externally referenced and facilitates its selection by placing it in a separate branch in the tree.

Another benefit of publishing data is seen when integrating with the 3DEXPERIENCE platform. During the lifecycle process of data creation, links can become disconnected from their references for a number of reasons. The use of publications places the geometry at a higher level of importance by giving the publication feature its own Universally Unique ID. Therefore, the publication is viewed with the same weight as an actual part file. This facilitates the management of links through the use of publications.

You can publish the following types of elements:

- Reference elements, such as points, planes, lines, and splines
- Features
- Sketches

- Bodies
- Surfaces
- Parameters
- Sub-elements, such as faces, edges, and axes

Identifying Elements in the Tree

Items can be published from the 3D shape (part). They can also be published at the product (assembly) level. In addition, an item already published in a 3D shape can be republished at the assembly level. Doing this yields a small shortcut arrow next to the publication icon in the tree, as shown in Figure 7–2.

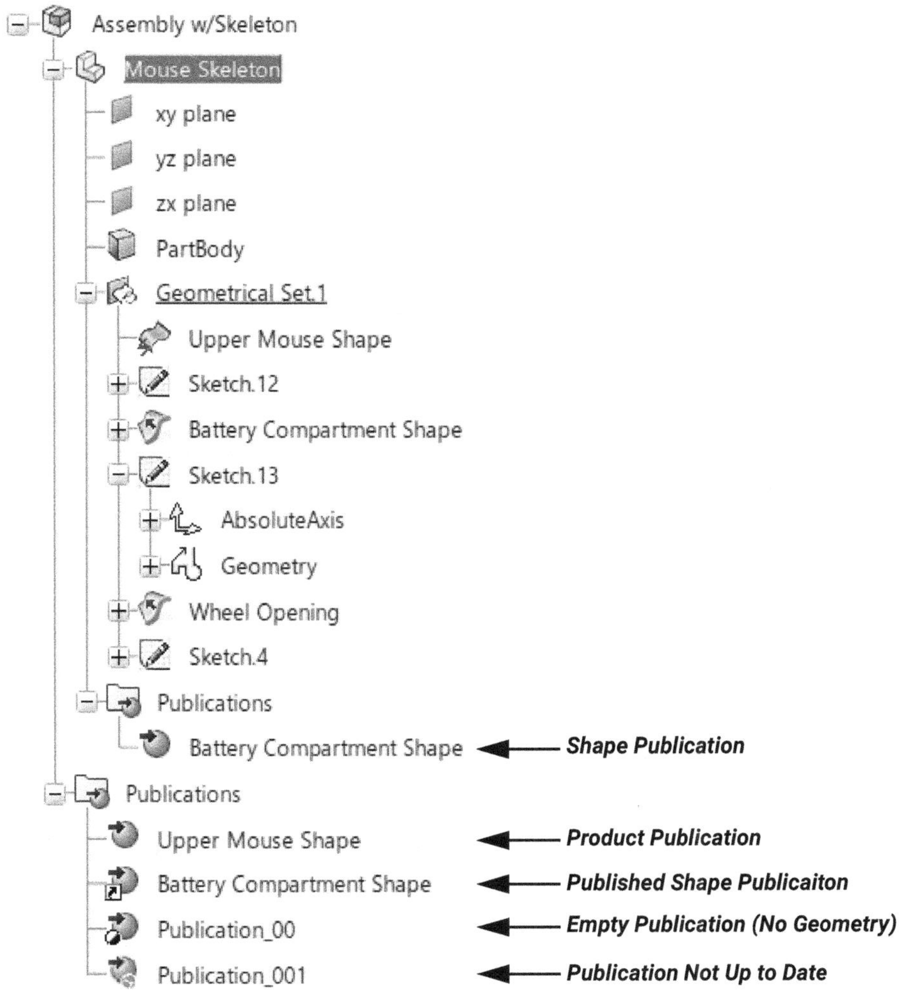

Figure 7–2

Creating a Publication

How To: Publish Elements

Use the following general steps to publish elements:

1. Select elements to publish, as shown in Figure 7–3.

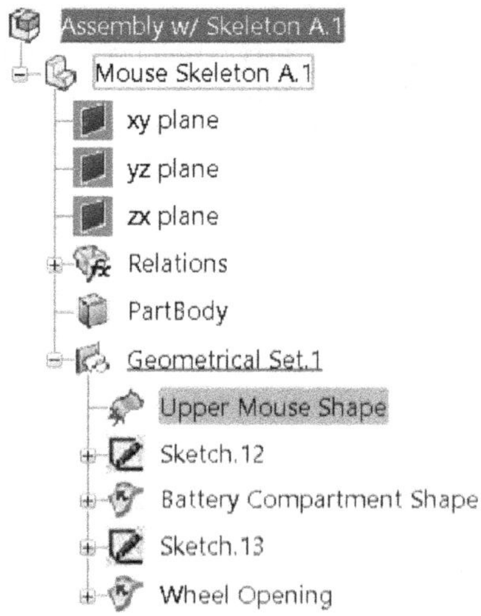

Figure 7–3

2. In the *Product Modification* section of the Action Bar, click (Create a Publication).
3. In the *Publication* dialog box, enter a name for publication. The default value is the name of the selected item, as shown in Figure 7–4.

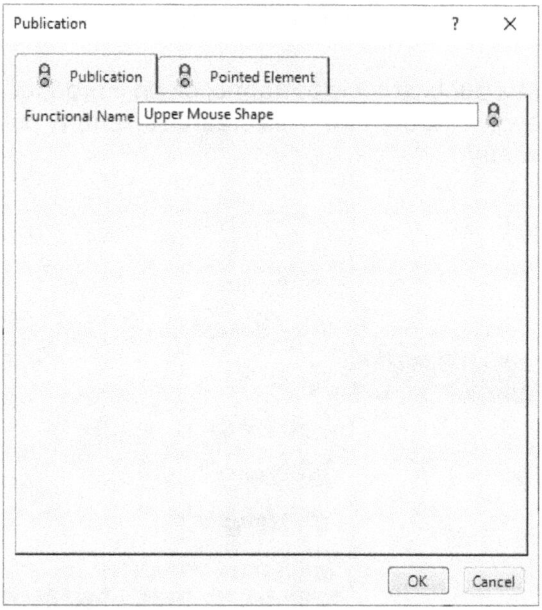

Figure 7–4

4. Click **OK** to complete publication. The publication is listed at the end of the specification tree, as shown in Figure 7–5.

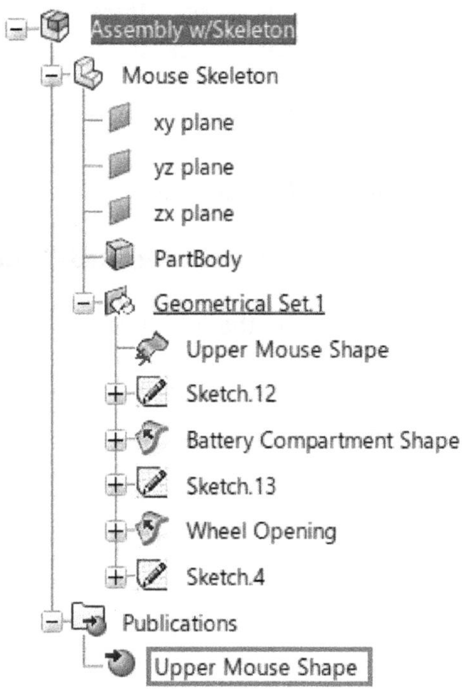

Figure 7–5

Associating Geometry to Publication

An alternative way to build a publication is to right-click on a product and select **Insert>Publication**, as shown in Figure 7–6. This creates an empty publication that will not yet be associated to any geometry.

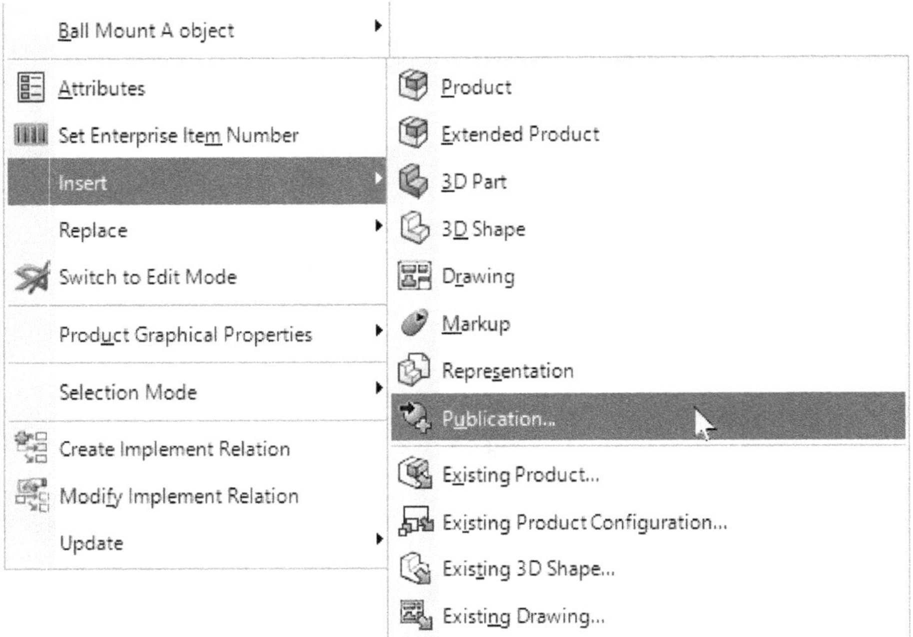

Figure 7–6

How To: Associate Geometry to the Publication

1. Click the publication in the tree and select **Modify Pointed Elements** in the context menu, or click  (Edit Publication Properties) in the Action Bar.

2. If necessary, switch to the *Published Element* tab, as shown in Figure 7–7.

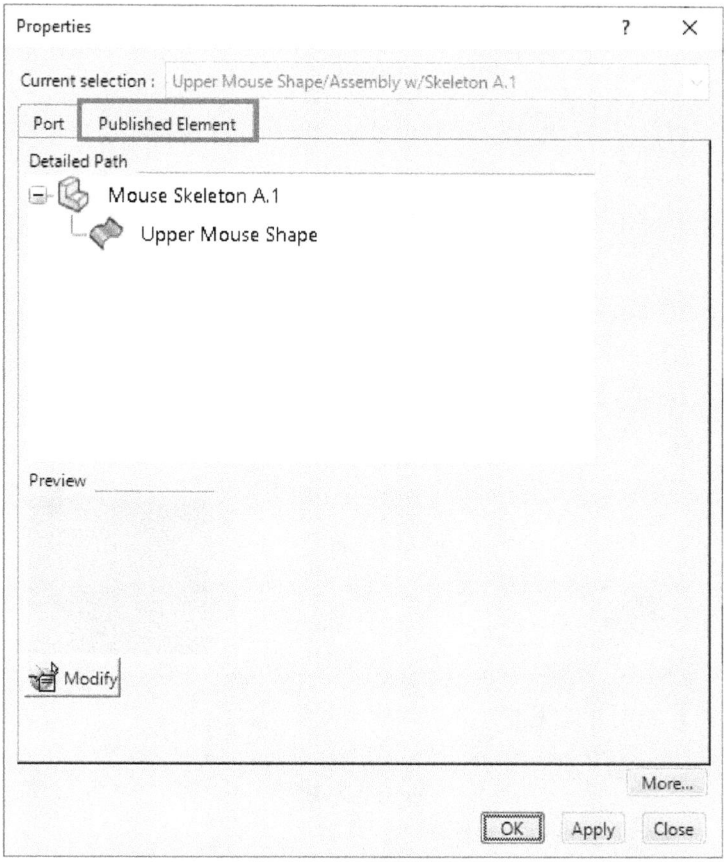

Figure 7–7

3. Click **Modify** and select the geometry that is to be published, as shown in Figure 7–8.

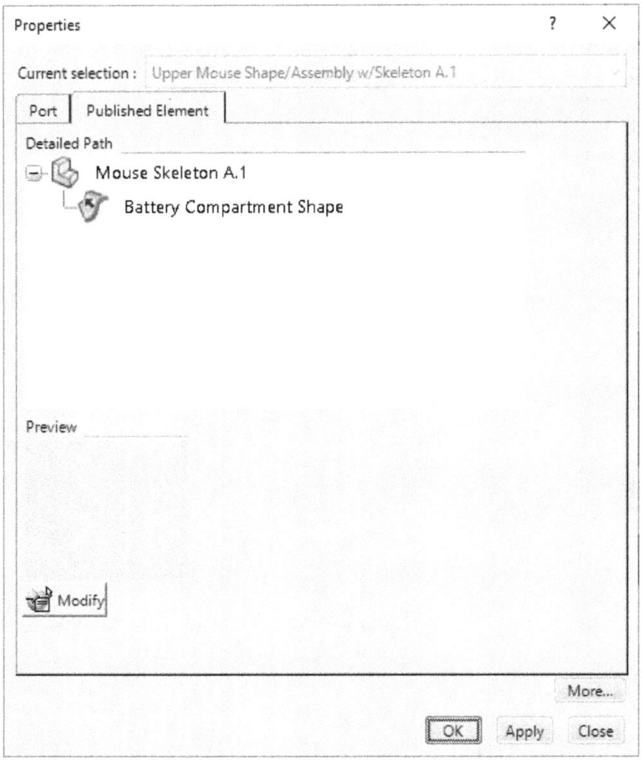

Figure 7–8

4. Click **OK**.

Publication Modifications

Options for modifying publications are available. Click on a publication directly to find these options in the context menu:

	Rename the Publication
	View Attributes – View attributes such as name, description, modification date, etc.
	Modify Pointed Elements – Link publication to differing geometry

You can also access the **Publication** commands in the *Action Bar*, as shown Figure 7–9.

Figure 7–9

Edit Publication Properties	Select or change the geometry to be published.
Optimize Publications	Minimize publications that point to the same object at different levels.
Export Publications	Creates a text file that contains a list of publications in the product.
Import Publications	Creates publications with names from a text file. These will need to manually be linked to the geometry in the part/product.

Publication Preferences

General settings regarding external links and publications are available in **Me>Preferences> Common Preferences>Object Properties>3D Shape>Infrastructure>External References**.

A common setting is **Restrict external selection with link to published elements**, as shown in Figure 7–10. Choosing this will ensure that links can only point to published geometry, minimizing the chance of accidentally creating links or linking to unintended geometry.

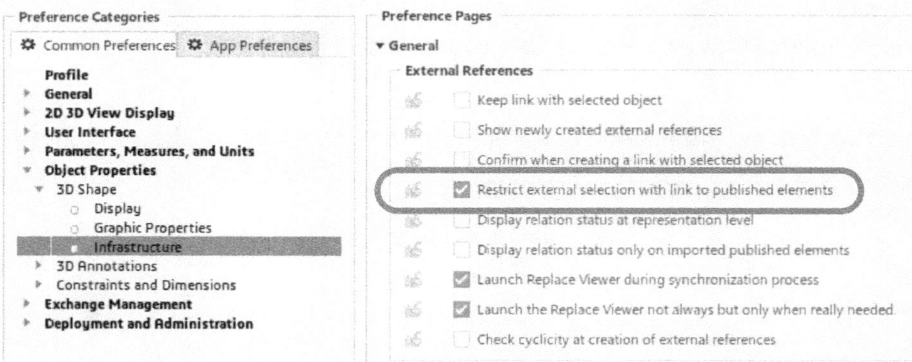

Figure 7–10

Constraint Creation

Assembly constraint options can be set to enable only the published elements to be referenced.

To access this option, as shown in Figure 7–11, select **Me>Preferences>App Preferences> 3D Modeling> Mechanical Systems>Assembly Design> Constraint Creation**.

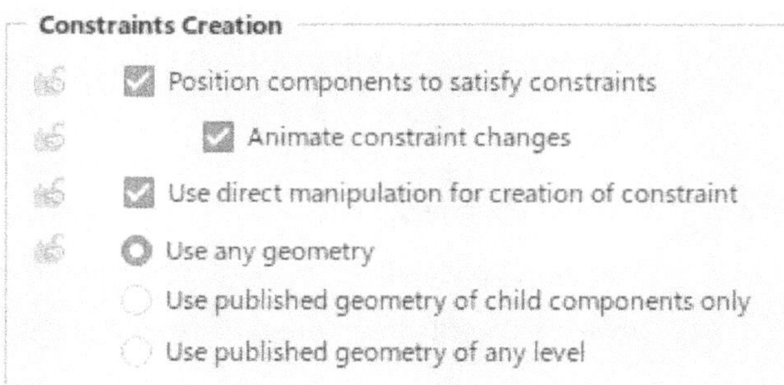

Figure 7–11

Replacing a Publication

Another advantage of using publications is that all external references are linked to the published element and not directly to the feature. As long as there is a publication with the same name, the link is valid and updated. This simplifies the replacement of data, because the referenced geometry can be replaced through the publication so that all of the references are automatically updated. An example is shown in Figure 7–12.

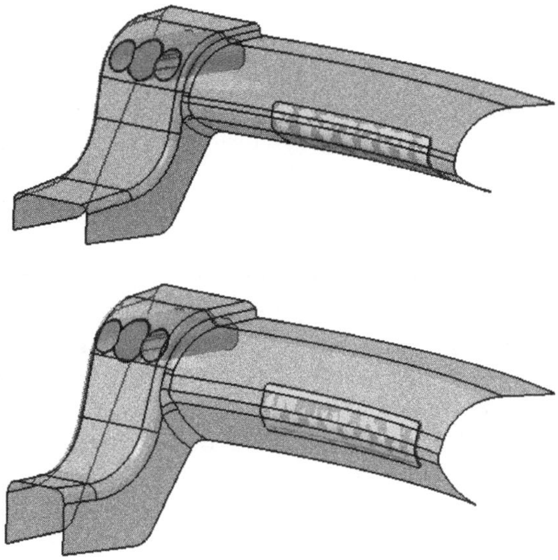

Figure 7–12

The process to replace a publication is identical to the steps listed in ***Associating Geometry to Publication***.

7.2 Skeleton Modeling

Skeleton models create an underlying structure for product files. The skeleton model is a 3D shape that acts as a three-dimensional layout of an assembly to facilitate a top-down design.

Skeleton models generally consist of wireframe features, surface features, and parameter information. Parts are then constrained to or created from them.

Parent/Child Relationships

Constraining parts to a skeleton model instead of to other parts reduces unwanted parent/child relationships. Deleting and replacing parts is also easier because fewer dependency relationships exist between parts.

Volume Control

Creating parts from a skeleton model ensures that they fit the location and volume requirements of the product. Skeleton models can be used to create a conceptual part that defines a region of a product. This region represents the volume to be occupied or avoided by one or more parts that have yet to be created. The skeleton model can then be referenced during the creation of these parts to ensure that they fit the location and volume limitations. For example, when designing a car, the frame or body is designed around the engine. The space claimed by the engine can be represented by a skeleton and the frame and body data can be designed around the constraint.

Styling Data

The skeleton model is also a central location for all of the styling data that is created. The surfaces or curves can then be used across a number of different components in the assembly to control their shape.

7.3 Creating a Skeleton

A skeleton model is created using the same techniques as a part, except that it cannot contain any solid geometry. A skeleton model is the first component placed in a product file. All other components are constrained to or created from it.

Consider the following tips when creating a skeleton model:

- A skeleton model should not contain any solid elements.
- A skeleton model should contain referencing elements, such as surfaces, planes, lines, and points. This helps place the solid geometry from other parts into the assembly.

General Steps

Use the following general steps to create a skeleton model:

1. Create a new part file.
2. Create the skeleton geometry.
3. Publish geometry for external reference selection.
4. Assemble parts into the product.
5. Reference parts to the skeleton.

Step 1 - Create a new part file.

Begin with an empty product file and use (Insert 3D Shape). Using **3D Shape** (instead of 3D Part) will ensure that the skeleton is not accidentally moved. Enter a name that indicates that this file is being used as a skeleton model (e.g., **Mouse Skeleton**), as shown in Figure 7–13.

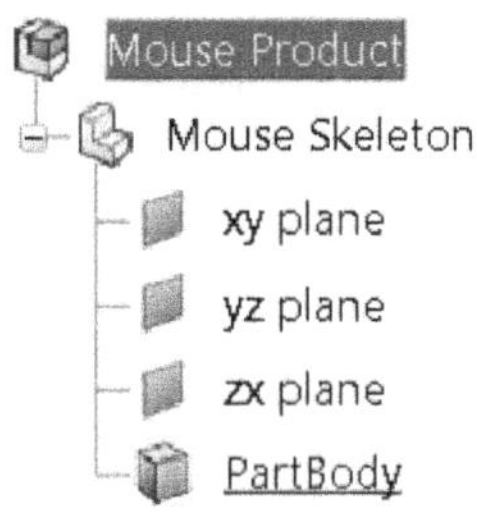

Figure 7–13

Step 2 - Create the skeleton geometry.

A skeleton model can be created using the options in the Surfacing apps, such as Wireframe and Surface Design or Generative Shape Design. The skeleton model for a wireless computer mouse is shown in Figure 7–14. The entire model consists of surfaces and reference geometry.

The battery compartment for the wireless mouse is located beneath a removal lid on top of the mouse. To ensure that both the upper lid and the rest of the body of the mouse use the same styling shape, a skeleton is created as separate surfaces; one for the overall shape of the mouse and others to mark important features, such as the break between the mouse body and lid, as well as a designated opening for the mouse wheel.

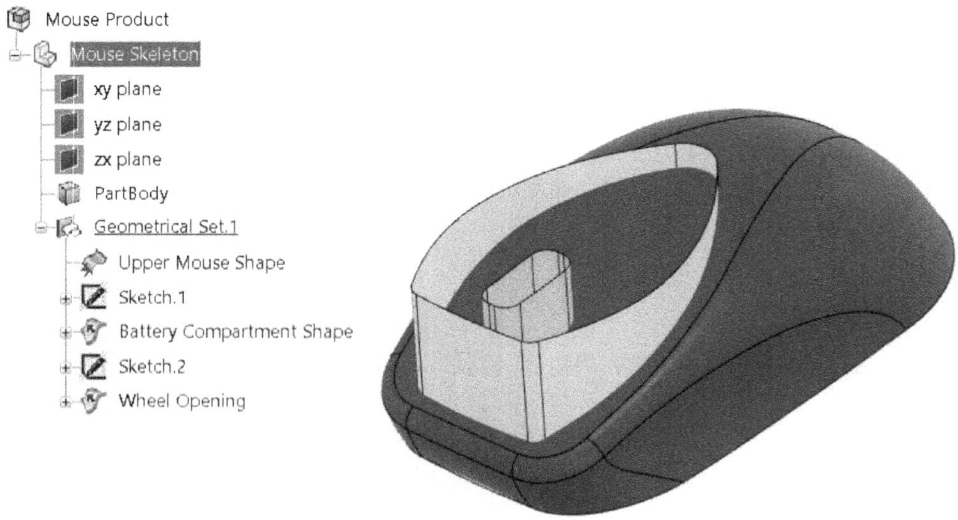

Figure 7–14

Step 3 - Publish geometry for external reference selection.

Once the skeleton geometry has been developed, it should be published before it is used as a reference to create geometry in other components. In this example, the top and bottom surfaces are published, as shown in Figure 7–15.

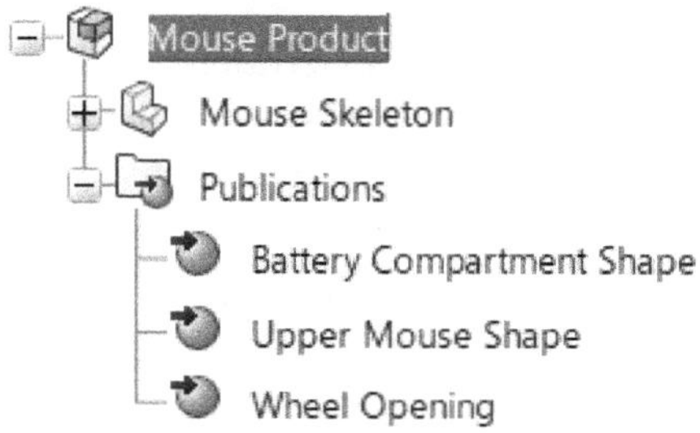

Figure 7–15

Step 4 - Assemble parts into the product.

The skeleton model is always the first part brought into a product. All other parts are then constrained to or created from it. Two 3D part files (**Mouse Main Body** and **Mouse Lid**) are then added to the product file (**Mouse Product**), as shown in Figure 7–16.

Figure 7–16

Step 5 - Reference parts to the skeleton.

To ensure that the mouse maintains the design intent, the geometry used for creating the various components should reference the skeleton model. This way, if a change to the remote is required, only the skeleton model needs to be adjusted.

> ***Note:*** *Any changes to the skeleton model are not reflected in the top or bottom parts if* ***Keep link with selected object*** *is not selected.*

Before creating the parts, you must create an external link between the part files. Select **Me>Preferences** to open the *Preferences* dialog box. Select **Common Preferences>Object Properties>3D Shape>Infrastructure**, then in the *External References* section, select **Keep link with selected object**, as shown in Figure 7–17.

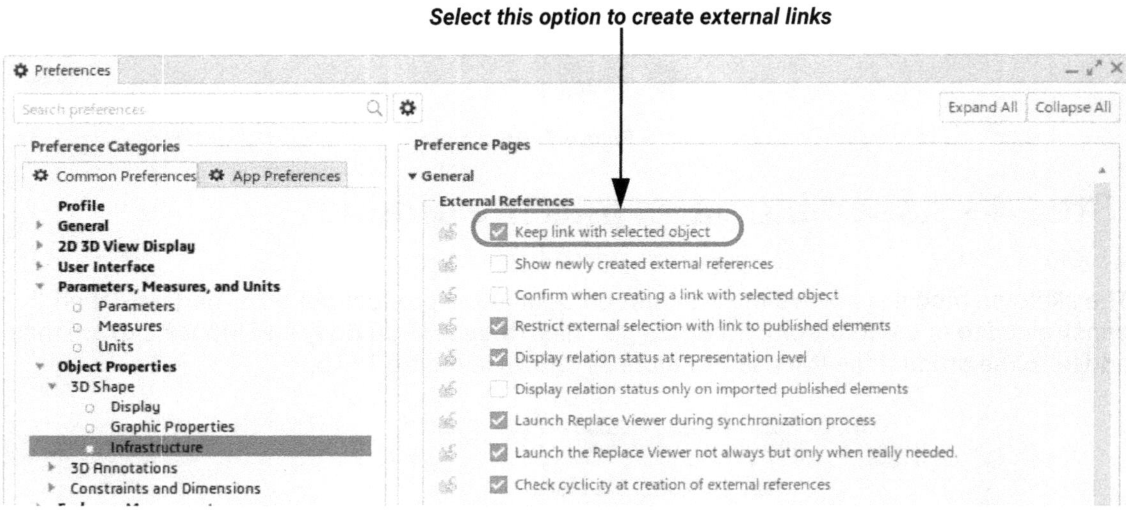

Figure 7–17

The main body of the mouse is created by thickening the upper mouse surface and removing the battery compartment shape, as shown in Figure 7–18.

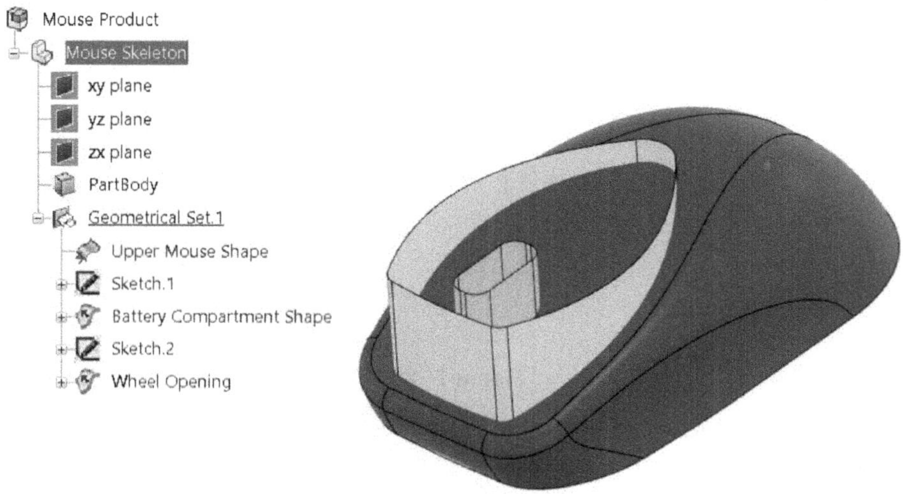

Figure 7–18

Once the top part has been created, 3DEXPERIENCE creates another geometrical set in the top cover part called **External References**. This geometrical set contains an external link to the Upper Mouse Shape and the Battery Compartment Shape surface, as shown in Figure 7–19.

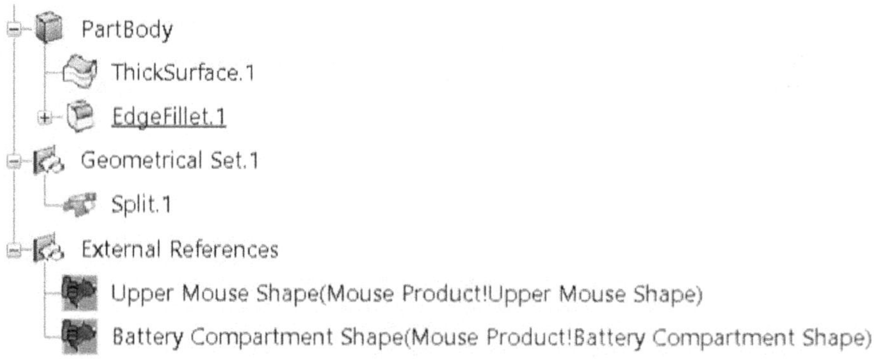

Figure 7–19

The mouse lid is built in a similar fashion. Once completed, any required changes to the size of the remote can be made from the skeleton model. By changing only the skeleton, all items linked to it are updated simultaneously. The part files display the changes once they have been updated, as shown in Figure 7–20.

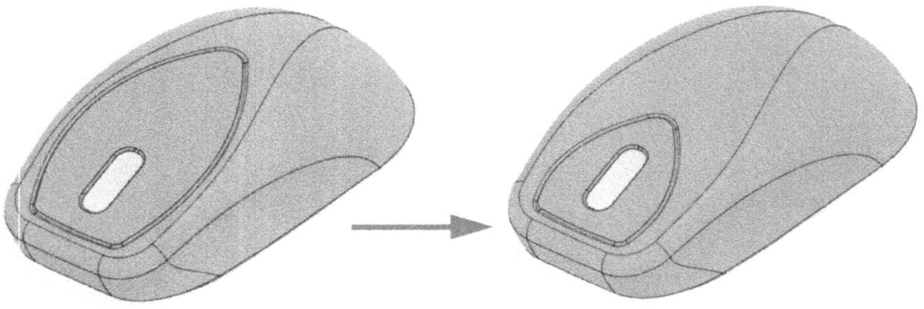

Figure 7–20

The bottom cover is created using the same technique as the top cover. Once completed, any required changes to the size of the remote can be made from the skeleton model. The part files display the changes once they have been updated.

Contextual Engineering Connections and Skeleton

A contextual engineering connection is a connection between assemblies and subassemblies that are nested, or at different levels, in the tree.

In Figure 7–21, bolts are placed in a separate sub product for easy organization. In V5, it would not be possible to constrain the individual bolts to the Plate Skeleton, since the skeleton is at a higher level branch of the tree. Instead, the entire Bolt Sub Assy would constrain to the Plate Skeleton, yielding incorrect results.

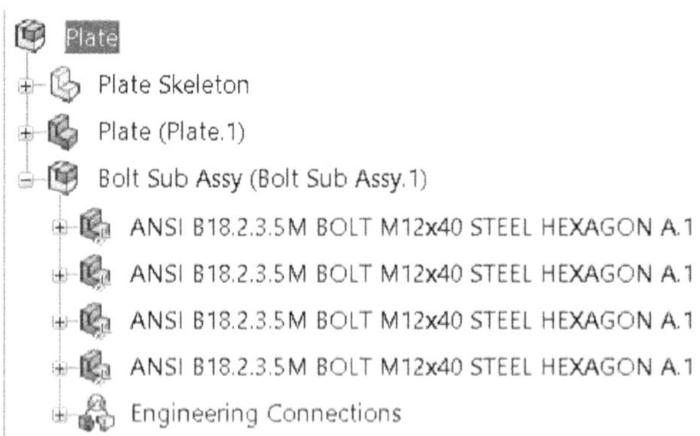

Figure 7–21

The 3DEXPERIENCE platform, however, will allow the individual bolts to be connected directly to the skeleton, reducing the need for sub-skeletons and simplifying the tree and number of components. To do so, activate (double-click on) the correct sub product before building the engineering connections.

3DEXPERIENCE and V5 Skeletons Compared

The skeleton concept remains the same, but the execution is slightly different, as shown in Figure 7–22. In V5, publications for skeletons can be created at the part level. In 3DEXPERIENCE, it is recommended to create publications at the assembly level for skeleton models. In V5, the skeleton would belong to a part in an instance. By using a 3D shape in 3DEXPERIENCE, a branch of the tree is removed, preventing accidental movement of the skeleton part. Sub-assembly elements can now be positioned without a sub-skeleton.

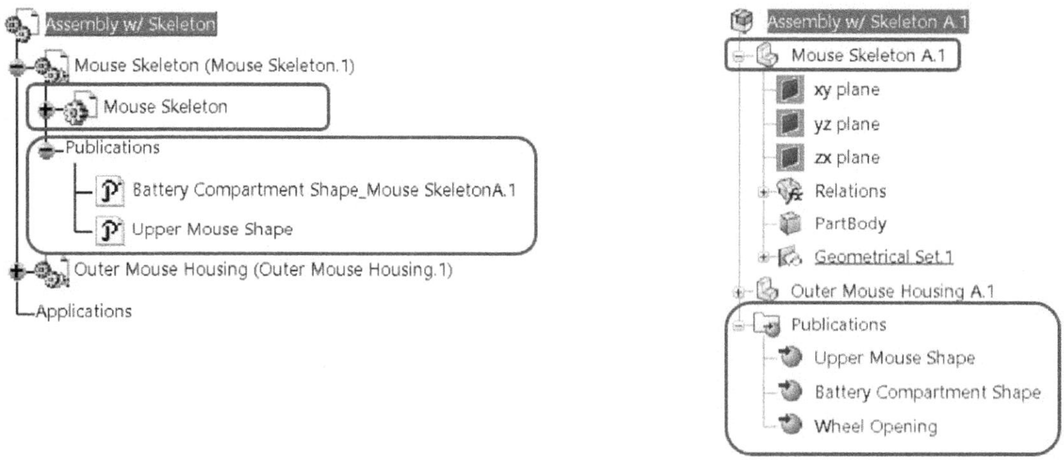

Figure 7–22

Managing Reusable Representations

By creating a skeleton as a 3D shape (instead of a 3D part), it is effectively locked inside the current product, both in assembly position and tree structure. Attempting to copy and paste to use the skeleton in a different product will yield an error, as shown in Figure 7–23.

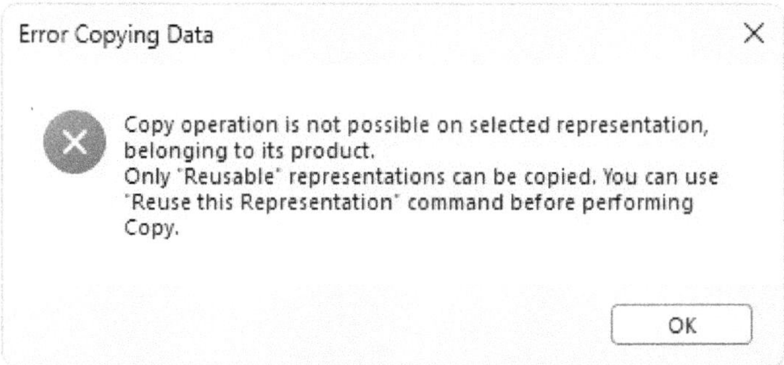

Figure 7–23

Right-click on the skeleton 3D shape and select **Enable Reuse of this Representation**, as shown in Figure 7–24, to allow the file to be copy/pasted elsewhere or inserted into another product.

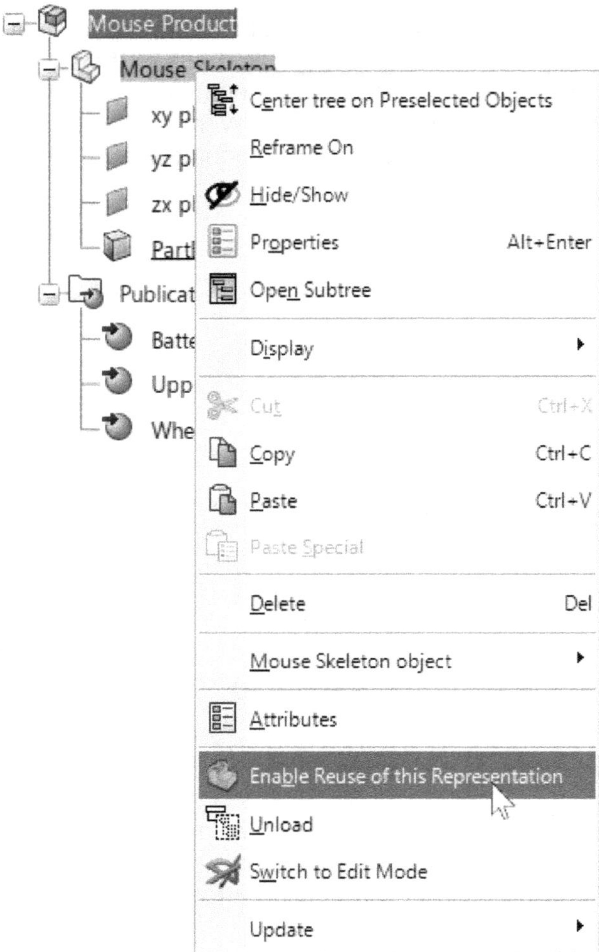

Figure 7–24

Practice 7a
Skeleton Models

Practice Objective

- Create a skeleton model.

In this practice, you will create reference features to create a skeleton model.

Task 1: Import the required files.

1. Import **Skeleton_Models.3dxml**.

Task 2: Create a new product with a 3D shape.

1. Create a new **Physical Product**.
2. In the *Physical Product* dialog box, enter ***Your_Initials*_UniversalJoint** in the *Title* field and click **OK**.
3. Right-click on **UniversalJoint** and select **Insert>3D Shape**.
4. In the *New Content* window, select **3D Shape**.
5. In the *3D Shape* dialog box, enter **Skeleton** in the *Title* field and click **OK**.
6. Rename the yz plane as **CenterLine**. The specification tree displays as shown in Figure 7–25.

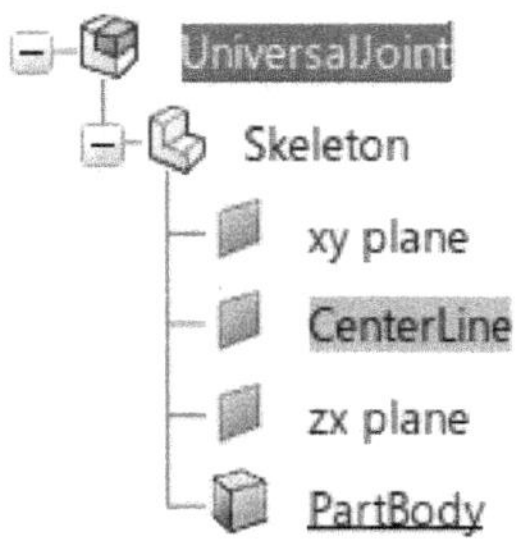

Figure 7–25

Task 3: Create reference geometry.

1. Activate the **Skeleton** 3D shape.

2. Create a reference point at the **0,0,0** location, as shown in Figure 7–26.

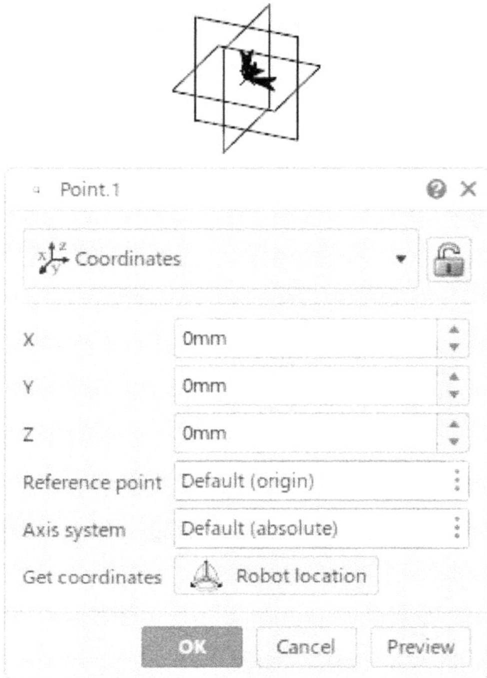

Figure 7–26

3. Create a reference line by selecting the references and entering the value as follows, as shown in Figure 7–27:
   - *Line type:* **Point-Direction**
   - *Point:* **Point.1**
   - *Direction:* **CenterLine**
   - *Line End - Offset:* **12.5**
   - *Length Type:* (Length)
   - Select (Mirror Element)

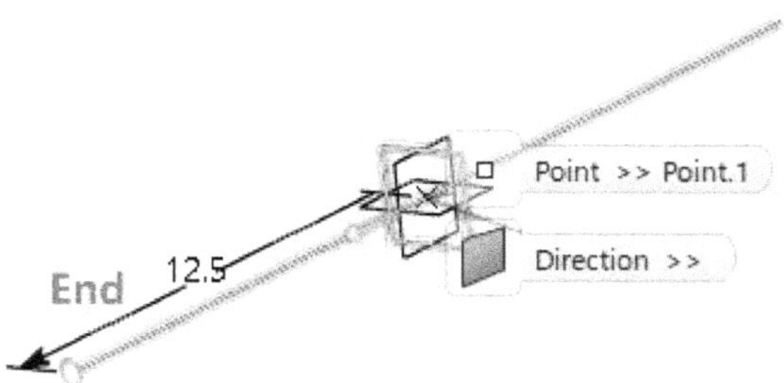

Figure 7–27

4. Click **OK** to complete the line.
5. Create another reference line by entering the information shown in Figure 7–28. If required, click (Reverse Direction) to create the line in the orientation shown in Figure 7–28.

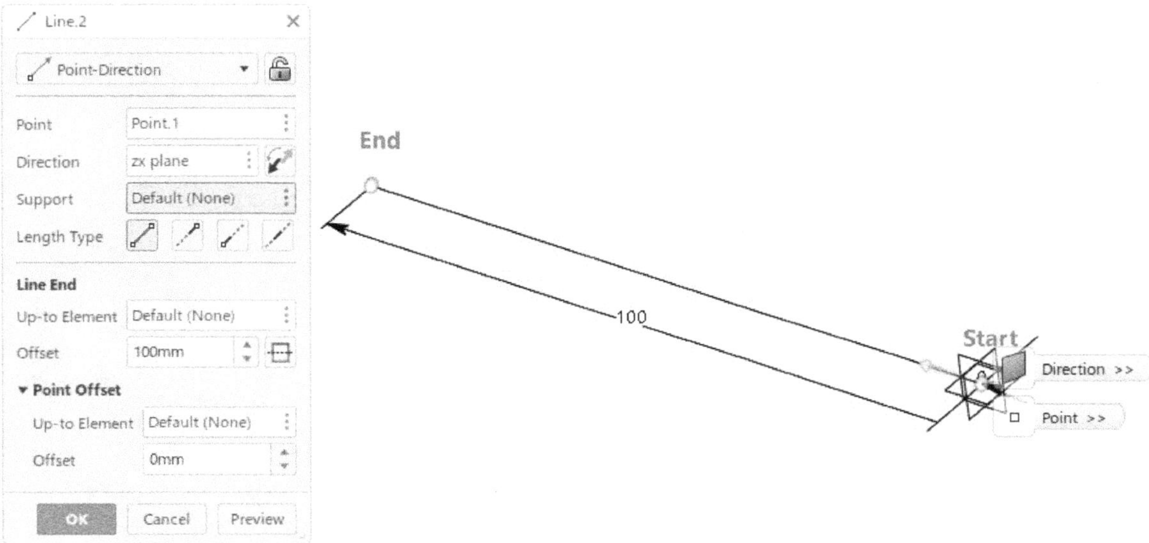

Figure 7–28

6. Create a reference plane as shown in Figure 7–29. The *Angle* is a negative value.

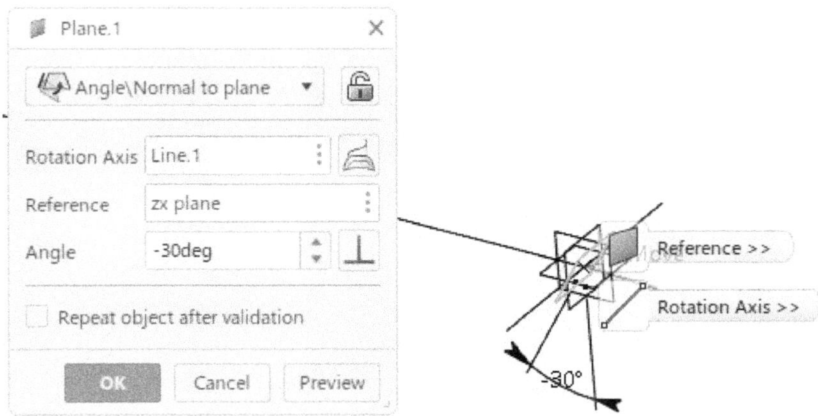

Figure 7–29

7. Create a third reference line as shown in Figure 7–30.

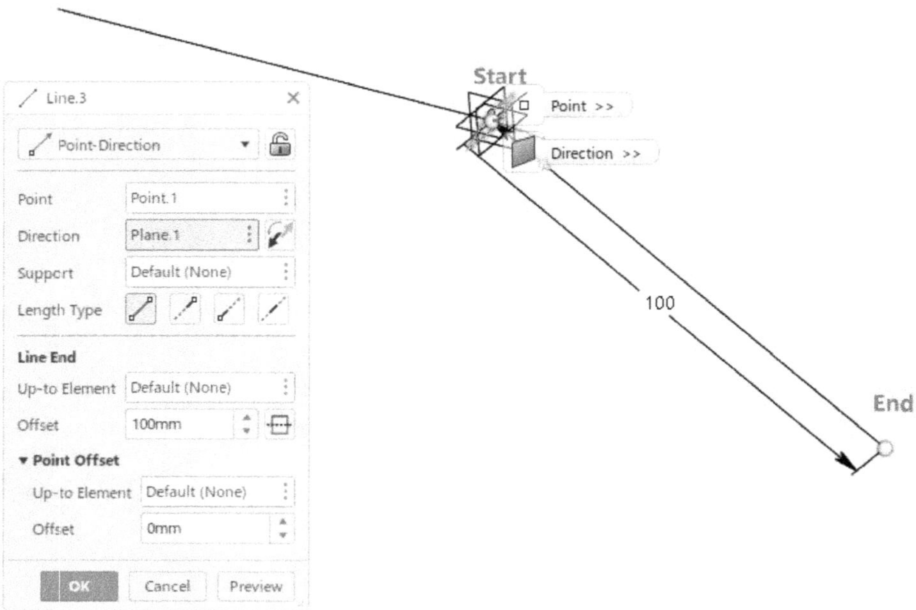

Figure 7–30

8. Rename *Line.2* as **OutputCenterLine** and *Line.3* as **InputCenterLine**, as shown in Figure 7–31.

Note: *Press <Alt>+<Enter> to open the Properties dialog box for a selected feature.*

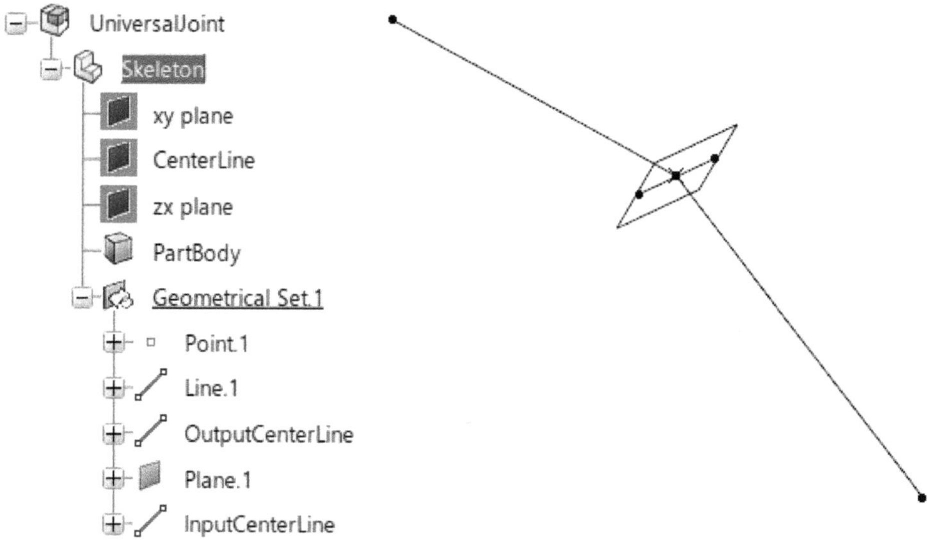

Figure 7–31

9. Hide the four reference planes and **Line.1**, as shown in Figure 7–32.

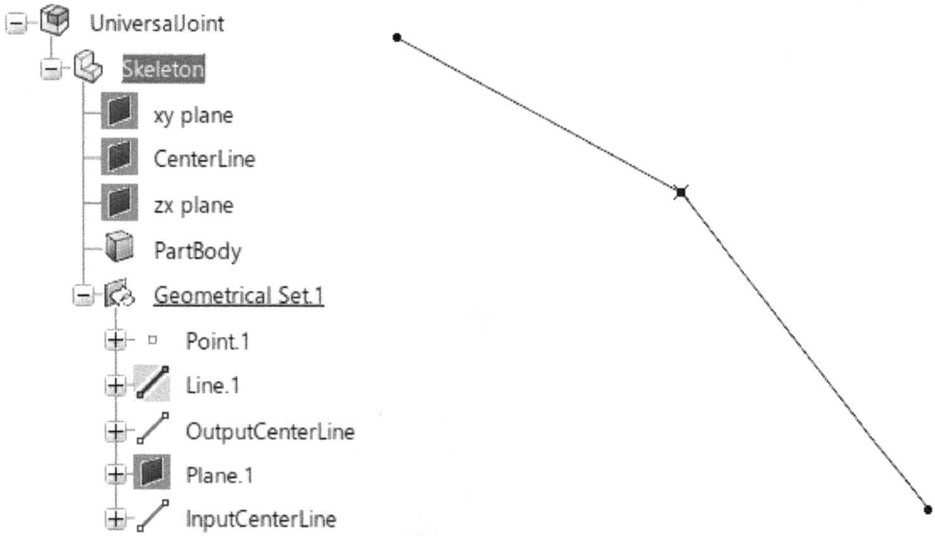

Figure 7–32

10. Save the product but leave the tab open.

Task 4: Assemble components to the skeleton.

1. Activate the **UniversalJoint** product.
2. Assemble the **1742** (Output Shaft) part from the *Bookmarks app - Skeleton_Models* tab. Use the Robot to reposition the part, as shown in Figure 7–33.

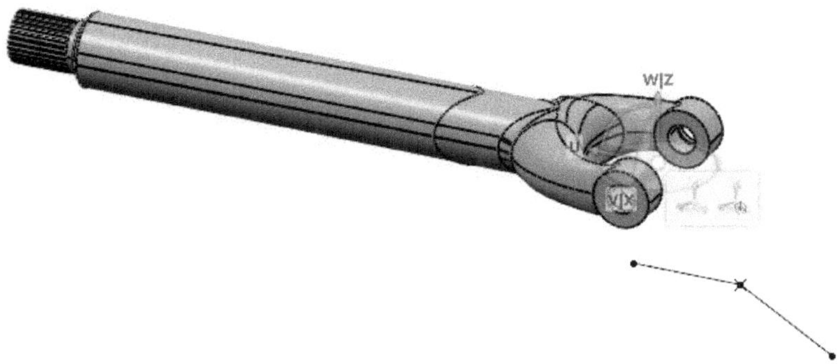

Figure 7–33

3. Create a **Cylindrical** engineering connection by applying a **Coincident** constraint between:
    - *OutputShaft:* (implicit axis)
    - *Skeleton:* **OutputCenterLine**

    Ensure that you zoom in on the area shown in Figure 7–34 to be able to select the implicit axis.

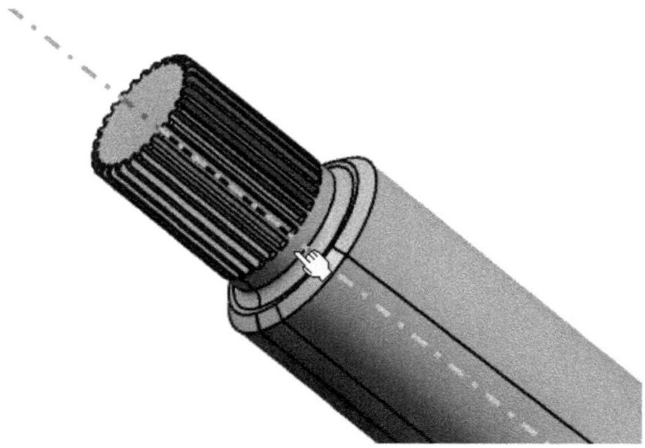

Figure 7–34

4. In the *Undefined Interference Specifications* dialog box, click **No**.
5. Assemble the **1652** (Spider) part from the *Bookmarks app - Skeleton_Models* tab.

6. In the specification tree, expand **Skeleton** and **1652** (Spider), as shown in Figure 7–35.

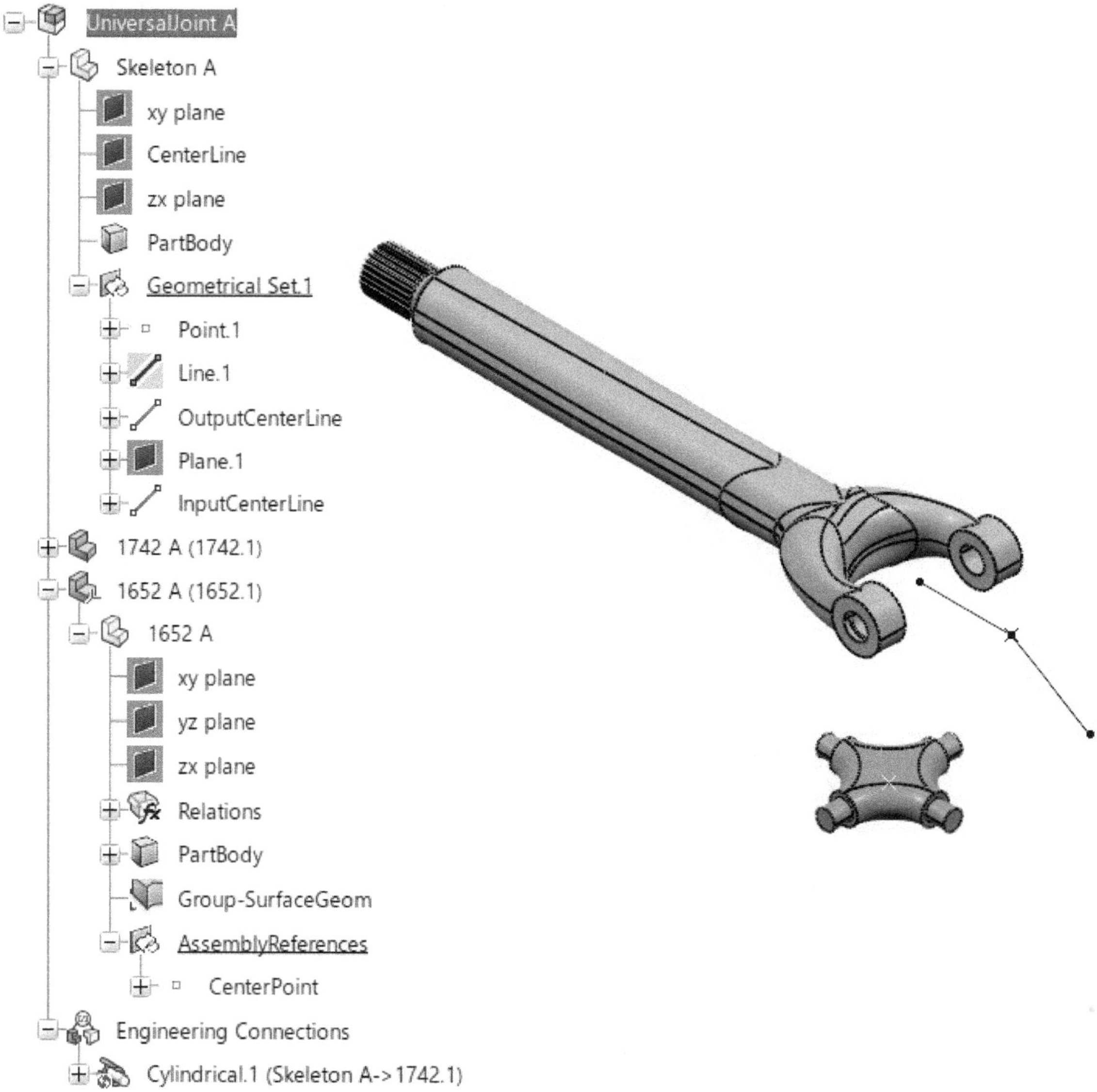

Figure 7–35

7. Create a **Spherical** engineering connection by applying a **Coincident** constraint between:
   - *1652:* **CenterPoint**
   - *Skeleton:* **Point.1**

   Select these references in the specification tree.
8. In the *Undefined Interference Specifications* dialog box, click **No**.

9. Click  (Update) to update the assembly.
10. Create a **Cylindrical** engineering connection by applying a **Coincident** constraint between:
    - *OutputShaft:* (implicit axis)
    - *Spider:* (implicit axis)

    Refer to Figure 7–36.

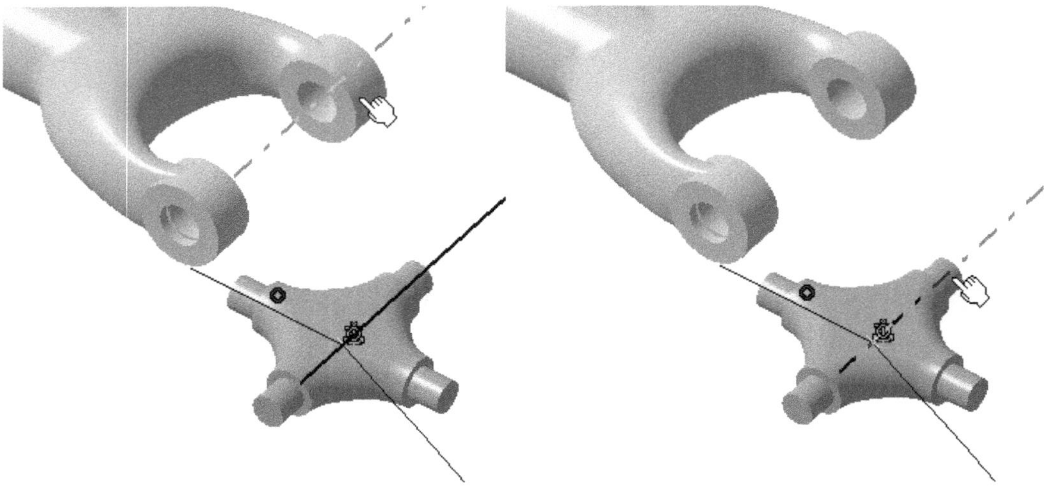

Figure 7–36

11. In the *Undefined Interference Specifications* dialog box, click **No**.
12. Click  (Update) to update the assembly. It displays as shown in Figure 7–37.

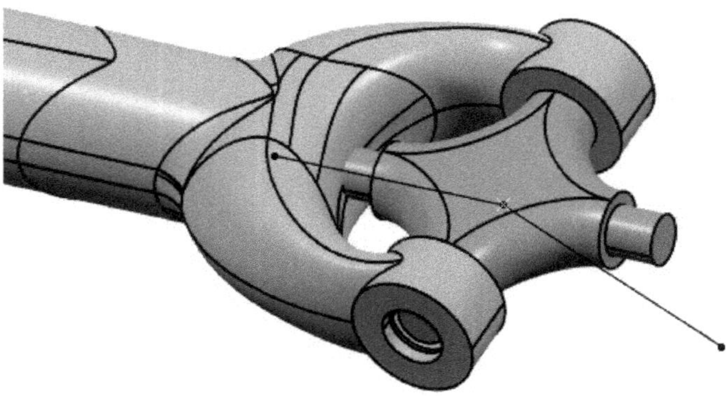

Figure 7–37

13. Assemble the **1741** (Input Shaft) part from the *Bookmarks app - Skeleton_Models* tab. Position the part as shown in Figure 7–38.

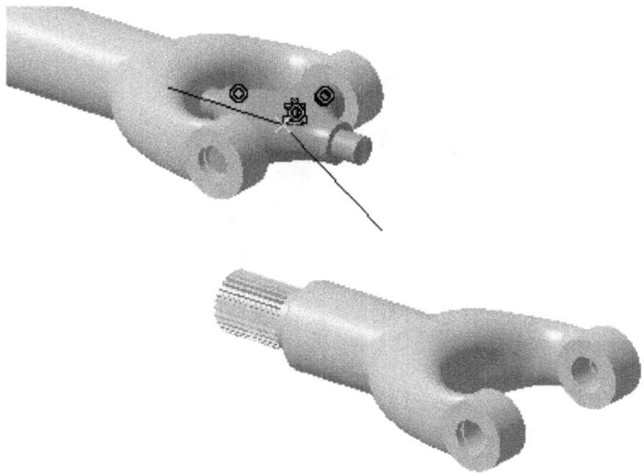

Figure 7–38

14. Create a **Cylindrical** engineering connection by applying a **Coincident** constraint between:
    - *InputShaft:* (implicit axis)
    - *Spider:* (implicit axis)

    Select the implicit axis shown in Figure 7–39.

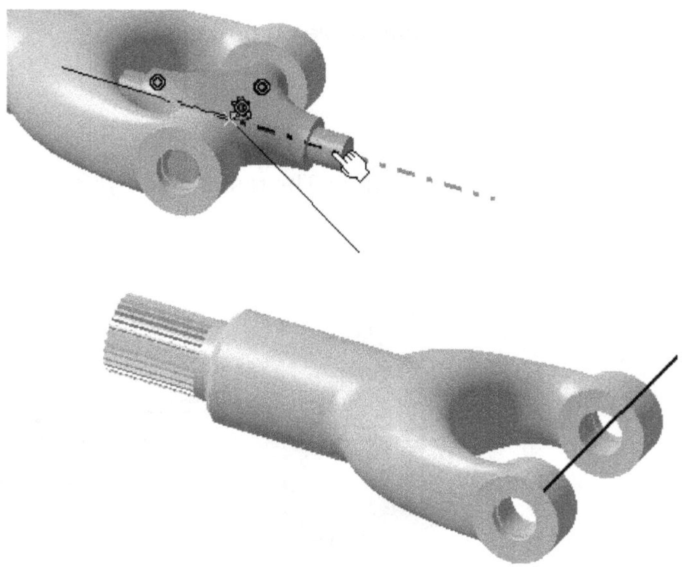

Figure 7–39

15. In the *Undefined Interference Specifications* dialog box, click **No**.

16. Create a **Cylindrical** engineering connection by applying a **Coincident** constraint between:
    - *InputShaft:* (implicit axis)
    - *Skeleton:* **InputCenterLine**

    Select the implicit axis shown in Figure 7–40.

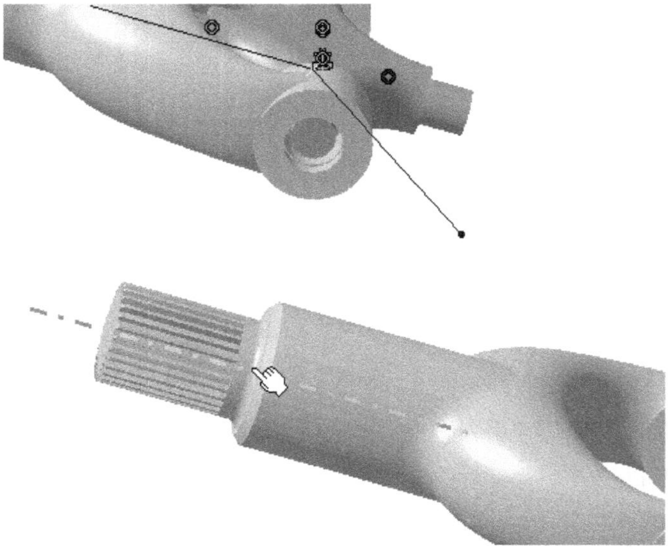

Figure 7–40

17. In the *Undefined Interference Specifications* dialog box, click **No**.

Task 5: Manipulate the assembly.

1. Click (Update) to updated the assembly. The result displays as shown in Figure 7–41.

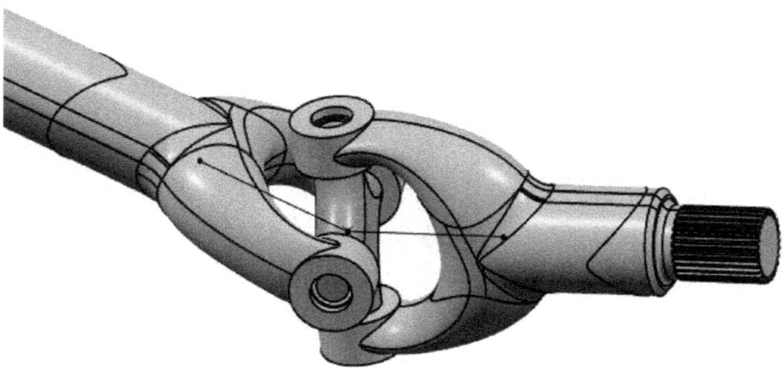

Figure 7–41

2. In the *Assembly* section of the Action Bar, click (Manipulate). The *Manipulation* toolbar displays, as shown in Figure 7–42.

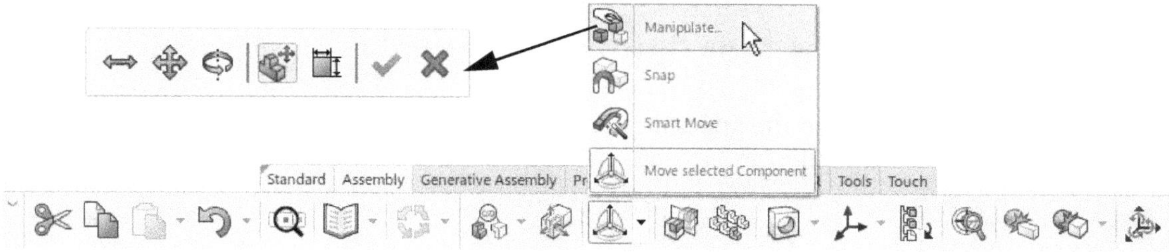

Figure 7–42

3. Click (Rotate) and select the implicit axis, as shown in Figure 7–43.

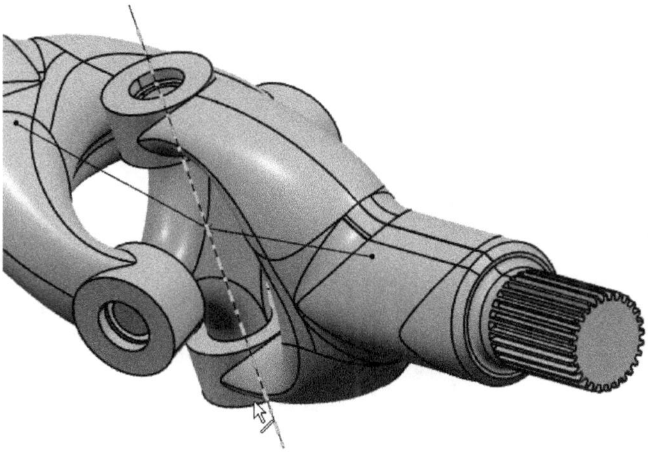

Figure 7–43

4. Select the **Input Shaft**, hold the mouse button, and drag the part to the location shown in Figure 7–44.

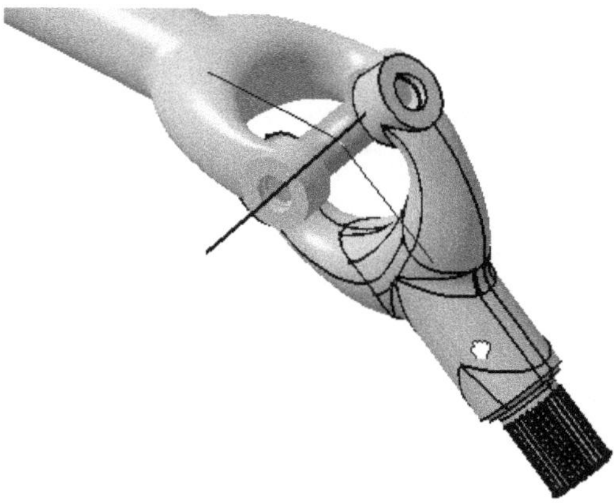

Figure 7–44

5. Click (Apply positions).
6. Click (Update) to update the assembly.
7. Another way to manipulate the assembly is to adjust the values of the reference elements in the Skeleton part file. In the specification tree, double-click on **Plane.1** twice, as shown in Figure 7–45. This enables you to edit the feature.

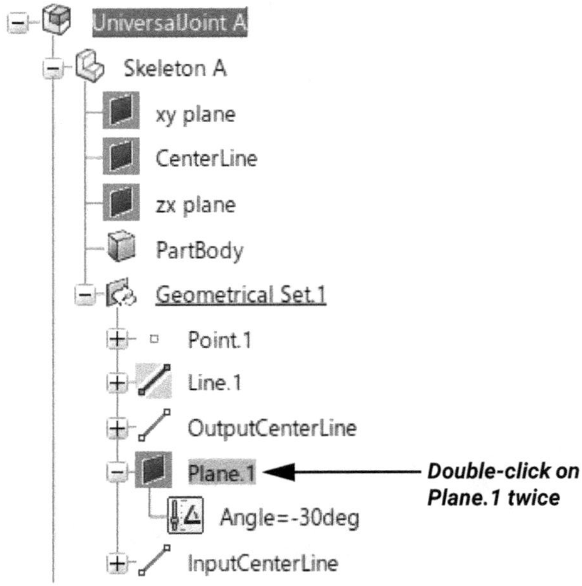

Figure 7–45

8. Set the *angle value* to **33 deg**.
9. Click **OK**.

10. In the specification tree, double-click on **UniversalJoint**, as shown in Figure 7–46. By doing so, you are sent back to the **Assembly Design** app.

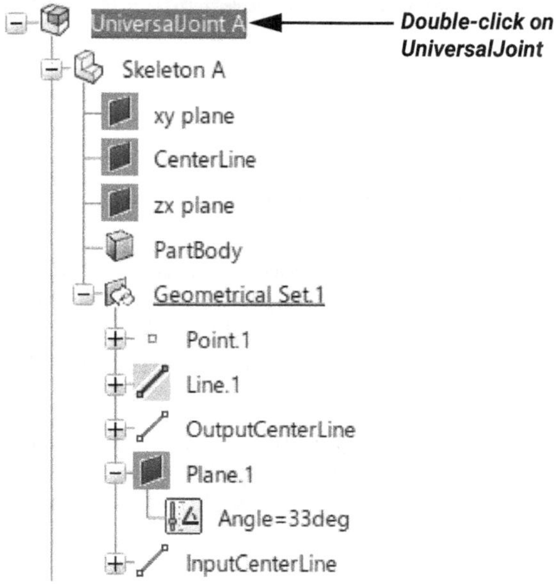

Figure 7–46

11. Click  (Update) to update the assembly. It displays as shown in Figure 7–47. The parts update based on the new **Plane.1** angle.

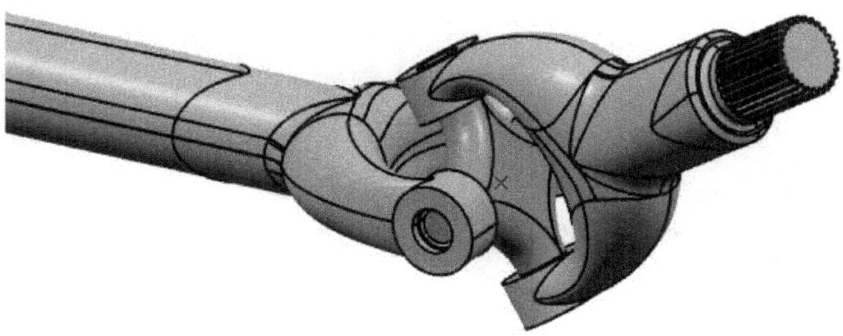

Figure 7–47

12. Save the assembly and close all tabs.

End of practice

Practice 7b
Design with Publications

Practice Objectives

- Publish a surface.
- Publish a parameter.
- Replace a publication with an updated feature.

In this practice, you will develop a frame component for the fuselage of an aircraft. The exterior skin of the aircraft has been defined by the Analysis team and will be used to control the shape of the frame component. This skin has been placed in a skeleton model along with some parameter information. To externally reference this information, the surface and a parameter will be published.

These publications will be used to develop a split and shell feature in the frame component. When the frame geometry has been defined, the published surface will be updated with a new exterior skin surface. The completed component is shown in Figure 7–48.

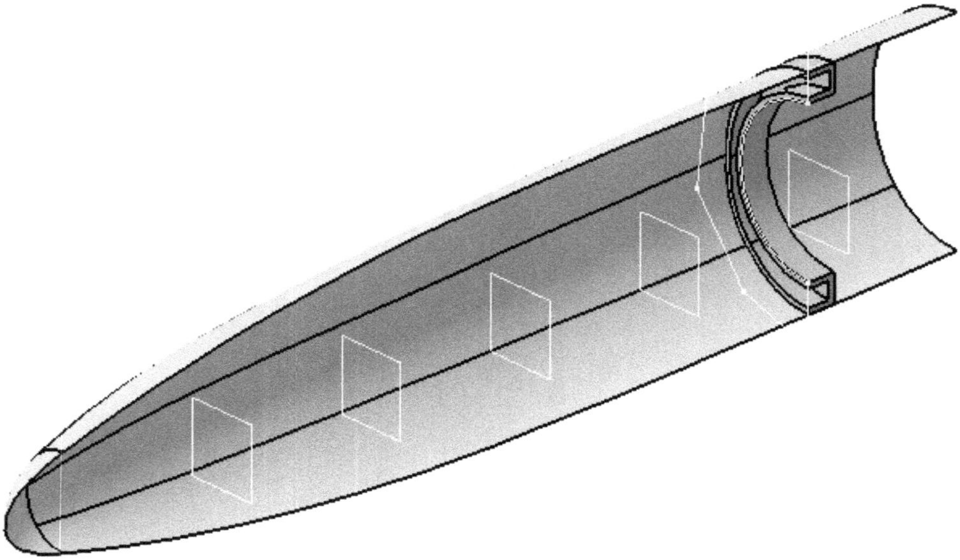

Figure 7–48

Task 1: Open ML_REF.3dxml.

In this task, you will open the skeleton model and investigate the wireframe, sketched and surface geometry, and parameter that have been developed.

1. Import **ML_REF.3dxml**.
2. In the specification tree, right-click on **ML_REF** and select **Open**.
3. Close the *ML_REF (Explore)* tab.
4. Orient the skeleton part as shown in Figure 7–49.

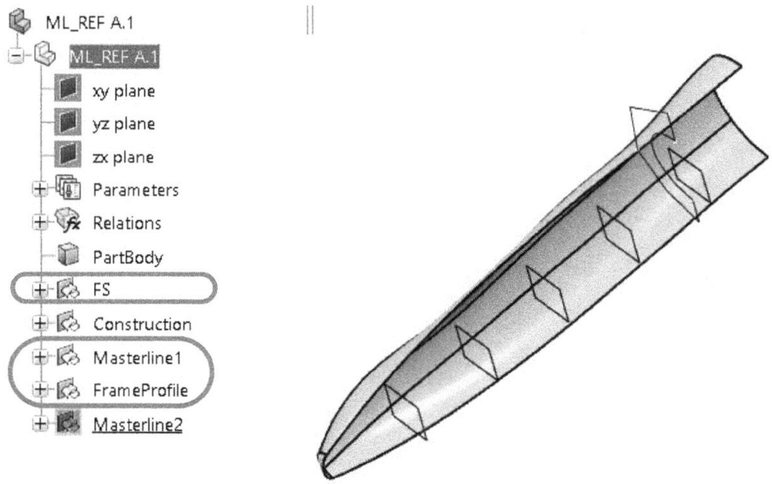

Figure 7–49

5. Investigate the geometry that resides in the skeleton part. This geometry is as follows:

Object	Description
Parameters	A **ShellThickness** parameter has been defined to control the thickness of each frame component.
FS	The geometrical set contains a reference plane to locate each of the frame components in the assembly.
Masterline1	The geometrical set contains the exterior skin surface that is used to trim the frame components.
FrameProfile	The geometrical set contains the profile for the frame component.

Task 2: Publish the Masterline surface.

In this task, you will publish the Masterline surface. This surface will be used to trim the frame components in the assembly to ensure that they always conform to the interior skin of the fuselage.

1. In the specification tree, double-click on the top-level product to activate it.
2. In the *Product Modification* section of the Action Bar, click  (Create a Publication). Select the **Masterline_Nov01** datum surface in the **Masterline1** geometrical set. The *Publication* dialog box opens, as shown in Figure 7–50.

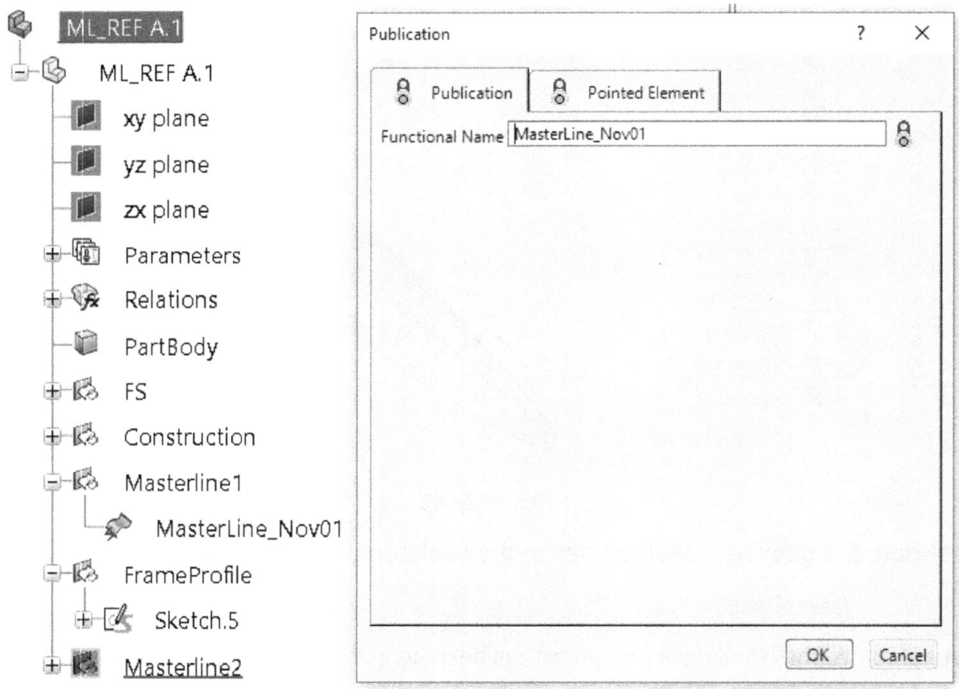

Figure 7–50

3. Edit the *Functional Name* to **MasterLineSurf**.

4. Click **OK**. The published element displays in a new *Publications* branch in the specification tree, as shown in Figure 7–51.

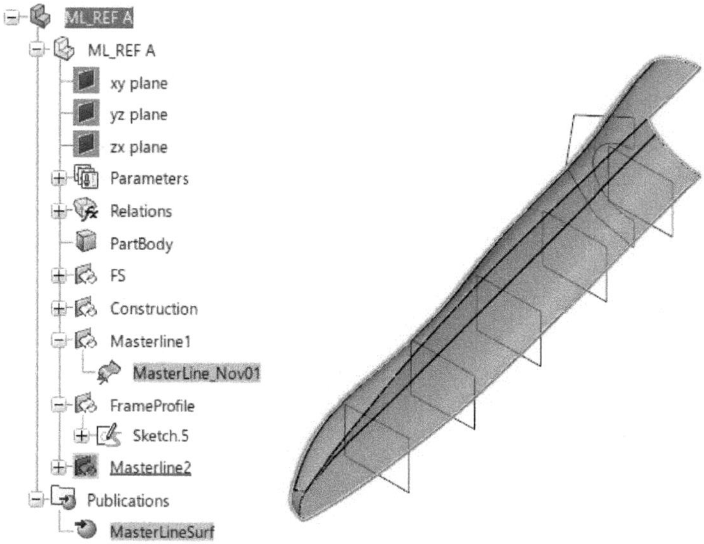

Figure 7–51

Task 3: Publish a reference plane and a sketch.

1. In the **FrameProfile** geometrical set, select **Sketch.5**.

2. Click  (Create a Publication).

3. Edit the *Functional Name* to **FrameProfile** and click **OK**. The sketch is published, as shown in Figure 7–52.

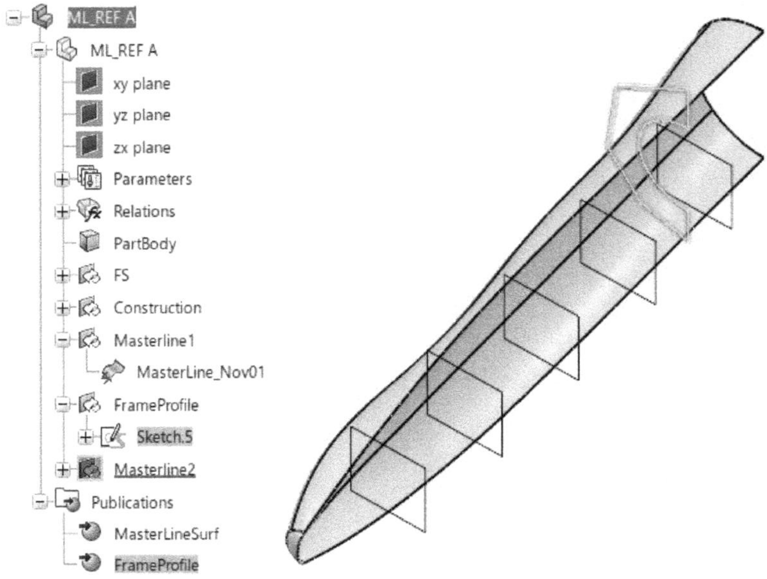

Figure 7–52

4. Publish the **Frame5** reference plane in the **FS** geometrical set. Leave the *Functional Name* as **Frame5** and click **OK**. The publication is added, as shown in Figure 7–53.

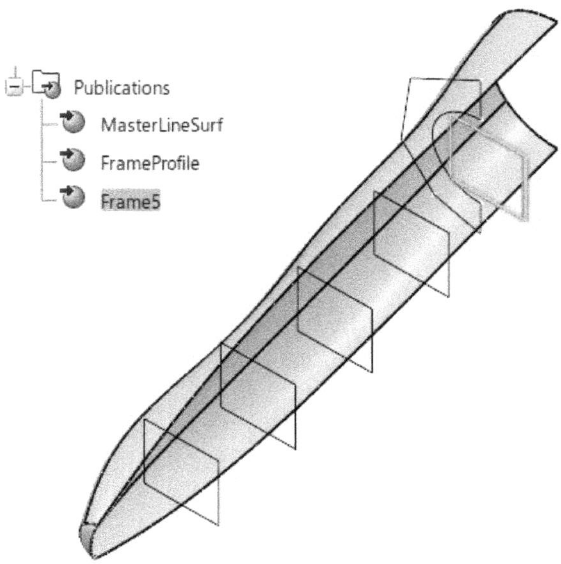

Figure 7–53

Task 4: Publish a parameter.

1. Click (Create a Publication).
2. Expand *Parameters* and select **ShellThickness**. The *Publication* dialog box opens, as shown in Figure 7–54.

Figure 7–54

3. Click **OK** to publish the **ShellThickness** parameter.

Task 5: Create a new product and assemble the skeleton.

1. In the Top Bar, select (Add/Create)>**Physical Product**.
2. In the *Physical Product* dialog box, type ***Your_Initials*_Fuselage** in the *Title* field.
3. Click **OK**.
4. Insert **ML_REF** and apply a **Fix in Space** engineering connection to the component in the assembly.

Task 6: Create a frame component.

1. Right-click on **Fuselage** and select **Insert>3D Part**.
2. For the *Title* on both the *3D Part* and *3D Shape* tabs, enter ***Your_Initials_*Frame5**.
3. Click **OK**.
4. Fix (Fix in Space) the new part so it is assembled at the origin of the assembly. The specification tree displays as shown in Figure 7–55.

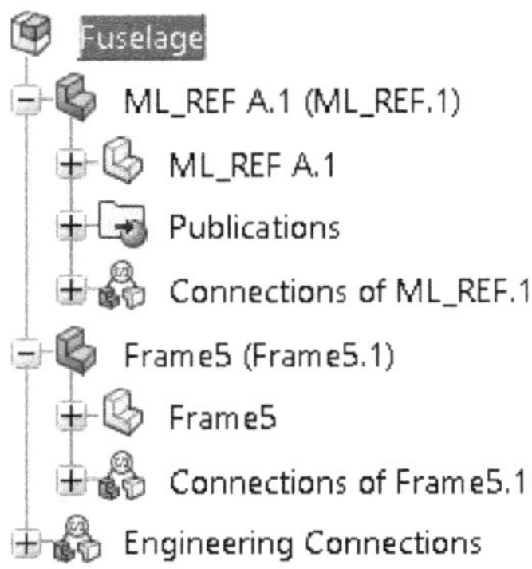

Figure 7–55

Task 7: Set options for contextual design.

1. Select **Me>Preferences>Common Preferences>Object Properties>3D Shape>Infrastructure**.
2. Expand the *General* section, if needed.
3. Enable the following options, as shown in Figure 7–56:
   - **Keep link with selected object**
   - **Restrict external selection with link to published elements**

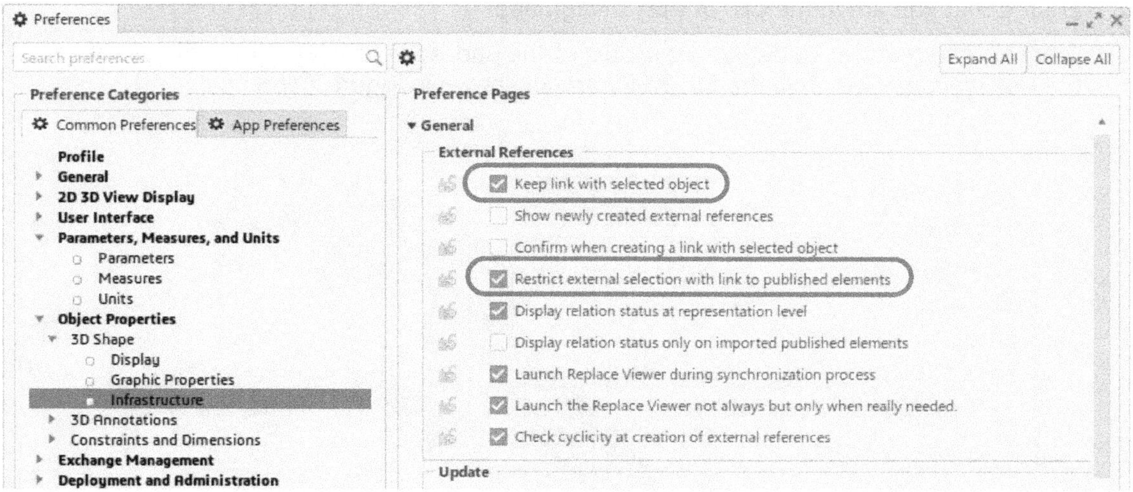

Figure 7–56

4. Click **OK**.

Task 8: Perform contextual design.

In this task, you will develop the geometry for the **Frame5** component. The part will be developed by creating a pad that references the published sketch. Next, the part will be trimmed to the published surface. Finally, a shell feature will be used to complete the geometry.

1. In the specification tree, expand **Frame5** and activate the part, as shown in Figure 7–57.

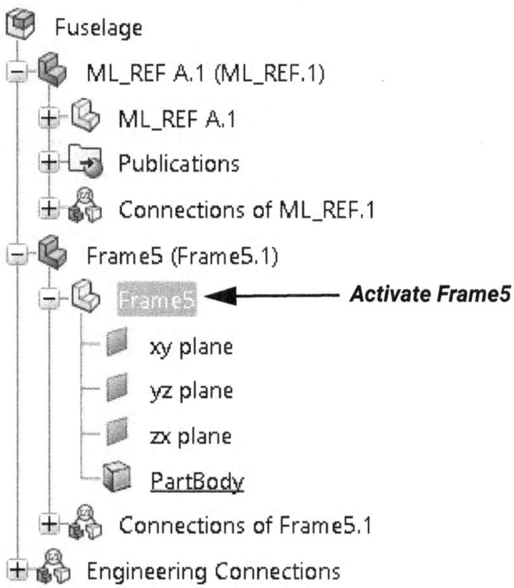

Figure 7–57

2. Ensure that you are in the **CATIA Part Design** app.
3. Create a pad feature. To define the profile of the pad, select the **FrameProfile** element in the *Publications* branch in the **ML_REF** part, as shown in Figure 7–58.

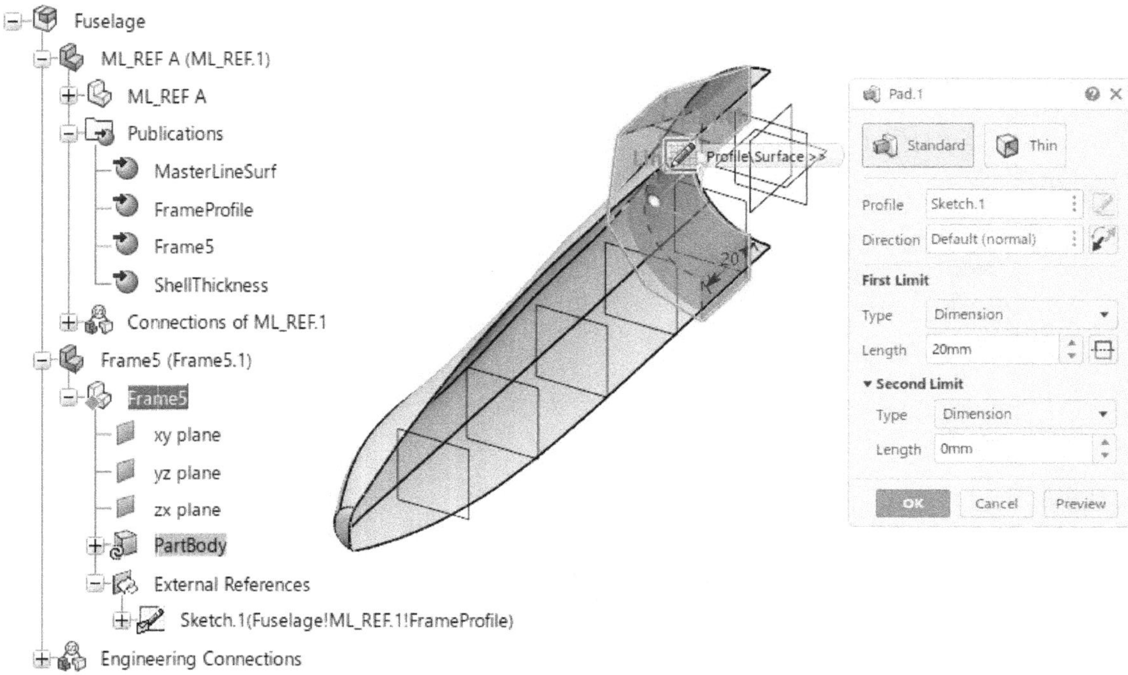

Figure 7–58

Design Considerations

When selecting an element from another model, the system will add an *External References* branch to the specification tree that contains the link to the referenced element. In this case, the system has locally named the element **Sketch.1**. This sketch is an associative link to the **FrameProfile** publication.

4. Enter a *length* of **5mm** and complete the feature. The model displays, as shown in Figure 7–59.

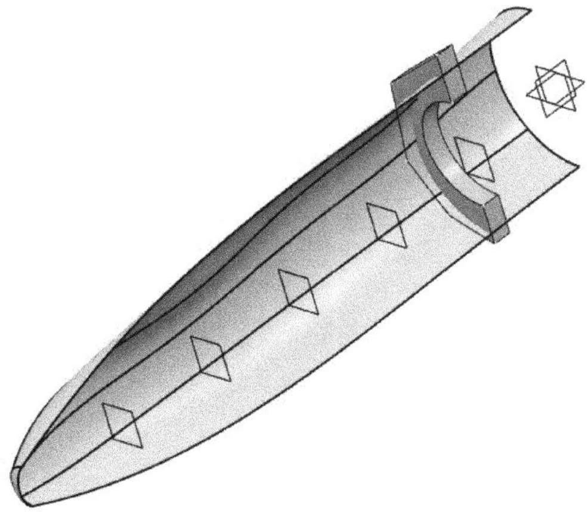

Figure 7–59

5. In the *Transform* section of the Action Bar, click  (Split). This feature will use the **Masterline** surface to trim away geometry from **Frame5**. The *Split* dialog box opens, as shown in Figure 7–60.

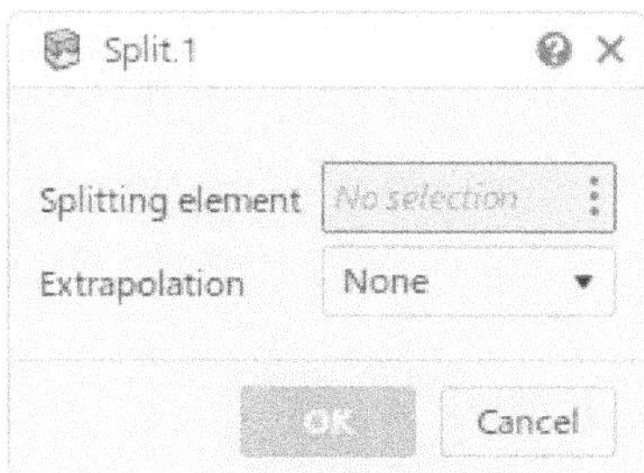

Figure 7–60

6. Select the **MasterlineSurf** publication.

7. Arrows display on the model, indicating the direction of material to keep. Ensure that the arrows point toward the center of the model, as shown in Figure 7–61.

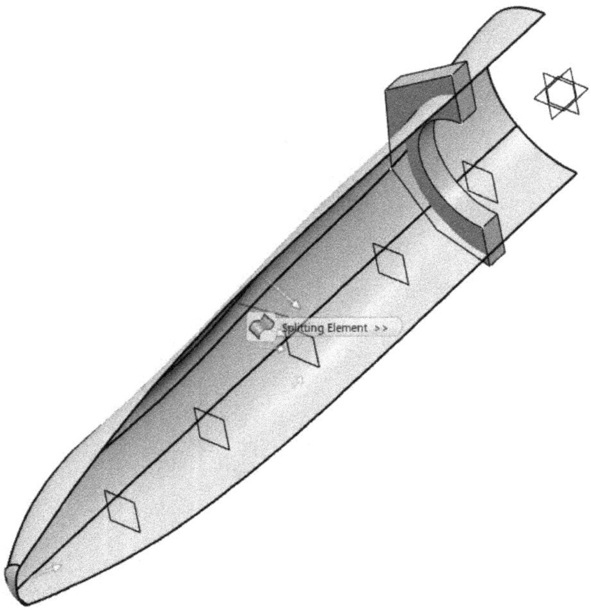

Figure 7–61

8. Click **OK** to complete the operation. The assembly displays, as shown in Figure 7–62.

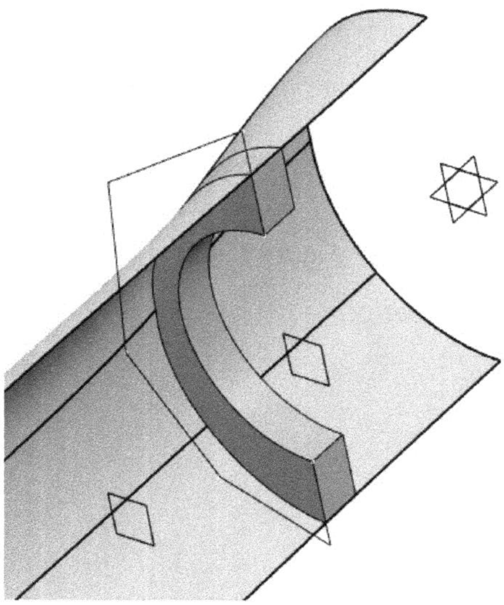

Figure 7–62

9. Create a shell feature with an inside thickness of 1mm that removes three faces to create the geometry shown in Figure 7–63.

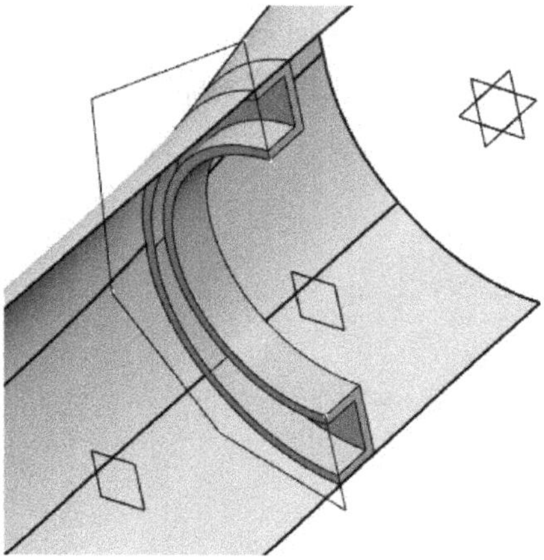

Figure 7–63

Task 9: Modify a publication.

In this task, you will modify the **MasterLineSurf** publication to reference an updated version of the surface from the design team.

1. Activate the **ML_REF** component.
2. Show the **Masterline2** geometrical set. It contains a second datum surface, as shown in Figure 7–64. This new surface must be used to create the frame components in the Fuselage assembly.

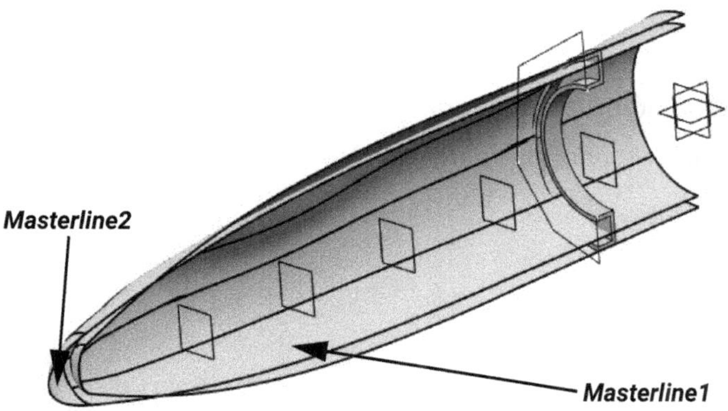

Figure 7–64

3. In the **Masterline01** geometrical set, hide the **MasterLine_Nov01** surface.
4. Activate the **Fuselage** product.

5. In the *Product Modification* section of the Action Bar, click  (Edit Publication Properties).
6. In the specification tree, select the **MasterLineSurf** element.
7. In the *Properties* dialog box, select the *Published Element* tab, as shown in Figure 7–65.

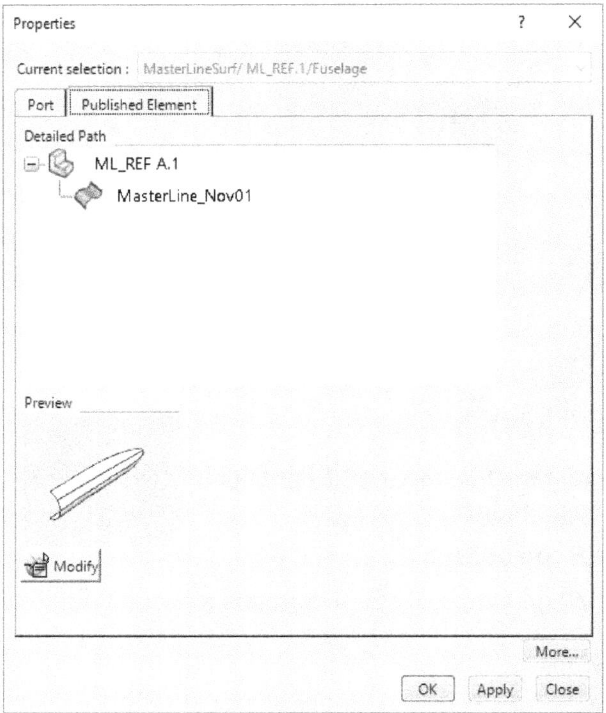

Figure 7–65

8. Click  (Modify) and select **Masterline_Nov23** from the **Masterline2** set.
9. Click **OK** to close the *Properties* dialog box.

10. Activate the **Fuselage** assembly and update the model. The assembly displays, as shown in Figure 7–66.

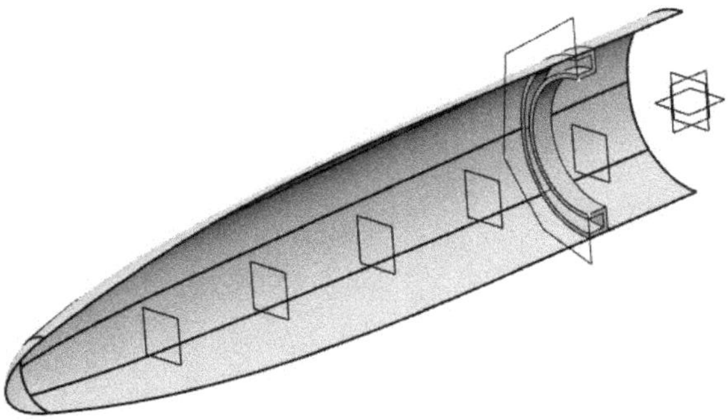

Figure 7–66

Note that the size of the Frame5 part has changed to fit within the newly published surface. The shell in that part also updated to fit the changes.

11. Save the objects and close all tabs.

End of practice

Chapter 8

Working with Assemblies

This chapter introduces the methods used to create, investigate, maintain, and remove links between assembly components.

Learning Objectives

- Understand how to manage links between components that are established when existing geometry from one component is used to help build another.
- Review the symbols used in the specification tree to indicate referenced geometry.
- Learn how to manage external links.
- Learn how to create assembly-level features.

8.1 Contextual Design

Contextual design is the process of creating part geometry in the context of an assembly model, rather than building parts separately on their own. This provides the advantage of being able to reference the geometry of other part and assembly models while developing geometry for the active part. Contextual design is the mechanism through which skeleton geometry can be used throughout the assembly.

When designing parts in context, you must be aware of any external references being created. An external reference can be created when a reference outside the active part is selected.

When you select geometry from Part A to create a feature in Part B, a dependency is generated. The feature in Part B cannot be modified or updated unless Part A is present. Therefore, it is important to only generate external references when they are required to drive the design intent of the model.

An external reference can be created in the following cases:

- Selecting a support
- Creating geometrical constraints
- Creating dimensional constraints
- Specifying a depth option requiring a selection
- Projecting 3D or silhouette edges

General Steps

Use the following general steps to create components in context:

1. Set external reference options.
2. (Optional) Publish elements.
3. Activate or create a part file.
4. Develop geometry in the context of the assembly.
5. Save the part.

Step 1 - Set external reference options.

Select **Me>Preferences>Common Preferences>Object Properties>3D Shape>Infrastructure**. Look for the *External References* category for the required options.

External Reference Settings

You can control how external references are created and handled. A company standard that requires everyone to use the same options is recommended to promote consistency.

To set external reference options, select **Me>Preferences>Common Preferences>Object Properties>3D Shape>Infrastructure**. Locate the *External References* area under the *General* section, as shown in Figure 8–1.

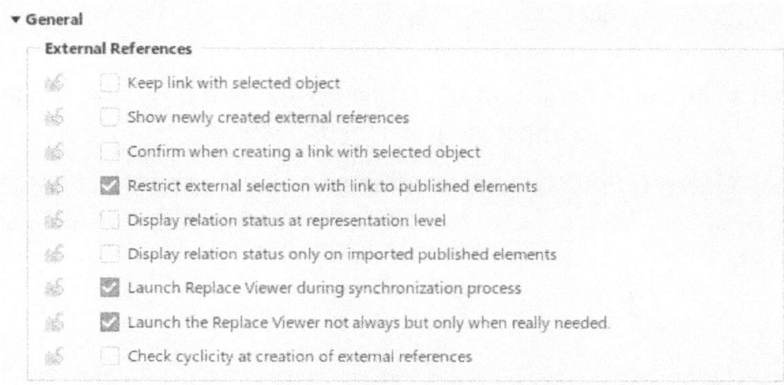

Figure 8–1

You can set the following options for external references:

- **Keep link with selected object:** Maintains a link between the source part and the target part. If this option is cleared, reference elements are copied to the target part as a geometrical set and do not associatively update.
- **Show newly created external references:** Displays external references that are created. If this option is cleared, external references are automatically hidden in the target part.
- **Confirm when creating a link with selected object:** Causes the *Selection In Context* warning dialog box to open, as shown in Figure 8–2.

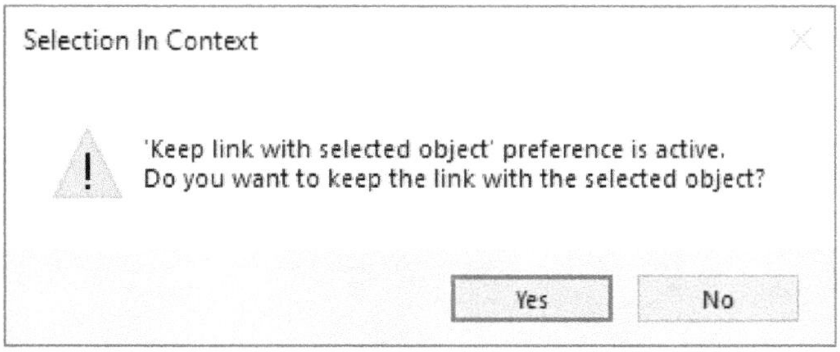

Figure 8–2

This dialog box indicates that a link is created when selecting an external reference. At this point, you can disable the **Keep link with selected object** option by clicking **No**.

- **Display relation status at representation level:** By enabling this option, an icon will appear at the representation level of the element displaying the current link status.

Icon	Description
	Reference object not loaded or synchronized
	Reference object loaded, but not synchronized
	Reference object deleted
	Reference object replaced by another version

- **Display relation status only on imported published elements:** Similar to the previous command, but only applies to imported published elements.
- **Launch Replace Viewer during synchronization process:** Enable the *Replace Viewer* (shown in Figure 8–3) to always be displayed when updating links or just when a change requires that items be reselected.

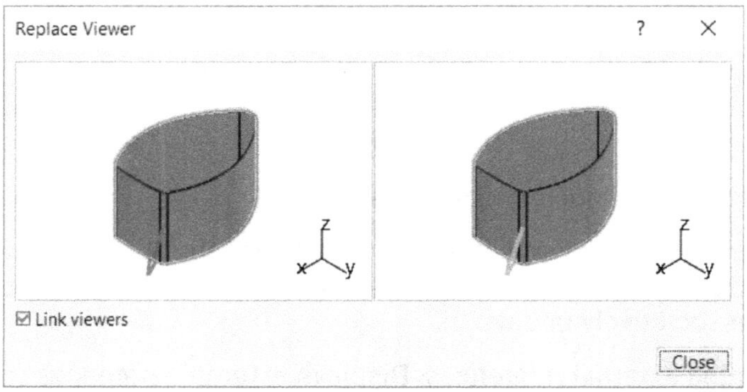

Figure 8–3

Update Settings

The *Update* area in the *General* section is shown in Figure 8–4. If the **Synchronize all external references when updating the 3D shape** option is selected, the system searches for any modifications to the source part and updates the target part accordingly. Selecting this option ensures that you are working with the latest version of the source part. However, this option also increases update time.

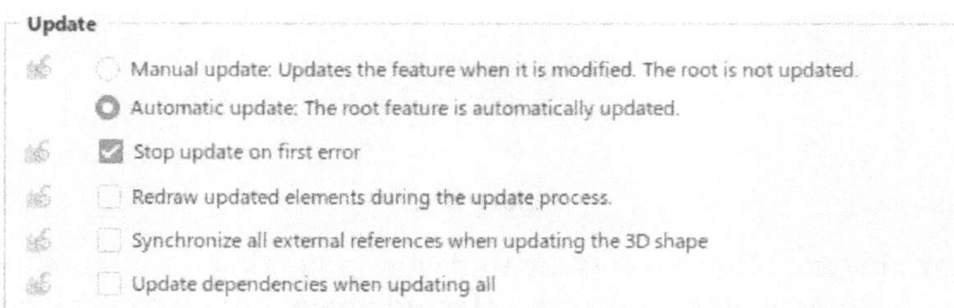

Figure 8–4

From the *Preference Categories* on the left, select **Object Properties>3D Shape**, then expand the *Display* section and select **External References** from the list of options, as shown in Figure 8–5. This will display the *External References* branch in the specification tree.

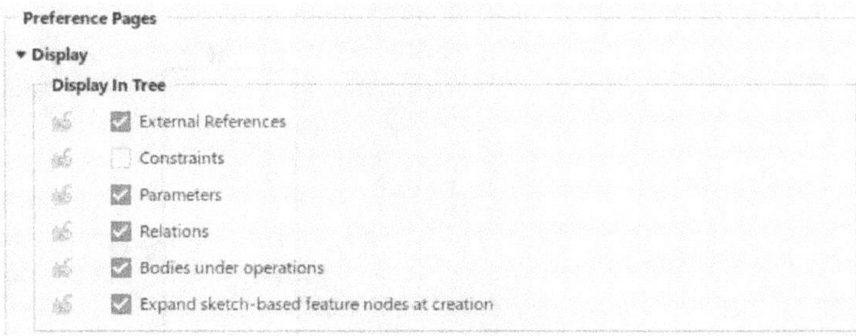

Figure 8–5

Step 2 - (Optional) Publish elements.

Publish elements of a component that you want to be used for external references.

Step 3 - Activate or create a part file.

Activate an existing part or click (Insert 3D Part) to create a part.

Step 4 - Develop geometry in the context of the assembly.

Once the part has been activated from the assembly, the system launches one of the part modeling apps (e.g., Part Design or Generative Shape Design), enabling you to use these modeling tools to add geometry to the active part.

When working in the context of a large assembly, it is a common practice to bring all of the required external references into the design part. Therefore, the part can be developed without needing to load the assembly.

For example, a sketch created in context is shown in Figure 8–6. The geometrical and dimensional constraints have been developed between the sketch and the surrounding geometry. With this sketch created in the assembly context, the part can now be opened in a separate window and completed.

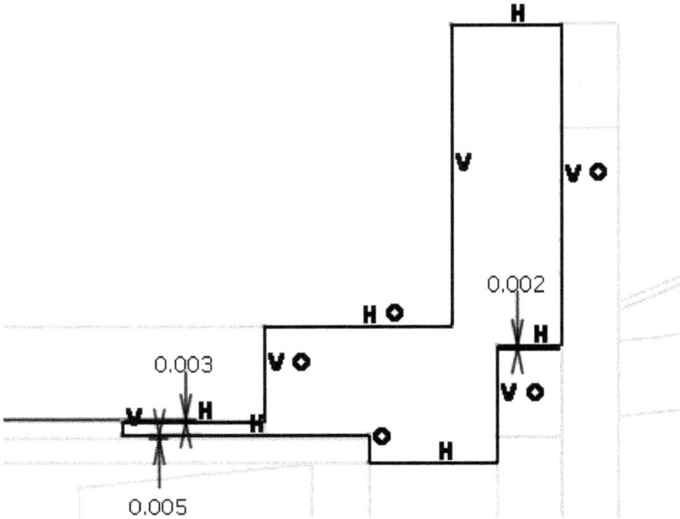

Figure 8–6

Step 5 - Save the part.

Once the external reference information is captured, enter a *3D Shape Title* and a *3D Part Title* if the part is new, and save it with a descriptive name.

Open the part in the **Part Design** app and create geometry to complete the design.

8.2 Link Management

Links between components are established when existing geometry from one component is used to help build another. Referencing geometry in one model to build new features in another can be an effective way of ensuring that geometry in several models is correct when changes are made. Preserving links between the original geometry and the copy enables multiple parts to be updated by modifying a single part.

An external reference can be created when referencing geometry in another component for the following reasons:

- Selecting a sketch support.
- Creating geometrical and dimensional constraints.
- Specifying a depth option that requires a selection.
- Projecting and intersecting 3D or silhouette edges.
- Copying geometry using the **Paste Special** and **As Result With Link** options.

When an external reference is established, it creates an additional branch in the specification tree, as shown in Figure 8–7. If the external reference is pasted into an existing geometrical set, the *External References* branch is not created and the reference is placed in the geometrical set.

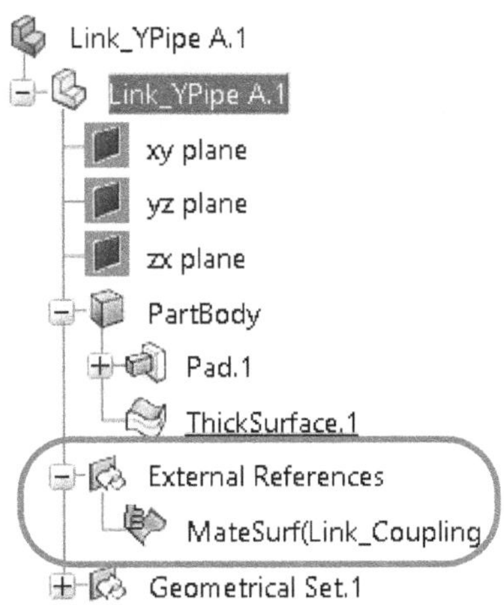

Figure 8–7

Carefully consider the use of external links. Links can create large file sizes and references to external documents. To modify linked geometry, the referenced file must be available and loaded into the 3DEXPERIENCE platform.

When creating external references, two types of links can be created: **Reference-Reference** and **Reference-Instance**.

Reference-Reference Links

A Reference-Reference link is created when geometry is copied from one part to another without the use of a product file. The geometry is pasted into the new part based on part origins and the instance positioning is lost. This method is convenient when instance positioning is not important or when a model has been designed using body coordinates, because these parts overlay with the same origin.

When pasting a published reference between parts in separate windows, the resulting feature name contains an exclamation mark, as shown in Figure 8–8. This can be used to determine that a Reference-Reference link has been defined.

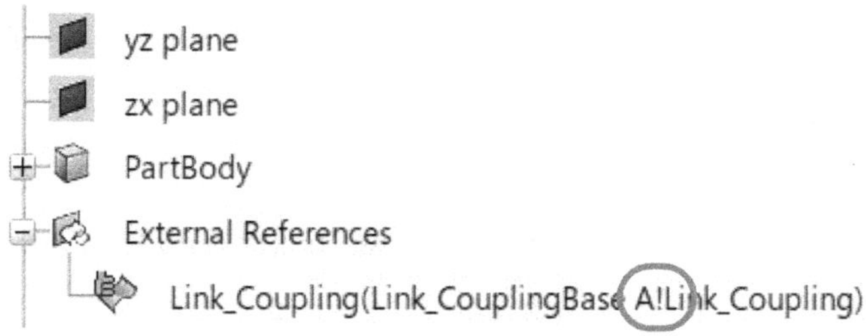

Figure 8–8

Reference-Instance Links

A Reference-Instance link is created when geometry is copied from one part to another in the context of an assembly. When copying geometry in an assembly, the instance positioning is maintained.

When pasting a published reference between parts in an assembly, the resulting feature name does not contain an exclamation mark.

8.3 Thumbnail Builder

The *Thumbnail Builder* is used to facilitate fast and easy exploration of large products, to view parts without expanding the specification tree, and to create images for search results.

To use the *Thumbnail Builder*, access the (ENOVIA Product Finder) app. In the app, you need to add (Thumbnail Builder) to the Action Bar or *Action Pad*. This can be done using the customize settings found when you expand preferences. Once added, you can select (Thumbnail Builder), which opens the *Thumbnail Builder* dialog box (shown in Figure 8–9).

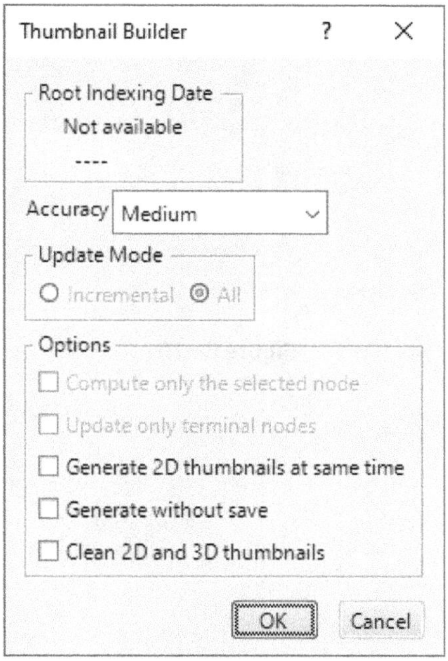

Figure 8–9

3D thumbnails are used to view the model on the turntable. 2D thumbnails are used to preview models during search. When you click **OK** in the *Thumbnail Builder*, the system generates thumbnails in the *Thumbnail Monitor*, as shown in Figure 8–10.

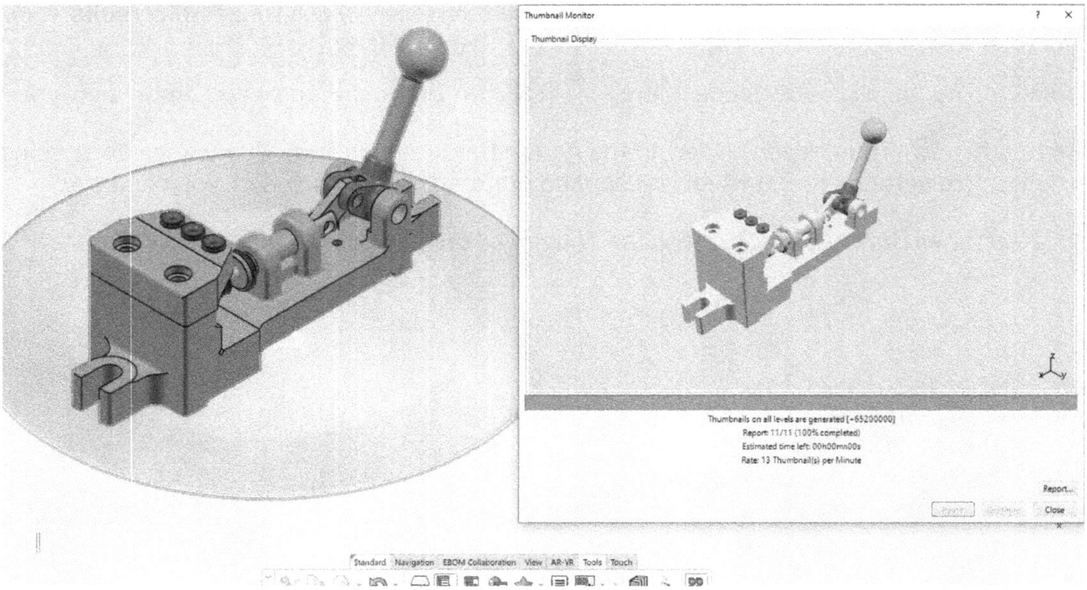

Figure 8–10

8.4 Loading Referenced Objects

Another tool that can be used to simplify the opening of large assemblies is **Open Advanced**, which allows for the selective opening of objects (with or without representations from the database).

When an assembly is opened in an Explore state, the objects are not fully loaded into memory, but are displayed on the turntable as thumbnails.

You can then use **Open Advanced**, as shown in Figure 8–11, to selectively bring objects into memory, thereby limiting the total memory used by your system. This is particularly helpful for large assemblies.

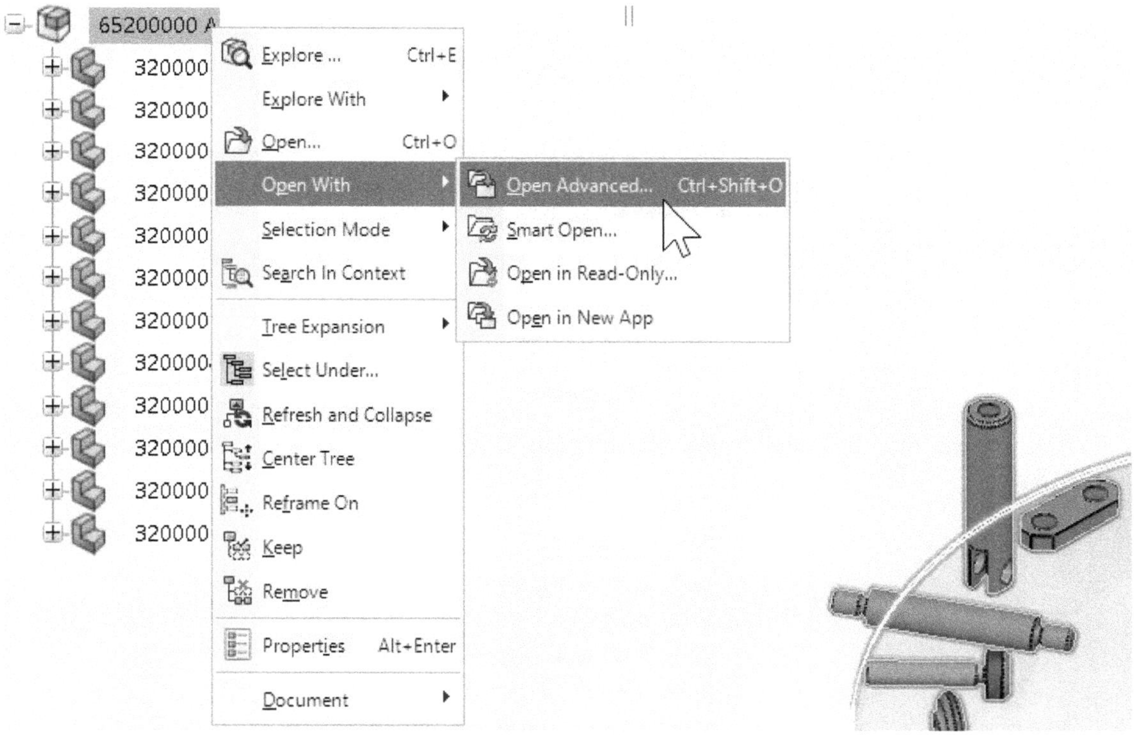

Figure 8–11

The *Open Advanced* dialog box opens. To open the assembly with only its tree structure and without loading any objects into memory, select the **Without any representation** option, as shown in Figure 8–12.

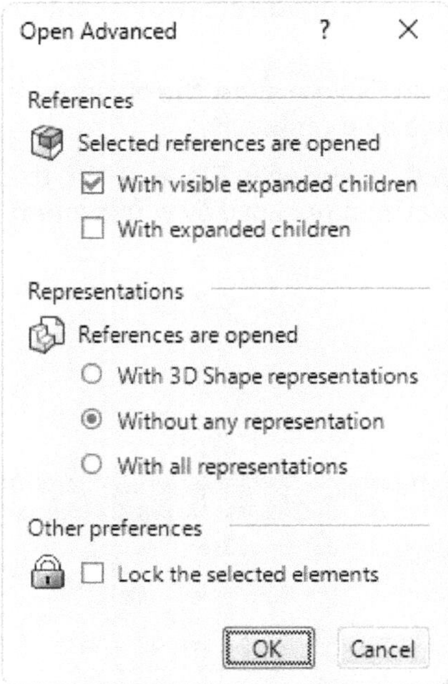

Figure 8–12

Click **OK**. The specification tree loads, showing the assembly structure, as shown in Figure 8–13.

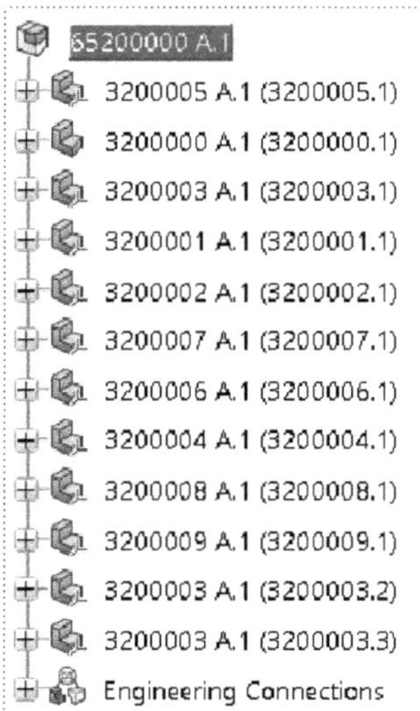

Figure 8–13

You can select the object or objects that you want to load from the tree, then in the *Tools* section of the Action Bar, click (Manage Representation). The *Manage Representations* dialog box opens. Select **Load all representations under selected objects**, as shown in Figure 8–14.

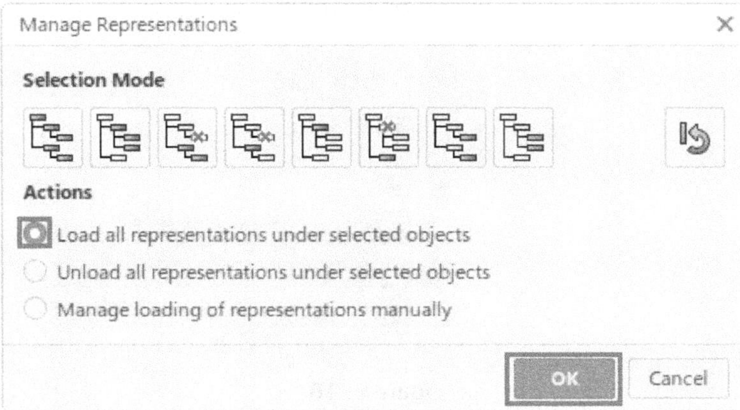

Figure 8–14

Click **OK**. The **Load** and the object are loaded, as shown in Figure 8–15.

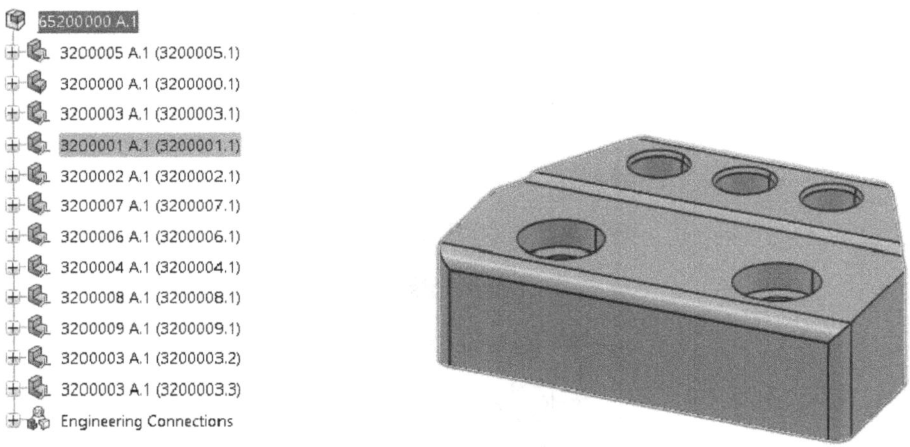

Figure 8–15

In the *Tools* section of the Action Bar, click (Unload) to remove the object from memory.

Using (Unload) reduces the amount of memory used by the system. You cannot use **Undo** for this option and instead must reload an object if you accidentally unload it.

8.5 Assembly Features

In CATIA V5, assembly features are based on the Part Design features and are accessed in the *Assembly Features* toolbar, as shown in Figure 8–16.

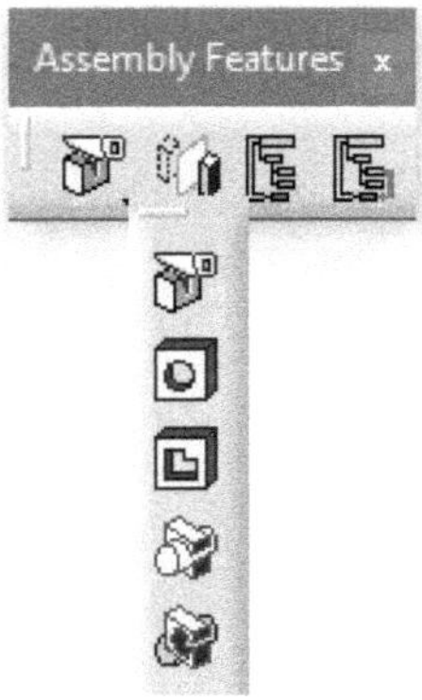

Figure 8–16

Assembly features are placed in a node at the end of the specification tree, as shown in Figure 8–17.

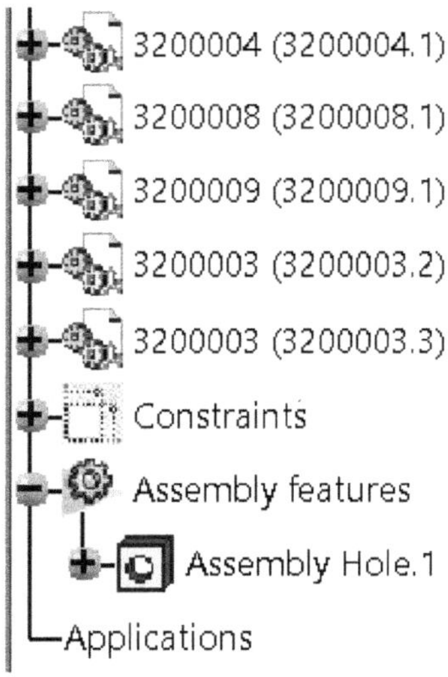

Figure 8–17

In 3DEXPERIENCE, assembly features are created using the options found in the *Assembly* section of the Action Bar, as shown in Figure 8–18.

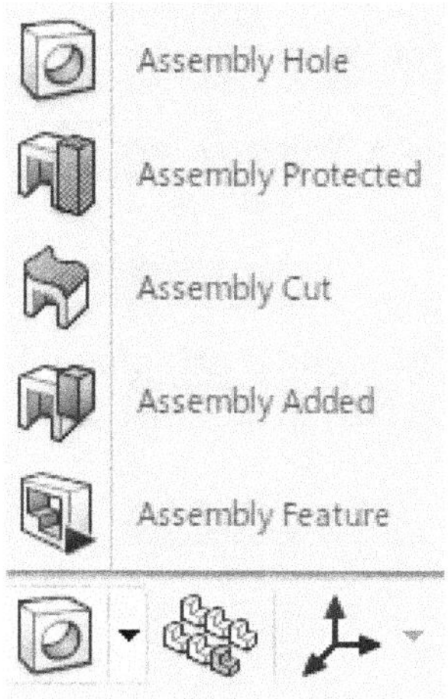

Figure 8–18

Assembly features are created as 3D shapes in the product, as shown in Figure 8–19.

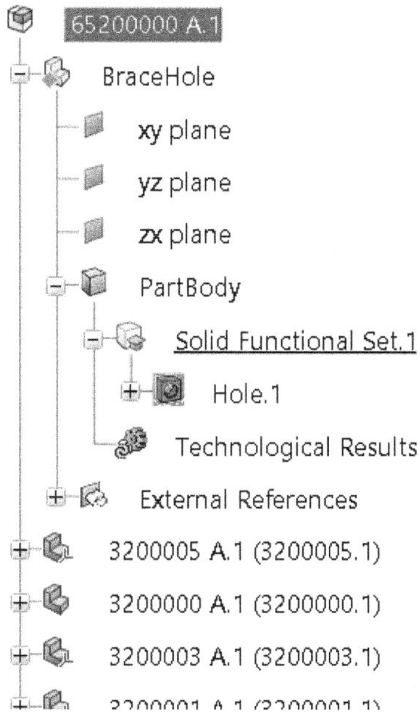

Figure 8–19

Creating an Assembly Hole Feature

Assembly hole features are created in a similar fashion to those created at the part level. The major difference is the selection of the parts the hole affects.

How To: Create an Assembly Hole Feature

1. In the *Assembly* section of the Action Bar, click (Assembly Hole).
2. In the *Choose a 3DShape* dialog box, either select an object from the assembly or click **Create new**, as shown in Figure 8–20.

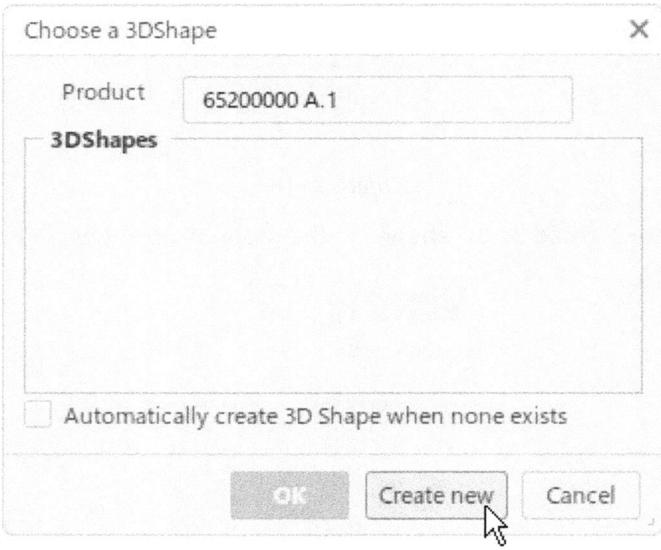

Figure 8–20

3. The *3D Shape* dialog box opens. Enter a title for the shape and click **OK**.
4. Select the surface on which to place the hole.

5. Specify the options in the *Hole* dialog box, as shown in Figure 8–21.

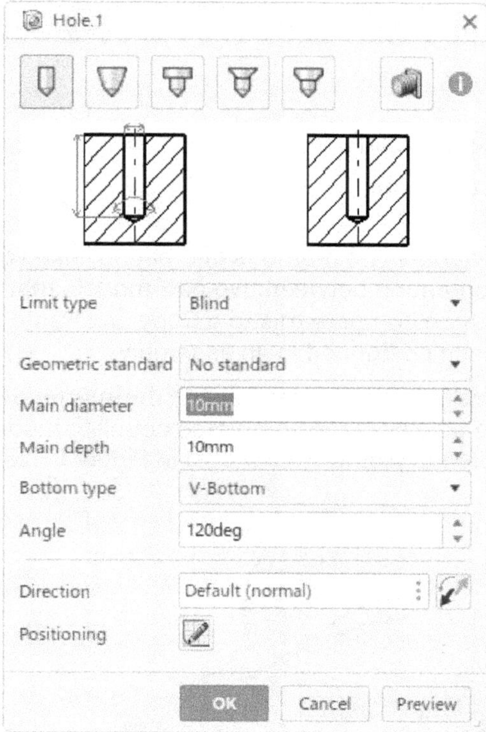

Figure 8–21

6. Click **OK**. In the *Assembly Features* dialog box (shown in Figure 8–22), select the components to be affected by the hole.

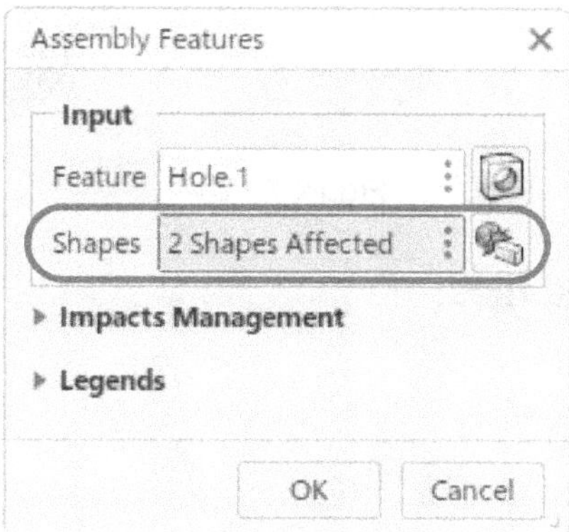

Figure 8–22

7. Click **OK** and **Update** the assembly.

Practice 8a
Link Types

Practice Objectives

- Develop a Reference-Reference link.
- Develop a Reference-Instance link.

In this practice, you will investigate two methods of creating linked geometry. The first method involves a **Copy** and **Paste** operation between two part models that have been opened in separate windows. You will then compare this to a **Copy** and **Paste** operation between the same two parts that have been positioned in an assembly.

The linked geometry you develop will be used to define the interface between the coupling base and y-pipe components. The face from the completed coupling model will be used to develop a pad in the y-pipe. The completed geometry is shown in Figure 8–23.

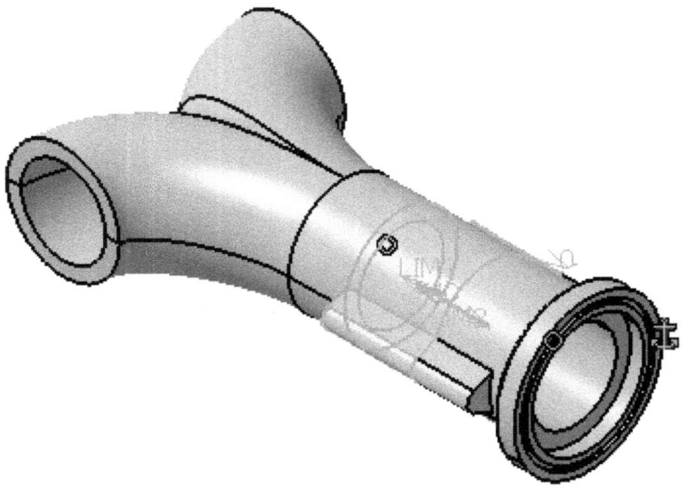

Figure 8–23

Task 1: Import the required files.

1. Import **Link_Types.3dxml**.

Task 2: Publish geometry.

1. In the specification tree, right-click on **LinkCouplingBase** and select **Open**.
2. Expand **Geometrical Set.1** and **Show** it. It contains an extract of the top face of the part, as shown in Figure 8–24. This surface will be used to develop geometry in the y-pipe mating part.

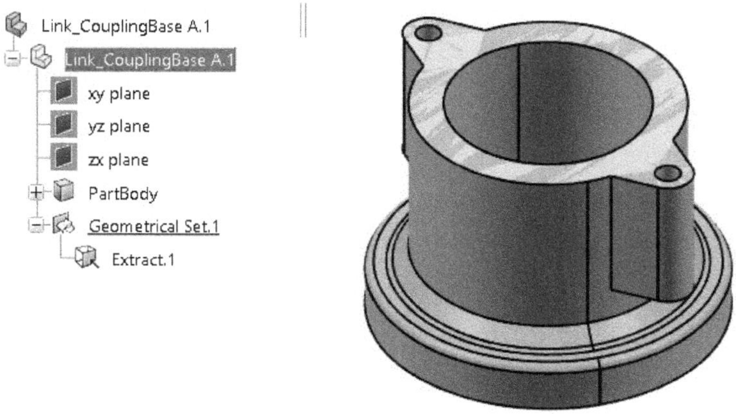

Figure 8–24

3. Double-click on the top-level product to activate it.
4. In the *Product Modification* section of the Action Bar, select  (Create a Publication) and select **Extract.1**.
5. Edit the name of the publication to **MateSurf** and click **OK**. The specification tree displays as shown in Figure 8–25.

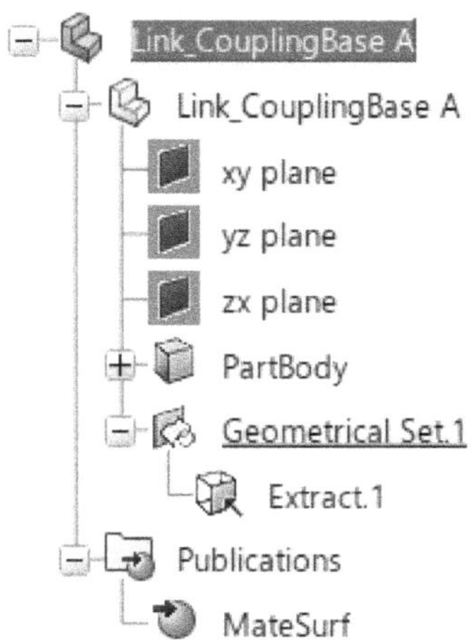

Figure 8–25

Task 3: Open the pipe model and manage the tabs.

1. Select the *Bookmarks app - Link Types* tab at the top of the graphics window.
2. In the specification tree, right-click on **Link_YPipe** and select **Open**.
3. Close the *Bookmarks app - Link Types* tab.

Task 4: Create a Reference-Reference link.

A Reference-Reference link is generated between two models that are open in separate tabs. In this task, a **Copy** and **Paste Special** operation will be performed to create the link.

1. Select the *Link_CouplingBase* tab.
2. Double-click on the **Link_CouplingBase** 3D shape to activate it.
3. Copy the **MateSurf** publication in the specification tree.
4. Select the *Link_YPipe* tab, right-click on the **Link_YPipe** 3D shape, and select **Paste Special**. The *Paste Special* dialog box opens, as shown in Figure 8–26.

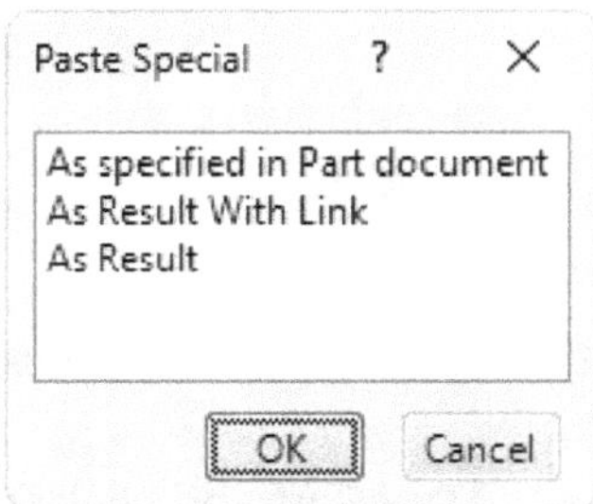

Figure 8–26

5. Select **As Result With Link** and click **OK**. The copied surface is added to the y-pipe model, as shown in Figure 8–27.

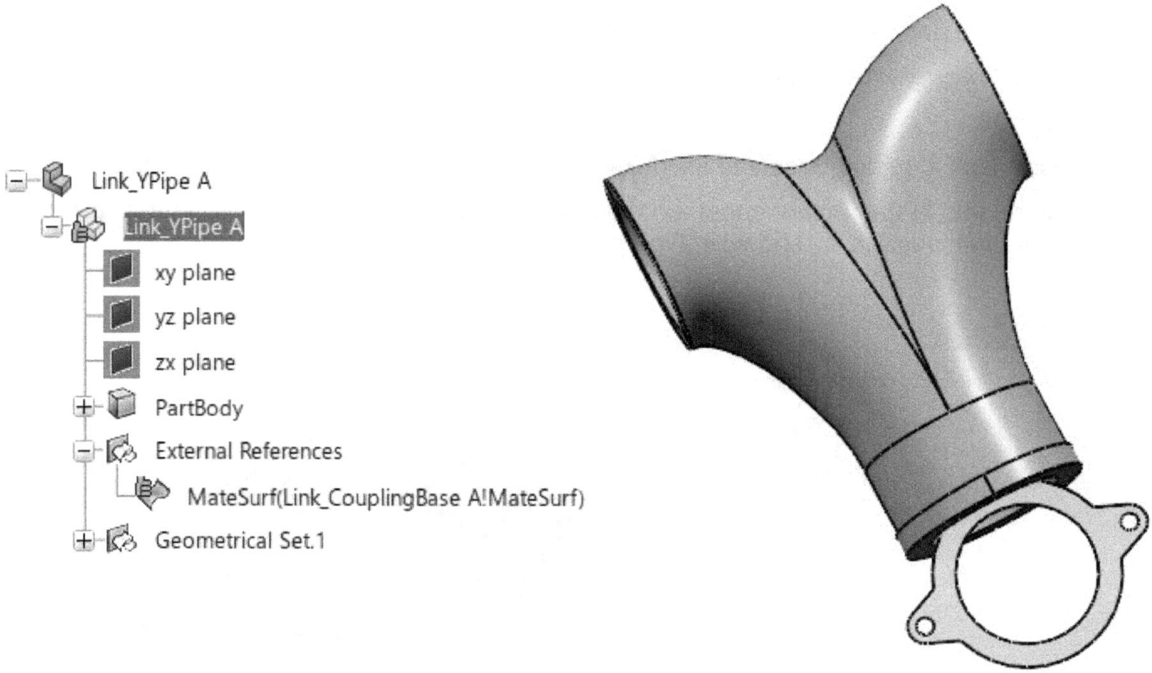

Figure 8–27

Design Considerations

A Reference-Reference link occurs when geometry is copied and pasted without the use of an assembly to define the positioning information. This results in the pasted data being placed at the same location with respect to the default axis system of the source model. This type of link is useful when positioning is not important (for example, when developing a linked parameter) or when the parts are to be developed using in-place modeling techniques.

The position of the copied geometry can be modified using the Robot. However, the end result is that all positioning is driven by the y-pipe part and will not change due to modifications to the coupling base.

6. In the Action Bar, click (Undo) twice to fully undo the paste operation.

   Note: *It might take more than two undos if extra clicks (unselect) were made on the screen.*

Task 5: Create an assembly.

1. In the Top Bar, select (Add/Create)>**Physical Product**.
2. In the *Physical Product* dialog box, type ***Your_Initials_*ReflnstLink** in the *Title* field.
3. Click **OK**.
4. Insert **Link_CouplingBase** and **Fix** (Fix in Space) the component in the assembly.
5. Insert **Link_YPipe**. Do not constrain the component in the assembly, so that it displays in its default location, as shown in Figure 8–28.

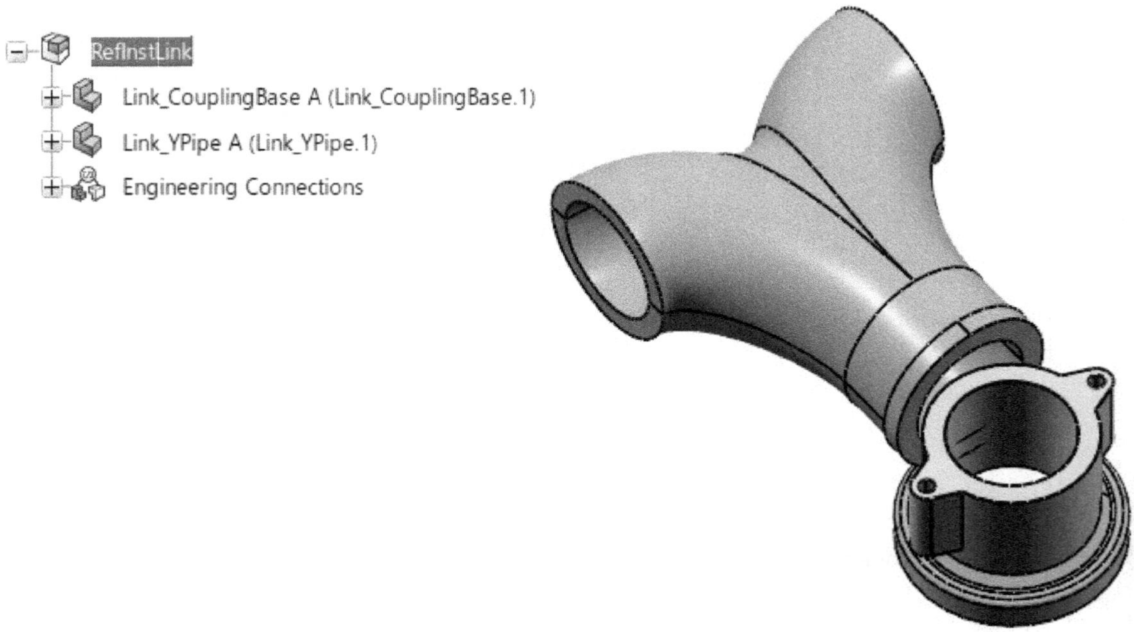

Figure 8–28

Task 6: Develop a Reference-Instance link.

1. In the specification tree, double-click on the **Link_YPipe** 3D shape, as shown in Figure 8–29, to activate it in the **Part Design** app.

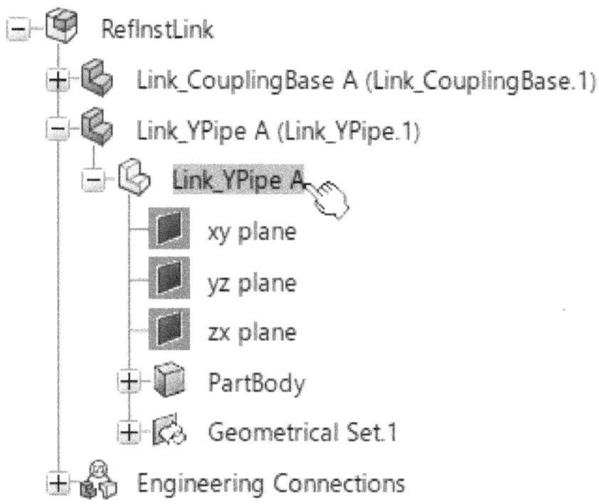

Figure 8–29

2. In the tree, expand the **Link_CouplingBase** component to display the *Publications* branch.
3. Copy the **MateSurf** publication and paste it into **Link_YPipe** using the **Paste Special** and **As Result With Link** options. The copied surface displays as shown in Figure 8–30.

Figure 8–30

Design Considerations

When generating a Reference-Instance link between two components in an assembly, the position of the linked geometry is driven by the position of the source component in the assembly. Therefore, moving the **Link_YPipe** component into its assembled location will reposition the copied surface in the **Link_YPipe** part. This is because its position relative to the **Link_CouplingBase** component has changed.

To demonstrate this, you will reposition the **Link_YPipe** component. You will open the **Link_YPipe** model in a separate window first so that you can see the direct impact of the reposition operation on the copied surface.

Task 7: Reposition Link_YPipe.

1. Activate the **RefInstLink** assembly.
2. In the specification tree, hide the *External References* node under **Link_YPipe**.
3. Create a **Revolute** engineering connection (**Coincidence** between axes and **30mm Offset** between faces) so that the updated assembly displays as shown in Figure 8–31.

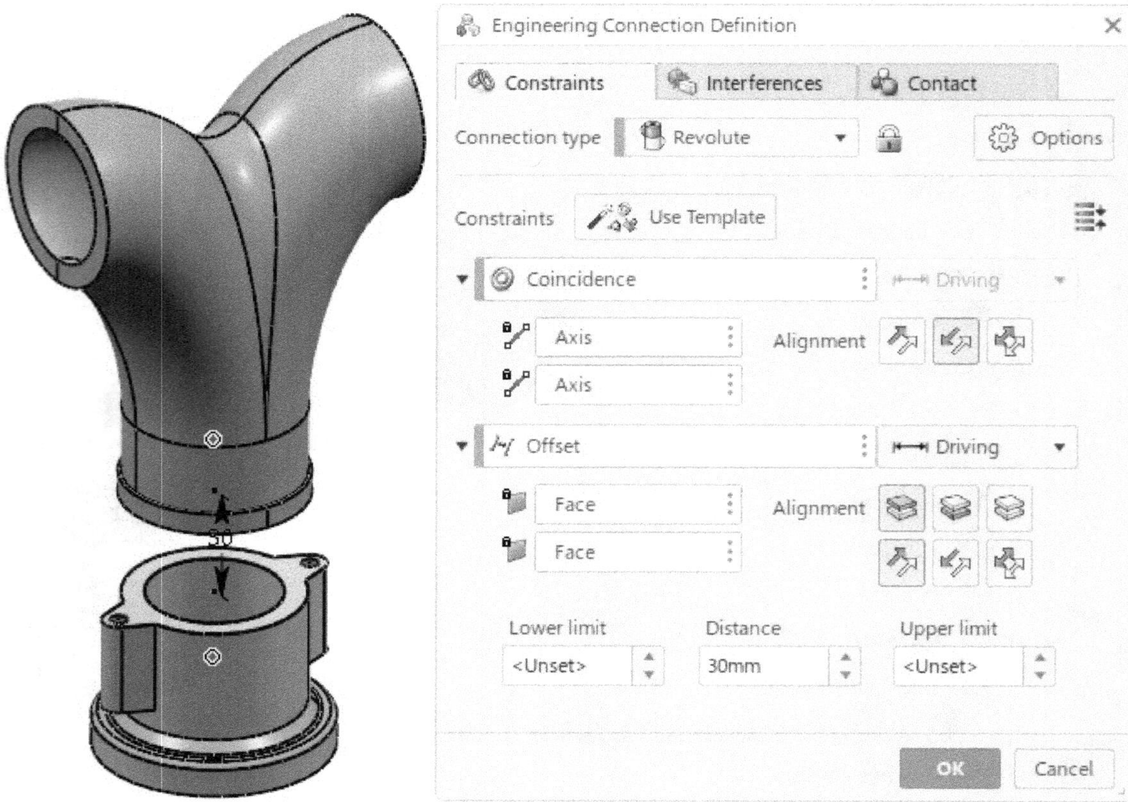

Figure 8–31

4. Click **OK** to complete the connection. In the *Undefined Interference Specifications* dialog box, click **No**.
5. If needed, in the Action Bar, click (Update).
6. Select the *Link_YPipe* tab. If required, show the **External References** geometrical set and note that the relative position of the copied surface has changed.

Task 8: Create a pad and modify the assembly positioning.

1. Create a **Pad** feature using the following parameters, as shown in Figure 8–32:
   - *Profile:* **MateSurf copied surface**
   - *Direction:* **yz plane**
   - *First Limit Type:* **Up to plane**
   - *Limit:* Select the face shown in Figure 8–32

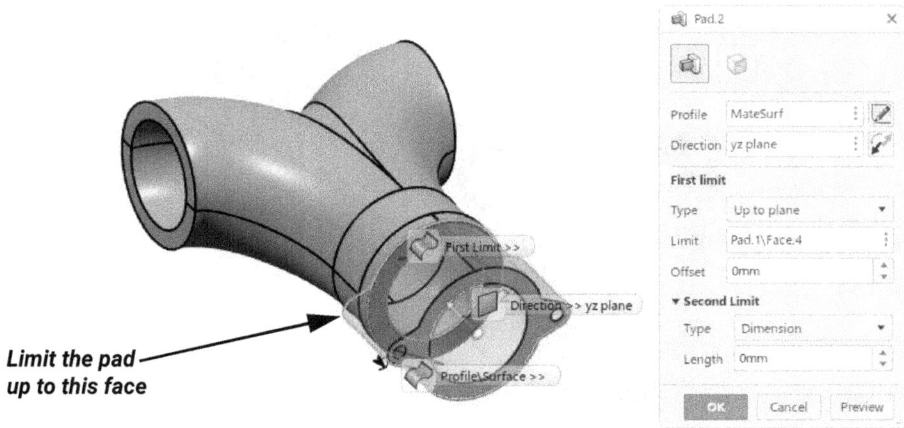

Figure 8–32

2. Click **OK** to complete the pad.
3. Select the *Assembly* tab and modify the value of the *Offset* constraint to **40mm**.
4. Update the assembly. The length of the pad has now increased. This is due to the position change of the copied surface in **YPipe**, based on the relative position change of the two components in the assembly.
5. Save the assembly and close the window.

End of practice

Practice 8b
Assembly Features

Practice Objective

- Add features to an assembly.

In this practice, you will modify the assembly shown in Figure 8–33 by adding holes at the assembly level. By creating the holes at the assembly level, all parts affected by the hole creation are automatically updated to reflect the creation of the holes.

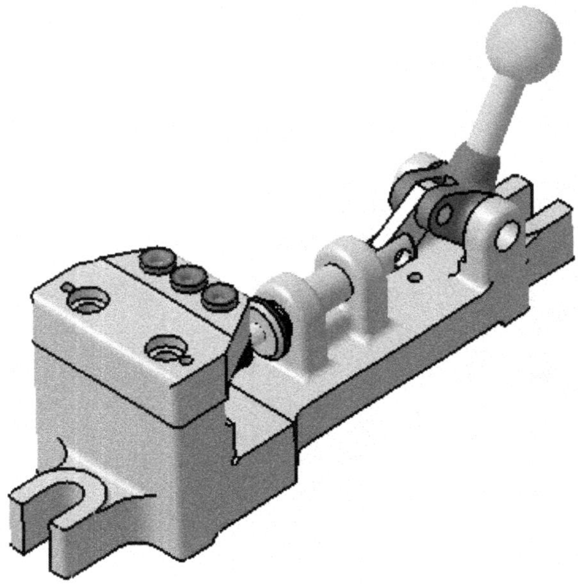

Figure 8–33

Task 1: Open the product and investigate some parts using Open Advanced.

1. Import **Bore-Device-2.3dxml**.
2. In the specification tree, right-click on **65200000** and select **Open With>Open Advanced**.

3. Enable the **With expanded children** and **Without any representation** options, as shown in Figure 8–34, and click **OK**.

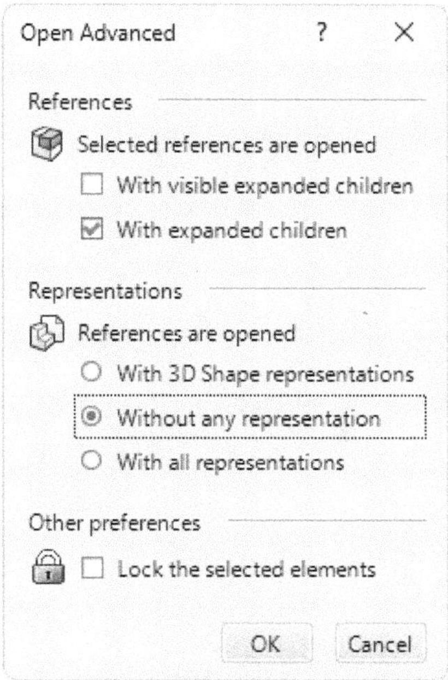

Figure 8–34

4. The specification tree loads, but no geometry is visible. Select the **3200000** object and click  (Manage Representation) in the *Tools* section of the Action Bar.
5. In the *Manage Representations* dialog box, under *Actions*, select **Manage loading of representations manually**. Note that when you have multiple objects to choose from, using this option is convenient as it allows you to select specific objects to load.

6. Check the box next to the **3200000** object to load the shape, as shown in Figure 8–35, and click **OK**.

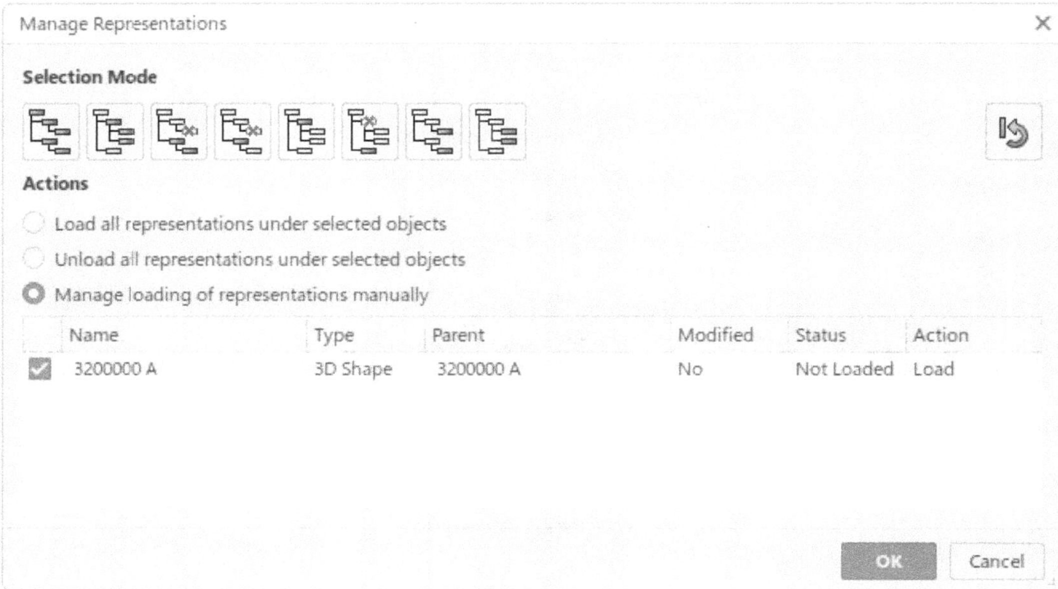

Figure 8–35

7. Click **OK** in the *Manage Representations* window that appears.
8. The model displays in the window. In the tree, expand the **3200000** node until you can see the part body. This will ensure that all references are selectable. Note that it has two small holes, as shown in Figure 8–36.

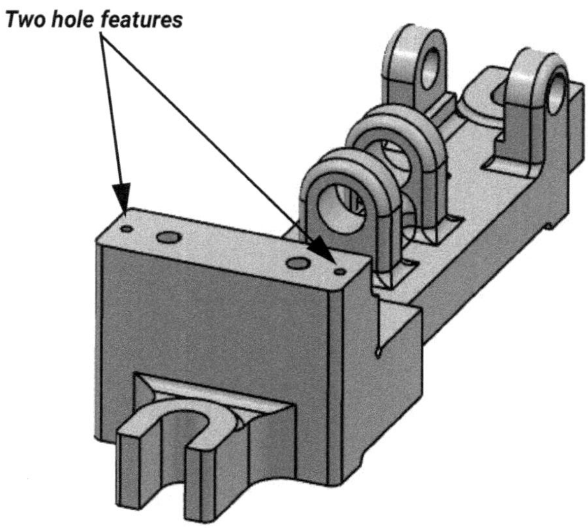

Figure 8–36

9. You will reference these holes to create the holes in another part, so in the *Product Modification* tab of the Action Bar, click (Create a Publication).
10. Select the surface of the hole shown in Figure 8–37.

    Note: *If you are unable to select the surface, try expanding the part in the tree first, and then select the hole's surface.*

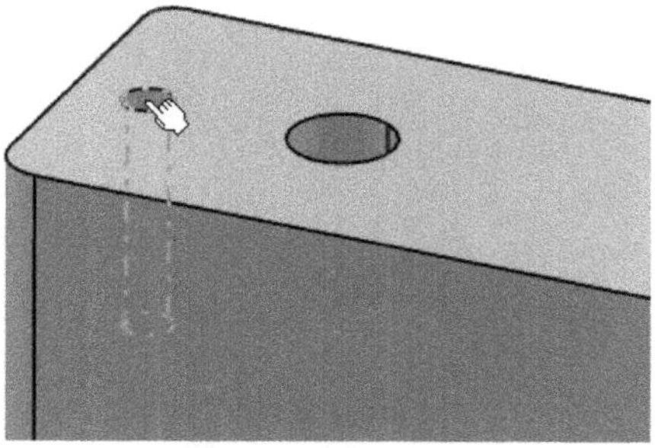

Figure 8–37

11. In the *Publication* dialog box, enter **Axis_1** for the *Functional Name* and click **OK**.
12. Click (Create a Publication).
13. Select the surface of the hole shown in Figure 8–38.

Figure 8–38

14. In the *Publication* dialog box, enter **Axis_2** for the *Functional Name* and click **OK**.
15. Select the **3200001** object and click (Manage Representation) in the *Tools* section of the *Action Bar*.
16. In the *Manage Representation* dialog box, if needed, click the radial button next to **Load all representations under selected objects** and click **OK**.

17. Select **Load** in the *Manage Representations* window. Note that the 3200001 part does not have the required holes to match the other part, as shown in Figure 8–39.

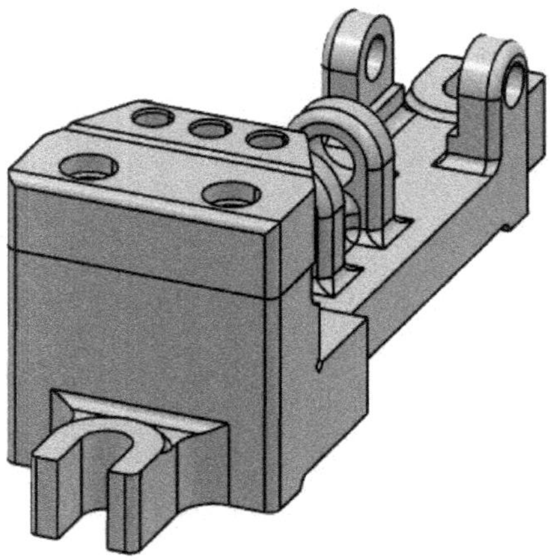

Figure 8–39

Task 2: Publish the surfaces to use for the hole starting surface and depth.

1. In the *Product Modification* tab of the Action Bar, click (Create a Publication).
2. Select the surface shown in Figure 8–40.

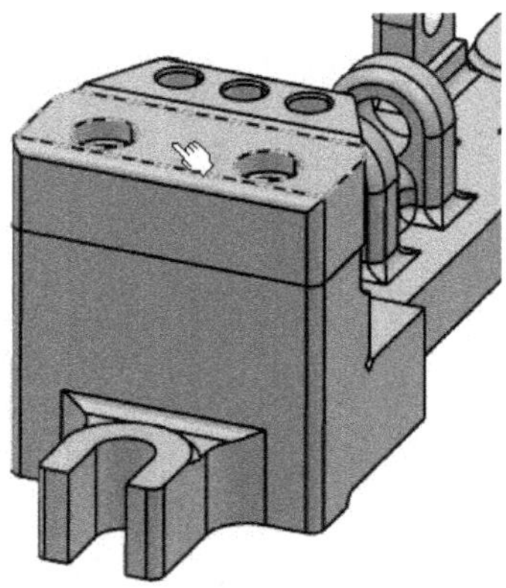

Figure 8–40

3. Enter **Start_Surface** as the *Functional Name* and click **OK**.
4. Click (Create a Publication).
5. Select the surface shown in Figure 8–41, then click the selection shown.

   Note: *Hidden surfaces can be selected more easily by hovering your cursor over the area of the object you want and pressing <Up Arrow> and <Down Arrow> to toggle through everything under the cursor.*

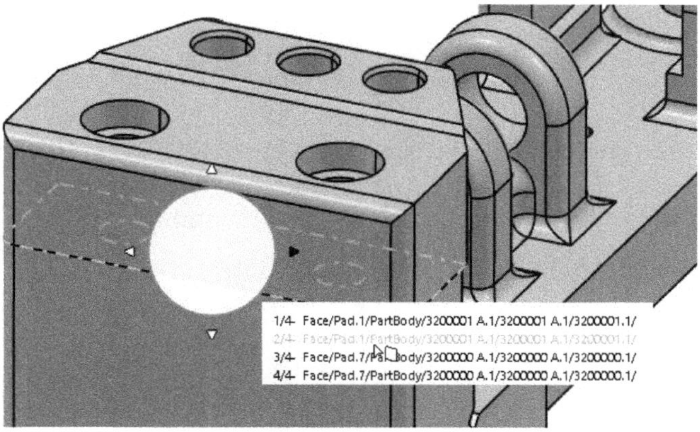

Figure 8–41

6. Enter **End_Surface** as the *Functional Name* and click **OK**.

Task 3: Create holes at assembly level.

1. Ensure that the external reference settings are correct by selecting **Me>Preferences> Common Preferences>Object Properties>3D Shape>Infrastructure>General>External References** and selecting the **Keep link with selected object** option, as shown in Figure 8–42.

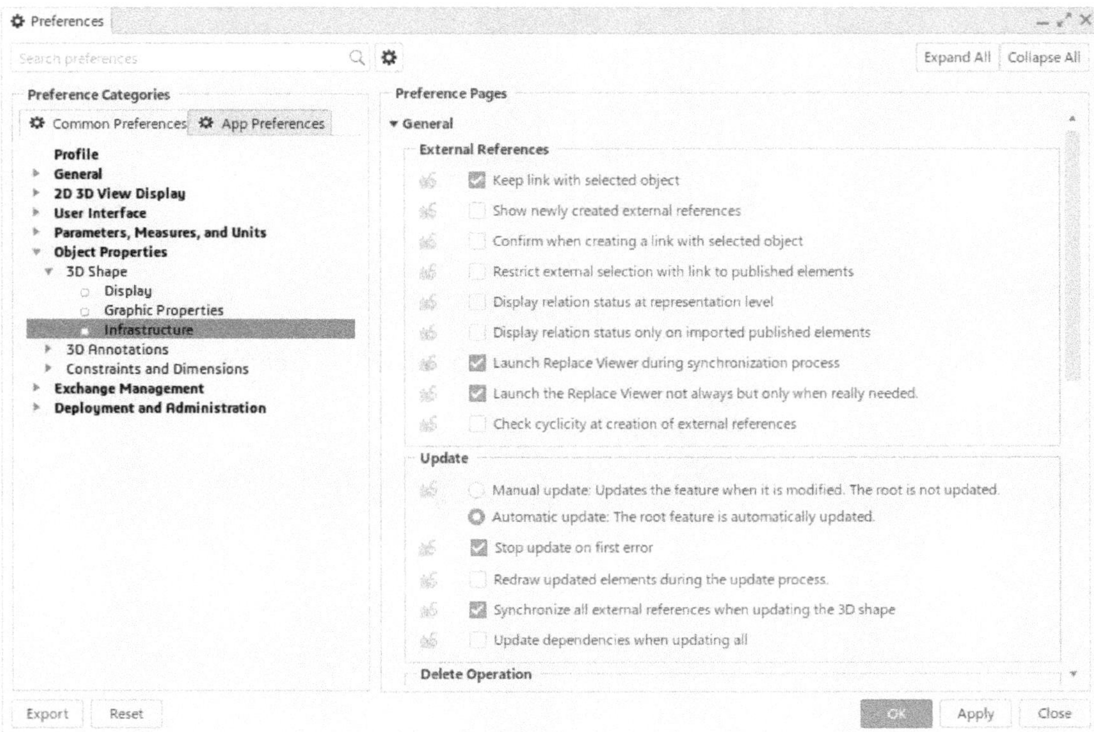

Figure 8–42

2. Click **OK**.
3. Change the display mode to **Wireframe** by clicking (View Modes) in the *View* section of the Action Bar, then selecting (Wireframe) from the *View Modes* window.
4. In the *Assembly* tab of the Action Bar, click (Assembly Hole) to create a hole feature.
5. In the *Choose a 3DShape* dialog box, click **Create new**.
6. Enter **Drilled Holes** for the *Title* and click **OK**.
7. In the specification tree, select **Start_Surface**, as shown in Figure 8–43.

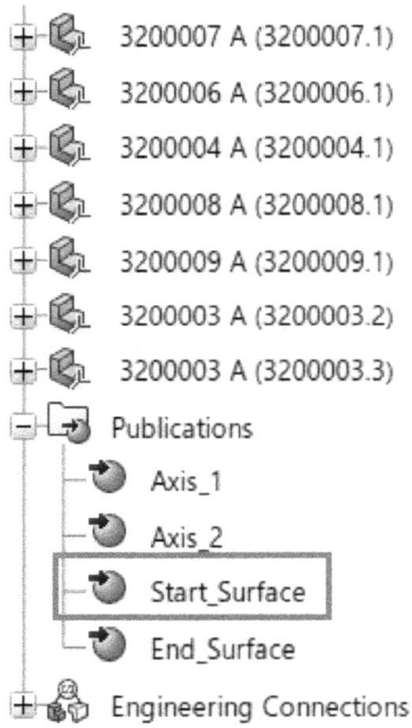

Figure 8–43

8. Click **OK** in the *Warning* dialog box, indicating that a link will be created.
9. Change the orientation to (* top).
10. In the *Hole* dialog box, click (Positioning Sketch).

11. Select the locating point shown in Figure 8–44.

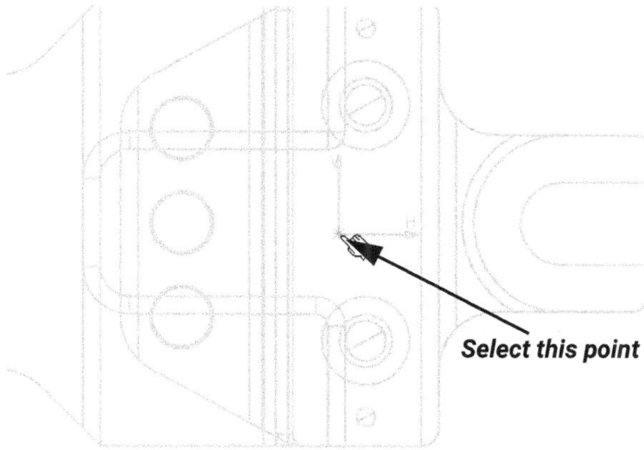

Figure 8–44

12. Click (Constraint) and select **Axis_2** in the specification tree.
13. Right-click and select **Coincidence**.
14. Click (Exit App) to complete the sketch.
15. Change the display mode to **Shading with sharp and smooth edges** by clicking (View Modes) in the *View* section of the Action Bar, then selecting (Shading with sharp and smooth edges).
16. In the *Hole* dialog box, click (Reverse) for the *Direction*.
17. Change the *Main diameter* to **5**.
18. Set the *Limit type* to **Up to Surface** and select **End_Surface** in the specification tree.
19. Click **OK** in the *Warning* dialog box, indicating that a link will be created.
20. Click **OK** in the *Hole* dialog box.
21. When the *Assembly Feature* dialog box opens, select **3200001** from the specification tree.
22. Click **OK**.
23. The hole is initially not visible. Select the *65200000* (Explore) tab, right-click on **6520000** in the specification tree, and select **Open**. This brings all the objects into session.
24. In the *Assembly* tab of the Action Bar, click (Update).
25. In the *Assembly* tab of the Action Bar, click (Hole) to create a hole feature.
26. In the *Choose a 3DShape* dialog box, select the **Drilled Holes** 3D shape listed and click **OK**.

27. In the specification tree, select **Start_Surface**, as shown in Figure 8–45.

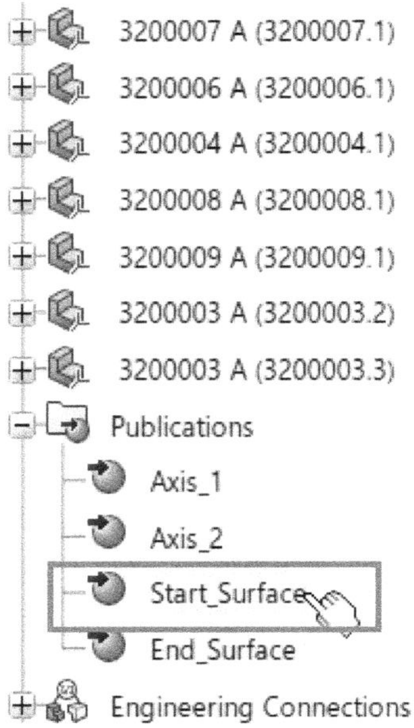

Figure 8–45

28. Click **OK** in the *Warning* dialog box, indicating that a link will be created.
29. Change the orientation to  (* top).
30. In the *Hole* dialog box, click  (Positioned Sketch).
31. Select the locating point shown in Figure 8–46.

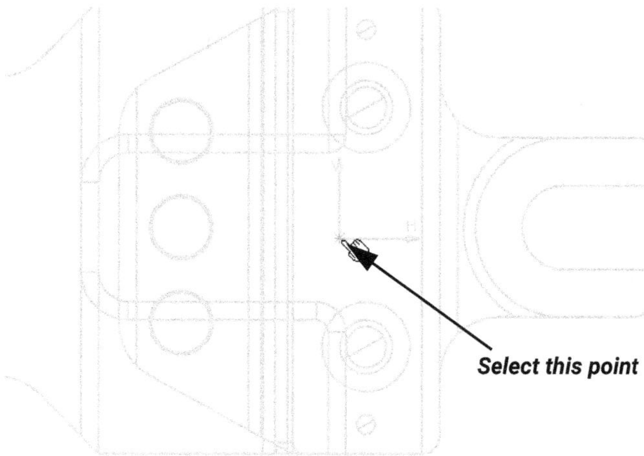

Figure 8–46

32. Click (Constraint) and select **Axis_1** in the specification tree.
33. Right-click and select **Coincidence**.
34. Click (Exit App) to complete the sketch.
35. Change the display mode to **Shading with sharp and smooth edges** by clicking (View Modes) in the *View* section of the Action Bar, then selecting (Shading with sharp and smooth edges).
36. In the *Hole* dialog box, click (Reverse) for the *Direction*.
37. Change the *Main diameter* to **5**.
38. Set the *Limit type* to **Up to Surface** and select **End_Surface** in the specification tree.
39. Click **OK** in the *Warning* dialog box, indicating that a link will be created.
40. Click **OK** in the *Hole* dialog box.
41. When the *Assembly Feature* dialog box opens, select **3200001** from the specification tree.
42. Click **OK**.
43. In the *Assembly* tab of the Action Bar, click (Update). The model displays as shown in Figure 8–47.

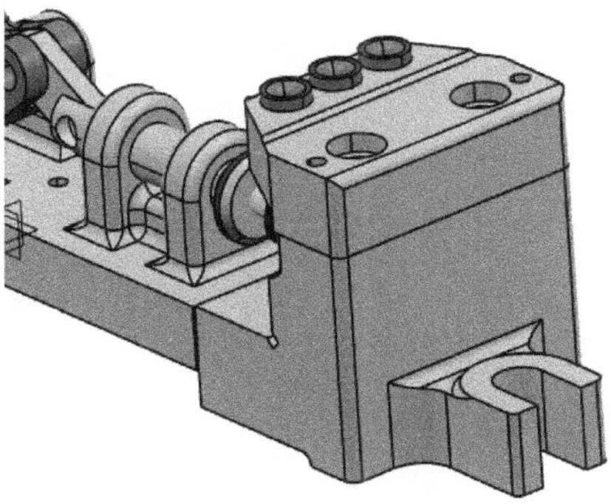

Figure 8–47

Task 4: Incorporate design changes.

1. A design change requires that the position of the referenced hole feature be modified. Double-click on **3200000** in the specification tree.
2. Modify **Sketch.23** of **Hole.4**. Change the *5* dimension to **7.5**, as shown in Figure 8–48. Exit the sketch.

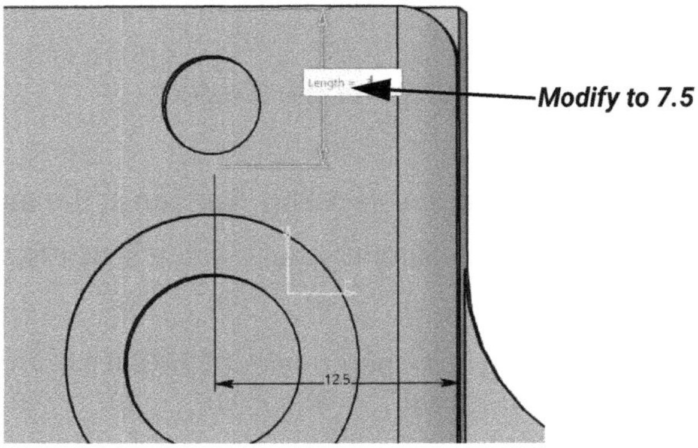

Figure 8–48

3. Complete the edit.
4. Activate the top level of the assembly.
5. Click (Update) to update the assembly.
6. The assembly displays as shown in Figure 8–49. View the assembly and note the updated position of the holes.

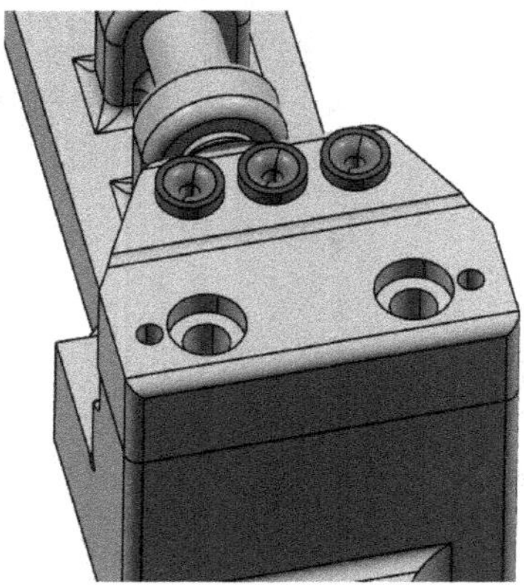

Figure 8–49

7. Save the assembly and close all tabs.

End of practice

Chapter

9

Catalogs

This chapter focuses on creating and working with custom catalogs to help reuse components.

Learning Objectives

- Understand the use of custom catalogs.
- Create custom catalogs.
- Assign keywords to describe a chapter or item.
- Create part family catalogs.

9.1 Catalogs

Catalogs provide a mechanism for reusing objects by classifying them according to user-defined keywords. You use structured custom catalogs to store and find common objects. This increases consistency and efficiency.

The catalog structure in the 3DEXPERIENCE platform has been simplified over CATIA V5. There is no longer a family node, and items can be directly inserted in the chapters, as shown in Figure 9–1.

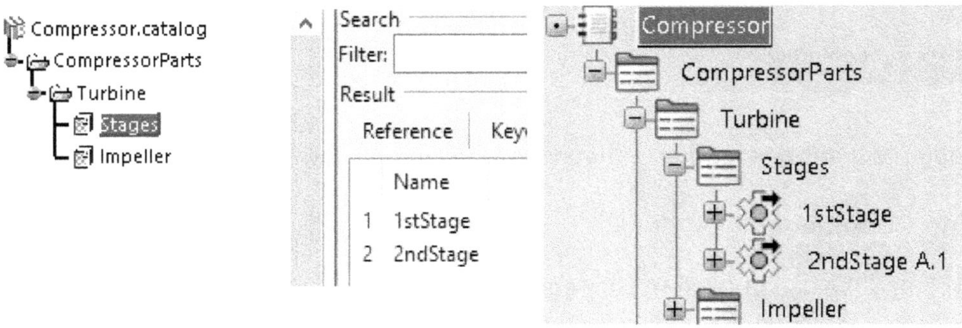

Figure 9–1

9.2 Creating a Catalog

You can use the 3DEXPERIENCE platform to create your own part catalogs based on company-specific requirements. In the Top Bar, click  (Add)>**New Content**. In the *New Content* window, select **Catalog**, as shown in Figure 9–2.

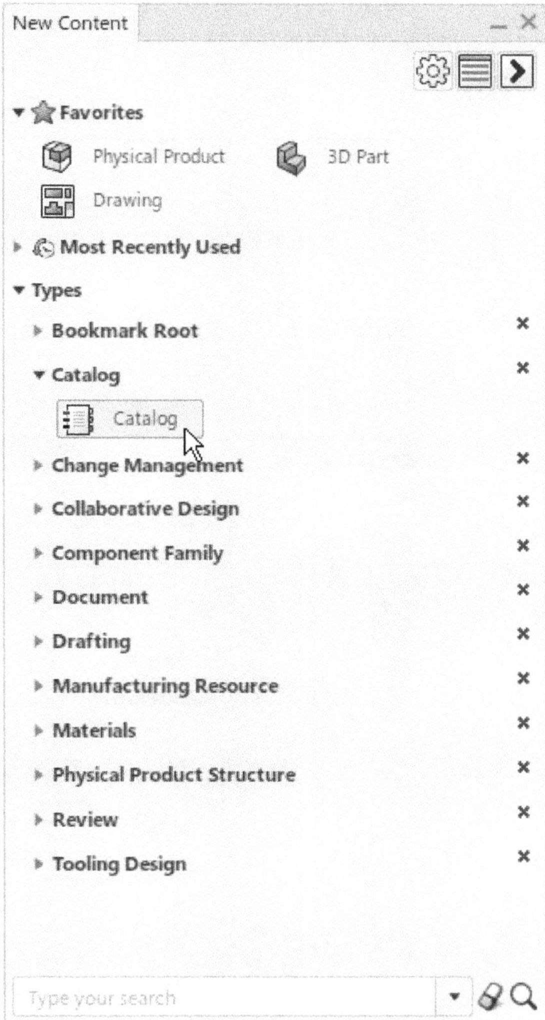

Figure 9–2

The *Catalog* dialog box opens, as shown in Figure 9–3. Enter a name for the catalog and click **OK**.

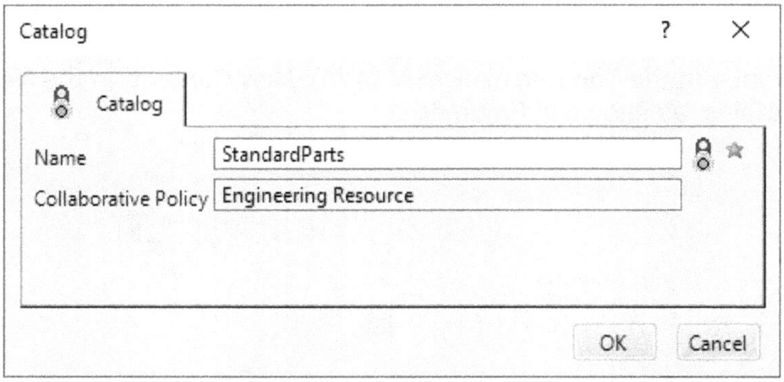

Figure 9–3

Ensure that you are in the (ENOVIA Design IP Classification) app, as shown in Figure 9–4.

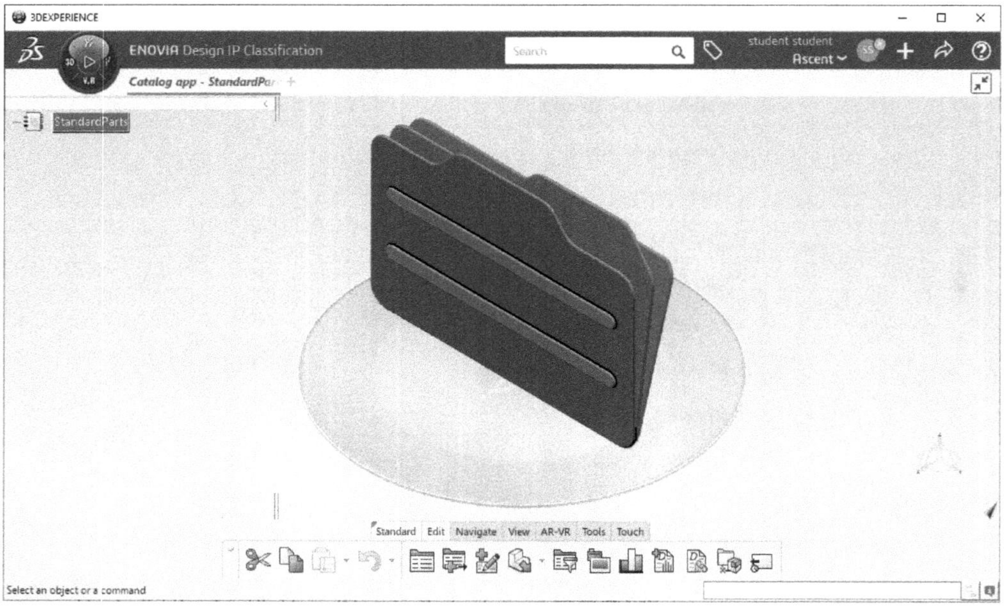

Figure 9–4

Once a catalog is created, you can add chapters. A chapter is a collection of other related chapters and/or families of parts in the catalog.

How To: Add a Chapter

1. Select the top-level chapter that you want the new chapter to follow.
2. Click (New Chapter). The *Catalog Chapter* dialog box opens, as shown in Figure 9–5.

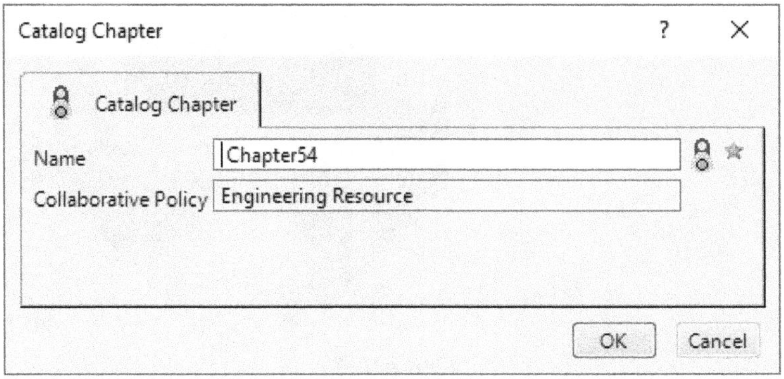

Figure 9–5

3. Enter the name of the chapter and click **OK**. The catalog opens with the new chapter in the tree, as shown in Figure 9–6.

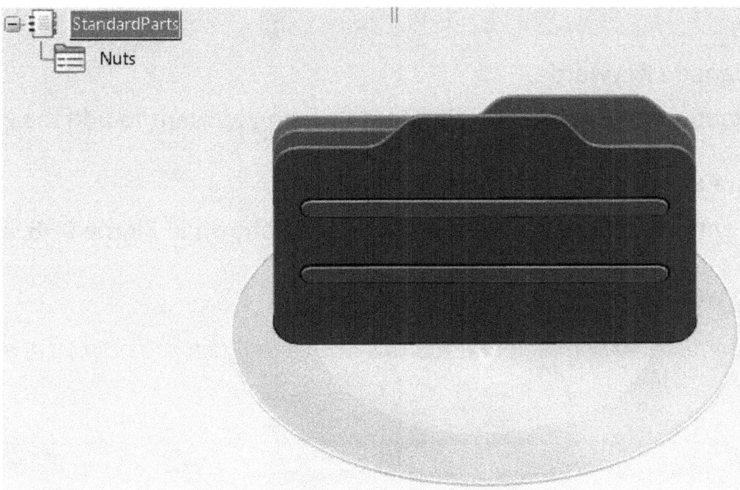

Figure 9–6

You can repeat the process to add multiple catalogs. The catalogs are added to the specification tree as well as the turntable, as shown in Figure 9–7.

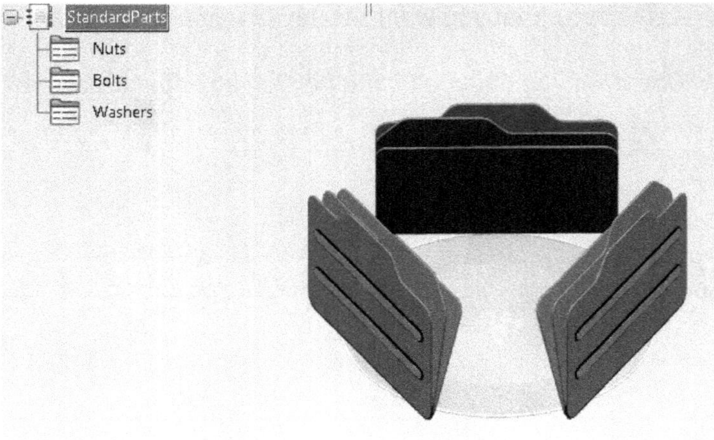

Figure 9–7

You can add keywords and attributes to the chapters so you can search for those attributes and filter the contents.

How To: Add a Keyword

1. Click (Manage Keywords).
2. In the specification tree, select the chapter to which you want to add the keyword.
3. In the attribute editor, click (Add Keyword).
4. In the editor, enter the *Keyword*, *Type*, and *Value*, as shown in Figure 9–8, and click (Add Keyword).

   Note: *It may be necessary to select the arrow above the editor to display it, as it may appear hidden initially.*

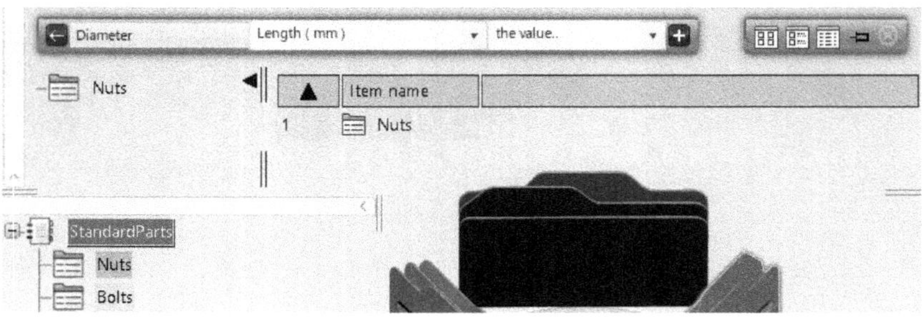

Figure 9–8

5. Repeat the previous steps to add additional keywords if required.

Once the keywords are added, you can add components to the catalog. In the specification tree, select the appropriate catalog, right-click, and select **Insert>Insert Existing Object**, as shown in Figure 9–9.

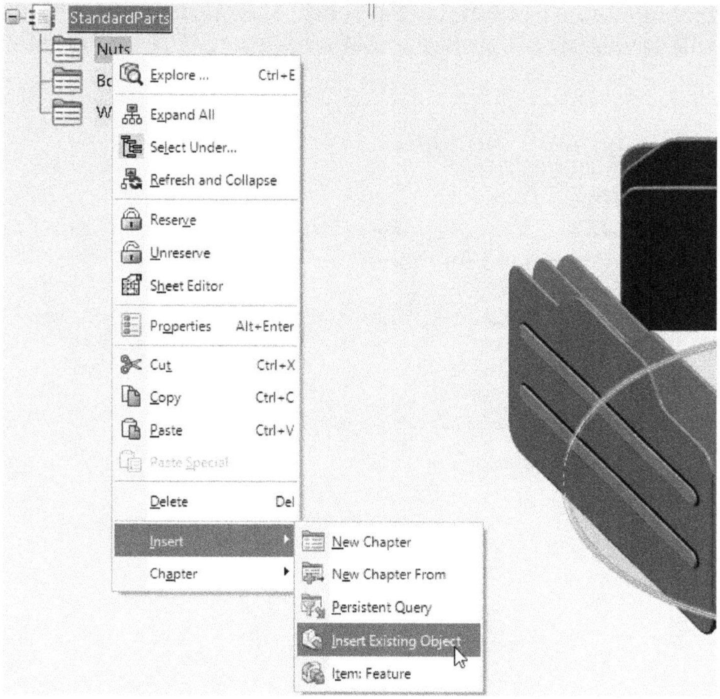

Figure 9–9

Alternatively, click  (Insert Existing Object) in the Action Bar.

In the search bar, enter the name of the object you want to add and select it in the search results. You can add as many objects as required to each of your catalogs.

9.3 Creating Part Family Catalogs

Once you create the design table, you can add it to a catalog where you can retrieve the different configurations as separate part objects.

You can add a part design table to a new catalog or an existing one. It is recommended that you become familiar with any existing catalog document structure before creating new catalog documents.

How To: Create a Component Family

1. In the Top Bar, click (Add/Create)>**New Content**. In the *New Content* window, select **Component Family**, as shown in Figure 9–10.

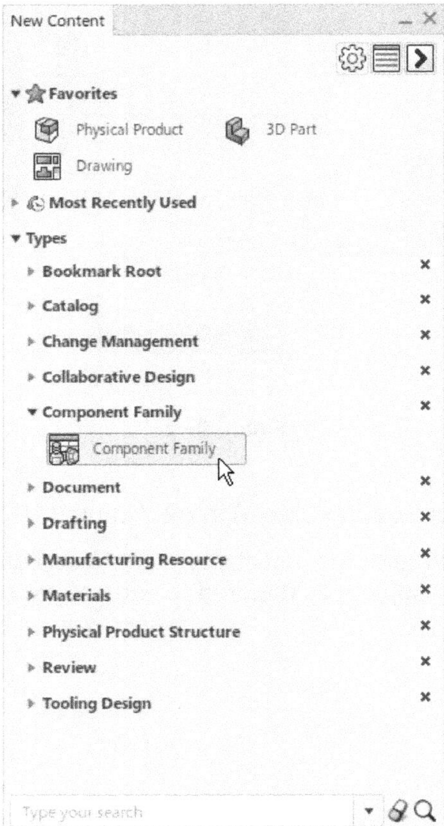

Figure 9–10

2. The *Component Family* dialog box opens, as shown in Figure 9–11. Enter a *Title*.

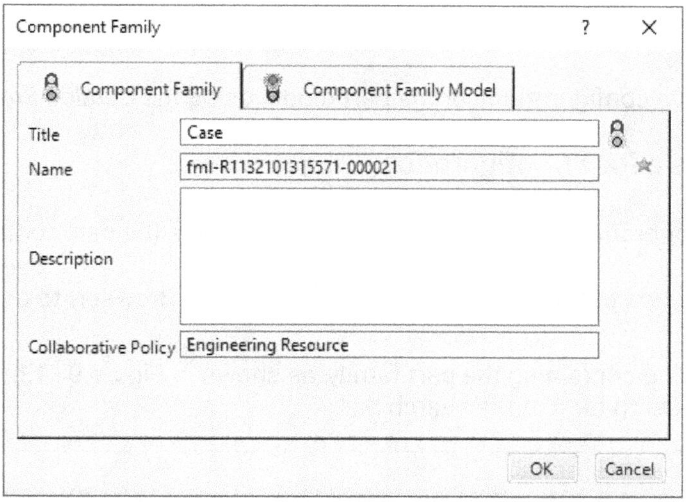

Figure 9–11

3. Select the *Component Family Model* tab, as shown in Figure 9–12, and set the appropriate options.

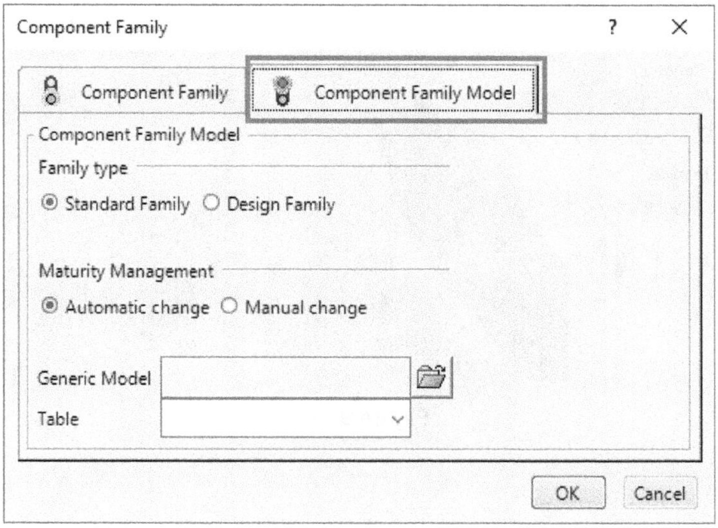

Figure 9–12

4. To select the appropriate model, click  (Choose Generic) and select or search for the object.
5. Click **OK** in the *Component Family* dialog box.

9.4 Adding Catalog Components to Assemblies

You can now retrieve configurations of the part model using the *Catalog Browser*.

How To: Retrieve a Part Configuration

1. Open the part or product file to which you want to retrieve the part configuration.
2. In the *Tools* section of the Action Bar, click  (Catalog Browser) to open the *Catalog Browser*.
3. Select the catalog containing the part family, as shown in Figure 9–13. If the catalog is not available, search for it in the search bar.

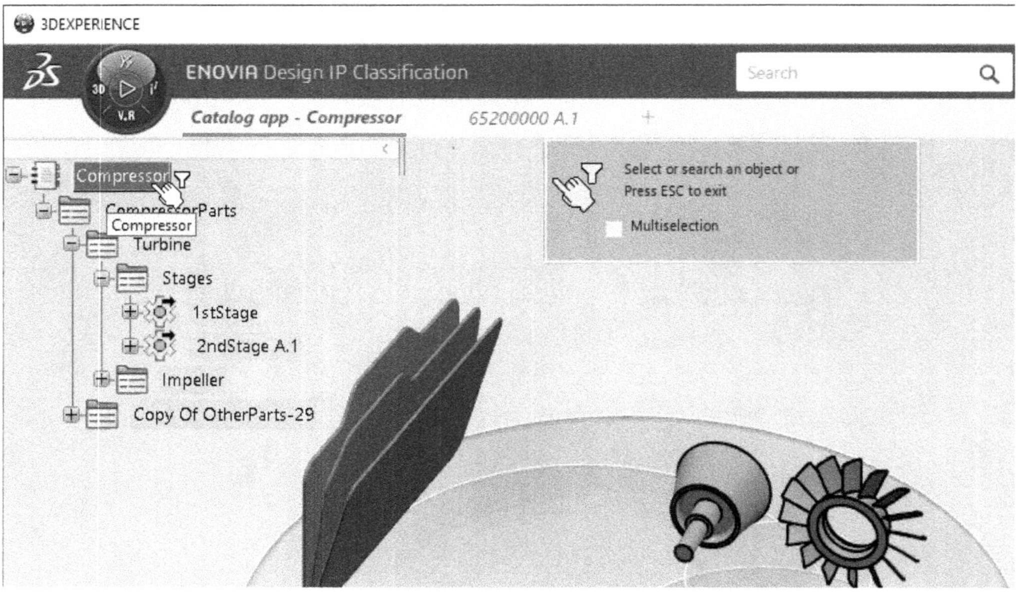

Figure 9–13

4. In the *Catalog Browser*, the available objects display. Select the required object, as shown in Figure 9–14.

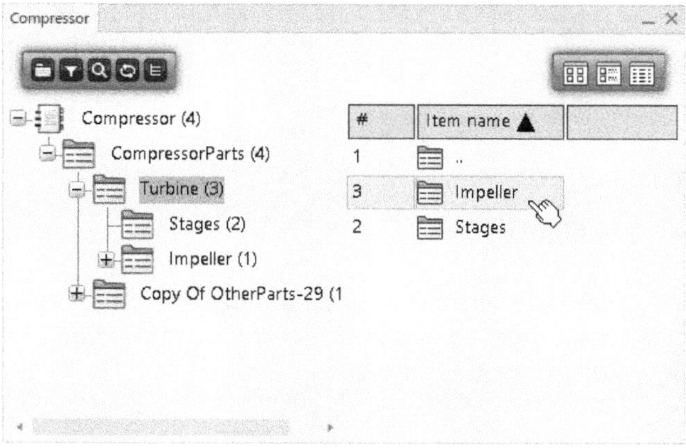

Figure 9–14

5. Once you locate the required configuration, double-click on the configuration to retrieve it and assemble it.

Note that you can insert object and features. The features you can insert are:

- Details
- Sketched
- User-defined Features
- Power Copies

Practice 9a
Catalogs

Practice Objectives

- Create a catalog.
- Add elements to a catalog.
- Link from one catalog to another.

In this practice, you will create the structure for a catalog. The parts are added to the catalog. Finally, you will generate a new catalog and create a link from the first catalog to the new one. The completed catalogs are shown in Figure 9–15.

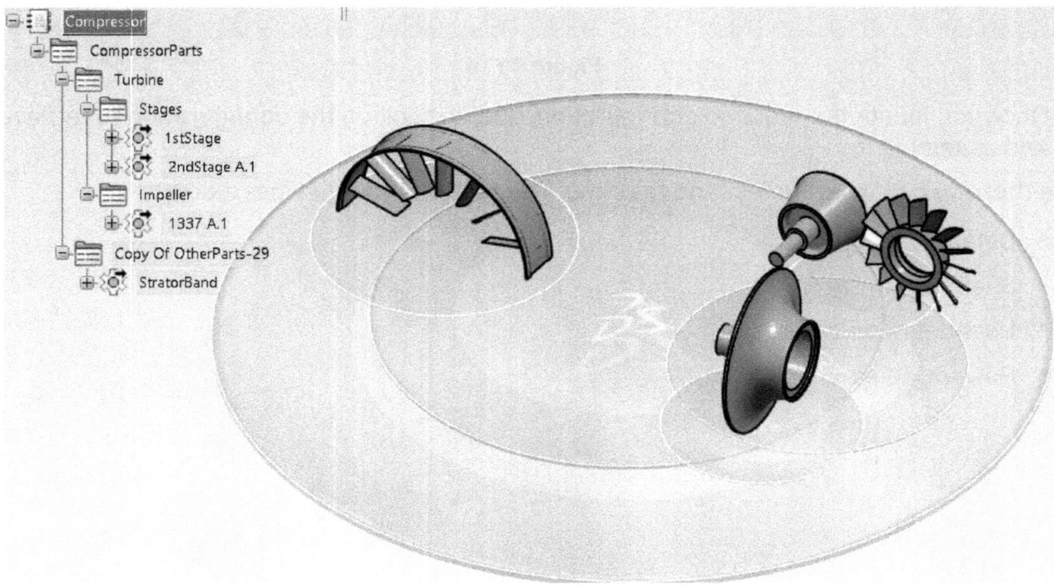

Figure 9–15

Task 1: Import the required files.

1. Import **Catalogs.3dxml**.

Task 2: Create a new catalog.

1. In the Top Bar, click (Add/Create)>**New Content**.
2. In the *New Content* window, select **Catalog**.
3. In the *Catalog* dialog box, enter the *Name* as ***Your_Initials*_Compressor** and click **OK**.

4. In the specification tree, right-click on **Compressor** and select **Compressor>Insert>New Chapter**. The *Catalog Chapter* dialog box opens, as shown in Figure 9–16.

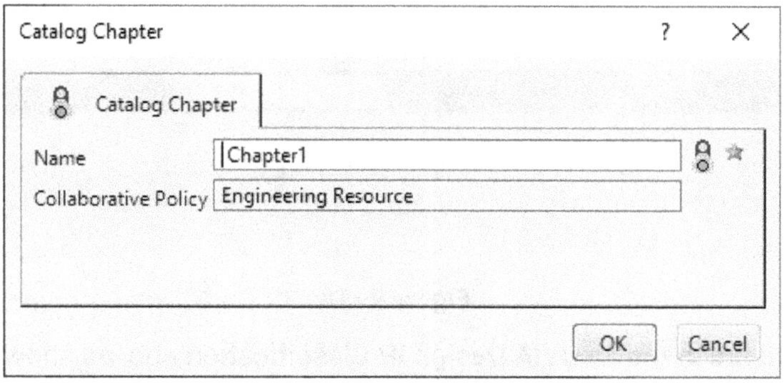

Figure 9–16

5. In the *Name* field, enter **CompressorParts**.
6. Click **OK**.
7. The **Compressor** catalog displays, as shown in Figure 9–17.

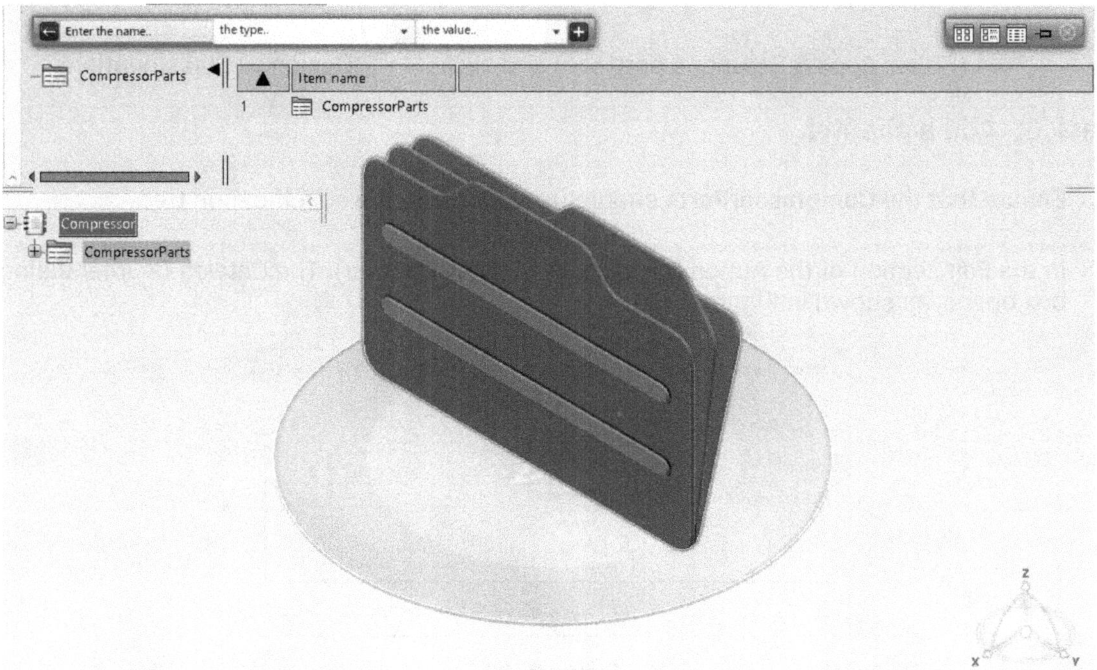

Figure 9–17

- If you do not see the attributes table in the upper right area of the window (as shown previously in Figure 9–17), click the icon shown in Figure 9–18 to expand the table.

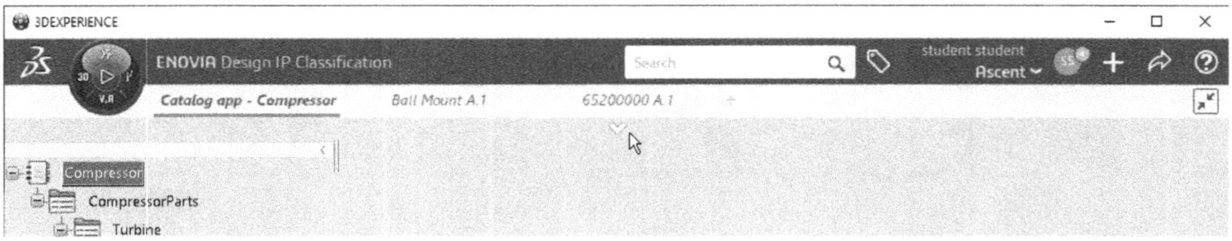

Figure 9–18

8. Ensure that you are in the **ENOVIA Design IP Classification** app, as shown in Figure 9–19.

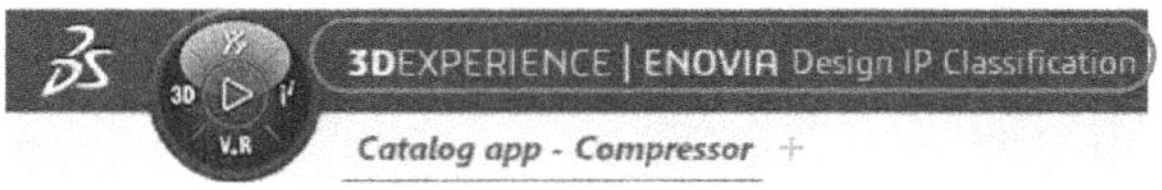

Figure 9–19

- If you are not in the **ENOVIA Design IP Classification** app, in the Compass, click (Roles, Apps & Solutions portfolio) and click (Design IP Classification).

Task 3: Add a chapter.

1. Ensure that the **CompressorParts** chapter is selected in the specification tree.
2. In the *Edit* section of the Action Bar, click (New Chapter). The *Catalog Chapter* dialog box opens, as shown in Figure 9–20.

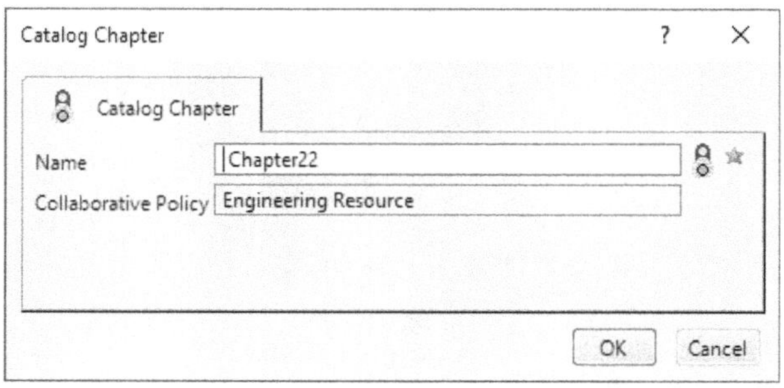

Figure 9–20

3. In the *Name* field, enter **Turbine**.

4. Click **OK**. The catalog displays as shown in Figure 9–21.

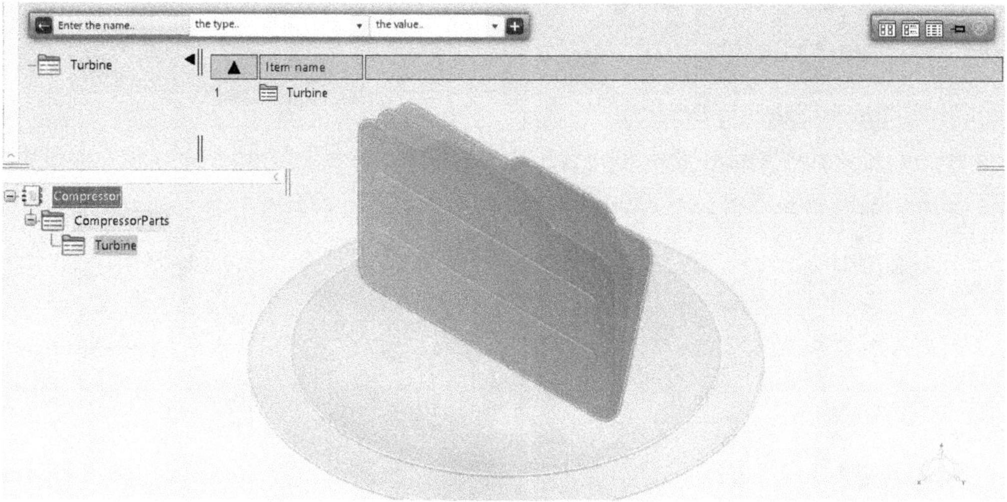

Figure 9–21

5. Ensure that the **Turbine** chapter is selected, then add a chapter called **Stages**, as shown in Figure 9–22.

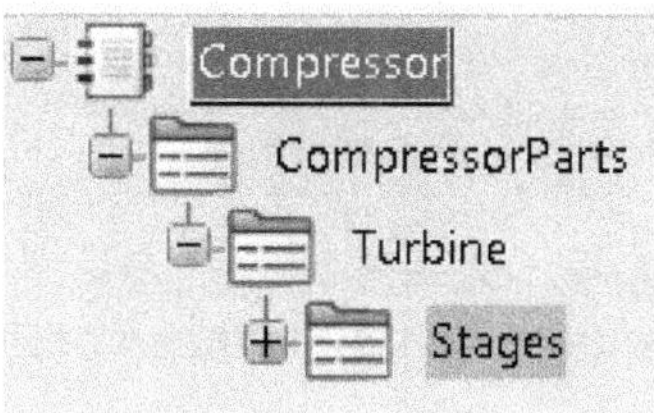

Figure 9–22

6. Select the **Turbine** chapter and add another chapter to it called **Impeller**. The *Compressor* catalog displays as shown in Figure 9–23.

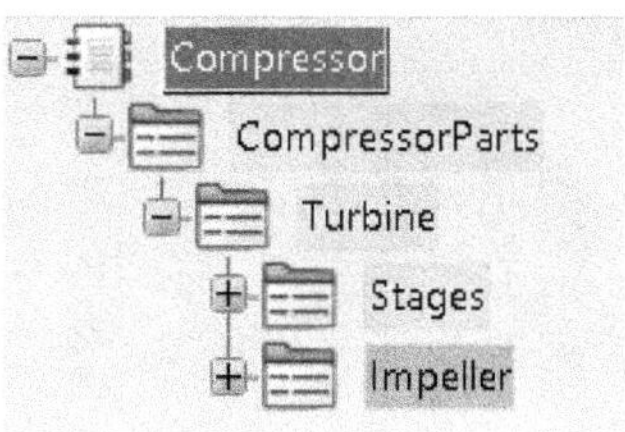

Figure 9–23

Task 4: Add components to a chapter.

1. Select the **Stages** chapter.
2. Click  (Insert Existing Object).
3. Select the *Bookmarks app - Catalogs* tab, expand the specification tree, and select **1292**.
4. The component is added to the catalog, as shown in Figure 9–24.

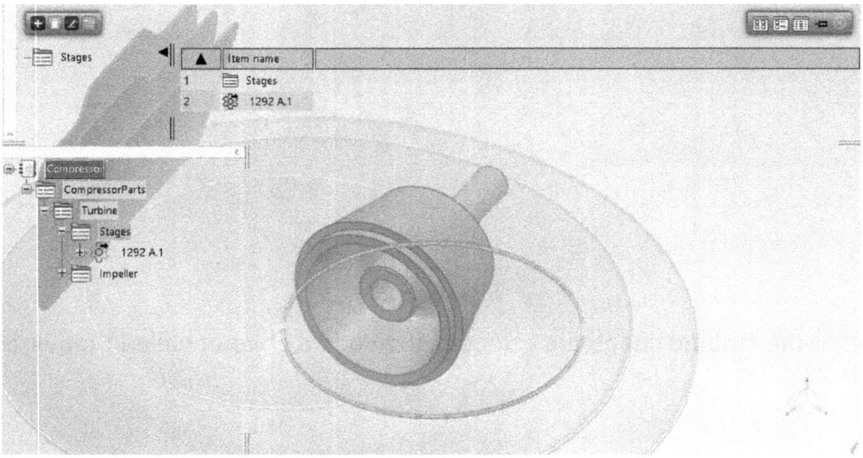

Figure 9–24

5. Close the attributes table.
6. Right-click on **1292** in the specification tree and select **Properties**.
7. Change the name to **1stStage**.
8. Repeat this procedure to add **2ndStage** to the *Stages* family. The catalog displays as shown in Figure 9–25.

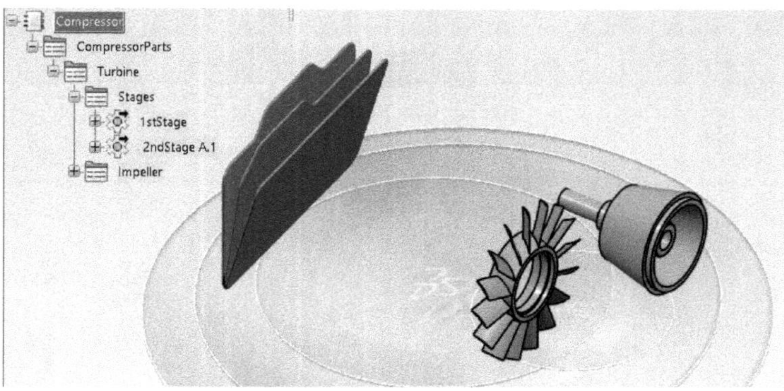

Figure 9–25

9. Select the **Impeller** family and add **1337**, then repeat Steps 6 and 7 to rename 1337 to **Impeller**. The *Compressor* catalog displays as shown in Figure 9–26.

Figure 9–26

Task 5: Create a new catalog.

1. Create a new catalog named **LinkedCatalog**.
2. Add a chapter called **CompressorParts**.
3. Create a chapter named **OtherParts** beneath the **CompressorParts** chapter.
4. Add the **1350** component from the *Bookmarks app - Catalogs* tab to the **OtherParts** chapter.

5. Close the attributes table, then rename the part to **StatorBand**. Once renamed, the catalog displays as shown in Figure 9–27.

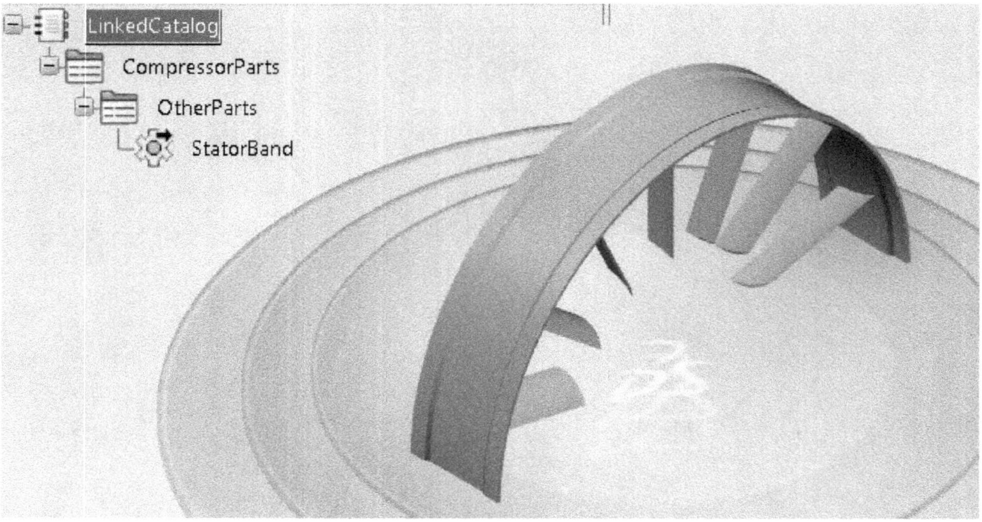

Figure 9–27

Task 6: Add a link to a chapter.

1. Select the *Catalog app - Compressor* tab.
2. Select the **CompressorParts** chapter.
3. Click (New Chapter From).
4. Select the **OtherParts** chapter from **LinkedCatalog**.

5. Expand **Copy of Other Parts** in the *Compressor* catalog, as shown in Figure 9–28.

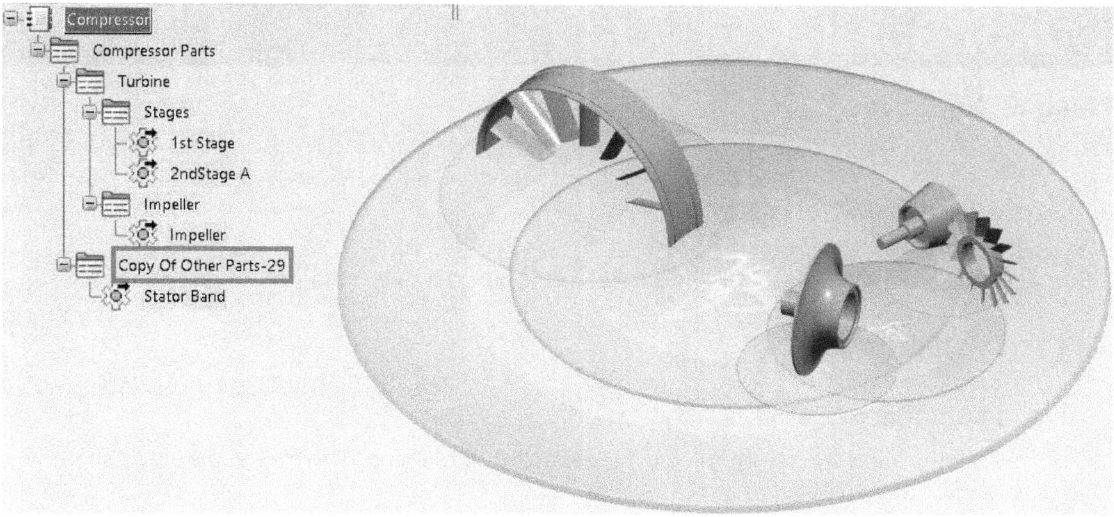

Figure 9–28

6. Save the catalogs and close all tabs.

End of practice

Practice 9b
Stator Band

Practice Objectives

- Create a design table.
- Add the design table to a catalog.

In this practice, you will create and add a design table to a new catalog.

Task 1: Open the part.

1. Import **StatorBand2.3dxml**.
2. In the specification tree, right-click on **1350** and select **Open**. The model displays as shown in Figure 9–29.

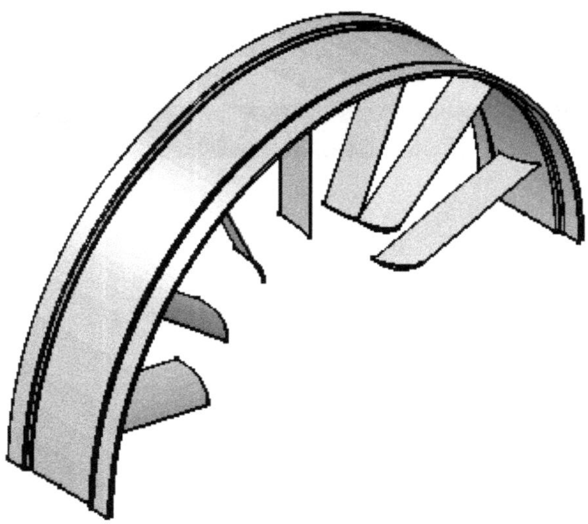

Figure 9–29

Task 2: Create a design table.

1. In the *Tools* tab of the Action Bar, click (Design Table). In the *Creation of a Design Table* dialog box, fill in the details as shown in Figure 9–30.

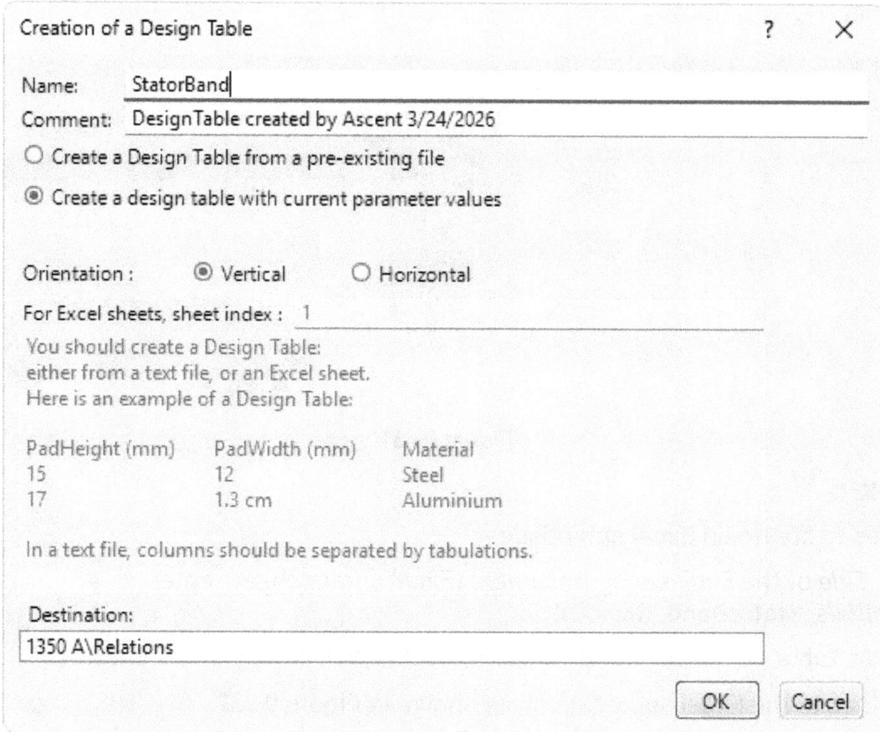

Figure 9–30

2. Click **OK**.

3. Insert the four parameters shown in Figure 9–31.

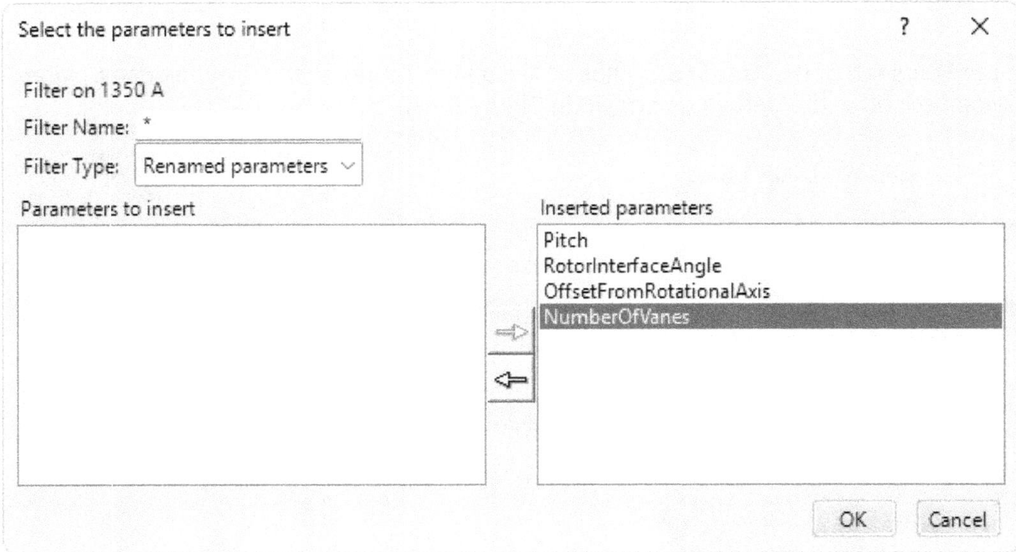

Figure 9–31

4. Click **OK**.
5. Click **Yes** to create an Excel spreadsheet.
6. For the *Title* of the *Engineering Document* (Excel spreadsheet), enter ***Your_Initials*_StatorBand**. Click **OK**.
7. Click **Edit Table**.
8. Add values to the Excel spreadsheet, as shown in Figure 9–32.

   Note: *When creating a Part Number column in a design table, it is important that you label it "PartNumber", without a space between the two words. If you include a space, 3DEXPERIENCE will not allow you to save it as a part family in a catalog.*

	A	B	C	D	E
1	PartNumber	Pitch (deg)	RotorInterfaceAngle (deg)	OffsetFromRotationalAxis (mm)	NumberOfVanes
2	1350	20	30	25.4	7
3	1351	25	18	30	13
4	1352	30	15	34.3	14
5	1353	35	11	37.3	16
6	1354	40	7	39.6	18
7	1355	45	2	40.6	15
8					

Figure 9–32

9. Save and close the spreadsheet. Close any messages that display in *Knowledge* dialog boxes. The *Design Table* dialog box updates, as shown in Figure 9–33.

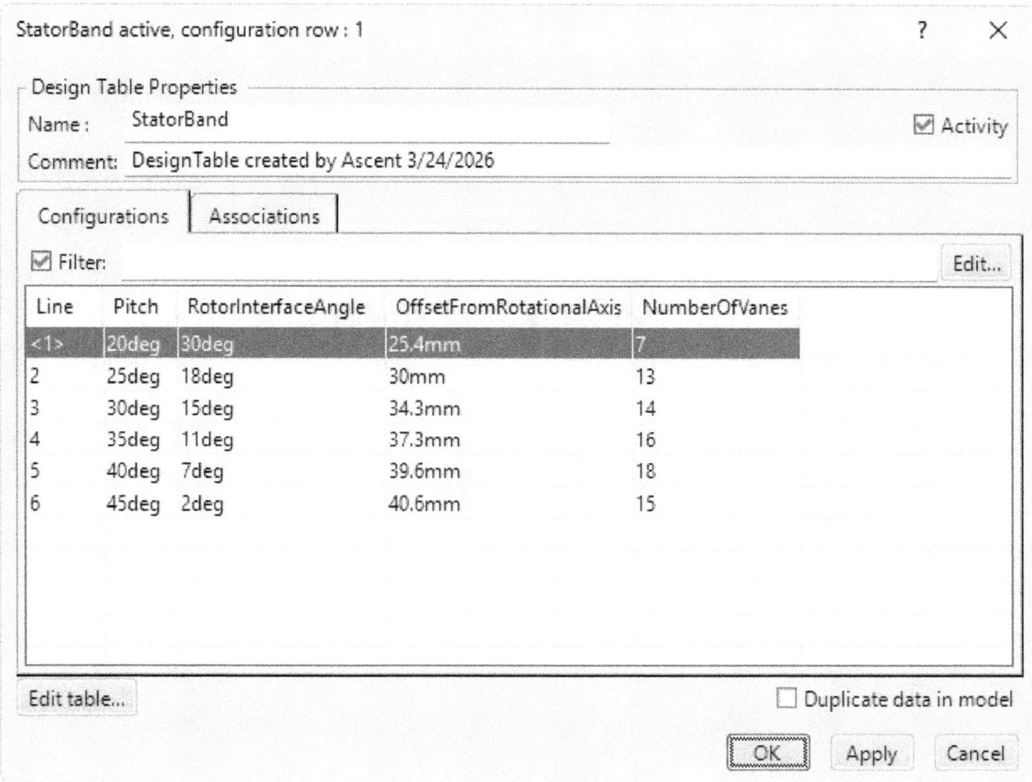

Figure 9–33

10. Select the *Associations* tab.

11. Click **Associate** to link the *Parameters PartNumber* value with the *Columns PartNumber* value. Reorder the *PartNumber* parameter so it displays at the top of the list.

12. Select the *Configurations* tab. The dialog box displays as shown in Figure 9–34.

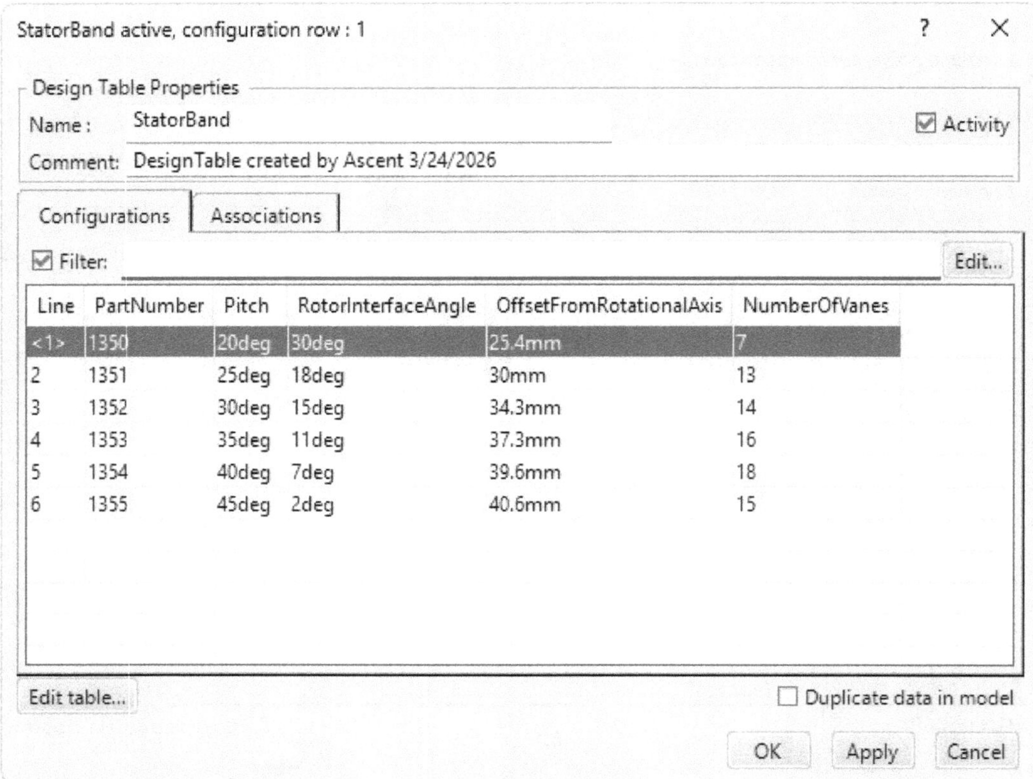

Figure 9–34

13. Select the configuration with **PartNumber 1355** and click **Apply**. The model displays as shown in Figure 9–35.

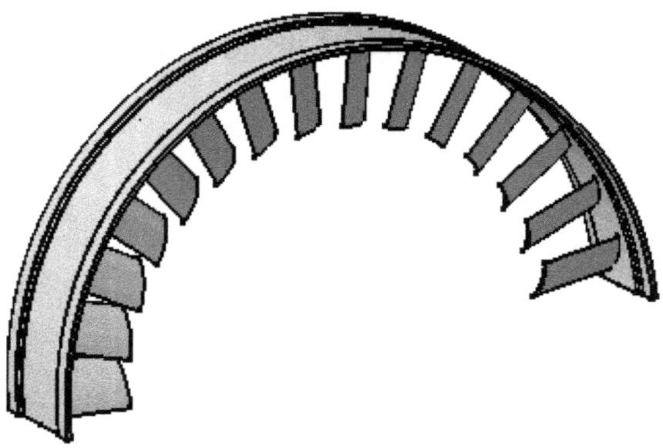

Figure 9–35

14. Open two other configurations in the part window to ensure that the parameter values are working correctly.
15. Reset the current model to **PartNumber 1350** and close the *Design Table* dialog box.

Task 3: Create a component family catalog.

1. In the Top Bar, click  (Add/Create)>**New Content**. In the *New Content* window, select **Component Family**, as shown in Figure 9–36.

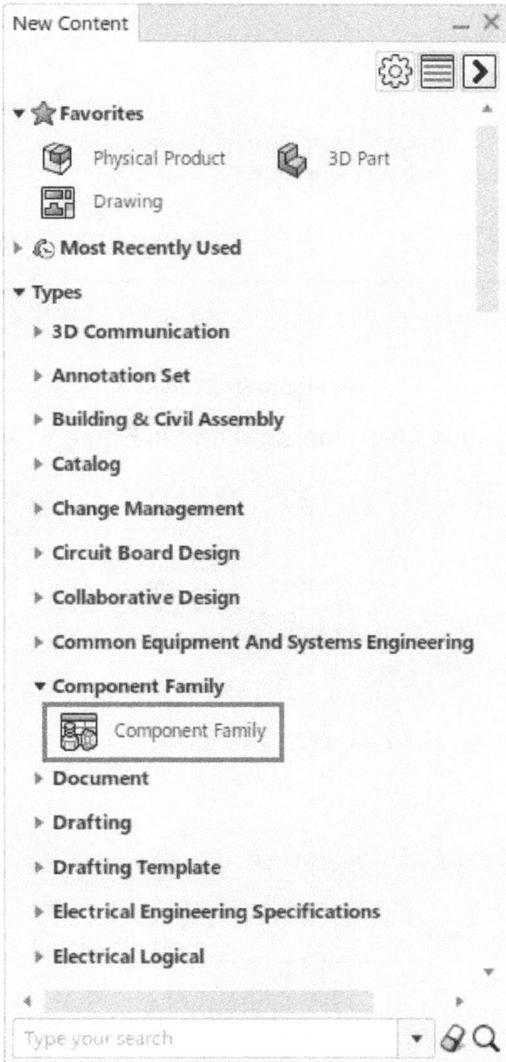

Figure 9–36

2. The *Component Family* dialog box opens, as shown in Figure 9–37. Enter ***Your_Initials*_StatorBand** as the *Title*.

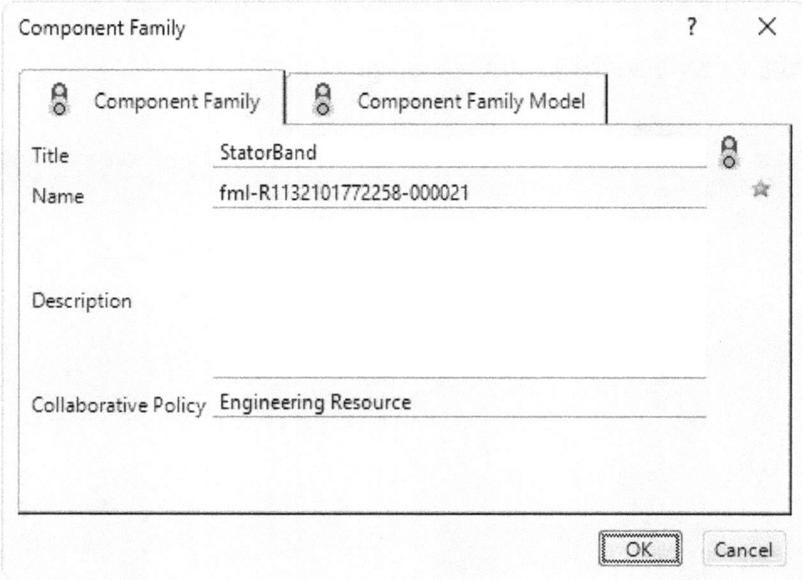

Figure 9–37

3. Select the *Component Family Model* tab, as shown in Figure 9–38, and set the appropriate options.

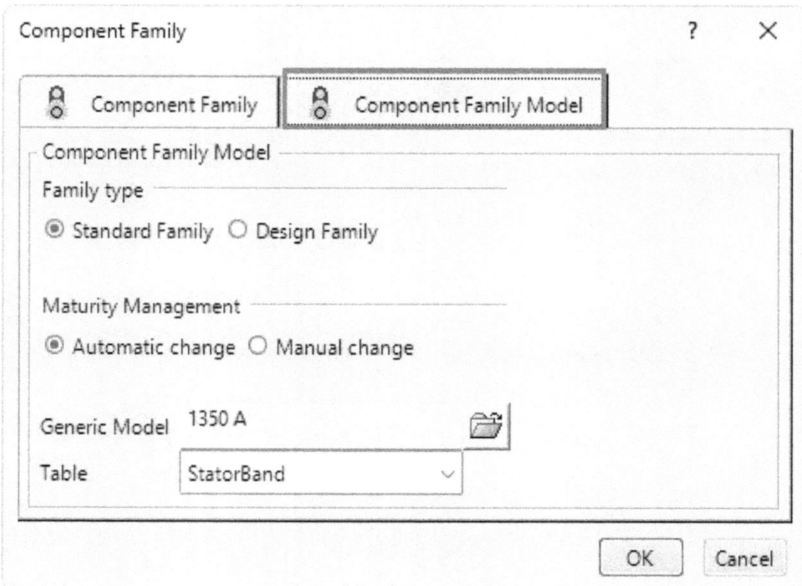

Figure 9–38

4. Click **OK** in the *Component Family Definition* dialog box. The system reads in each instance from the design table.

   - Once complete, the *Component Family Definition* window displays as shown in Figure 9–39.

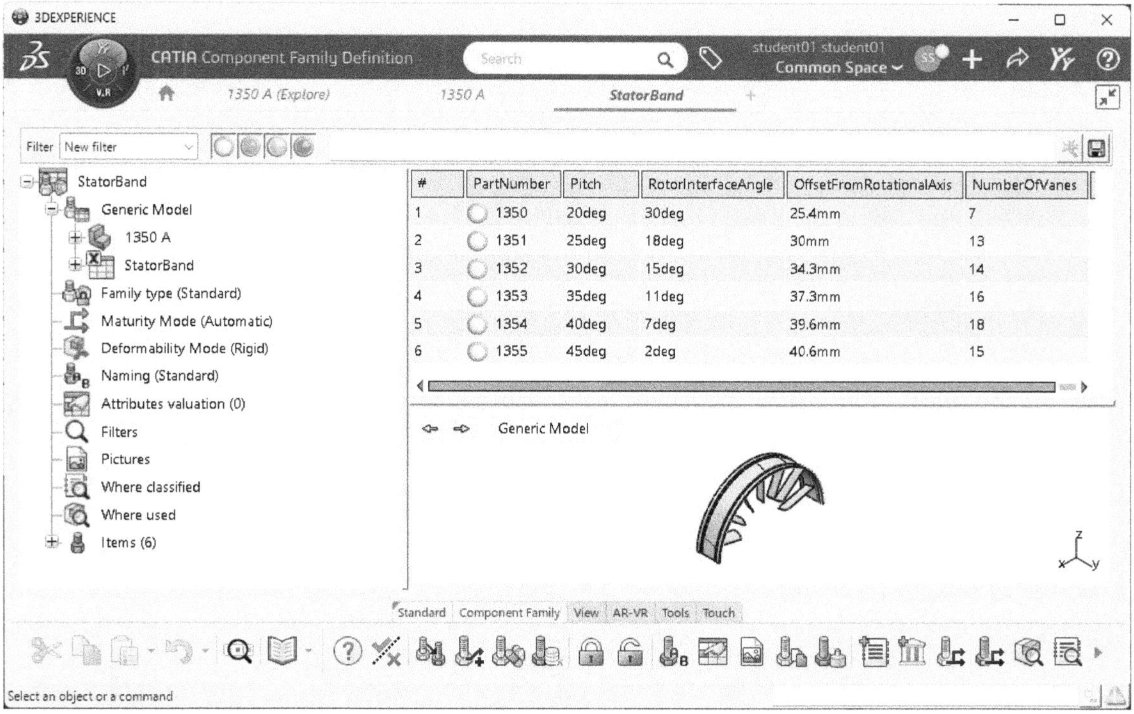

Figure 9–39

5. Save the component family and close all tabs.

End of practice

Chapter 10

Assembly Analysis

This chapter covers the techniques that you can use to analyze an assembly. The **Interference Analysis** tool enables you to determine whether any interference is present in the assembly.

Learning Objectives

- Determine whether interference exists in an assembly.
- Analyze assembly degrees of freedom.

10.1 Interference

When creating an assembly, the system permits interference between components. There are two tools that are used to evaluate an assembly for interference and related conditions:

- Engineering connection interference checks
- **Interference Check** app

Comparing V5 to 3DEXPERIENCE

In CATIA V5, interference analysis results are stored in a single node, as shown in Figure 10–1. Multiple interference results are stored under this node.

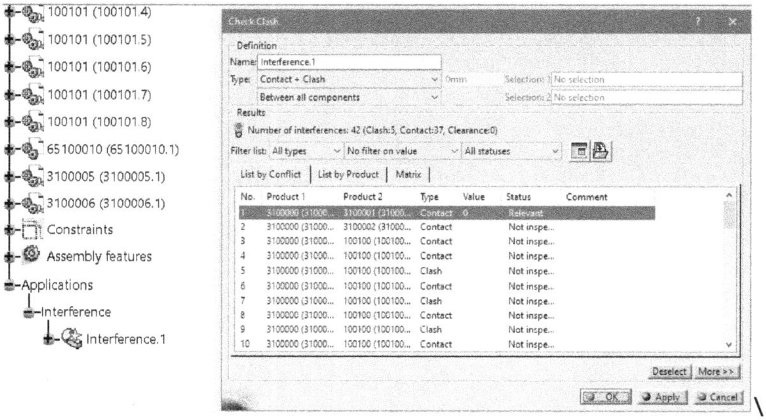

Figure 10–1

In the 3DEXPERIENCE platform, interference results are stored in a *Interference Simulation* object, as shown in Figure 10–2. The results are stored separately under the *Result* node.

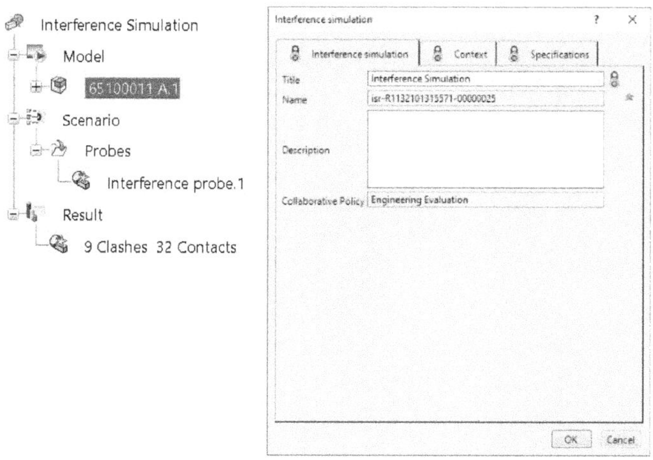

Figure 10–2

Engineering Connection Interference Check

During the definition of engineering connections, the *Interferences* tab in the *Engineering Connection Definition* dialog box (shown in Figure 10–3) provides the ability to define a check for clash/contact/clearance conditions between the related components as the engineering connection is created.

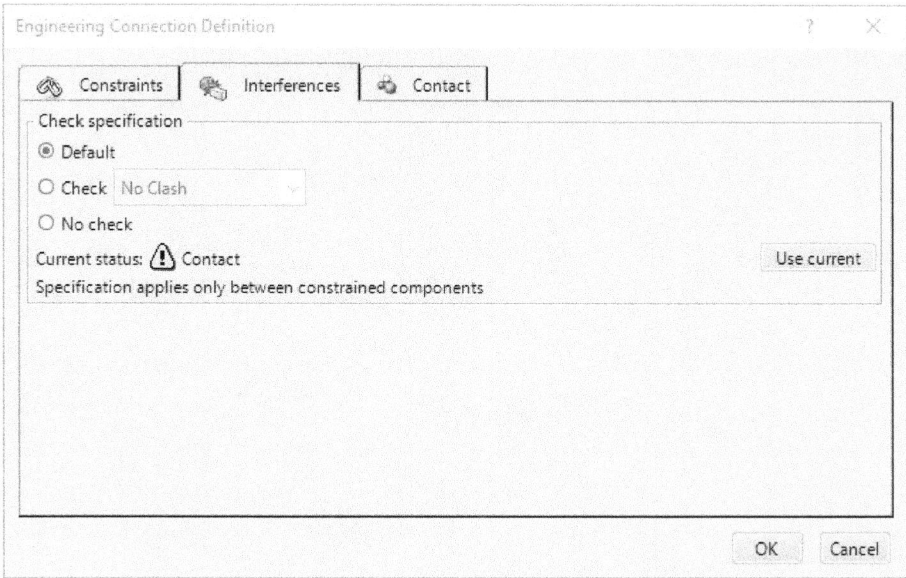

Figure 10–3

If the *Check specification* value is set to **Default**, the *Undefined Interference Specifications* dialog box is triggered, as shown in Figure 10–4. This enables a warning to be generated if downstream modifications result in the engineering connection components violating the check specification condition.

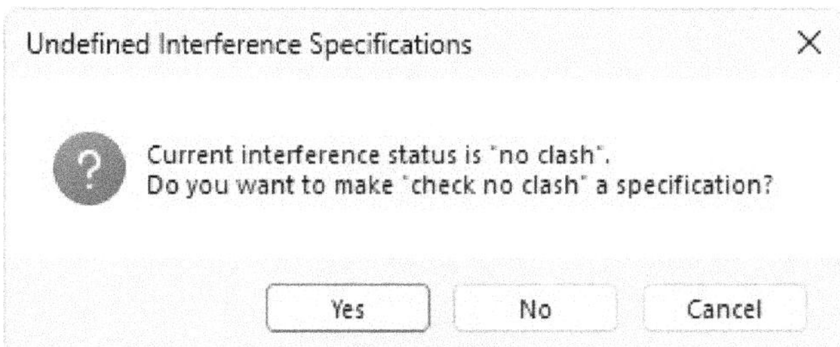

Figure 10–4

Interference Check App

The **Interference Check** app enables the analysis of conditions including clash, contact, and clearance between two or more components. It is used to determine whether interference exists, and if so, the degree of interference. To access the app, do one of the following:

- Click (Create Interference Simulation) in the *Assembly* section of the Action Bar. The *Interference simulation* dialog box opens, as shown in Figure 10–5. Enter a *Title* and click **OK**. The system places you in the **ENOVIA Interference Check** app.

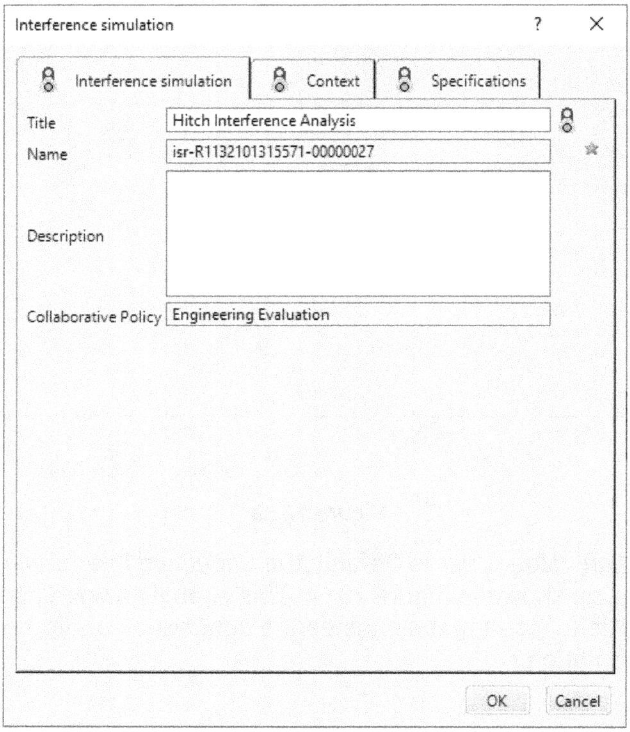

Figure 10–5

- Click **Roles, Apps & Solutions portfolio** in the Compass, as shown in Figure 10–6. In the list of apps, click (Interference Check).

Figure 10–6

In the *Interference Analysis* section of the Action Bar, click (Analyze Interference). To see the results of this analysis, click above the Action Bar. The results expand and display as shown in Figure 10–7.

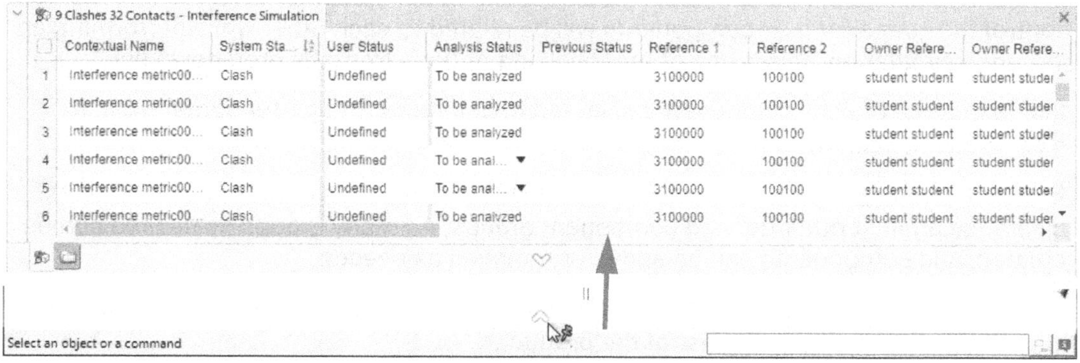

Figure 10–7

If any conflicts occur, you can select and view the result, as shown in Figure 10–8. The pair of interfering components is visible and all other components are displayed in a transparent state. Transparency can be adjusted by dragging the context transparency slider.

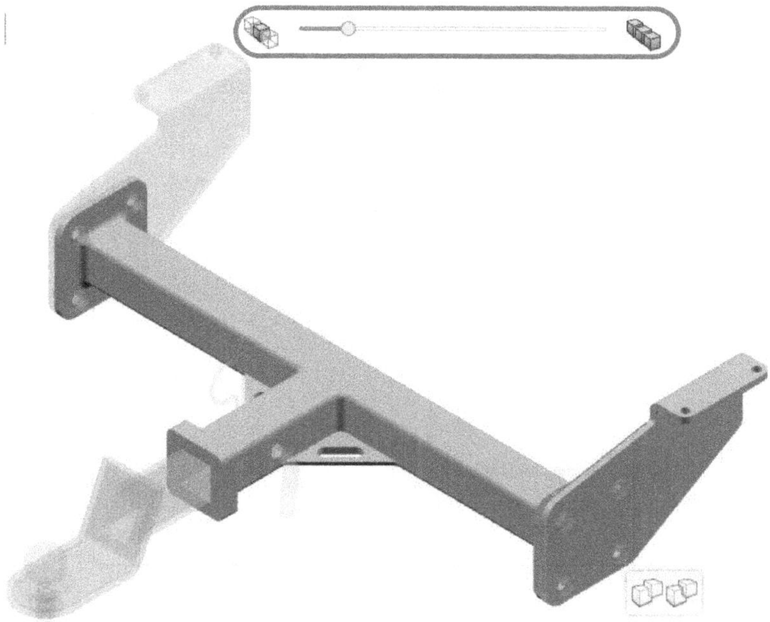

Figure 10–8

By default, interference analysis checks between all components for **Clash** and **Contact** (and **Clearance**, if selected). The scope of the analysis might be restricted through the options available in the *Context* tab, as shown in Figure 10–9.

To access the *Interference Simulation definition* dialog box, click  (Edit Specification) in the *Interference Analysis* section of the Action Bar.

To control the scope for how components will be related to each other while performing an interference simulation, select one of the following options from the drop-down list:

- **Inside groups:** Checks components selected to belong to Group1 for contact/clash/clearance between them.
- **Groups against groups:** Checks components that belong to a group for contact/clash/clearance against other defined component groups. As many groups as desired can be created, and components can be added or removed as needed.
- **Groups against context:** Checks components selected to belong to Group1 for contact/clash/clearance against the rest of the product.

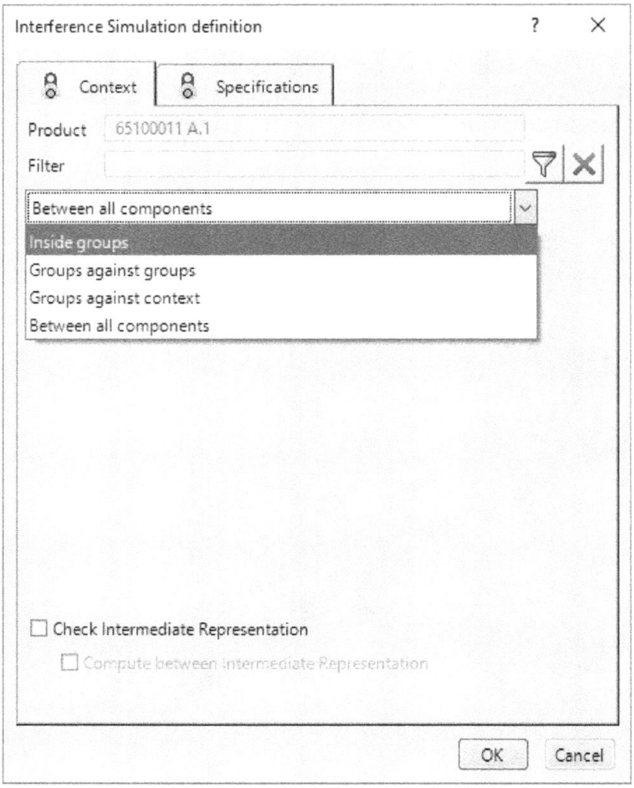

Figure 10–9

10.2 Degrees of Freedom

When a component is inserted into an assembly, the unconstrained model is positioned in a default location and orientation with respect to the rest of the assembly. This component can translate to any position or rotate to any orientation. The ability to translate or rotate is known as *degrees of freedom* (DOF). An unconstrained component has six degrees of freedom: three translation and three rotation with respect to a coordinate reference framework, as shown in Figure 10–10.

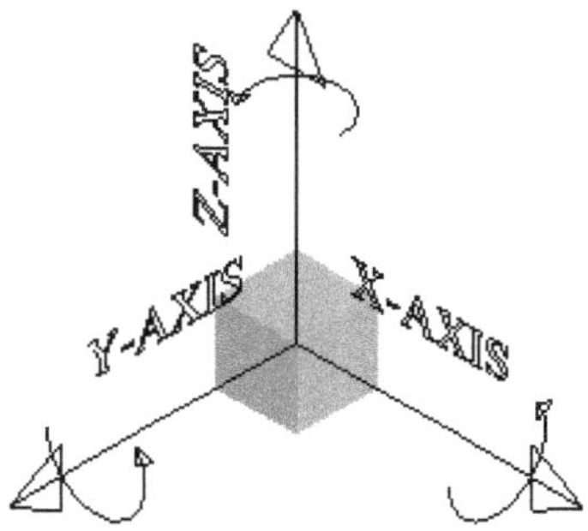

Figure 10–10

As constraints are added to a component, they restrict degrees of freedom.

Analyzing Degrees of Freedom

When constraining a component to complete a design, ensure that it does not have any unconstrained degrees of freedom. You can check the degrees of freedom of a component by right-clicking on a component and selecting **Component object>Component Degrees of Freedom**. Three possible results can occur:

- The component is unconstrained.
- The component is fully constrained.
- The component is constrained but has degrees of freedom.

Component Is Unconstrained

If the component does not have any constraints defined, the message dialog box shown in Figure 10–11 opens.

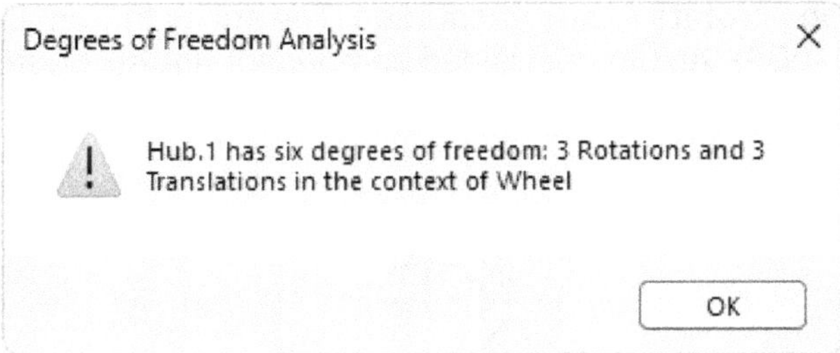

Figure 10–11

Component Is Fully Constrained

If the component is constrained in all six degrees of freedom, the message dialog box shown in Figure 10–12 opens.

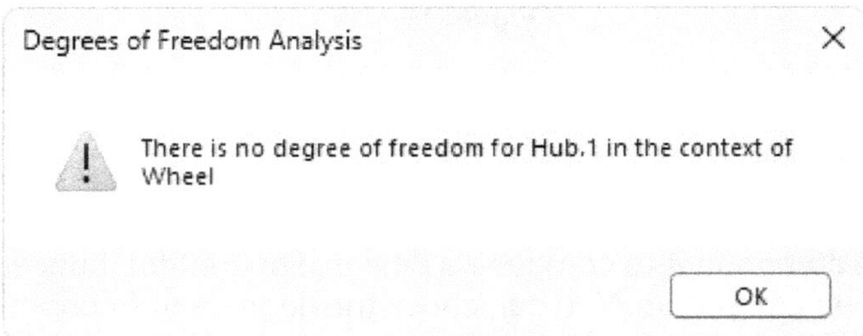

Figure 10–12

Component Is Constrained But Has Degrees of Freedom

If the model has between one and five degrees of freedom, the *Degrees of Freedom Analysis* dialog box opens, as shown in Figure 10–13.

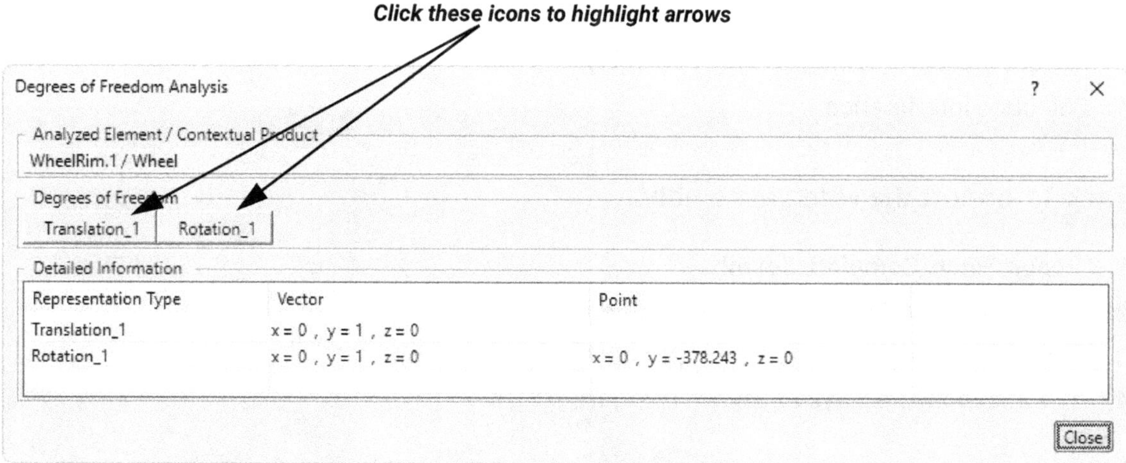

Figure 10–13

The dialog box lists the degrees of freedom of the component and enables you to display vector arrows on the model to see their directions.

Practice 10a
Assembly Information

Practice Objectives

- Extract measurements from the assembly.
- Calculate interference.

Task 1: Import the Hitch assembly.

1. Import **Hitch_Complete.3dxml**.
2. Right-click on **65100011** and select **Open**.
3. In the *View* section of the Action Bar, click (Fit All In).
4. The assembly displays as shown in Figure 10–14.

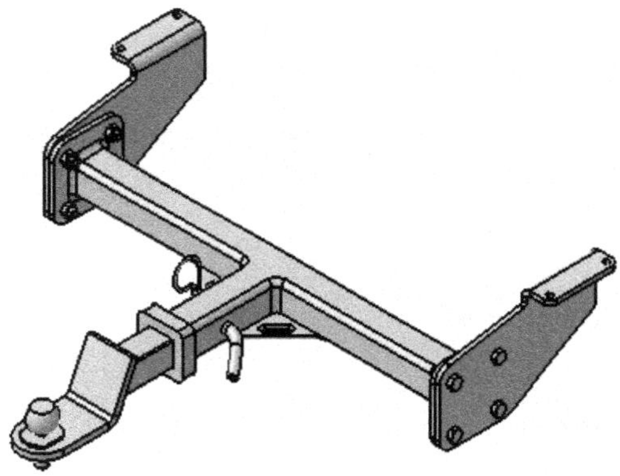

Figure 10–14

Task 2: Check for interference.

1. Ensure that you are in the **Assembly Design** app.
2. In the *Assembly* section of the Action Bar, click (Create Interference Simulation).
3. In the *Interference simulation* dialog box, enter ***Your_Initials*_Hitch Interference Analysis** for the *Title* and click **OK**.
4. The system places you in the **ENOVIA Interference Check** app. In the *Interference* section of the Action Bar, click (Edit Specifications).
5. In the *Interference Simulation definition* window, on the *Specifications* tab, ensure that **Class** and **Contact** are turned on. Click **OK**.

6. In the *Interference* section of the Action Bar, click (Analyze Interference).
7. If needed, click above the Action Bar. The results of the interference analysis are shown in Figure 10–15.

9 Clashes 32 Contacts - Hitch Interference Analysis

	Name	System Status	User Status	Analysis Status	Previous Status	Reference 1	Reference 2	Owner F
1	Interference metric00000711	Clash	Undefined	To be analyzed		3100000	100100	SS stu
2	Interference metric00000712	Clash	Undefined	To be analyzed		3100000	100100	SS stu
3	Interference metric00000713	Clash	Undefined	To be analyzed		3100000	100100	SS stu
4	Interference metric00000714	Clash	Undefined	To be analyzed		3100000	100100	SS stu
5	Interference metric00000715	Clash	Undefined	To be analyzed		3100000	100100	SS stu
6	Interference metric00000716	Clash	Undefined	To be analyzed		3100000	100100	SS stu
7	Interference metric00000717	Clash	Undefined	To be analyzed		3100000	3100003	SS stu
8	Interference metric00000718	Clash	Undefined	To be analyzed		3100000	3100006	stu

Figure 10–15

8. Note the detected clash conditions listed in the *System Status* column.
9. Select the first row where a clash is indicated. The model zooms in to display the location of the clash on the model. The clash is between the **T-Support** and the **Bolt**, as shown in Figure 10–16.

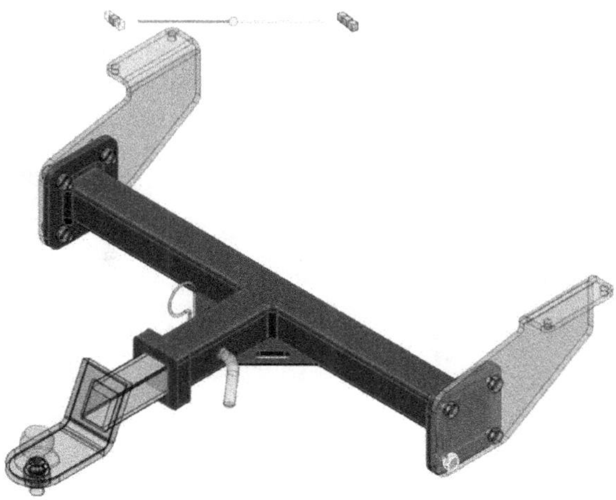

Figure 10–16

10. Continue to review the other clashes in the model. There is a problem with the placement of some of the bolts, and possibly the retaining pin, and the **Ball_Mount** product.
11. Click the X in the upper-right corner of the results panel to close it.

Task 3: Investigate the cause of the clash with measurements and sectioning.

1. In the *Interference* section of the Action Bar, click (Sectioning) to investigate the location of the first clash.
2. In the context toolbar, click (Specify Position). Select the center axis of each bolt, as shown in Figure 10–17.

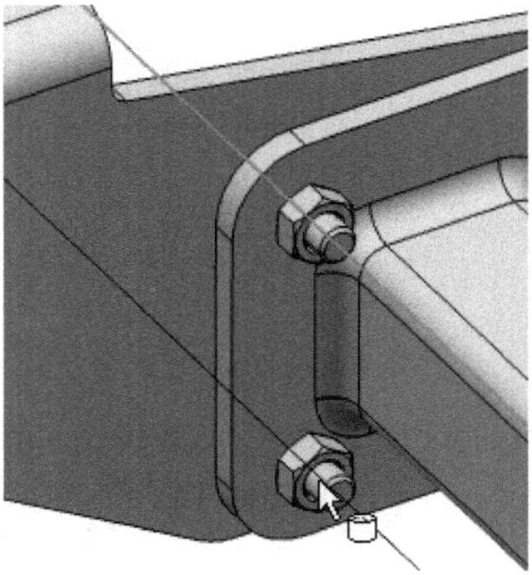

Figure 10–17

3. Zoom in and rotate if necessary on the clash location, as shown in Figure 10–18, to examine the reason for the clash. The upper portion of the intersection should display interference and the lower portion of the intersection should display clearance.

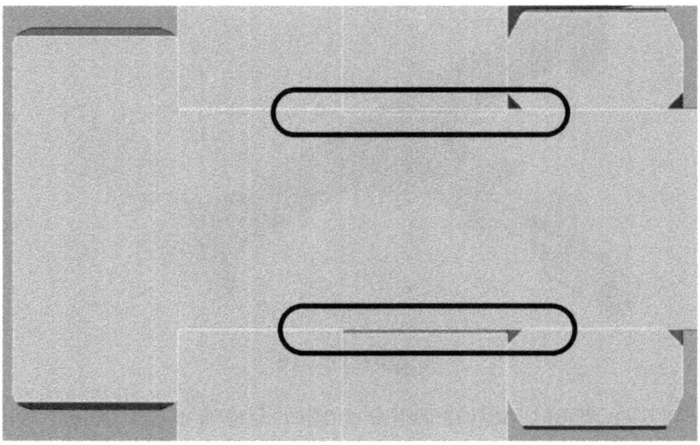

Figure 10–18

4. Click (Measure Item) to investigate further.

5. Select the edge of the support shown in Figure 10–19. Its value is **89.2mm**.

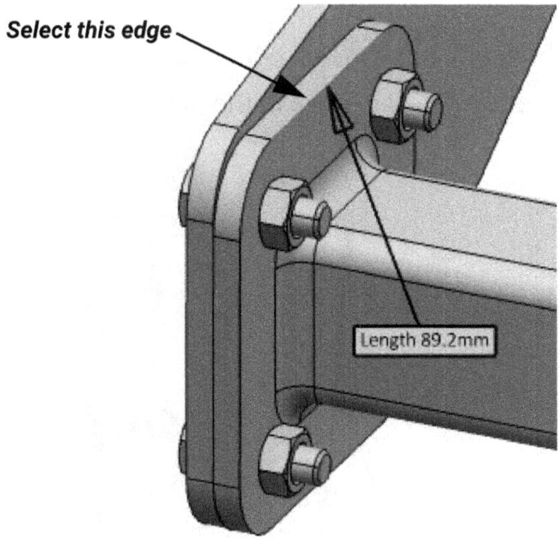

Figure 10–19

6. Select the edge shown in Figure 10–20. Its value is also **89.2mm**. These dimensions are used for the increment of the hole pattern.

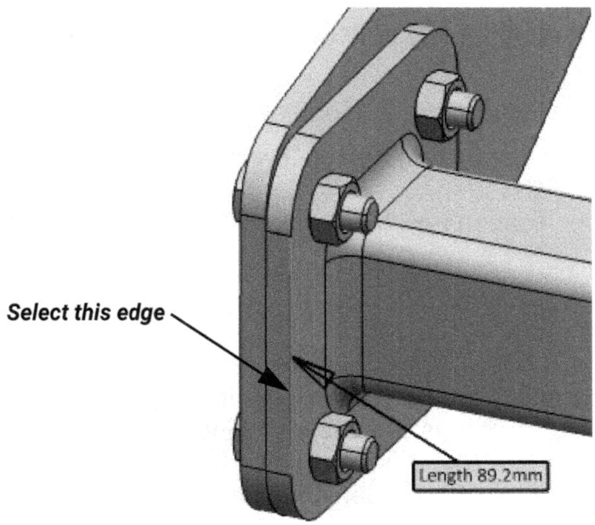

Figure 10–20

7. Verify that the dimensional increment of **RectPattern.1** and **RectPattern.2** for part **3100000** is **89.2mm** in both directions.

   Note: *You might have to close the Measure Item dialog box to verify the dimensional increment of RectPattern.*

8. Confirm that you are in the **Interference Check for Native Apps** application. If not, double-click on the model, then expand the node in the specification tree.
9. Click (Measure Between) in the *Measure Item* dialog box.
10. Measure between the spacing of the holes in the brace, as shown in Figure 10–21.

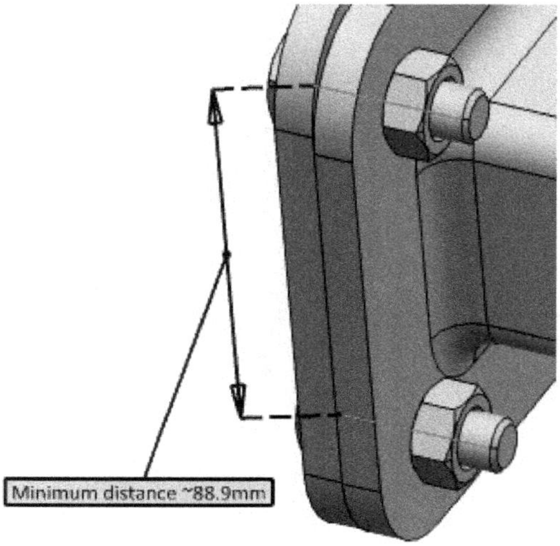

Figure 10–21

11. Note that the hole spacing for this pattern is **88.9** and not **89.2**, which is the dimension used by the pattern.
12. Modify the spacing of **RectPattern.1**, in both the **3100001** and **3100002** parts, to [**89.2**].
13. To update the assembly, verify that the top-level assembly is active by double-clicking on **65100011** in the specification tree, then click (Update) in the *Standard* section of the *Action Bar*.

    Note: *The tree will collapse when you double-click on it. To expand it again, double-click a second time.*

14. You will also need to update the simulation by switching back to the **Interference Check for Native Apps** app (you can do this by double-clicking on **Hitch Interference Analysis** at the top of the tree) and clicking (Update Simulation) in the *Interference* section of the Action Bar.
15. Check for clash again. There should not be any clash involving the bolts.
16. Save the analysis file and close all tabs.

End of practice

Practice 10b
Degrees of Freedom

Practice Objective

- Analyze degrees of freedom.

In this practice, you will create a product and assemble the **Hub** part as the base component. The **WheelRim** part is assembled to the **Hub** part. The resulting configuration is shown in Figure 10–22. You will analyze the degrees of freedom throughout the assembly process to demonstrate how applying assembly constraints affects the degrees of freedom of a component.

Figure 10–22

Task 1: Import the required files.

1. Import **DegreesOfFreedom.3dxml**.

Task 2: Create a product file.

1. In the Top Bar, select (Add/Create)>**Physical Product**.
2. In the *Physical Product* dialog box, type ***Your_Initials*_Wheel** in the *Title* field.
3. In the *Description* field, type **Front-end wheel assembly**.
4. Click **OK**.

Task 3: Assemble the base component.

1. Assemble **Hub** from the *Bookmarks app - DegreesOfFreedom* tab and apply a **Fix** (Fix in Space) engineering connection.
2. Orient the assembly as shown in Figure 10–23.

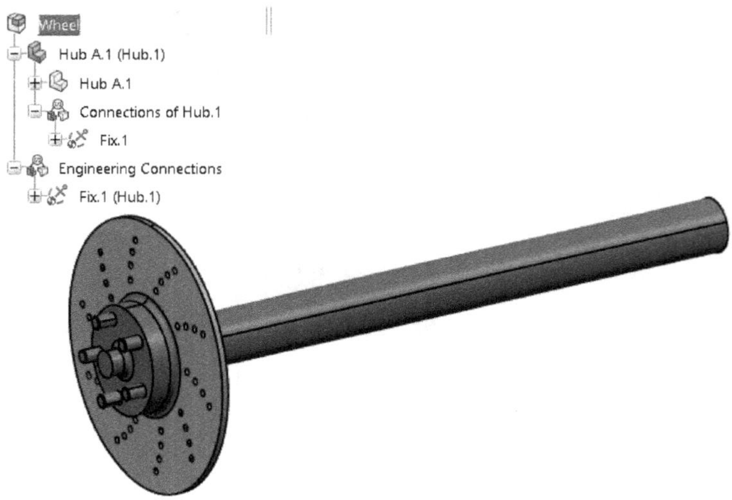

Figure 10–23

Task 4: Analyze component degrees of freedom.

1. In the specification tree, right-click on the **Hub** part and select **Hub.1 object>Component Degrees of Freedom**.

   The *Degrees of Freedom Analysis* message dialog box opens, indicating that there is no degree of freedom for **Hub.1**, as shown in Figure 10–24. This is because the **Fix** engineering connection has been applied.

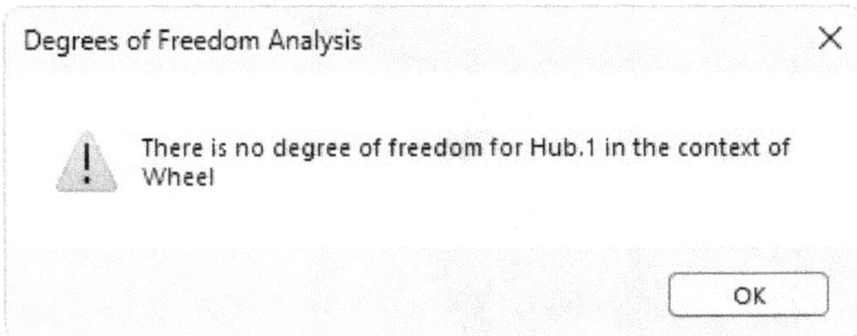

Figure 10–24

2. Click **OK** to close the dialog box.

Task 5: Assemble the second component.

1. Assemble **WheelRim** into the **Wheel** assembly from the *Bookmarks app - DegreesOfFreedom* tab.
2. In the specification tree, right-click on the **WheelRim** part and select **WheelRim.1 object> Component Degrees of Freedom** to analyze its degrees of freedom.

   The system reports that **WheelRim** has six degrees of freedom, as shown in Figure 10–25.

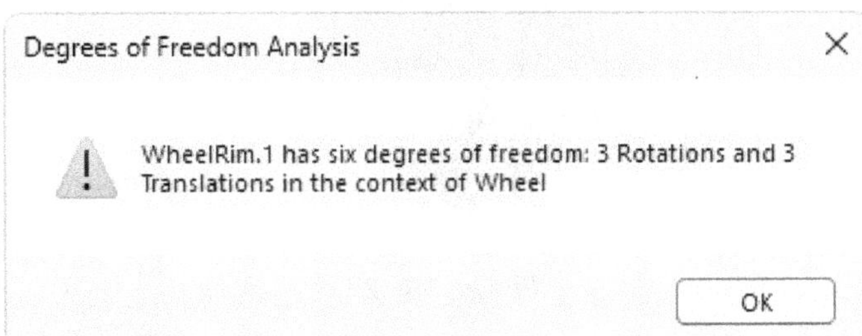

Figure 10–25

3. Click **OK**.

Task 6: Apply a constraint to the WheelRim.

1. Apply an engineering connection using a **Coincidence** constraint between the axis of the **Hub** part and the axis of the **WheelRim** part, as shown in Figure 10–26 and Figure 10–27.

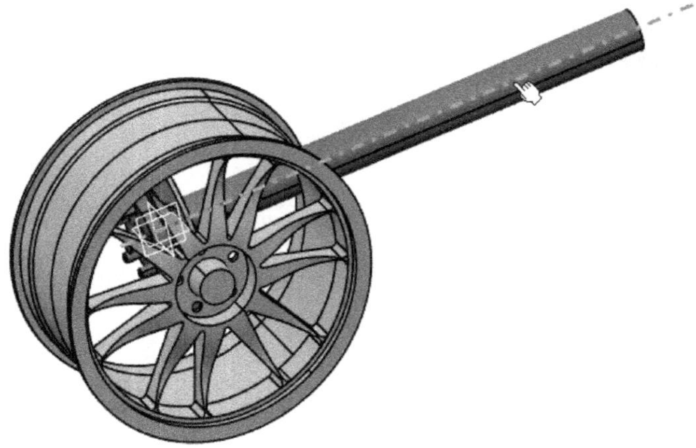

Figure 10–26

Note: *You can select the cylindrical surface of the hub as well, which will also select the axis.*

Figure 10–27

2. When completing the engineering connection, click **No** in the *Undefined Interference Specification* dialog box.

3. Click  (Update) to update the assembly.

4. Analyze the degrees of freedom for the **WheelRim** part. The *Degrees of Freedom Analysis* dialog box opens, as shown in Figure 10–28, indicating two degrees of freedom. The **WheelRim** currently has a rotational and a translational degree of freedom.

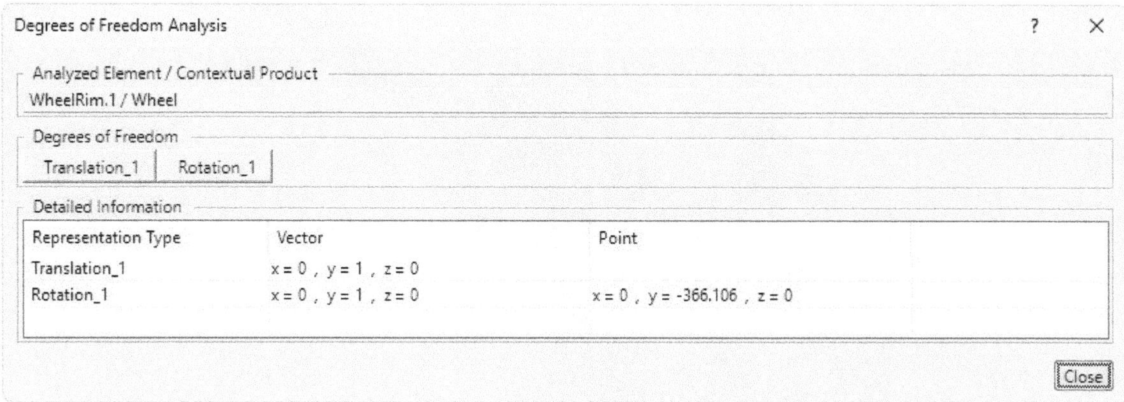

Figure 10–28

5. Click **Close**.
6. In the *Assembly* section of the Action Bar, click (Degrees of Freedom Display).
7. The *B.I. Essentials* dialog box opens, and the degrees of freedom are displayed in the color scheme shown in Figure 10–29.

   Note: *The hub is shown as* ***Fixed*** *and the wheel is shown as* ***Partially constrained****.*

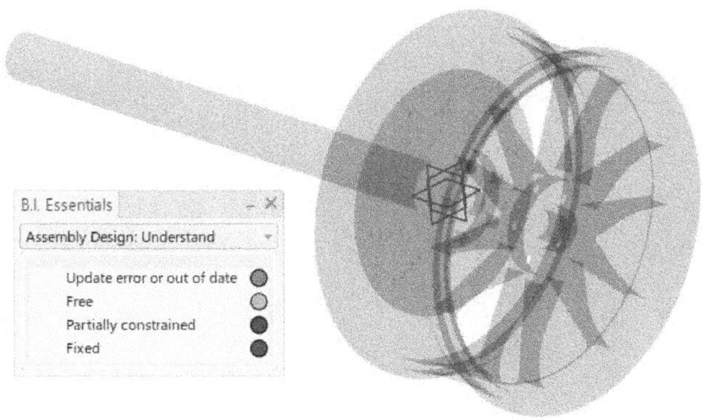

Figure 10–29

8. Close the *B.I. Essential* dialog box.

9. Reposition the **WheelRim** part, as shown in Figure 10–30, using the Robot.

Figure 10–30

10. Apply an engineering connection using a **Contact** constraint between the back surface of the wheel and the front of the hub, as shown in Figure 10–31.

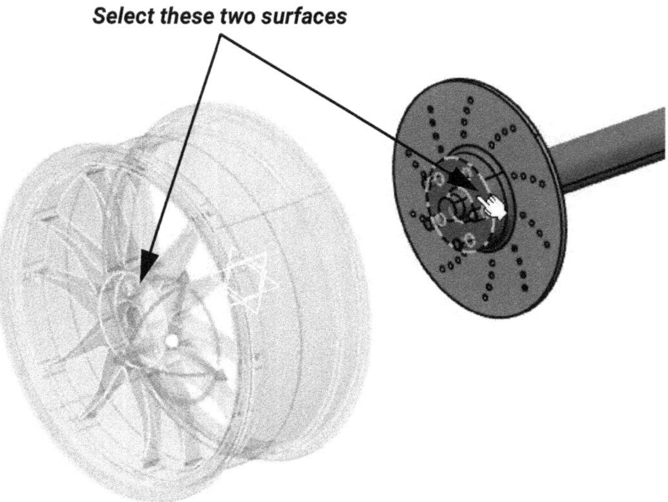

Figure 10–31

11. When prompted to enrich an existing connection, as shown in Figure 10–32, click **Enrich**.

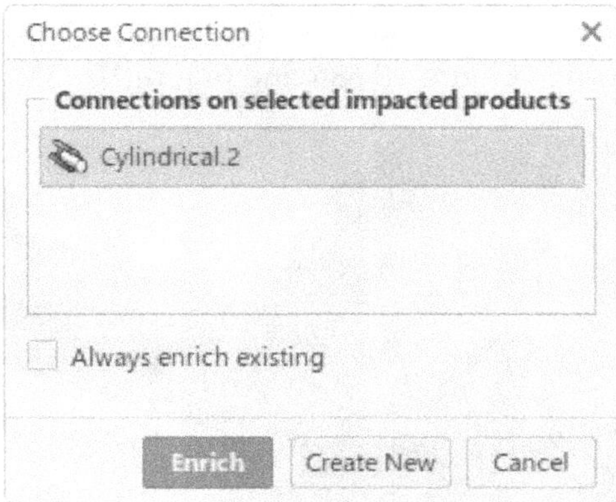

Figure 10–32

12. Click **OK** to complete the engineering connection.
13. An *Invalid engineering connection configuration* dialog box appears. This is because the *Connection type* of **Cylindrical** that worked with one constraint does not work when both are applied. Click **Edit connection**.
14. Click (Unlock) to free the engineering connection to change its type. It automatically changes to **Revolute**, which is acceptable.
15. Click **OK**.
16. If prompted regarding kinematic degrees of freedom, click **Yes**.
17. Analyze the degrees of freedom for the **WheelRim** part. This part should only have one (rotational) degree of freedom, as shown in Figure 10–33.

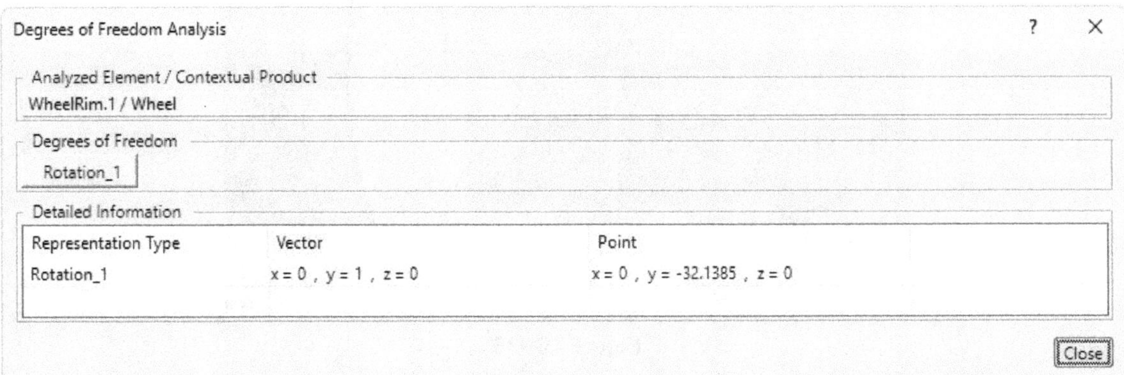

Figure 10–33

18. Double-click on the **Revolute.2** engineering connection under the *Engineering Connections* node in the specification tree.

19. Click (Unlock) to free the engineering connection to allow more constraints to be added.
20. Create a **Coincidence** constraint between the axis on one of the **Hub** studs and one of the **WheelRim** holes, as shown in Figure 10–34 and Figure 10–35.

Figure 10–34

Figure 10–35

21. Click **OK** to complete the engineering connection.

22. Perform a **Component Degrees of Freedom** analysis for the **WheelRim** part. It should not have any degrees of freedom, as shown in Figure 10–36.

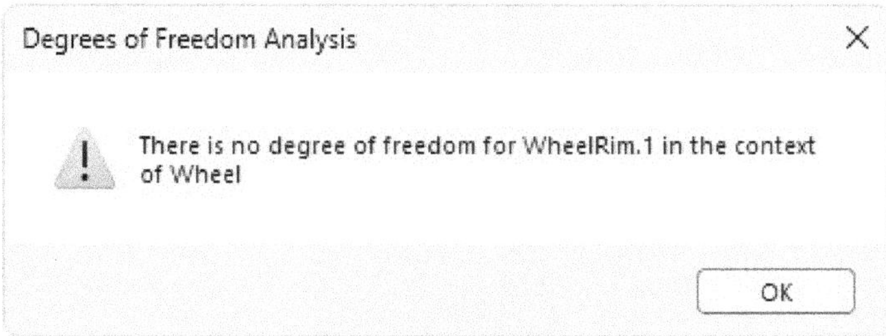

Figure 10–36

23. Save the model and close the tabs.

End of practice

Chapter 11

Drawings

This chapter introduces the **2D Drafting** app by outlining the drawing creation process. You will learn how to create, modify, and manipulate drawing views.

Learning Objectives

- Understand the steps required to create a drawing.
- Review the **2D Drafting** app interface.
- Add views and create a drawing frame and title block.
- Understand the view orientation compass.
- Review the available view properties.
- Learn how to manipulate views.
- Learn how to update a drawing when geometry changes.

11.1 Creating a New Drawing

All drafting view geometry and dimension information comes from the 3D model. The 3D model must be open to create a drawing.

How To: Create a New Drawing

1. Open the model that is to be included in the new drawing, as shown in Figure 11–1.

Figure 11–1

2. With the 3D part or the product level active, right-click on the 3D part level in the specification tree and select **Insert>Drawing**, as shown in Figure 11–2.

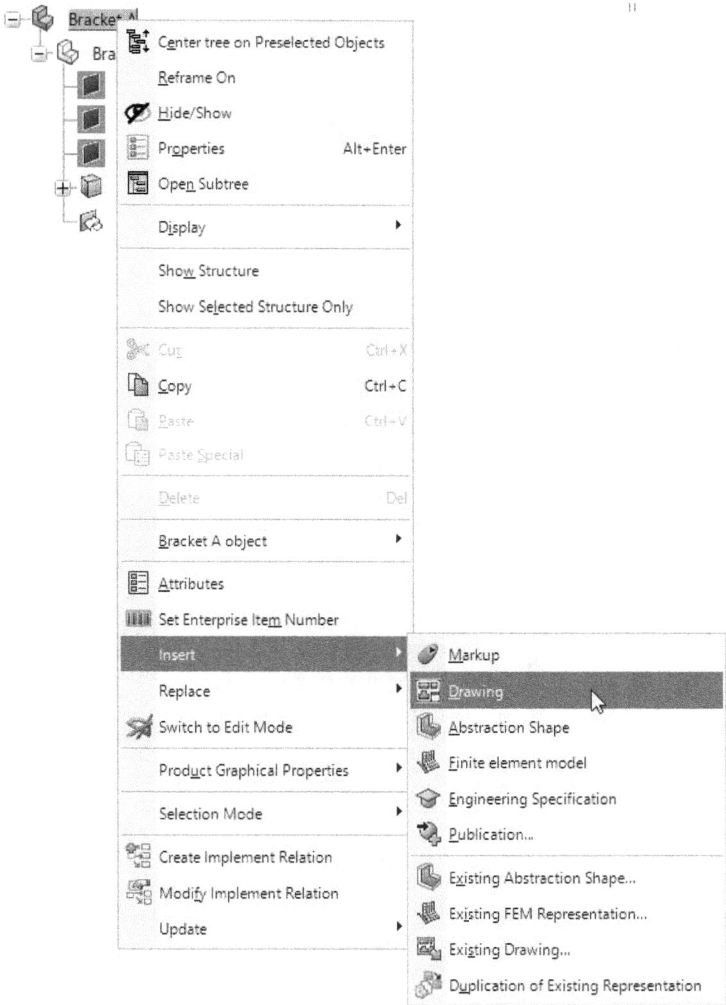

Figure 11–2

3. In the *Drawing* dialog box, enter a *Title* for the new drawing, as shown in Figure 11–3.

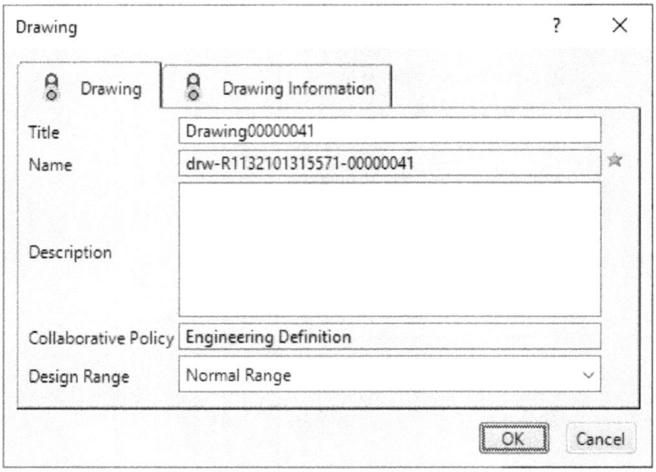

Figure 11–3

4. Select the *Drawing Information* tab and select the drafting *Standard* and *Sheet Style* options, as shown in Figure 11–4.

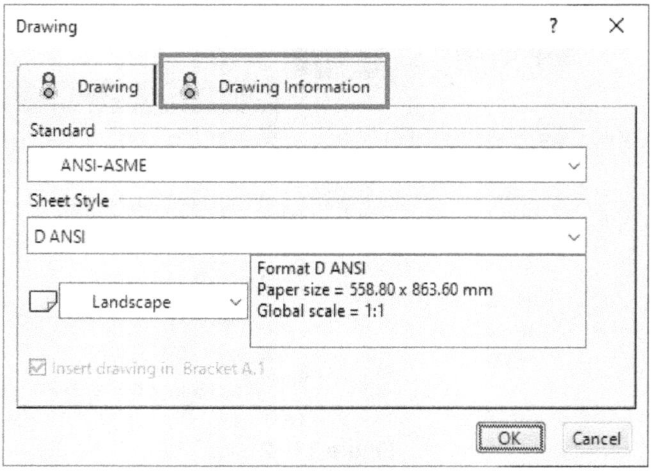

Figure 11–4

5. Click **OK** to begin with an empty drawing. The drawing displays in the specification tree, as shown in Figure 11–5. Double-click on the drawing entity in the specification tree to open the drawing.

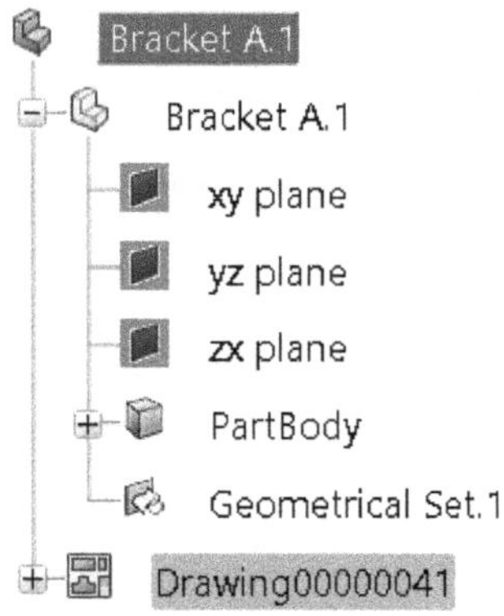

Figure 11–5

11.2 Drafting App Interface

The user interface of the **Drafting** app is shown in Figure 11–6.

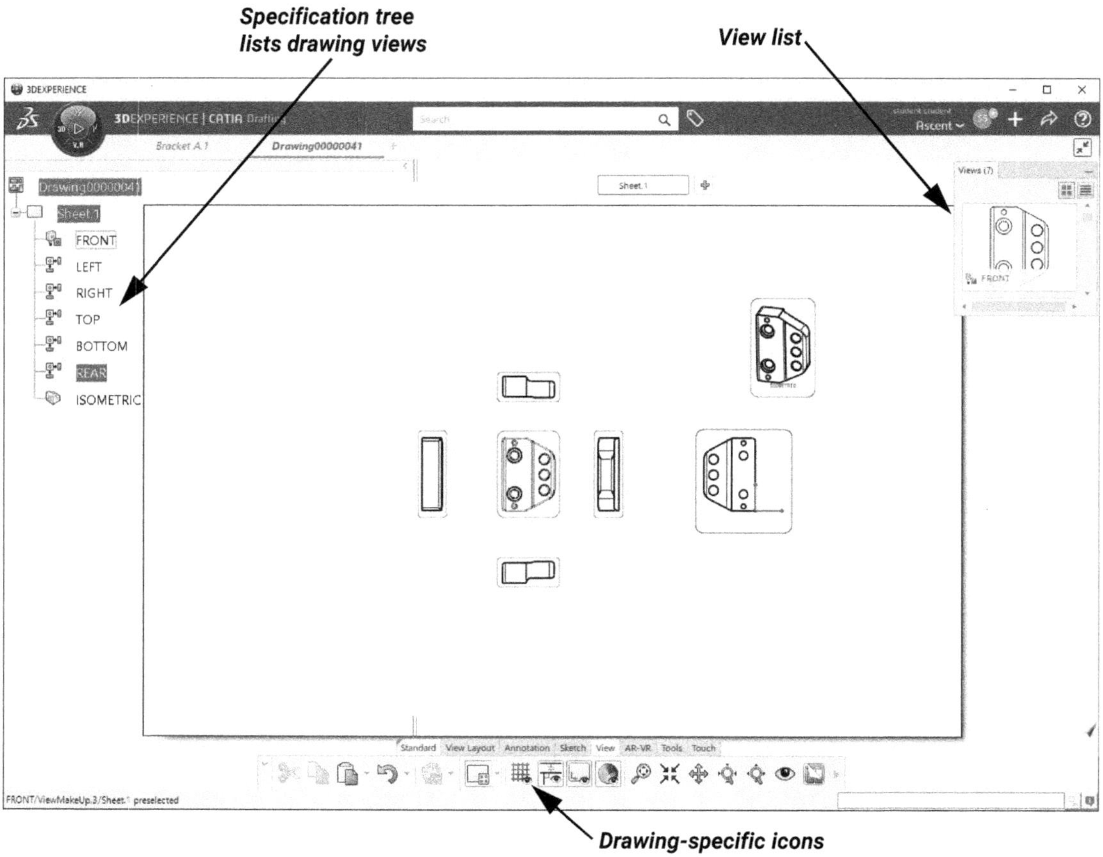

Figure 11–6

11.3 Adding Views

Views are added to the drawing using the icons in the *View Layout* section of the Action Bar, as shown in Figure 11–7.

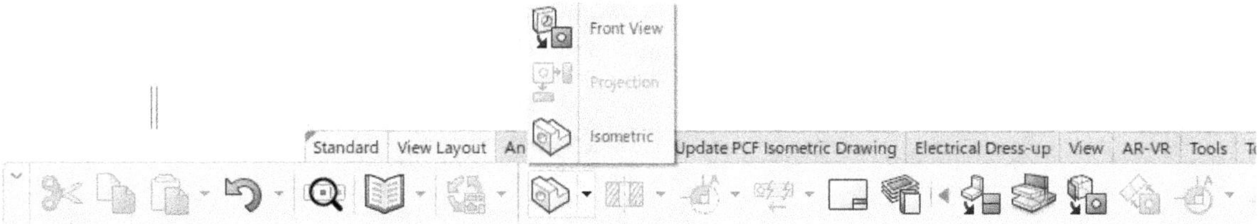

Figure 11–7

The placement and orientation of the first drawing view requires the selection of a reference from the 3D model. To facilitate this selection, you can click between tabs to move from the drawing to the part and back, as shown in Figure 11–8.

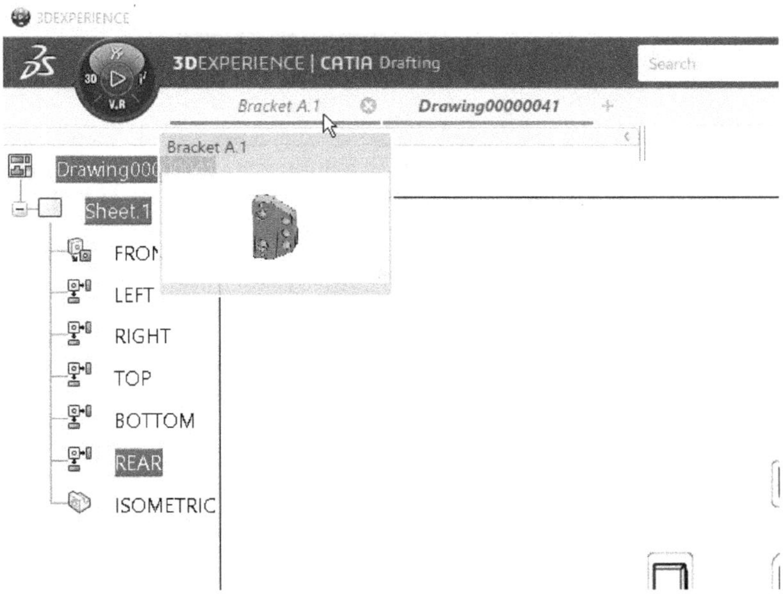

Figure 11–8

The first drawing view can be one of the view types listed in the table below. Select the appropriate icon in the *Projections* toolbar to initiate the creation of the first view.

View Type	Description
(Front View)	The front view (shown in Figure 11–9) is also known as the main view. You can use the view compass to orient it. 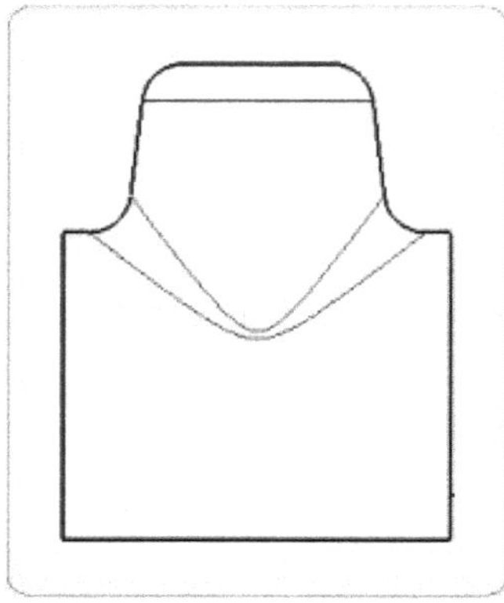 **Figure 11–9**
(Isometric)	An isometric view is used as a reference view (as shown in Figure 11–10) and is typically set at a smaller scale. A reference surface must be selected from the 3D model. You can use the view compass to orient this view. 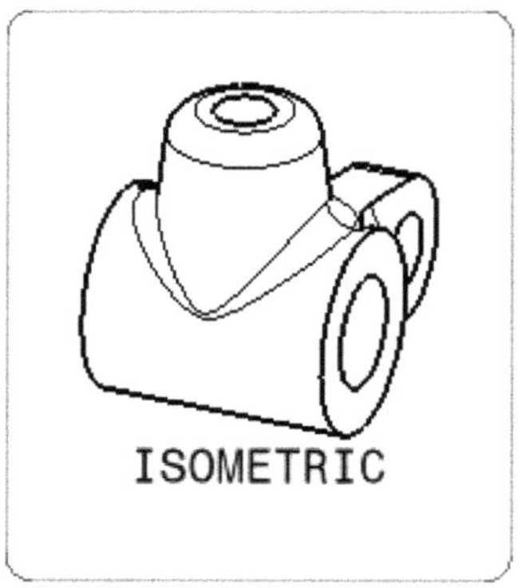 **Figure 11–10**

Once a view icon has been clicked, switch to the model window and select a planar surface, face, or reference plane. As you move your cursor over each surface, a preview displays to help you select the proper surface, as shown in Figure 11–11.

Figure 11–11

Once a reference surface is selected on the 3D model, the view orientation compass displays in the top-right corner of the display, as shown in Figure 11–12.

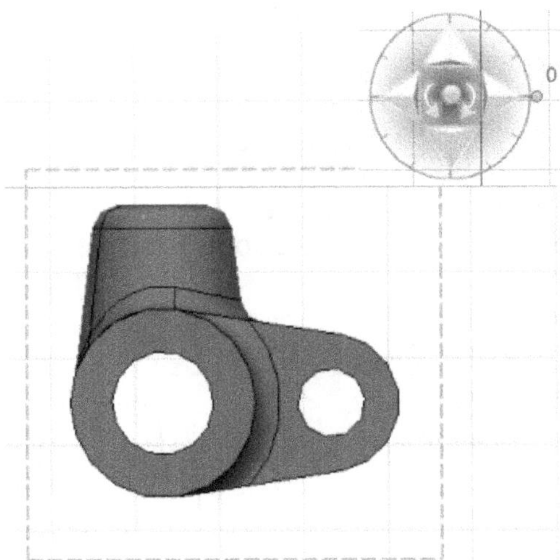

Figure 11–12

View Orientation Compass

The view orientation compass enables you to rotate and flip the front view until the correct orientation displays. The view compass functionality is shown in Figure 11–13.

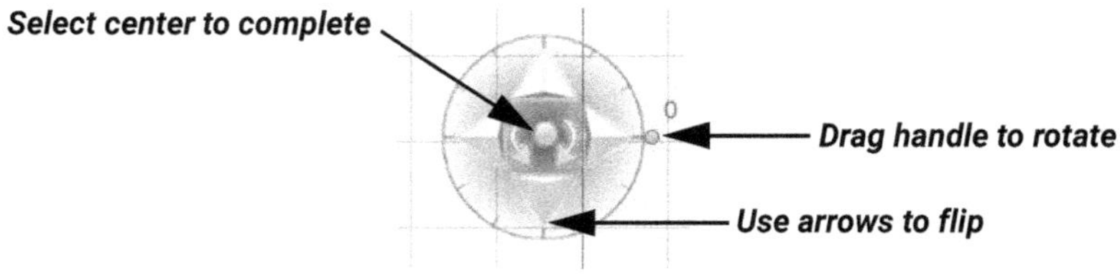

Figure 11–13

Use the right-click menu to change the compass properties, as shown in Figure 11–14 (right-click over the rotate handle).

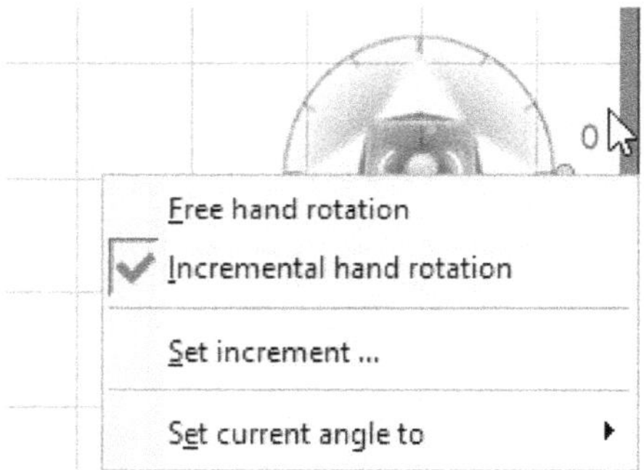

Figure 11–14

When you reach the required view orientation, select the center of the compass or select the active view to complete the view definition. The completed view definition is shown in Figure 11–15.

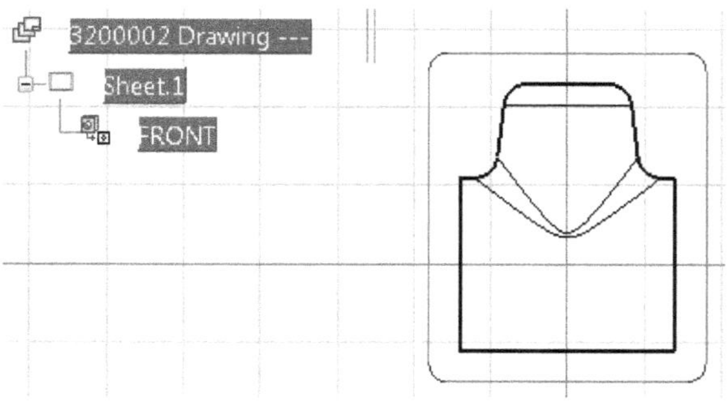

Figure 11–15

The view is added to the sheet in the drawing specification tree. The view displays on the drawing with a red border, indicating that it is the active view. When more than one view is present, a view can be activated by double-clicking on its border.

A variety of view types can be added to complete the drawing. Three of these view types are described in the table below.

View Type	Description
 (Projection)	Projects a view perpendicular from the front view. It creates views, such as top, right, left, and bottom, and is placed by selecting a location on the screen. The system applies the proper label (name) based on its position relative to the front view. It maintains the same scale value as its parent view, as shown in Figure 11–16. 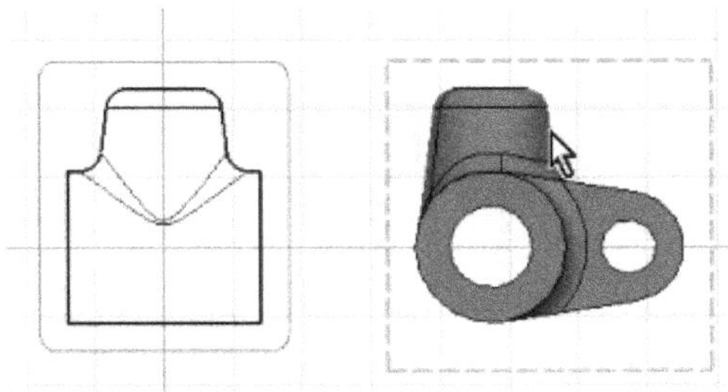 **Figure 11–16**
 (Quick Detailed View)	Creates a scaled view focusing on a specific area of an existing view, as shown in Figure 11–17. It is created by sketching a circle on an existing, active view that encloses the geometry to be represented. To complete the view, assign a name, boundary type, and note location. The system automatically assigns a label identifying the scale value and view name of the detailed view. Orientation of this view corresponds to its parent view. 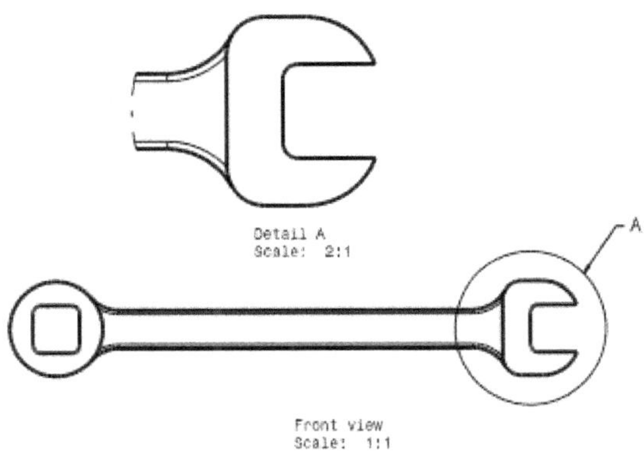 **Figure 11–17**

View Type	Description
 (Offset Section View)	The offset section view creates a section that displays all of the edges that are behind the cutting plane. You can create this view as planar (as shown in Figure 11–18) or as a sketched cutting plane (as shown in Figure 11–19).

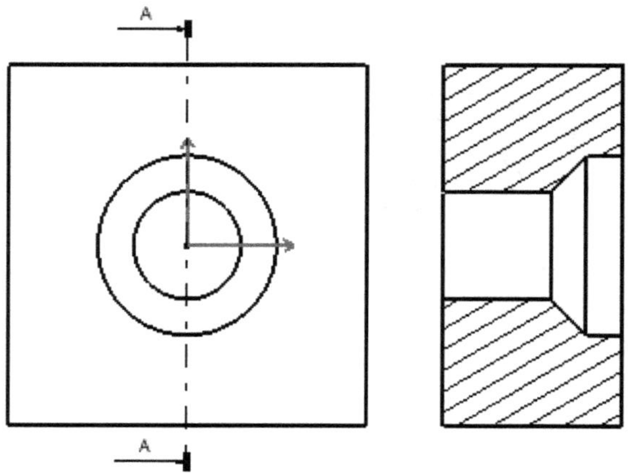

Figure 11–18

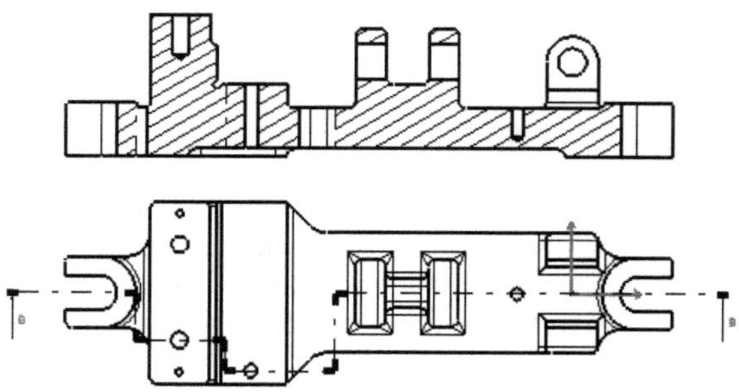

Figure 11–19

11.4 Changed Geometry

Updating a Drawing

If a drawing has been created from a 3D model and the model geometry has changed, the drawing must be updated to reflect the changes.

To update the drawing, click (Update Current Sheet) or press <Ctrl>+<U>. A grayed-out icon ( ) indicates that the 3D model has not changed, and that the drawing does not need to be updated.

Links to 3D Models

If a drawing is open and the 3D model it references is not open, the drawing cannot be updated. To open the referenced model, right-click on a drawing view and select **Open 3D Data**. The 3D part/product opens in a new window.

Practice 11a
Create a Drawing

Practice Objectives

- Create a new drawing.
- Place views using the *View Wizard*.
- Manipulate the views in various ways.

In this practice, you will use a part to create a new drawing. The drawing will consist of two sheets and multiple views. One of the sheets is shown in Figure 11–20. You will use the *View Wizard* to place and modify the views.

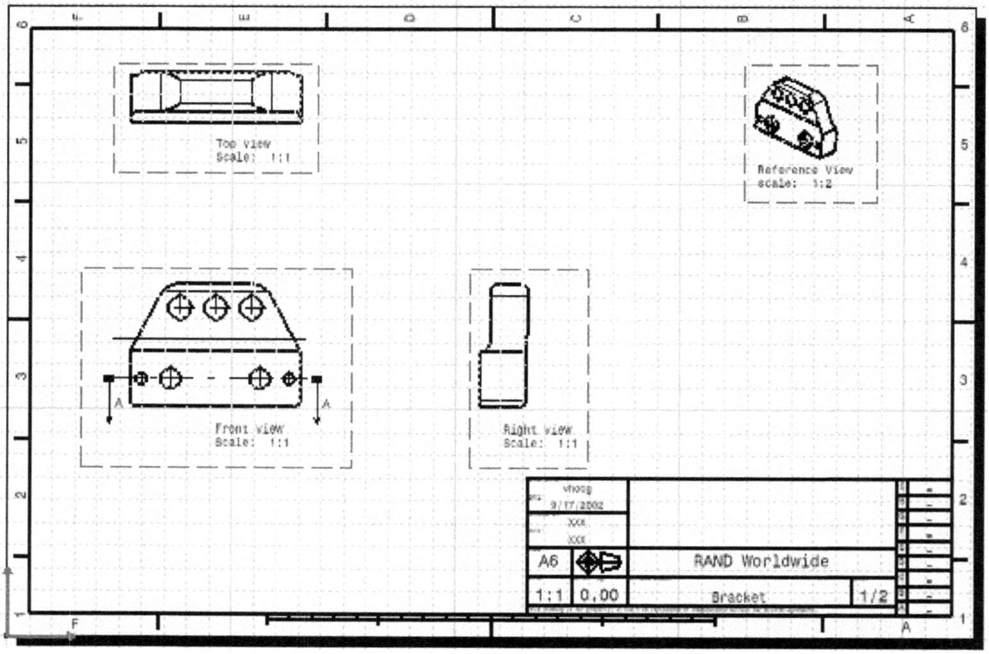

Figure 11–20

Task 1: Import the Bracket part.

1. Import **Bracket.3dxml**.
2. Open the part. The model displays as shown in Figure 11–21.

Figure 11–21

Task 2: Insert a drawing in the 3D part.

1. Double-click on the top level of the specification tree. The specification tree should display as shown in Figure 11–22.

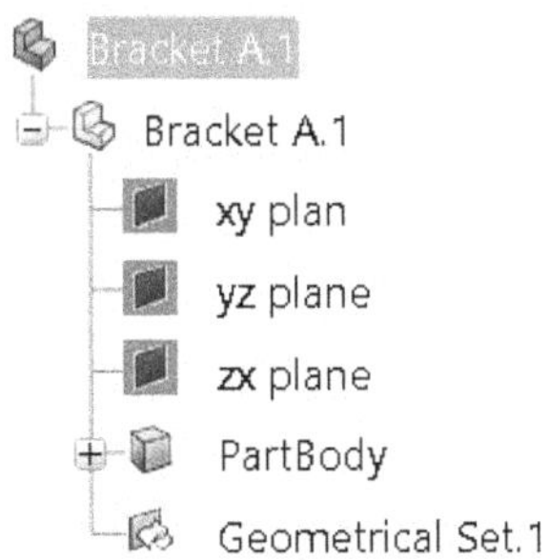

Figure 11–22

2. Right-click on the top line of the specification tree and select **Insert>Drawing** in the context menu, as shown in Figure 11–23.

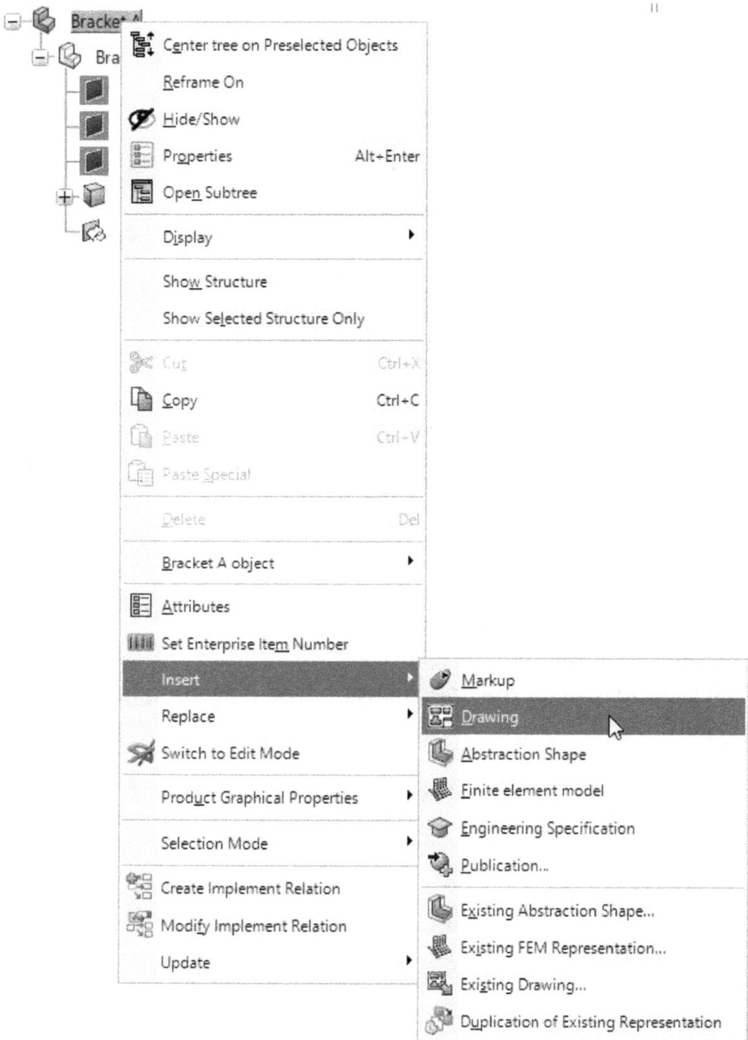

Figure 11–23

3. In the *Drawing* dialog box, enter the name ***Your_Initials*_Bracket** for the *Title*, as shown in Figure 11–24.

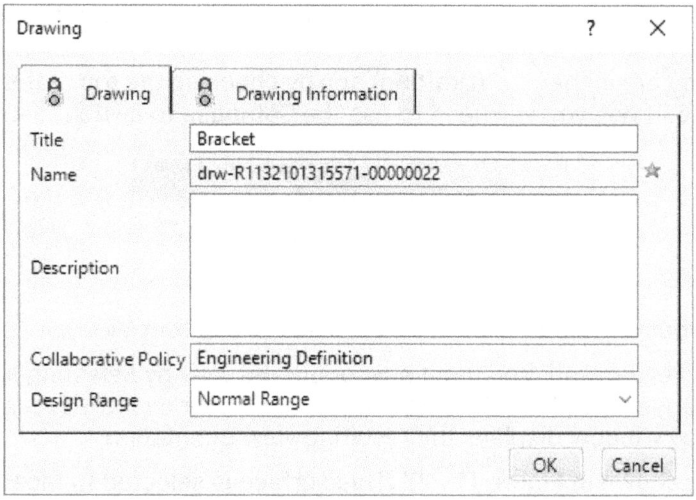

Figure 11–24

4. Select the *Drawing Information* tab.
5. Select the following options so the dialog box updates as shown in Figure 11–25:
   - *Standard:* **ANSI-ASME**
   - *Format:* **B ANSI**
   - *Orientation:* **Landscape**

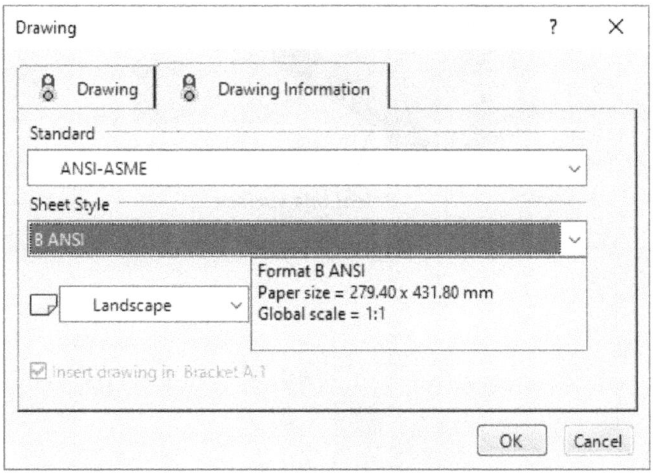

Figure 11–25

6. Click **OK** to finalize drawing creation.

Task 3: Create a front view.

1. Double-click on the drawing name in the specification tree to open the drawing.
2. Confirm that you are in the (Drafting) app by checking the top of the screen, as shown in Figure 11–26. If not, you will need to use the Compass to switch to it.

Figure 11–26

3. In the *View Layout* section of the Action Bar, click (Front View).
4. Select the *Bracket* part tab. You must now orient the view by selecting a face from the model. Select anywhere in the **Bracket** window and hover over the faces of the model. An *Oriented Preview* window displays the resulting view orientation.
5. Select the face shown in Figure 11–27. This surface is selected to face the front of the screen in the front view.

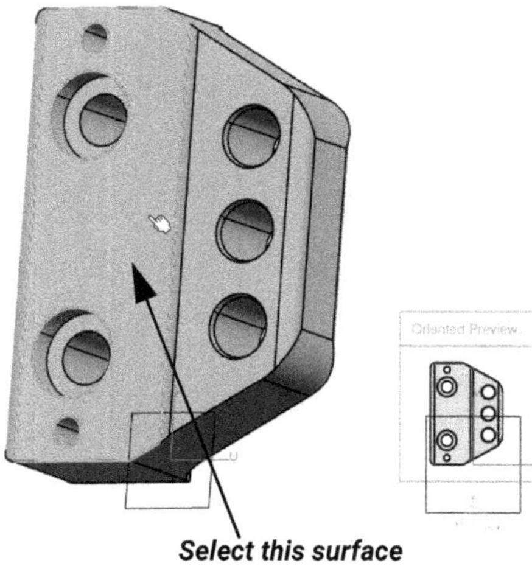

Figure 11–27

6. The display automatically toggles back to the drawing sheet. A view orientation compass displays in the top-right corner of the display. Use the cursor to drag the green handle to the 90° location. The front view is oriented as shown in Figure 11–28.

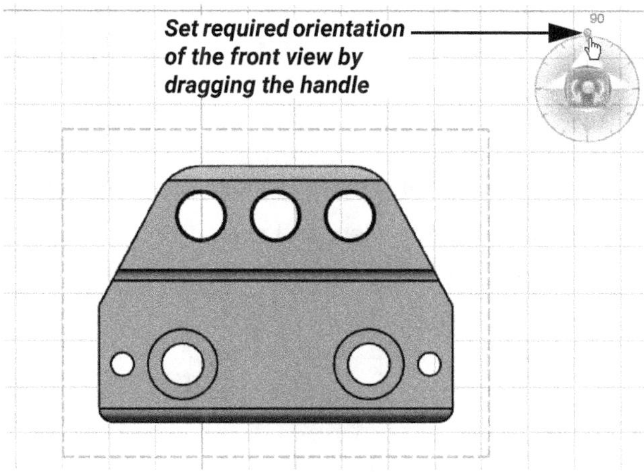

Figure 11–28

7. Click the center of the compass (or a blank space of the screen) to complete the orientation. The drawing sheet is shown in Figure 11–29.

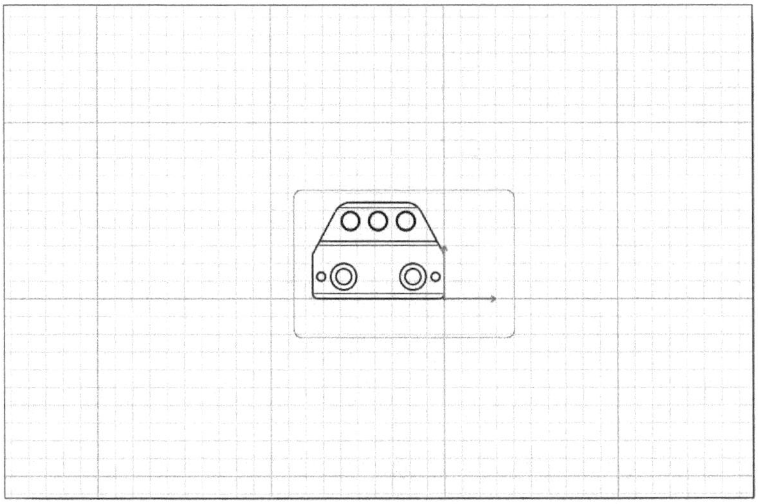

Figure 11–29

Task 4: Create an isometric view.

1. In the *View Layout* section of the Action Bar, expand the arrow next to  (Front View) and select  (Isometric).
2. Activate the *Bracket* tab and select a face on the model. The system orients the isometric view using the current model orientation. Therefore, the face selected is not important. The system places the view on the drawing and the view orientation compass displays.
3. Select the dashed green border of the view and drag it to the upper-right corner of the drawing, as shown in Figure 11–30.

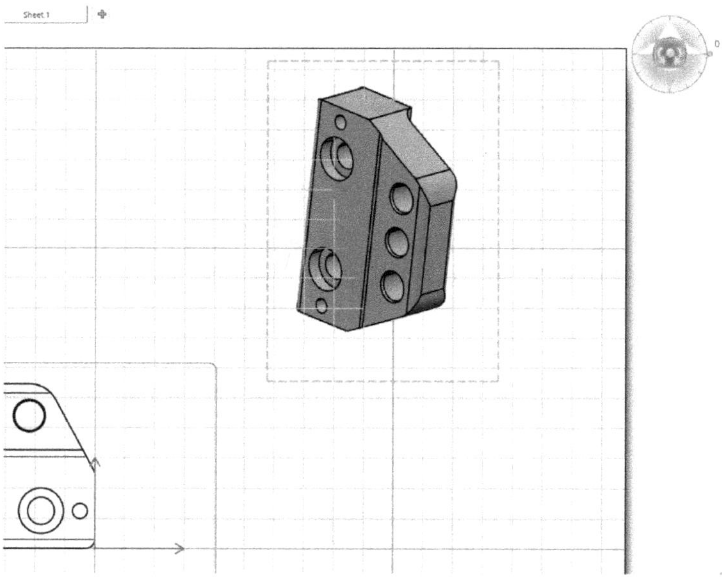

Figure 11–30

4. Click anywhere on the drawing to complete the creation of the view.

Design Considerations

The border of the front view is currently red, while the border of the isometric view is blue. The red border indicates that it is the active view. Any view operations are always performed on the active view. As well, the creation of a section or projection view will reference the active view. Double-click on the view border to activate a view.

Task 5: Create a projection view.

In this task, you will project a view from the front view. The front view must be active.

1. Ensure that the front view is active.
2. Click (Projection).
3. Position the cursor around the front view. Four possible projections can be created, as shown in Figure 11–31.

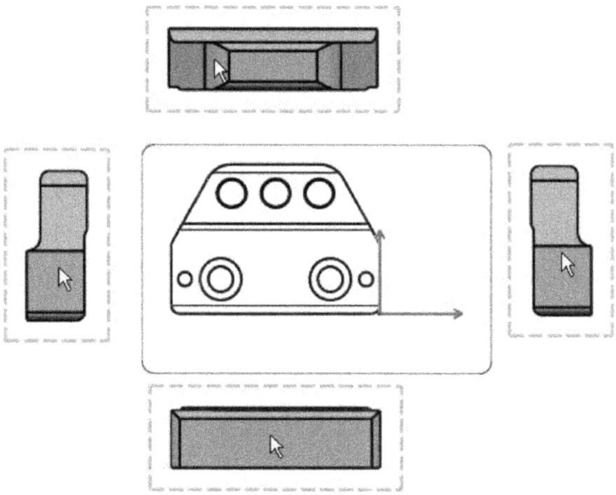

Figure 11–31

4. Create the projection to the right of the front view. The drawing view displays as shown in Figure 11–32.

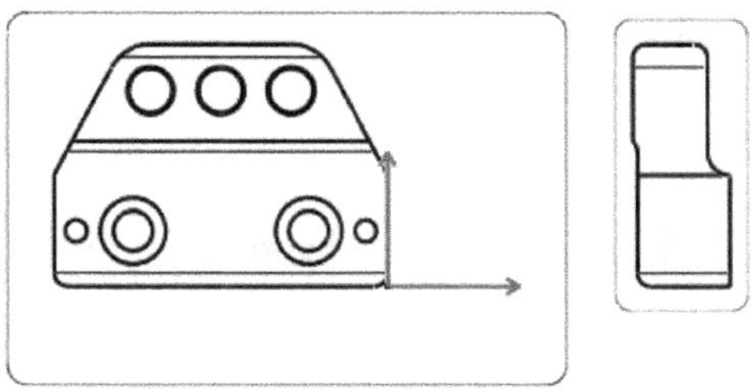

Figure 11–32

Task 6: Move the views.

1. Select the view frame of the front view and drag it to the bottom-left corner of the sheet.
2. Experiment by moving the right view. Move the isometric view as well and note the differences between the linked and unlinked views.

Design Considerations

The projected right view is a child of the front view, so it maintains an aligned position with it. The isometric view can be moved independent of the front view.

Task 7: Change the properties of a view.

1. Right-click on the **FRONT** view in the specification tree and select **Properties**.
2. In the *Properties* dialog box, on the *Generation* tab, select **Center Line** and **Axis** in the *Dress-up* area, as shown in Figure 11–33.

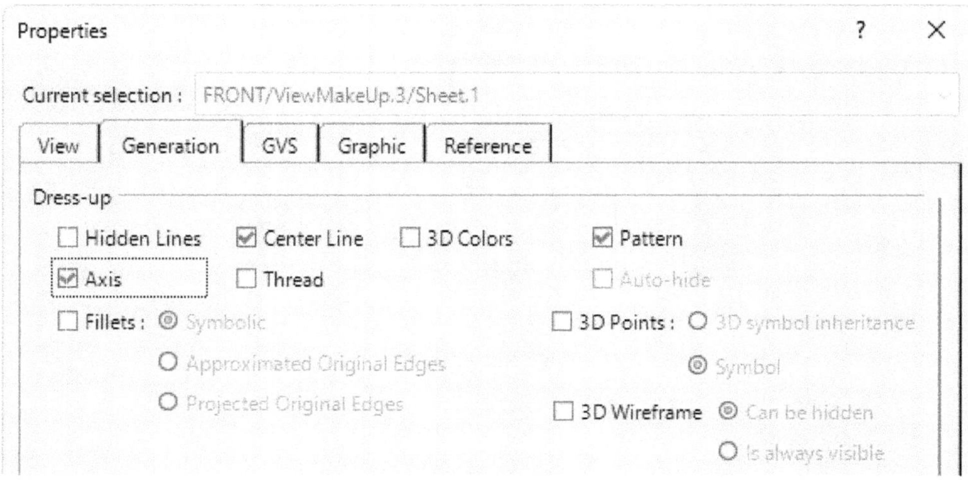

Figure 11–33

3. Click **OK**.

Task 8: Create a section view.

1. Zoom in on the front view.
2. Click  (Offset Section View) in the *View Layout* section of the Action Bar.

3. Sketch a line that starts approximately one grid square space to the left of the view, as shown in Figure 11–34. Enable the system to assume an alignment with the axis of the hole feature.

   Note: *To align the start of the section line with the hole, try positioning the cursor over the hole to create a coincidence constraint before starting the creation of the line. (Snap to Point) can be disabled under the Sketch tab to make the cursor ignore the grid in the background.*

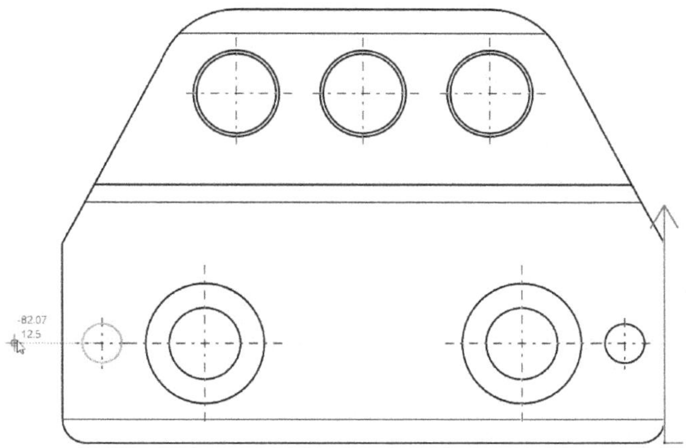

Figure 11–34

4. Drag the line across the front view and select a location approximately one grid square space to the right of the view, as shown in Figure 11–35.

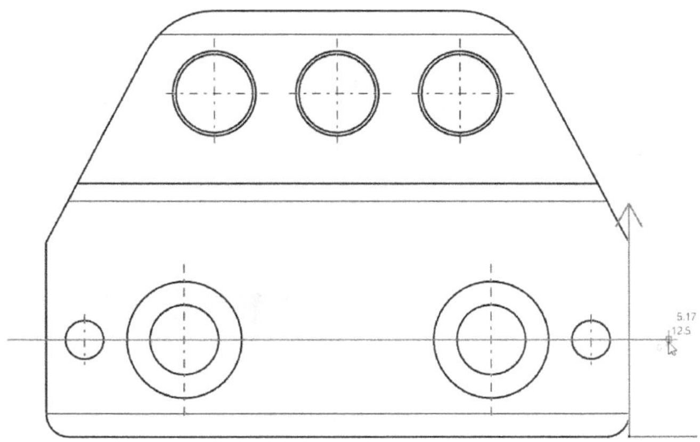

Figure 11–35

5. Double-click to complete the x-section definition.

6. Select a location above the front view. The view displays as shown in Figure 11–36.

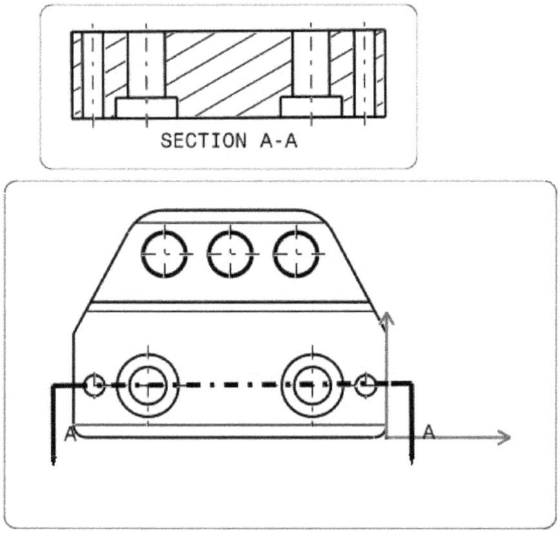

Figure 11–36

- If the section view callout arrows are pointing in the wrong direction, right-click on the arrow and select **Callout (Section View).x object>Definition**, as shown in Figure 11–37.

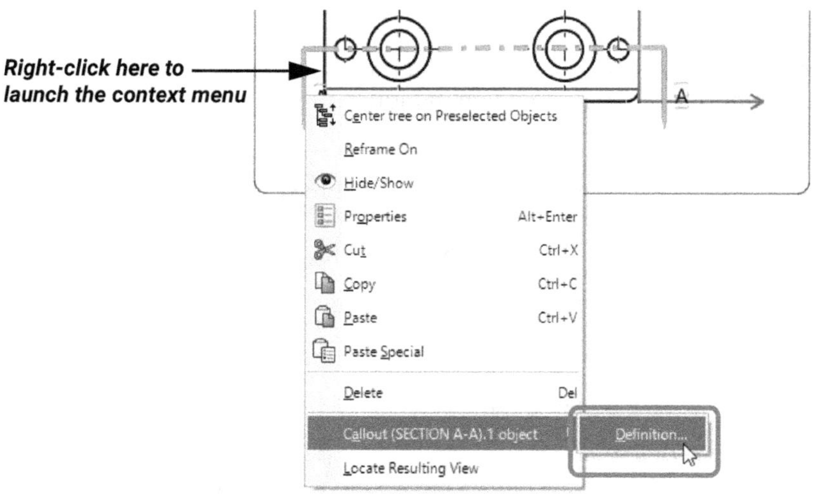

Figure 11–37

7. The Profile Edition mode is displayed. In the *Edit/Replace* toolbar, click (Reverse View Direction).
8. Click on the screen to complete the action.

Task 9: Add a detail view.

1. Zoom in on the section view.
2. Double-click on the frame of the section view to make it active. The border turns red and the name of the view in the view tree is underlined, indicating that this view is the active view.
3. In the *View Layout* section of the Action Bar, expand (Expand) and select (Quick Detail View).
4. Select a location on the right side of the counterbored hole feature and drag the cursor to create a circle callout, as shown in Figure 11–38.

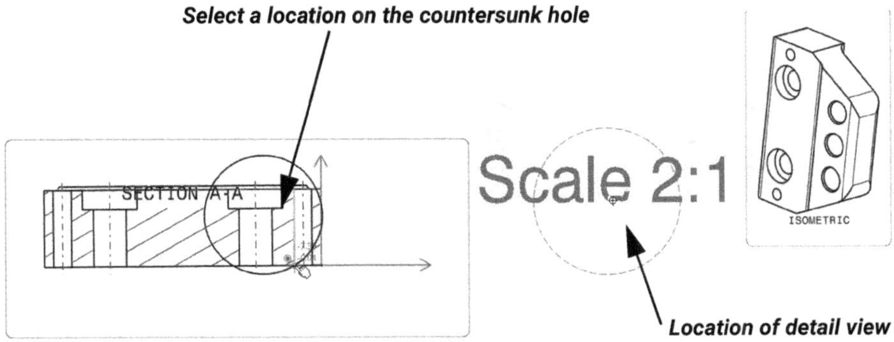

Figure 11–38

*Note: If the axis is not visible, right-click and select **Properties**, then in the Properties dialog box, select the **Axis** option on the View tab.*

5. Select a point to the right of the section view to define a location for the detail view. The complete detail view containing the callout is shown in Figure 11–39.

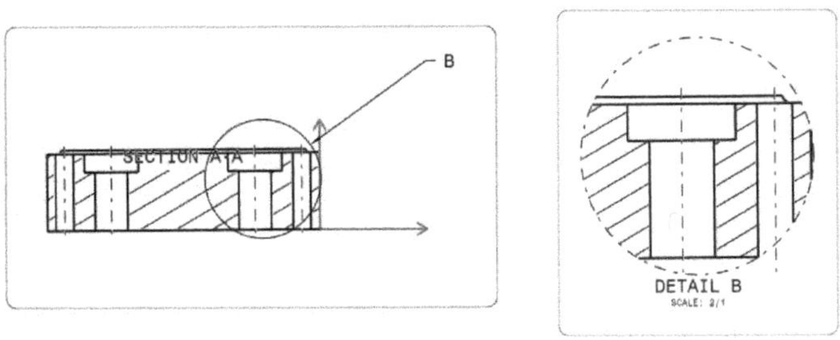

Figure 11–39

6. Right-click on the arrows in the front view and select **Callout (Section View).x object> Definition**.
7. Click (Reverse View Direction) in the context toolbar.

8. Click on the screen and note that the circle defining the detail view has moved.
9. Double-click on the section circle to activate it.
10. Move and resize the section circle as shown in Figure 11–40.

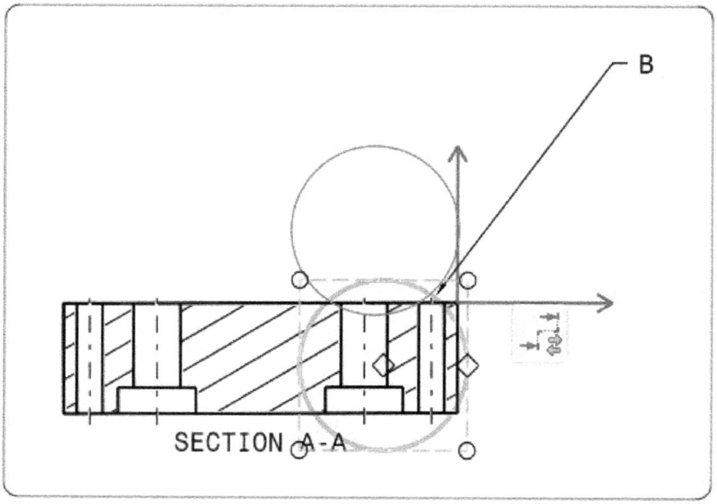

Figure 11–40

11. Click on the screen to complete the edit.
12. Move the detail view to an appropriate location.

Task 10: Insert a frame and title block.

1. In the *View Layout* section of the Action Bar, click (Page Layout). In the *Page Layout* dialog box, in the *Dress-up* drop-down list, select **Drawing Titleblock Sample 1**, as shown in Figure 11–41.

Figure 11–41

2. Click **Apply**. The frame and title block are displayed.
3. Click **OK** to close the *Page Layout* dialog box.
4. Save the drawing.

End of practice

www.ingramcontent.com/pod-product-compliance
Lightning Source LLC
Chambersburg PA
CBHW061156240926
51846CB00006B/1029
9781967625789